W. Draw

W9-CKE-357

Restoring the Power of Unions

Restoring the Power of Unions

It Takes a Movement

Julius G. Getman

Yale UNIVERSITY PRESS

New Haven & London

To Vinnie Sirabella,
union visionary

Yale University Press books may be purchased in quantity for educational, business, or promotional use. For information, please e-mail sales.press@yale.edu (U.S. office) or sales@yaleup.co.uk (U.K. office).

Set in Adobe Garamond type by The Composing Room of Michigan, Inc.
Printed in the United States of America.

Library of Congress Cataloging-in-Publication Data

Getman, Julius G.
    Restoring the power of unions : it takes a movement / Julius G. Getman.
        p. cm.
    Includes bibliographical references and index.
    ISBN 978-0-300-13700-2 (cloth : alk. paper)
    1. Labor unions—United States.   2. Labor movement—United States.
I. Title.
    HD6508.G38 2010
    331.880973—dc22

                                                            2010003820

A catalogue record for this book is available from the British Library.

This paper meets the requirements of ANSI/NISO Z39.48-1992 (Permanence of Paper).

10 9 8 7 6 5 4 3 2

Contents

Preface

LESSONS FROM LIFE

The son of a garment-industry cutter, I grew up with the knowledge that we were union people. Although I knew little about the complexities of labor relations and collective bargaining, I knew that the International Ladies' Garment Workers' Union (ILGWU) had provided what little schooling my immigrant father ever got. It helped him earn decent wages, and the benefits that it provided included home visits by Dr. Lamstein for $2.

It was not until I attended Harvard Law School and studied labor law with the noted scholar Archibald Cox that I began to understand how complex the issues of labor law and labor relations were. Cox, like most of the Harvard faculty, discouraged emotional commitment and emphasized rigorous legal analysis. He did not care whether a particular opinion helped or hurt unions. Instead, he would ask, Was it consistent with statutory language, policy, and history? Did it follow established precedent? Cox was rigorous, stately, nonpartisan, knowledgeable, the model of an impartial expert, labor arbitrator, and mediator trusted by both unions and management. I realized in his class that my earlier views had been one-sided and uninformed. By the time I graduated, my goal was to become like Cox, a labor expert above the fray.

I soon got my chance. After graduation from law school, I went to work for the National Labor Relations Board (NLRB). It was a great place to work. The attorneys with whom I worked were dedicated and able. Many went on to distinguished academic and government careers. I thought them as tough and impartial as sheriffs in Western movies. They were neutral labor-law experts, like Archibald Cox.

When I left the Board to enter law teaching, I was determined to carry on this tradition of neutral expertise. My first labor-law students at Indiana University wondered whether I was pro-union or pro-management. My first scholarly article was a complex exposition and criticism of the *Midwest Piping* doctrine, which required an employer to withhold recognition from either of two competing unions. I argued that the doctrine did not protect employees and that it unnecessarily hindered employers. My article was carefully reasoned and researched. It betrayed no partisan bias. It supported changes in a technical labor-law issue that nobody really cared about.

My first connection with the labor movement, and the realities of labor law, occurred in the fall of 1965 when I was asked to teach labor law to a group of steelworkers who had been selected for academic potential from among hundreds of applicants. The program that brought them to campus was an experiment jointly developed by the United Steelworkers, Indiana University, and the Ford Foundation. The fellows chosen studied a full range of academic subjects, including English literature, political science, speech, and history, in addition to labor law. Once on campus they had the time of their lives. They eagerly read the assigned material and held heated debates about its significance. After class hours they could be found arguing the merits of unions with the conservative business students with whom they shared dormitory space.

I realized after a few weeks that I was learning a lot about industrial regulations from their questions. The fellows teased each other constantly and after a while began to tease me, focusing mainly on the irrationality of the law, much of which made no sense to them. They were not a group easily cowed by credentials—not mine and not any of the other faculty who taught in the program. I admired their eagerness to learn and envied their evident sense of commitment to the union and to each other. Their solidarity and devotion to the union made me less satisfied with my above-the-fray style of teaching and scholarship.

At the end of the graduation ceremony that marked the program's end, they locked arms and sang "Solidarity Forever," several with tears in their eyes. The fellows returned to their mills and factories, inspired and eager to repay the union for its support. But many soon became disillusioned. They had expected recognition of their learning and the opportunity to play a prominent role in their local unions using the skills that they had acquired at the university. But instead of new respect, they were met with resentment. The union's professional staff worried that their role was being preempted and their status undercut by the willingness of the fellows to state contrary opinions. The fellows quickly came to be resented as "wise asses" and "know-it-alls." The resentment on both sides became strong enough that several of the fellows began exploring new career paths and the union's district leadership demanded the right to name the fellows for the next year's program. This was my first, but far from last, encounter with the harmful effects of internal union political battles on the goals and performance of organized labor.

When the program ended, I was asked to teach at a leadership training program for leading members of Steelworkers District 30's staff, including the district director. I accepted immediately. I was eager to demonstrate my pedagogic skill to this important union group. The class, however, was a fiasco. Unlike the fellows, the staff members did not appreciate Socratic questioning. They were uncomfortable when I asked them to suggest answers to difficult issues. Worst of all, they overwhelmingly deferred to positions taken by their superiors in the union's hierarchy. Speaking truth to power was not part of their agenda. The district director himself answered a few of my questions, but when I prompted him for his reasoning, he simply restated his conclusions. It was, I realized, as hierarchical as the army in which I had served as an enlisted man.

From time to time during the 1960s, I served as a labor arbitrator. Arbitrators are private judges hired by employers and unions to interpret their agreement when disputes arise. They decide whether management has just cause to discharge workers, whether seniority is being properly acknowledged in promotions, and whether employees are being laid off, given vacation time, or paid in accordance with the agreement. What I learned as an arbitrator is how profoundly collective-bargaining agreements change the nature of the employment relationship. Collective bargaining, when it works properly, gives unions status and workers dignity. In the late 1960s I also became active in the American Association of University Professors (AAUP), which had a large and active chapter on campus. The AAUP, although it neither engaged in nor advocated collective bargaining for professors, was as close to a union as faculty at major universities came in those days. Our chapter was large, active, contentious, and quite effective in promoting its major causes—academic freedom and faculty governance. The concept of academic freedom had been developed and defended by the AAUP in the aftermath of World War I. A team of major scholars had given the term practical meaning through a complex process that involved censuring universities that violated the rights of faculty members to teach, study, and publish the truth as they saw it. University administrators were eager to avoid censure by the AAUP on issues of academic freedom, and they wanted the goodwill of the local chapter because it was highly respected by the faculty, had access to the press, and could initiate the process of investigation and censure.

In 1969, with Professor Stephen B. Goldberg of the University of Illinois, I undertook to write a treatise on the law of union organizing. Organizing campaigns were then, as they are now, an area of complex legal regulation. Goldberg and I quickly realized that we did not know enough to properly evaluate the rationality of existing law. In a moment of academic daring facilitated by ignorance, we decided to investigate the relationship between the law and the realities of union organizing campaigns. It took us four years and six test studies to develop our research design. We wanted to identify elections likely to involve hard-fought, possibly illegal election campaigns by employers and their lawyers and consultants. Much to our surprise, the NLRB, where we both had worked and which regularly stressed the desirability of academic inquiry into Board rules, opposed our study. The Board argued that employees would be intimidated by our presence and that they would assume that we were employer spies and either refuse to talk to us or not tell us the truth. The Board's concern with the effect of our presence was based on assumptions very similar to those that the Board used in regulating campaign conduct—namely, that employees were attuned to nuances of coercion and could in fact be easily coerced into voting against union representation.

To get the names of the employees eligible to vote in the elections we wished to study, we were forced to sue the NLRB under the newly enacted Freedom of Information Act. We were the first of many academics to use the Act in support of our research and were rewarded with a strong favorable opinion by Judge J. Skelly Wright.[1]

From the first test study, our experience talking to workers was far different from the Board's prediction in almost every way. The employees answered honestly and fully. They had things to say about their jobs, their employers, and the unions that sought to organize them. They were pleased that we were genuinely interested. Indeed, it is difficult to overstate their eagerness to help make the law fairer generally. Our data further undermined my belief in the Board's expertise. What we concluded is that NLRB rules about what employers may say do not reflect an understanding of employee voting behavior. This conclusion, which I still believe to be true, has been questioned by many subsequent scholars. I explain in chapter 17 why I believe that subsequent research purporting to undermine our results is untrustworthy.

Quite apart from the careful statistical analysis of NLRB rules, I came away with a sense of the decency and intelligence of the workers whom we talked with. I also concluded sadly that the union organizers whose campaigns we studied, although invariably decent people, were often incompetent. They relied too much on canned handouts and did not spend enough time talking to and listening to the workers they were attempting to organize.

In our book *Union Representation Elections: Law and Reality,* we recommended less regulation of employer speech and greater access to employees for union organizers. Our study made something of a stir, but it was sharply criticized by union lawyers and pro-union academics who insisted that employer rhetoric required far more regulation than we suggested.

I joined the Yale law faculty in 1977. About a year after I arrived, I received a call from the police union, which was seeking a lawyer to help with its upcoming negotiations with the state. I agreed to meet with members of the union's bargaining committee at the bar of the Sheraton Hotel. When I arrived, I had no trouble picking out the members of the police union even though they were out of uniform—leather jackets, bright sports coats, and shirts opened at the throat. Their manner was boisterous. Despite the laughter and drinks, their posture suggested wariness rather than relaxation.

They told me about their union, which had only recently been organized when the troopers had become dissatisfied with the traditional role of the Policemen's Benevolent Association. They had negotiated a contract once before, but the troopers remained discontented. The department was rife with favoritism. Assignments were based on getting along rather than on ability. Police were punished unfairly on the basis of unproven allegations. Senior members of the force were denied legitimate opportunity. No career ladder existed, and training was inadequate. The police were subject to arbitrary discipline. The police auxiliaries they had to work with were a joke and a menace. Each accusation was illustrated with stories that brought forth knowing laughter and expressions of anger.

The officers of the union wanted me to draft proposals and actually conduct the negotiations on their behalf. The offer was tempting. It seemed a wonderful way to learn both about police and about the intricacies of collective bargaining, a subject that I had taught but something that I had never engaged in. Also, the group was surprisingly appealing with their camaraderie, toughness, and cynical humor.

I spent at least a day each week during the next few months meeting with the troopers and learning about their jobs, concerns, and attitudes. I got a sense of how the world looked from the vantage point of those compelled to deal with human beings at their worst and to confront violent death, tragedy, hostility, and deception on a regular basis. They saw themselves as guardians of a society that did not appreciate them and as workers for a government that underpaid, scorned, and regularly mistreated them.

The negotiations proceeded slowly. The hardest part for me was not the discussions across the table but the free-for-all battles that occurred during the union caucuses when it was time to make concessions. It was during the caucuses that I earned my money and really learned about the art of compromise. But despite the tension in the bargaining committee, the state made a series of important concessions so that after a month of negotiations the outline of a fine contract had been agreed to. The cops were pleased and attributed far more of the success to my tough negotiating style than I deserved. It was their anger and militancy that worried the state negotiator, not my eloquence.

After a month of meetings, negotiations stalled. The cops, without my involvement, decided on a job action—one that had no precedent. During the weekend before the July 4 holiday, they stopped issuing tickets to motorists. They didn't stop patrolling. They arrested drunk drivers, and they continued to stop speeders, whom they warned to slow down. But the delighted motorists were let go with a verbal warning. It was a responsible job action, and the newspapers mostly pointed this out in their editorials. Theoretically, the cops who weren't issuing tickets were subject to discipline, but the sergeants and lieutenants never issued a single reprimand. After two days I got a frantic call from the state's lawyer, who desperately wanted an agreement before the July 4 weekend. We met the following Monday and quickly came to an agreement.

I learned a lot during that negotiation: most significantly, that the strike or strike threat is a powerful weapon; second, that imaginative job actions can sometimes be as effective as strikes; and third, that a union can gain more power when it has low-level supervisors on its side.

While at Yale, I was invited to spend a week at the Polish Academy for State and Law. I accepted eagerly because I knew that the country was being profoundly changed by the Solidarity labor movement. While in Poland, I met with many of the movement's leaders. I was particularly struck by the former factory worker Zbigniew Bujak and his close relationship with the dissident intellectual Jan Letinski. I realized that the alliance between workers and intellectuals mediated by the Catholic Church was what gave Solidarity its admirable vision.

When I returned to Yale, I saw that the worker-intellectual alliance that I so admired in Poland existed in Local 34 of the Hotel Employees & Restaurant Employees International Union (HERE), which was seeking to organize Yale clerical and technical workers. The alliance was marvelous, illustrated in the relationship between the ninth-grade dropout Vincent Sirabella and his disciple, John Wilhelm, an honors graduate of Yale. I conducted a series of interviews with them and published an article about what I thought of as their inside-outside approach to organizing and collective bargaining. The organizing drive was dramatic and very well led. It was followed by an equally dramatic strike that ended in a surprising union victory. I spoke out on behalf of the union and conducted a series of interviews with its leaders. I became convinced that they were onto something valuable for the labor movement generally.

When I left Yale and joined the faculty at The University of Texas, I continued to study the organizing efforts of HERE, then directed by Sirabella.

The book on union organizing that I was planning to write was placed on hold in the 1990s as I turned my scholarly attention to the issue of strike replacement. It all began innocently enough when a former student, James Brudney, then staff counsel to the Senate labor committee, asked me to testify on proposed legislation that made it unlawful for an employer to hire permanent strike replacements. During the hearing I began talking with a group of permanently replaced paperworkers from Maine. Their story moved me, and I decided to find out more about the strike. This led to a ten-year study of the strike of Local 14 of the United Paperworkers International Union (UPIU), which represented workers at International Paper's Androscoggin mill in Jay, Maine. During the course of the sixteen-month strike, Local 14 used a version of the inside-outside strategies previously employed by HERE. The local had superb leadership, widespread grassroots involvement, and highly creative strategies. It also had inspiring solidarity: fewer than 70 of the 1,200 strikers crossed the picket line. Local 14 also won over the media and enlisted the support of national political figures. Despite Local 14's heroic struggle, the strike was unconditionally called off in October 1988. The local has since been decertified and the community destroyed.

Two things about the union's loss were particularly disheartening. First, the international union's leadership mishandled the strike. Many were hostile to the local's leadership and their outside advisors. Some seemed worried that the local leaders, who were heroes to the union's rank and file, would try to take over the unions.

The other disheartening aspect of the strike was the unfairness of the National Labor Relations Act, which was, according to its preamble, designed to "enhance collective bargaining." Collective bargaining can work effectively only if there is a robust right to strike.

Since the mid-1980s, the union movement has been in a precarious situation. It has been confronted by increasingly hostile employers. Union jobs have moved overseas. Under the malevolently anti-union Bush Labor Board and the conservative courts, the law has grown dramatically more hostile. Unions have been sued under the Racketeer Influenced and Corrupt Organizations Act (RICO) and state tort law. They have been burdened with new reporting requirements, and their political efforts have been restricted. Inevitably, the once-powerful union pay advantage has shrunk. Major organizing efforts by once-powerful unions like the United Auto Workers and the United Mine Workers have failed.

But HERE, the union that organized Yale workers during the late 1980s and through the 1990s, developed a new and powerful approach to organizing and bargaining that depended on mobilizing the passion of its rank-and-file membership. Other unions seemed to be experimenting with new approaches as well. It was with the hope that organized labor was becoming more effective and that the mood of the country might be right for union growth that I undertook to write this book.

Acknowledgments

Many thanks to all the people who agreed to be interviewed for this book. I hope I have done justice to your experience and ideas.

The basic idea for this book originated in a series of interviews conducted between 1985 and 1995 with Vincent Sirabella, who for most of that time was Director of Organizing for the Hotel Employees and Restaurant Employees Union (HERE). Vinnie's first disciple was John Wilhelm, now President of UNITE HERE, whom I first saw in action and came to admire during the organizing drive of Yale's clerical and technical workers. During the writing of this book John was steadfast in his encouragement, support, and friendship. My research for this book brought me into contact with the legendary union strategist Jeff Fiedler, the guru of the comprehensive campaign. He was enormously helpful by providing ideas, information, insights, and humor.

Another grateful nod to the paperworkers of Jay, Maine, and their families. Their story is relevant to the basic concept of this book—the need for organized labor to become a movement once again. Peter Kellman and Roland Samson were especially helpful.

I had many conversations with Judy Scott, the able and innovative General Counsel of SEIU. I am thankful for her help and her friendship. She was consistently willing to share ideas and explain strategy. Kirk Adams and Tom Woodruff, SEIU's insightful organizing leaders, were gracious and helpful. I am grateful to Andy Stern and Anna Burger, SEIU's top leaders, for taking the time to speak with me. They made me aware of the union's multifaceted approach to organizing and collective bargaining.

It was particularly gratifying, twenty years after the Yale clerical and maintenance strike, to renew contact with Paul Clifford, Andrea van den Heever, Karl Lechow, and Warren Heyman—each played a major role during the strike. I also had the opportunity to interview Sherri Chiesa and D. Taylor, both of whom Vinnie Sirabella had brought to my attention as up-and-coming union leaders more than twenty-five years earlier. They have lived up to his expectations. Chiesa is now Secretary Treasurer of UNITE HERE, and Taylor is General Vice President, and leader of the Culinary Union in Las Vegas. Richard McCracken, whom I first met as a young lawyer, is now HERE's creative legal strategist. He has been the guiding force behind the union's rejection of the NLRB election process.

I learned a lot from Donna Schneider and Willie Gonzalez, who are heading UNITE HERE's fascinating organizing effort in Texas.

I am grateful once again to Ray Rogers for telling me about the early days of the corporate campaign.

Many people at AFL-CIO were of help, including former President John Sweeney, and then General Counsel John Hiatt. I had several enlightening conversations with Director of Organizing Stuart Acuff.

Cecil Roberts, the eloquent President of the UMW, was willing to describe for me in detail the union's efforts to utilize comprehensive campaign tactics. Thanks to organizer Sarah Julian and management attorney Katie Lev, both daughters of former colleagues and both now skilled professionals. I learned much from each of them.

My special thanks to Crystal Lee Sutton, for speaking to me with her passion and frankness while fatally ill. She remains an inspiration long after the events memorialized in the film *Norma Rae*.

I was fortunate to have excellent labor experienced student assistants Brooke Lierman and Mike Murphy. They and I were supported by student Ryan Lovell.

I received excellent, more than customary, support from my faculty assistants Gale Hathcock and Marsha Moyer.

Thanks to Associate Dean Michelle Dickerson for providing me with a light teaching load at the start of the project.

Everyone that I dealt with at Yale University Press has been competent, interested, and supportive—starting with Mike O'Malley, who first encouraged me to take on another book about labor. Margaret Otzel, a former shop steward for Yale's Local 34, was the ideal in-house editor for this book, and the copy editing by Karen Schoen was splendid; former Yale Local 34 organizer Aldo Cupo (who worked for the union after the strike) was my production controller at the Press.

Finally I'd like to express my long-time scholarly and personal debt to the late Jerome R. Mintz, of Indiana University, a marvelous scholar and writer who has served for many years as an academic model.

Introduction

BASIC CONCEPTS

Organized labor needs to rekindle the spirit of the activist member-powered movement that has guided its past successes. Organized labor today is a progressive interest group, but it is not a workers' movement. A "movement" entails something more than money, members, and economic power—significant though all these factors are. A movement requires activating and using the energies of workers. It means fostering solidarity across unions and occupations. It requires leaders who are willing to trust and who are committed to sharing power with the union's rank and file. The spirit of movement also requires a concern for issues beyond the economic well-being of the members, such as environmental justice, racial equality, and the rights of immigrants. Organized labor regularly approaches this goal and just as regularly retreats from it.

This book tells the story of labor's struggles, both external and internal, by tracking the history of the Hotel Employees & Restaurant Employees International Union (HERE). I have chosen HERE (currently UNITE HERE) as my focus because I believe that today it, more than any other union, has focused not only on organizing and bargaining but also on creating a spirit of movement. Unfortunately it (like all unions) has been hindered by the law, corruption, and internal strife.

As the HERE story illustrates, even with its membership mobilized and alliances established, organized labor would face major obstacles in organizing the unorganized and advancing the well-being of its members. It would still face the opposition of employers and the law's inadequacy, hostility, and complexity. The rules of labor law in every major area give an advantage to employers and make organizing and striking dangerous activities. The law should be amended to give workers greater voice. In this book I consider various proposals for reform, ranging from card-check organizing to eliminating the right of employers to permanently replace striking workers. In the aftermath of the 2008 election, labor leaders spent large sums of money and devoted great resources to passing the Employee Free Choice Act (EFCA), which provides for card-check recognition and mandatory first-contract arbitration after impasse. Despite the near unanimity of support for the EFCA from labor leaders and pro-labor scholars, I argue that the focus on EFCA was a mistake and that, even if ultimately passed, it would not achieve the optimistic goals that labor's spokespeople envision. I argue that protecting the right to strike, so that striking workers could not be permanently replaced, would be considerably more valuable and far more in keeping with building a sense of movement.

Not all the obstacles to labor's advance come from outside. Internal divisions—some ideological, some political, and others personal—have been a major obstacle to worker solidarity, as HERE's history demonstrates with depressing regularity.

OUTLINE OF CHAPTERS

In chapter 1 I illustrate why a strong, vital, and progressive labor movement is important for our society, both economically and politically. When unions were strong, the United States had the longest period of equitably shared prosperity in U.S. history—a sharp contrast with our current situation of a weak labor movement and growing economic discontent and gross disparities in wealth. The weakness of organized labor has had a negative impact on our political culture. It has made it relatively easy for right-wing demagogues to shamelessly appropriate the banner of populism and to turn to their own advantage the feelings of working-class people that they are invisible to those in power.

In chapter 2 I explain the decline of the labor movement and why it has failed to organize the unorganized, has lost strikes, and has become more professional but less militant and less inspiring. My explanation places less emphasis on the law and more on the problems inherent in the structure of the current union movement and the attitudes of its leaders. I believe that the labor movement bears more responsibility for its decline than most union leaders, liberal commentators, and scholars have been willing to acknowledge. To demonstrate this point I focus on the law and the practice of organizing.

The National Labor Relations Act (NLRA) has provided a system of representation elections for determining whether a group of workers is to be represented by a union. Chapter 3 explains how this election process works in practice. I describe the strategies of the parties and show the hurdles that must be overcome before a union is certified as the bargaining agent for a unit of employees.

Chapters 4–7 trace the history of HERE from its early days to the mid-1980s. I demonstrate that along the way the union has faced virtually every problem that has confronted the labor movement generally, including corruption, mob infiltration, weak leadership, fear of change, political divisions, racism, sexism, anti-immigrant prejudice, and economic catastrophe. It has successfully overcome its internal problems through a remarkable collaboration between up-from-the-ranks working-class leadership and progressive, college-trained political activists with roots in student and civil-rights movements. The collaboration began when Vincent Sirabella, a longtime union dissident who headed the union's local of maintenance workers at Yale, hired and trained John Wilhelm, a Yale graduate and longtime political activist. Together with a remarkable group of organizers and activists, they won a series of victories culminating with the successful organizing campaign and strike by Yale's clerical and technical workers. The Connecticut and Yale locals of HERE in the early 1980s represented a return to a model of collaboration between workers and intellectuals that had been absent from organized labor for many years. Its main architect was Sirabella, whom Ed Hanley selected as the director of organizing for the union. Sirabella believed that the model that he developed at Yale could transform the labor movement, and he began a national organizing campaign, which failed.

Chapters 8–13 trace the development of corporate and comprehensive campaign techniques by unions generally and HERE in particular. The lessons learned from Vincent Sirabella's failed national organizing campaign have turned out to be a major benefit to HERE. The union has abandoned the National Labor Relations Board (NLRB) and instead developed a comprehensive-campaign model based on mobilizing workers, forming committees, and pressuring employers to sign neutrality and card-check agreements. I explain why these tactics provide great advantages over the representation-election system—HERE and other unions using similar methods have organized successfully during the past decades as a result of these advantages. These chapters also discuss how HERE, under the leadership of John Wilhelm, became a major advocate within the labor movement for the rights of immigrant workers.

I also explore why HERE and UNITE (the Union of Needletrades, Industrial and Textile Employees, an amalgamation of garment unions) merged to form UNITE HERE. The problem of internal union politics, which this merger illustrates, is one of the major obstacles to recreating a powerful and effective labor movement. It was an understandable merger of two unions with progressive histories and complementary needs and resources. However, the merger resulted in a major battle between Bruce Raynor, the president of UNITE, who became the general president of the union after the merger, and John Wilhelm, who became the union's copresident. Wilhelm is now the union's president, and Raynor is no longer affiliated with UNITE HERE. The battle was made far more bitter and potentially destructive by the involvement of Andy Stern, the president of the Service Employees International Union (SEIU).

Chapters 14–17 explain why the NLRA election process has made organizing difficult. That the NLRA election process does not work well for unions is well recognized by commentators and union spokespeople, most of whom focus on unlawful employer resistance and the law's system of woefully inadequate remedies. The prohibition against unfair labor practices has done little to deter employers from threatening or retaliating against union supporters. To avoid the harmful impact of illegal employer behavior, unions have focused much effort on the passage of the EFCA. I suggest, on the basis of earlier field studies, that unions and academic commentators have exaggerated the impact of the threats and reprisals. I also argue that they have for too long limited themselves to what is called "hot-shop organizing."

In chapters 18–20 I demonstrate why an effective right to strike is critical to the labor movement and why the law, particularly the right of employers to hire permanent replacements, has turned out to be a significant hindrance to labor's effective use of the strike. I show that the secondary-boycott laws are both harmful and unconstitutional. I also explore the potentially devastating effect of the Racketeer Influenced and Corrupt Organizations Act (RICO) on the strength of the strike weapon.

In chapters 21 and 22 I discuss the strengths and weaknesses of different proposals to change the NLRA. I suggest that the EFCA is unlikely to provide the great boost to organizing that its proponents look forward to and its opponents dread. I argue that the EFCA would not do away with organizing campaigns in which the employer's advantage in terms of access to employees would remain a critical factor. I also argue that passage of the Act would lead many employers to conduct anti-union campaigns earlier than they might otherwise. In these chapters I make the case for amending the NLRA to prohibit employers from hiring permanent replacement workers in place of strikers. The regular use of permanent replacement during the 1980s has made organized labor fearful, with good reason, of striking.

In chapters 23 and 24 I consider whether the NLRA, administered by a supposedly expert agency, is a worthwhile scheme or whether it should be scrapped and replaced by a different federal Act or by state law. I conclude that the NLRA is worth saving but that it needs a fundamental overhaul. I suggest that Board members be chosen from a limited pool of neutral experts, possibly from the National Academy of Arbitrators, and that a special court review Board decisions. Among the needed amendments to the NLRA, I argue, are the following: The Board's remedial power needs to be increased. Injunctions against employers' unfair labor practices need to be regularly issued, just as they are currently issued against union secondary boycotts. Unions need to be given equal time to respond to employer speeches and meetings, and the election process should be accelerated. Employees unlawfully fired during an organizing campaign should be quickly reinstated. Most significantly, strikers who engage in no serious misconduct should not be risking their jobs when they lawfully walk out.

In chapter 24 I consider the impact of various alternatives to traditional collective bargaining. A frequently made suggestion is to permit minority bargaining. Several prominent labor scholars believe that the NLRA, properly interpreted, permits minority bargaining. I disagree. I argue that minority bargaining violates the law and that permitting it would not do much to strengthen the labor movement.

Chapter 25 focuses on the difference between organized labor and a labor movement. I argue that too often, union leaders have failed to take needed chances or to accept responsibility for their organizing and bargaining failures. It is possible to organize in the face of employer opposition and a hostile NLRB, as several unions—especially UNITE HERE—have demonstrated. Fear of failure has made unions too cautious and unwilling to depart from the hot-shop model. Taking chances is critical. Indeed, failed efforts such as HERE's national organizing drive of the late 1980s have provided the basis for later success.

Part I **Overview**

Chapter 1 The Need for Unions

"If a man tells you he loves America, yet hates labor, he is a liar!"
"There is no America without labor, and to fleece the one is to rob the
other." That is what Abraham Lincoln said.

It is not surprising that the man who spoke eloquently of government of, by, and for the people believed in the cause of labor, for the
two are inevitably intertwined. When organized labor is strong, workers become visible to those in power. A strong labor movement also assures those who toil a fairer share of the wealth that they help produce. That is why the cause of labor is worth fighting for and why its
failures are often failures of the American ideal.

Given the enormous power of corporations and corporate executives, the need for a powerful voice for labor is greater today than it
has ever been. Yet organized labor is in a state of crisis. Its percentage
of the working force has shrunk.[1] It is besieged by enemies, critics,
and self-appointed saviors. Many believe that the day of unions has
come and gone. Some believe that they are outdated—rendered unnecessary by legislation and useless by globalization, employer opposition, and the relentless working of the market. Some explain the de-

clining role of unions as the result of failures, weaknesses, and misdeeds—violence, prejudice, corruption, and indifference to the interests of workers. Some applaud the demise of unions because their absence gives the market a chance to work without interference.[2]

But for workers, the unregulated market is a disaster zone. As organized labor has struggled for survival, workers and their families have seen their standard of living decline, maintaining their real income only by making the one-wage-earner family a thing of the past.[3]

Finally, in the wake of populist outrage, sympathetic interest in unions is increasing, fueled by the inescapable facts of corporate plundering, widespread economic distress, the gross and growing inequality between workers and executives,[4] and the realization that millions of working people are only one medical crisis from financial disaster.[5] Progressive economists have long pointed out that unions bring needed balance to the distribution of economic benefits —that they improve wages for workers throughout the economy and that they make the entire economy stronger. The traditional role of unions was explained by Paul Krugman in his book *The Conscience of a Liberal:* "Unions were once an important factor limiting income inequality, both because of their direct effect in raising their members' wages and because the union pattern of wage settlements—which consistently raised the wages of less-well-paid workers more—was, in the fifties and sixties, reflected in the labor market as a whole. The decline of the unions has removed that moderating influence."[6]

The wage benefit to workers of unionization has been conservatively estimated as around 15 percent. In addition, as Michael Yates has pointed out, "the compensation advantage, which includes the benefits, is greater than the wage advantage. This is because union members enjoy both more and better fringe benefits than do nonunion workers. The union advantage is greater for blue collar workers than for all workers, reflecting the fact that unions are of most benefit to workers of lower status."[7]

There are those who believe that productivity suffers when employers must pay higher wages and are forced to give up their discretion to discharge and promote at will. This argument has been refuted by a series of economic studies, recently summed up by Lawrence Mishel, the president of the Economic Policy Institute:

> Decades of research show that unions can have substantial positive effects on firm performance.
>
> At least four factors account for the positive impact on performance:
>
> 1. Unions give employees a voice in the workplace, allowing them to complain,

shape operations, and push for change, rather than simply quitting or being fired. . . .

2. Union employees feel freer to speak up about operations, leading to improvements that increase productivity. . . .

3. Higher pay pushes employers to find other ways to lower costs—with new technology, increased investment, and better management.

4. Union employees get more training, both because they demand it and because management is willing to invest more to get a return on their higher pay.[8]

The strength or weakness of organized labor also affects public policy generally. As the noted labor economist Harley Shaiken has pointed out, "the decline of the labor movement exacerbates income inequality not only directly but also because it diminishes the role of unions in shaping public policy. For example, partly as a result of labor's diminished clout, an increase in the minimum wage has been blocked in recent years. Tax policy, to take a second example, has favored the rich, leading to smaller revenues to invest in health care, education, and other public programs that benefit the middle class. A stronger labor movement would have produced different tax and spending policies."[9]

Unions play an important role in bringing out underlying progressive attitudes among their members. Through political education they explain to workers the significance of public-policy choices. And union leaders like Cecil Roberts of the United Mine Workers of America and Maria Elena Durazo, head of the Los Angeles County Federation of Labor, are effective in shifting attitudes and getting workers to the polls. They are trusted by workers because of their history of battling on behalf of the underprivileged, and they speak in a voice that workers can easily relate to.

In recent years unions have been very effective in getting their members to vote. In 2000, 2004, and 2006, a high percentage of union members voted, and they voted overwhelmingly for Democrats.[10] People with similar backgrounds and income who were not members of a union were far more likely to vote Republican. If organized labor had more members, George Bush would not have been in a position to claim victory in 2000, and he would have lost to John Kerry in 2004.[11] The labor movement played a key role in Barack Obama's victory in 2008.

The political contributions of organized labor have a long and distinguished history. As Paul Krugman noted:

Not only did unions provide a reliable source of campaign finance; . . . they provided Democrats with a standing army of campaign workers who distributed lawn signs, bumper stickers, and campaign literature, engaged in door-to-door canvassing, and mobilized for get-out-the-vote efforts on election day.

A more subtle but probably equally crucial consequence of a powerful union movement was its effect on the political awareness and voter participation rates of lower- and middle-income Americans.[12]

Union leaders have long played a key role in responding to right-wing extremists who use populist clichés, a phenomenon that currently pervades our political discourse.[13]

Although organized labor for many years included unions that discriminated on the basis of race and sex, activist unions played a key role in the passage of civil-rights legislation, including both the Voting Rights Act of 1965 and the Civil Rights Act of 1964. Walter Reuther marched with Martin Luther King Jr. and shared the podium with him when King delivered his famous "I have a dream" speech.[14]

Unions have made and continue to make a significant contribution to racial harmony among the different ethnic strains of the working poor. It was through the International Ladies' Garment Workers' Union (ILGWU) that poor immigrant Jews and Italians learned to work and battle together for their mutual benefit. Today in Las Vegas, the Culinary Workers Union effectively joins together black and Hispanic, African and Caribbean, Anglo and immigrant workers. HERE's Local 6 has one of the longest and most distinguished records of battling for equality of any organization in the country. Not only did it join together all of New York's diverse working-class minority groups, but, when it won its first contract in 1939, it included one of the first nondiscrimination clauses in U.S. employment history. It forbade any discrimination based on "race, ethnicity, or religion."[15] In the 1940s "the union was also successful in equalizing the wages between waiters and waitresses." In the 1950s Local 6 gave great support to the Little Rock Nine, the students who integrated Little Rock Central High School. Elizabeth Eckford, one of the group, was the niece of Scotty Eckford, then the recording secretary of Local 6. "When Ernest Green and several other members of the group were denied jobs during the summer, Local 6 and the ILGWU (now part of UNITE HERE) found summer jobs in New York for Green and several of the other Little Rock Students. Local 6 also led the battle for pay equity between women and men, raising it as a negotiating issue, filing a grievance about it and finally bringing a law suit which was settled by an agreement to pay maids the same as housemen."[16]

Michael Yates points out: "Again and again, when workers are asked why they support the union or what the union has meant to them, they say that their fight for a union was a fight for dignity and respect. . . . In scholarly language, what a union does is give workers a 'voice' in their workplaces, a way to put themselves on a more equal footing with their employers."[17]

It is the collective bargaining process augmented by a grievance system, the final step of which is a decision by a neutral party, that regularly redeems the promise of dignity. At the unorganized workplace, employees' rights against the employer are severely limited and in many areas nonexistent. Employers have the right to hire and fire largely at will. They have almost unlimited discretion in structuring and altering job structures. Workers have almost no defense against management demands, no matter how unfair or ill conceived.[18] Management determines what is to be done, how it is to be done, when it is to be done, and what constitutes success or failure. It can punish failure by any means it chooses, up to and including discharge. Management decides what to pay for particular jobs and can cut wages or increase hours. It can regulate hours, determine holidays, and decide whom to lay off during periods of downturn.

To be sure, employer discretion is limited by the market, but the market dictates that workers be paid as little as possible and that their benefits be limited in order to increase profits. The market provides no protection against layoff during periods of downturn; nor does it ensure that workers will get a fair share of the profits when things are going well. As I once heard former labor secretary George Shultz say, "When it comes to labor relations the market is all thumbs."[19] It is the largely unregulated market that has kept worker income static while executive salaries have soared.

It is of course true that under the law, management discretion is not absolute. The Fair Labor Standards Act (FLSA) sets limits on hours and requires overtime pay for nonsupervisory employees. The anti-discrimination laws require that hiring and firing be done without regard to race, gender, religion, or national origin, and the NLRA prohibits employers from punishing employees for engaging in protected concerted activity, including protesting against working conditions and providing support for unions. The difficulty with these laws is twofold: their scope is fairly limited and enforcement mechanisms are inadequate. An employee who is fired because he or she protests an employer's policy is unlikely to get that job back even if the firing is ultimately held by the Labor Board to be unlawful—something that rarely happens.

Where collective bargaining between a responsible union and a law-abiding employer occurs, the result is likely to be a workplace in which power is to a significant degree shared. Collective-bargaining agreements are instruments of change. They replace discretion with rules of the shop. They contain a series of promises by the employer to abide by agreed-upon rules in dealing with the union. In return for a union promise not to strike, employers make a series of important promises—promises about promotions, layoffs, discharges, work schedules, and vacations, among other things. As pointed out by Lawrence Mishel:

> In our workplaces, unions promote opportunity, security, and fundamental fairness.
>   Through training programs and requirements that job openings be posted and filled fairly, unions help working Americans enjoy a fair chance to get ahead.
>   Unions make sure that workers are rewarded for their years of service and have regular hours that allow them to plan ahead and spend time with their families.
>   Union employers are less likely to violate civil rights laws, less likely to violate minimum wage and overtime laws, and more likely to follow workplace safety standards. Twenty-eight percent of coal miners, for example, work in union mines. Yet from 2004 to 2006, only 14 percent of fatalities occurred in union mines. The odds of dying in a non-union mine were more than twice as great as in a union mine.[20]

Collective-bargaining agreements typically cover wages and working conditions for a period of several years. They are therefore generally lengthy, complex, and ambiguous. When an employee or the union believes that rights under an agreement have been violated, a grievance may be filed. Once filed, the grievance is handled by the union through shop stewards and the grievance committee. If pursued, it is dealt with by successively higher levels of management in consultation with their union counterparts. At each stage, management may affirm its original decision, grant the grievance, or offer to grant it in part. At any stage the union may withdraw the grievance or accept a compromise. If the grievance is not resolved through negotiation, the union has the option of demanding arbitration.

A significant number of arbitration cases deal with the propriety of discipline or discharge. To enhance its chances of winning at arbitration, a company needs to establish careful disciplinary procedures consistent with arbitration awards defining the concept of just cause. Arbitrators generally insist on equal punishment for the same offense, and they require that employees be given advance notice of company rules and a chance to explain their behavior before they are disciplined. This increases the need for a sophisticated labor-relations staff that will respond appropriately to arbitration decisions and creates a disincentive to dealing with infractions on an ad hoc basis.

This is not to say that unions are always an unalloyed blessing for workers. Unions sometimes make life more difficult—sometimes for individuals, and sometimes and in some ways for the workforce generally. Because unions almost invariably favor tying benefits and promotions to seniority, they limit opportunities for junior employees. Employees are generally required under union agreements to pay the costs of union representation. Unions also bring the danger of striking, which I discuss in later chapters.

But the overwhelming majority of unionized workers believe that the costs and dangers are outweighed by the gains in money, retirement benefits, and workplace dignity.[21]

Chapter 2 The Fall of Organized Labor: A Brief Overview

In 1964, in the conservative heartland state of Indiana, the power of organized labor was at, or near, an all-time high. Union members made up nearly half the workforce. The legislature had more union officials than lawyers or lobbyists. The state's major industry was steel, and the United Steelworkers had a major voice in the day-to-day operation of the mills. Union stewards had status comparable to that of management officials, as did business agents of the carpenters, sheet-metal workers, and electricians at building sites throughout the state. Dallas Sells, an official of the United Auto Workers and head of the State Federation of Labor, was regularly quoted in the papers, even on issues far removed from strikes and organizing. Union officials served on the boards of public and charitable institutions, and they had constant access to the governor and to major political figures. Indiana University[1] had a large labor education program, which was controlled by a board of advisers that included university administrators and top union officials. The state's attorney general issued an opinion holding that a form of collective bargaining was permissible for state agencies. Collective-bargaining agreements shaped the salaries and benefits of union and nonunion workers alike.[2]

Indiana was far from unique. From the Northeast to the Midwest and along the Pacific coast, unions were powerful and seemingly secure. They had reached a state of general acceptance and no longer considered themselves to be under serious attack from management. Unions frequently acted to support their industries. They helped employers get tax breaks and promoted the products that they manufactured. Top union leaders rejected notions of class struggle, which was thought to be a relic of a bygone era. According to Vincent Sirabella of HERE, "It was common for labor leaders in the fifties, the sixties, and even into the early seventies to say that the major battles with management were over, that the labor movement had arrived, that management respected and accepted us, and all we needed to do was cooperate with them."[3]

The smugness of that era is long gone. Unions today have far fewer members and far less power.[4] They are under constant attack from employers, courts, and commentators. In many places they are fighting for survival.[5]

The labor movement has been hurt by major changes in the U.S. economy. The decline in U.S. manufacturing in key industries—steel, autos, apparel—cost hundreds of thousands of union jobs.[6] But the loss of manufacturing jobs is only part of the story. The economy kept growing, adding new jobs, particularly in construction, transportation, and service industries. Unions failed to organize successfully in those growing areas of the economy. And their share of the manufacturing sector declined. Why did they fail?

Conservative economists argued that private-sector unions were no longer relevant in the new economy—that they harmed the economy and did not bring significant gains to workers. According to Leo Troy, "The twilight of the Old Unionism is rooted in Schumpeter's theory of Creative Destruction and the New Age of Adam Smith. Capitalism and free markets spawned trade unions, but as these business processes evolved trade unions have not kept pace."[7]

This statement was written in 2004, and Troy, like many economists, believed that the forces set in motion by the "New Age of Adam Smith" were bound to intensify and force what he called "the Old Unionism" "deeper into the Twilight Zone." But the faith in unrestricted business reflected in Troy's statement has in the few years since he wrote those words largely disappeared, even among economists. Today, far fewer people accept the idea that business processes have evolved in a way that makes resistance to its goals and processes unnecessary and undesirable. People are searching once again for ways to control the predatory practices of corporate leaders, and unions are the one group with a record of having done this successfully.

Liberal economists and union supporters blame the decline of unions on a combination of employer hostility and the law's inadequacy. According to Nobel laureate Paul Krugman: "The answer is simple and brutal: Business interests, which seemed to have reached an accommodation with the labor movement in the 1960s, went on the offensive against unions beginning in the 1970s. And we're not talking about gentle persuasion; we're talking about hardball tactics, often including the illegal firing of workers who tried to organize or supported union activity. During the late seventies and early eighties at least one in every twenty workers who voted for a union was illegally fired; some estimates put the number as high as one in eight."[8] A similar point has been made by Dorothee Benz: "The reason this [union decline] is so is in significant measure the result of U.S. labor law, and in particular its inability to guarantee the right to organize it proclaims on paper. There is widespread agreement in labor and academic circles alike about the failure of the law to protect the right to organize, and there are numerous studies and countless examples documenting the role of weak labor laws in encouraging virulent anti-union campaigns, both legal and illegal, by employers. . . . 'Particularly problematic are NLRB policies that allow employers to wage no-holds-barred anti-union campaigns.'"[9]

Management opposition has played a big role in thwarting unions. In the public sector, where management has remained neutral, unions have fared much better and now represent somewhere around 35 percent of eligible workers. Also, since the 1980s, polls have consistently shown that a far higher percentage of workers favor unionization than the percentage unionized.

But attributing the failure to organize solely to management opposition and illegality is a simple and comforting explanation for a complex process. Unions bear significant responsibility for their own demise. When the need for organizing new members arose, they were not ready. They did not heed the warning voices from their own ranks urging them to prepare. During the 1960s and 1970s, unions focused their activity and resources on serving their existing membership through collective bargaining, contract enforcement, and a range of supplementary services. Collective bargaining is interesting, exciting, and obviously meaningful. During the days of union power, each agreement was generally a small triumph that produced higher wages, better health care, more free time, more benefits for family members. For most union staff, handling grievances was effective, satisfying work. They were directly responsible for making sure that members received the benefits of the negotiated contracts. When members were unfairly discharged, the union could generally get them returned to work. In carrying out their assignments, union staff did not need passionate member involvement, did not expect it, and generally did not seek it. Nor were union members generally eager to take on serious responsibilities in addition to their regular work. It was a system of professional service that met the goals of both union staffs and union members.

The trend toward professionalism in unions was given additional impetus by the complexity of legal regulation in both organizing and bargaining. The technical role of union representative or business agent served to separate the staff from the membership. As said by Daisy Rooks, "Under the direction of professional staff, many unions often ceased to be militant, class-based social movements. Instead, many evolved into reactive and often stagnant service-providing institutions."[10]

The shift in focus from organizing to servicing is understandable and consistent with union democracy. Nevertheless, the leadership of organized labor was blameworthy for losing sight of the need to organize and the need to maintain the spirit of a movement. They ignored warnings from within their own ranks and marginalized those who issued the warnings. They let the interests of the staff take precedence over the goals of the movement.

From the 1960s onward, most unions failed to give organizing the high priority that it required. They failed to hire a sufficient number of organizers, and they didn't adequately train those they hired. They routinely assigned their ablest staff members to collective bargaining and those least able to articulate and inspire to organizing. As a result, too many organizers ran unimaginative campaigns in which they relied on dated handouts replete with portraits of a fat, smug, cigar-smoking "boss," which had little relevance for workers dealing with young, sophisticated human-relations professionals. Poorly run campaigns gave some workers the impression that their opinions did not count, that decisions were made solely by the organizer or by the organizer and a small group of his or her favorites. As John Wilhelm, the president of UNITE HERE and one of the movement's best organizers, told me in 1985, "Organizing is not a priority for organized labor. It's not surprising that something that is not a high priority doesn't do very well. It hasn't been a priority in the last thirty years." Even after losses in membership and power were clear, most unions continued to engage in isolated organizing efforts using outdated methods and poorly trained organizers. Through the 1980s, less than 4 percent of the funds available to unions were devoted to organizing.

This is not to ignore the unfortunate contribution of our labor laws to the problems besetting unions. As I discuss in later chapters, the rules governing union representation campaigns give management a major advantage in resisting efforts to organize. The law governing striker replacement regularly makes the right to strike a misnomer. The law dealing with secondary boycotts and organizational picketing seems to make union activity a special disfavored class under the First Amendment. Our laws badly need amendment. Nevertheless, as Wilhelm recognized, unions could have significantly reduced their losses had they focused more effort and imagination on organizing and made a greater effort to mobilize their membership. As Dorothee Benz has explained, for example, the Culinary Workers Union (Local 226 of HERE) managed to sidestep the Labor Board and successfully organize in Las Vegas over determined management opposition. The Culinary used movement tactics—membership involvement, street and job protests, and where possible alliances.[11]

Movements are often nourished by outside attention and support. In the 1930s and 1940s, the labor movement was given great support by intellectuals and artists. Labor's struggles were the subjects of books, dramas, films, articles, and countless stirring songs. The children of New York garment workers and Midwest laborers sang the songs of Appalachian mine workers and believed that they were involved in a common struggle.

During the 1960s and 1970s, the onetime powerful alliance between unions and liberal intellectuals began to fade. The rise of the civil-rights movement inevitably turned attention away from unions. The successes of the labor movement made the cause of workers seem less compelling. By the late 1960s and early 1970s, radical students, liberals, and some minority leaders began to consider unions with their high salaries and desirable jobs protected by seniority as part of the power structure that perpetuated injustice and inequality. Seniority, once recognized as a major impediment to discrimination, was suddenly perceived as one of the reasons that black workers were "last to be hired, first to be fired." Union leaders came to be viewed with suspicion. Many were corrupt. Some unions, like the Teamsters, were gangster ridden and ready to sell out the interests of the members for the good of the leaders.[12]

The divisions between unions and liberal intellectuals were exacerbated by the Vietnam War. Unions supported the war, encouraged in part by the efforts of the Johnson administration and U.S. diplomats to build a democratic labor movement in Vietnam. Union families too supported the war, and their sons helped fight it. They were stunned to see college students carrying the Vietnamese flag and insulting veterans just back from combat. On the other hand, to many intellectuals in the anti-war movement, labor's support for the war simply illustrated that union leaders had sold out to capitalist exploiters.[13]

By the 1980s, with unions weakening, employers went on the offensive in bargaining. According to Richard E. Walton, Joel E. Cutcher-Gershenfeld, and

Robert B. McKersie, "During the 1980s anywhere from one-third to one-half of all labor-management agreements in the Untied States were characterized by some form of concessions."[14] Many organized employers began to see in the collective-bargaining process an opportunity to rid themselves of unions. The bargaining process easily lent itself to abuse through a three-step process. First, when a collective-bargaining agreement was due to expire, the company would demand major concessions it knew the union could not possibly accept and would steadfastly reject all major union counterproposals. This could easily be done without violating the law. Unions would be forced to strike to prevent the employer from implementing its proposals, which it could do once the negotiation was at an impasse. Second, when the union struck, the employer would permanently replace the strikers. Third, the replacement workers would then vote to decertify the union.[15] Management-provoked strikes—used by Phelps Dodge, Hormel, Boise Cascade, and International Paper Company, among others[16]—were a common part of the 1980s labor-relations scene.

When management provoked strikes, unions did not know how to respond. They did not have in place alliances with other movements. They did not know how to apply economic pressure on employers beyond that which they could achieve through the establishment of a picket line. They relied on occasional advertising and statements from union leaders in the struggle to win over public opinion. They did not know how to harness the enormous potential of their membership during strikes.

The problem of organizing became a crisis when unions were faced with the massive challenge of globalization. Jobs in union-organized heavy industry moved overseas. The heavily organized steel industry was probably the hardest hit.[17] The auto industry, once American dominated and fully organized, underwent massive changes as American companies were forced to compete with less expensive, more fuel-efficient cars from around the world. And in the mid-1980s, the problem became acute when Japanese and Korean carmakers built plants in the United States and defeated the United Auto Workers (UAW) in a series of representation elections.[18] The Big Three automakers employ far fewer workers, and competition from Japanese carmakers, especially Toyota and Honda, is now being conducted from nonunion plants in the United States. Indiana is a prime example. The auto industry once provided thousands of union jobs. Those are fast disappearing. New automaking jobs coming into the state are nonunion. The largest new facility is the 5,000-worker Toyota manufacturing and assembly plant in Princeton, Indiana, built in 1996. It remains steadfastly nonunion. Throughout the country, new factories owned by foreign car companies have defeated the UAW's organization efforts. By the end of the first decade of the twenty-first century, both ordinary people and right-wing political figures blamed the UAW for the crises in the U.S. auto industry.

Over the past decade, unions have begun to concentrate once again on the need to organize. The most successful have begun to switch from single-unit campaigns (referred to as "hot shop" organizing) to broader, longer actions known as "comprehensive campaigns." They have learned to use their economic power as an aid to organizing. They have tried to use their considerable political influence to change the law to make organizing in the face of employer opposition less difficult. Despite these welcome signs of renewed interest in organizing, however, there are serious differences in approaches among unions dedicated to organizing. Simply put, the issue is this: Should unions insist on organizing from strength, using their members and developing a strong support in the target workforce? Or should they organize wherever possible, recognizing that in many cases they will have to build strength and solidarity after recognition has been achieved?

Chapter 3 The NLRA

Organizing Process

Section 9 of the NLRA provides for secret-ballot representation elections to determine whether the majority of workers in a potential bargaining unit wish to be represented by a particular union. The Board's process has dominated organizing for over sixty years. It was established to promote the Act's basic policy: free choice. Free choice requires that employees feel free to choose or reject union representation without fear of economic reprisal by the employer or unlawful acts by the union. Although each individual worker is entitled to free choice, the wishes of the majority of the voters determine whether collective bargaining occurs. If a union wins a representation election, it is certified as the bargaining representative of the employees in the bargaining unit. The employer is then required to bargain with the union over the wages, hours, and conditions of employment for all employees in the unit. If the union loses the election, no collective bargaining takes place and the employer can continue to operate as it sees fit as long as it complies with the law generally. Since employers are eager to avoid unions and collective bargaining, the election is typically preceded by a campaign in which the employer seeks to persuade its employees to vote against representation and the union makes the case for it. These election campaigns generally follow a predictable pattern.

Organizing drives typically begin in response to employee discontent that is communicated to the union. Workplaces where workers are known to be unhappy are called "hot shops" and are considered by union organizers to be prime targets for the union message of increased power and dignity for workers. Not all unions limit themselves to hot shops. Some unions pick their targets in terms of maintaining, obtaining, or increasing power in a particular location or with a particular employer. But hot-shop organizing has been, and remains, the primary organizing technique of most unions.

When a hot shop is located or brought to the attention of the union by an employee, an organizer is dispatched to evaluate the situation by talking with employees and trying to get a measure of the degree of discontent. Once the union decides to begin an organizing drive, it may enlist additional organizers. To establish employee ownership of the campaign and to spread the union's message more easily, organizers generally form employee organizing committees. Thereafter, either the organizer or the organizing committee will ask employees to sign authorization cards designating the union as the workers' representative for purposes of collective bargaining. Signing a card of this type is a major commitment that few employees make unless they want union representation. To get workers to sign up, the organizer or committee will stress the increased power and dignity that comes with worker solidarity. They will point out that union workers have higher wages and better working conditions. Union organizers will hand out union literature that stresses the power of the union and the value of collective-bargaining agreements. Often, union organizers will ask the employees about the changes they would like to see and then show them contracts from other bargaining units that have achieved those improvements.

When the union obtains signed authorization cards from a substantial majority of the employees it is seeking to organize, it will typically write a "recognition letter" to the company's chief executive officer advising that the union has signed up a majority of employees, offering to prove this to an impartial observer, and requesting that the company enter immediately into a bargaining relationship with the union. Employers rarely agree to bargain at this point. Instead, if they have not already done so in response to rumors or supervisory warnings, they will contact a management lawyer or labor-relations consultant who will advise them to refuse recognition[1] and to undertake a preelection campaign to reduce the union's support.

When its request for recognition is rejected, the union will file an election petition with the NLRB specifying the unit of employees that the union claims to represent. When the petition is filed, the employer can, and in most cases will, challenge the proposed unit, claiming that, for one technical reason or another, it is "inappropriate" under Board standards. The employer might argue that some of the included employees are actually supervisors and thus ineligible for representation or that the unit wrongly excludes employees who have a common interest with those included. Before the Labor Board proceeds to an election, the unit issue must be resolved either by Board decision or by agreement of the parties. Raising the unit issues gives employers the ability to delay the election and mount a campaign to turn employees against the union. Eventually, the terms of the election and questions of eligibility are typically worked out by agreement of the parties. Almost invariably it is the union, fearful of losing its majority, that makes concessions and accepts the company's proposed unit. Employers may seek to reduce the number of employees in the unit and to eliminate key employees in order to weaken the union in subsequent bargaining or in the event of a strike. They may also seek to increase the unit in order to include employees whom they believe to be resistant to the union's message.[2]

The end result of the process is a secret-ballot election in which the employees vote either "yes" for unionization or "no" to reject it. Historically, for most elections, the union campaign was designed and controlled by the outside organizer who enlisted and signed up the workers, responded to management attacks, and calmed the fears of union supporters. It was the organizer who decided when it was time to petition for an election. And it was the organizer who initially determined whether the employer had violated the NLRA and if so, what action to take. Thus, the professional skill of the organizer was crucial to union success. Today, organizers tend to share responsibility with inside organizing committees, which makes campaigns more worker controlled.

Employer campaigns are usually directed by a labor-relations professional, either an attorney or a management consultant. At one time, most employer representatives would conduct moderate campaigns, trying to stay within the law. Moderate campaigns had two advantages from the employers' point of view. If the employees voted no and there was no illegality, the matter ended with the election. If the union won the election, it would be easier to come to a reasonable agreement without the hostility likely to be created by threats or acts of reprisal. Employer lawyers who stayed within the law were convinced that they could run as successful anti-union campaigns as management representatives who relied on threats and reprisals.

But according to experienced organizers, the era of the moderate campaign is largely past. The lawyers and consultants now most likely to be employed by management are those whose campaigns are always on the border of illegality or regularly go beyond it.

The themes struck in formal employer campaigns have been remarkably similar across elections and time. They focus on four main areas: the likelihood of a strike; the cost of union dues; the uncertain outcomes of collective bargaining; and the fact that the union, by threatening the profitability of the employer, might cause harm to the employees.

The emphasis on dues is intended to suggest that workers will pay a heavy price for union benefits and to attribute a mercenary motive to the union, thereby undercutting the idea that the union organizer is motivated by the desire to help workers. "Why is this union interested in you? Why does this organizer who does not even live in this community care about whether or not you join the union? The answer is that you are a source of money to permit union bosses to live the high life they are now living." Employer campaigns often make the amount of the loss concrete. For instance, sometimes employers give the employee his or her pay in two checks, one reflecting the current wage minus expected dues and the other the amount of expected dues. Some employers put on display a large quantity of groceries that cost the same amount as monthly or yearly dues.

Employer campaigns always stress that if the union wins the election, there is no assurance that the employee will obtain higher wages or increased benefits. The employer announces during the typical campaign that it will exercise its legal right to resist "unreasonable demands." The employer will point out that, under the law, it is not required to sign a contract that it considers harmful to its business. And the employer will argue that if the union does not agree, the union's only recourse is to strike.[3]

The possibility, indeed the likelihood, of strikes is a constant theme of all employer campaigns. Typical is the following excerpt from an actual campaign: "Strikes are a brutal and unpleasant experience. You get no wages, no unemployment compensation, and new employees may be hired to permanently replace you. Strikes generate ill will. Violence is not uncommon. Management loses during a strike too. In a strike everyone loses, except the union organizer. He will draw his pay fifty-two weeks a year."[4] Focusing on strikes permits the employer to draw a sharp distinction between the needs of the workers and the motives of the unions. The employer typically seeks to paint union leaders as essentially indifferent to the welfare of the workers, whose lives they damage by forcing them to go on strike.

Employer campaigns invariably seek to convince the employee that they have a stake in the business's profitability, a stake that the union threatens. The employer will claim that it is paying the workers as much as it can afford. The employer will either say or suggest that if the union harms profits, it threatens wages and ultimately the business itself.[5] Some variation of the following speech is almost always used: "In the past, the company has given you all the wage increases and fringe benefits it could afford and still stay competitive. We have given you these things voluntarily and without your having to pay one cent to any outsider or having to strike. We have done this because we want this to be as good a place for you to work as this company's financial ability and business will permit." An implicit part of this argument is that the financial interests of the employees are inevitably tied to the employer's profitability. That the union does not realize this endangers both the employer and the employees. As one employer put it, "We are not ashamed of being interested in profits. After all, if it wasn't for profits, there would be no reason for us to stay in business or provide jobs for you."

Most employer statements leave the source of the harm likely to result from unionization somewhat ambiguous. Roland Samson, formerly the Northeast organizing coordinator of the United Steelworkers, told me that most employers "imply really bad things are going to happen if the union wins. You know—read between the lines." Some are more explicit in suggesting that the employer will retaliate against employees if they vote for the union. Explicit threats rarely come from top management but are sometimes made by supervisors in one-on-one situations. Some employers go further and fire employees whom they know to be active union supporters. According to Samson, this technique has become increasingly frequent: "One thing I'm now seeing quite a bit is they will find out who the leader is immediately, and they will find a way to terminate that person as soon as they can. They'll make up another excuse for the discharge, but the employees are not fooled."

Such reprisals have two purposes. They remove a union supporter from the premises and from the voting rolls. They are also intended to intimidate the remaining employees. Of course, discharges undertaken for such purposes are unfair labor practices, but they are almost impossible to fully correct. The union must file charges with the NLRB to get the matter addressed. The employer will inevitably claim that the discharge was based on a legitimate cause having nothing to do with the organizing drive. A time-consuming process that may take years to finish ensues. In the meantime, the discharged employee is removed from the premises and the voting rolls.

Even when the employer conducts an illegal campaign that includes reprisals and threats, it is common for the campaign literature to take a friendly tone, using first names in salutations and closings as if to demonstrate the employer's other, more humane, side. Frequently, employer literature purports to correct factual errors in the union's campaign or to convey information about the election process in a disinterested fashion. Such propaganda might be titled "fact sheet" or "information bulletin" to contrast it with "irresponsible" union claims. If wages are low and working conditions poor, the company will stress job security or the fact that management has been willing to do small favors for employees, such as giving them time off in emergencies, lending them money, or permitting them to exchange shifts. The employer will claim that such behavior will become impossible once a union is on the scene and a collective-bargaining agreement in force.

Another standard management argument is that the union organizers are outsiders, angry mercenaries who make their living by promoting class warfare that will create a less friendly and more adversarial relationship between management and workers. Employers rarely attack the basic concept of unionism. They frequently acknowledge that unions once did good work—but always at other times, in other industries with other, less worker-friendly, employers. But, they insist, unions are no longer needed—not today; not here; not in this industry, this plant, this workforce. Unions have become too big, too rich, and too removed from the true interests of working people. Employers' campaigns frequently disclaim a general anti-union bias and instead characterize the union conducting the organizing drive as particularly corrupt, strike prone, inappropriate for the employees, or insensitive to their needs.

Employer campaigns are rarely completely negative. Management will suggest that it is sensitive to the concerns that led the employees to consider unionizing and that, given a chance, it will improve things on its own. Management will blame the law, which prohibits promises of benefits, for its inability to be more specific.

Management campaigns are conducted through a variety of techniques—prepared speeches to the assembled employees, letters (written by management's lawyer but signed by someone in management), and often one-on-one conversations between supervisors and workers. Although the traditional arguments continue to be made regularly, according to union organizers that I have interviewed, management campaigns today are far more intense than they were in the 1970s or 1980s.

Almost every management consultant or lawyer has certain tactics that he or she regularly uses: the double paycheck, the movie depicting the horror of a strike, and the guarantee letter that contains a place for the union organizer to sign pledging that workers will get more money or other benefits if the union wins. Some professionals like to conduct a survey in which employees are asked questions about their job attitudes in a way that suggests that changes will be made. If the professionals are good, they can survey without falling into the legal traps of soliciting grievances or promising benefits. A professional consultant often urges employers to get tough, to discharge employees thought to be union sympathizers as soon as they step out of line in any way. Some professionals urge their clients to act friendlier and more accommodating, but most suggest a business-as-usual approach.

There is nothing in any of the management arguments that cannot be answered effectively by an experienced union spokesperson. Union organizers will counter management's contention that workers will be dragged out on strike by pointing out that strikes are rare and (in most cases) that they require a vote of the membership—often a two-thirds vote. Union organizers can point out that decisions concerning bargaining positions are made by the employees themselves. "You are the union" is a line that appears in almost every union campaign. Union spokespeople will argue that management can afford increased wages and benefits. Increasingly, unions will point to the great disparity between what the workers are paid and what top executives receive in salaries and bonuses. Often, the union will affirm its desire to be reasonable and permit the employer a fair profit. Unions usually waive dues until the new benefits are obtained.

Able organizers have ready responses to the argument that they are unable to guarantee improvements. One organizer presented with an employer's guarantee letter explained his refusal to sign as follows: "What you get from the company isn't up to me; it depends on how strong you are and what you want. It's your local union, and if you support it, you'll be successful."[6] Through songs, literature, films, and meetings, unions try to convey a picture of the power of working-class solidarity and its ability to empower workers, giving them a voice at work that they never had before.

Unions scoff at management reminders of personal favors to employees, arguing that such favors would not have been necessary in a unionized shop. Unions point with pride to their history, and their literature includes positive quotes from famous people. Which quotes they use in a particular election depends on the makeup of the workforce: for example, papal statements for Catholic workers and, for minority workforces, Martin Luther King Jr.'s comment that "the labor-hater and labor-baiter is virtually always a twin-headed creature spewing anti-Negro epithets from one mouth and anti-union propaganda from the other mouth."[7]

Where suggestions of improvements are made, the union will claim credit for them. A typical union letter argues that "it took Local 561 to make the company discuss your needs, but have you been promised anything definite? Is it in writing? Is it signed? Whose word do you have that conditions will improve? The word of the company? Up to now that word hasn't been worth much to you."[8]

Unions regularly criticize the employer's campaign, claiming that it was designed to frighten and confuse. The union will seek to reassure employees fearful of losing their jobs by pointing out that the NLRA forbids employer retaliation against union supporters. The union will emphasize that it will take whatever steps are necessary to protect its members and card signers. The union will also emphasize that the company campaign was designed by an outside union-busting lawyer or consultant whose exorbitant fees would have been far better spent on salary increases—"It's a shame that the tremendous fee being paid to Mr. Flynn is not used as pay raises for you, instead of for scare letters." The campaigns of particular lawyers and consultants are sufficiently standardized that skillful organizers can predict the substance and sequence of their management campaigns in advance and rebut management's claims.

The great advantage that employers have is not the strength of their arguments but their ability to make sure that all their employees hear them and hear them often and in different ways.[9] Another advantage that employers have is that unions stand for change and that for many, perhaps most, people— even those locked into situations that they find unsatisfactory—the thought of substantial change in their lives is frightening. Finally, because remedies are slow and inadequate, employers as a practical matter have the ability to discharge union leaders and thereby weaken or even destroy the inside organizing effort.

Even in the absence of discriminatory discharges, it is very difficult for an outside organizer to give the employees needed reassurance with respect to the employer's arguments and the employees' concerns about change. For an organizing effort to be successful, the union campaign must be conveyed in part through well-respected fellow workers. This is a crucial part of the union campaign. The best organizing efforts constantly put forward the employee voice as the voice of the union. As Roland Samson explained to me, "The key under the operating conditions we have in this country is to have a well-trained informed organizing committee. Then we have a good shot at winning."

Every employer campaign seeks to exploit employee fears of the consequences of unionization. Efforts to create or exploit fear inevitably carry some suggestion of possible reprisals. But it is not clear how this fear affects votes. An employee who fears reprisal and believes that the vote is secret—and the great majority of voters do—might well conclude that his or her interest would be best served by voting for a union that can provide needed protection against reprisals.

Employees evaluate the union during the campaign. Will it be fair, reasonable, and democratic? Since the organizer initially stands for the union, employees will be likely to study the organizer's behavior for clues as to how the union will perform. In a typical campaign, at least some employees who are mildly in favor of unionization as an abstract concept will conclude on the basis of such observations that the particular union is unworthy of support. This is another reason unions today rely increasingly on internal organizing committees of respected employees to deliver their message. If the members of the organizing committee are not well respected, the union's chances of winning are substantially reduced.

Unions that have secured card majorities often lose election campaigns. The gap between card majority and final outcome has helped generate two related, but as yet unproven, hypotheses: first, that employers generally win representation campaigns by frightening employees into voting against representation; and second, that management consultants are particularly skillful in devising means of frightening employees. I have my doubts. I interviewed over a dozen management consultants at length during the course of my study on union organizing (discussed in chapter 17). I found them to be, in general, earnest but not terribly imaginative people. The campaigns that they conducted were based on simplistic models of employee behavior and did not depart from predictable themes and tactics.[10] I believe that the reputation of virulent anti-union consultants as having great skill in manipulating employee voting behavior is one of the myths of labor relations, a myth that persists and expands because its propagation is in the interests both of the consultants, who derive business from being perceived as tough and effective, and of the union organizers, who can then explain their failures in terms of the skill, resources, and ruthlessness of their opponents.

This is not to say that union organizers are being dishonest but rather that intimidation is a handy and, to some extent, self-exculpating way to explain an otherwise surprising loss.

The NLRB election process applies only occasionally in the construction industry, where employers and unions are permitted to enter into recognition agreements before a construction project is undertaken. When such an agreement is entered into, employers generally agree to hire employees through union hiring halls. Employers sign these agreements for two reasons: to avoid labor strife in areas where unions are strong and to use the union hiring halls as a good place to get skilled workers. Also, the line between employers and workers and between supervisors and workers in the construction industry is not as clear as it is in other areas. Many small construction firms are owned by workers who maintain their union affiliation and sometimes work as employees. Union business agents in the industry are a part of management and often see their role as making sure that the job is properly staffed and well run.

Unions are experimenting today. Even those unions that regularly use the NLRB election process are seeking new ways to organize. John Hiatt, the general counsel of the AFL-CIO, told me of a campaign by the United Steelworkers to organize 10,000 car-wash workers in Los Angeles. The campaign arose out of an affiliation between the Steelworkers and community groups: "The community groups were starting a labor-standards-enforcement campaign. They had been working on it for a year. They came to realize that even if they were successful in getting these five hundred employers who are all sub–minimum wage up to minimum wage, that when the spotlight disappeared and the labor enforcement agencies backed off, standards would revert unless there was unionization and collective bargaining as an ongoing enforcement mechanism. And so they came to us and invited us to find a union that would go in and partner with them to make this a joint community-labor campaign. Foundations are very interested in this, and I think it's potentially a wonderful model of community-labor cooperation."

Experimentation is likely to continue as long as the current system remains in force. All union organizers agree that this system is badly in need of reform.

Part II **The Story
of UNITE HERE**

Chapter 4 HERE and Its History

UNITE HERE is dedicated to organizing and motivated by a powerful sense of movement. How it came to this position is an important, sometimes inspiring, sometimes frustrating story. The union has overcome employer opposition, legal harassment, and internal schisms. Its story is illustrated primarily by the history of its major component, HERE.

HERE began in 1891 as the Waiters and Bartenders National Union, affiliated with the American Federation of Labor (AFL).[1] Many of its members were immigrants, and meetings were often conducted in German and French as well as in English. It began as a union of skilled craftsmen with little interest in the unskilled and exploited—often immigrant—workers who staffed the ",back of the house" in both restaurants and hotels. The union's early development was controlled largely by Jere Sullivan of St. Louis, the secretary-treasurer. Sullivan was honest and dedicated but far from a supporter of inclusive unionism. Slight and carefully groomed, with piercing eyes and a stern, no-favors-asked expression, Sullivan was not interested in bringing the great mass of immigrant workers from eastern and southern Europe into the union's ranks.

Twenty years after its founding, the union had barely scratched the surface of the hotel and restaurant business. Its membership made up less than 10 percent of the restaurant workforce, and it had little impact on wages and working conditions. Despite its claims to represent hotel and restaurant employees generally, it was known by most as the Irish Bartenders Union.[2]

In 1912 the Industrial Workers of the World (IWW)—often referred to as the Wobblies—established the rival Hotel Workers Industrial Union to compete with HERE, and in the second decade of the twentieth century they had considerable success, focusing on low-wage, mistreated immigrant workers. The success of the Wobblies forced HERE to pay greater attention to the less-skilled workers in the industry but always over the determined opposition of Jere Sullivan, who referred to the Wobblies as "loud mouthed demagogues . . . [destined for] dark dismal failure."[3] However, acting on their own, local leaders of HERE enlisted some of the IWW leaders and members in new locals.

The union slowly expanded during the period leading up to World War I. However, the advent of Prohibition in 1920 had a catastrophic impact on its membership. Prohibition cost jobs, and unemployed waiters and bartenders were inevitably drawn to speakeasies and to association with bootleggers and organized crime. The influence of criminals in the union was to remain a problem throughout the twentieth century. By the middle of the 1920s, the union's total membership was below 40,000.

The limited force of HERE nationally contrasted with the broad-based organizing on the West Coast—San Francisco in particular. Its Local 2 was led by Hugo Ernst, a classically educated immigrant from Croatia. Ernst, the son of a rabbi, was elected secretary of the San Francisco Waiters Union in 1910 as the result of a grassroots uprising against the incumbent leadership.[4] Ernst, like Sullivan, was a dedicated and ambitious union leader and was honest and tough. But he was far to the left of Sullivan politically. In 1922 he ran for Congress as a Socialist against an anti-labor Republican incumbent and "had the satisfaction of rolling up a very large protest vote."[5] In 1923 he traveled across the country visiting state and local HERE headquarters. He issued a report that highlighted the problems that the union would experience for most of the twentieth century—indeed, many of these problems continued to trouble the union fifty years after Ernst issued his report.

In St. Louis Ernst commented about the absence of cooperation "between the waiters and waitresses. They seem to have inaugurated a system of catch as catch can, and when the girls organize a house the boys try to take it away from them and vice versa. The consequence is that no one has anything." He also pointed out that the new "monster" Statler hotel had hired mainly "non-union Negro and Mexican workers and girls," whom the union ignored. In Cincinnati he reported that "there is no union House card in Cincinnati. The waiters . . . are continually fighting with the cooks. Girls are absolutely unorganized." He commented on the lack of organizing in Washington with only 375 members and the weak state of the union in Baltimore, Philadelphia, and Atlantic City.[6]

In almost all the cities he visited, Ernst was disturbed by the long-term impact of the union's relationship with racketeers and bootleggers, which was forged because of Prohibition. He described Local 5 in New York as more of a speakeasy than a union. In Chicago he detailed in a sarcastic, angry tone how one of two gangsters vying for the presidency of Local 7 had shot and killed the other.

To his credit, Sullivan was galvanized by Ernst's report and took action against some of the abuses that Ernst had discovered. For example, after a follow-up investigation, Sullivan concluded that "the moral atmosphere surrounding the headquarters of Local 7 is wholly repugnant to decent men. . . . Soon its charter was revoked."[7]

For his troubles Ernst was physically attacked at the next union convention. Sullivan was one of the first to speak up on his behalf.

Sullivan died in 1928 and was replaced by Robert Hesketh of Seattle. Hesketh and longtime union president Edward Flore were eager to expand the union's organizing efforts. But they faced enormous problems, including the corrupting influence of Prohibition and the connection between locals in major cities and the racketeers and bootleggers. The union also had to contend with resistance from established locals and battles with rival unions. From 1929 onward, it was confronted with the Great Depression, which almost destroyed all hotel and restaurant business.

Several hotel associations used the Depression as an occasion for union busting.[8] Hotel chains at or near bankruptcy demanded wage cuts and ignored existing contracts. Workers without funds were in no position to strike, and on those occasions when they struck, they were replaced by desperate, unemployed workers forced to apply for jobs as scabs. Even Ernst's Local 2 was almost wiped out.[9] The union's membership dropped from about 40,000 in 1929 to below 25,000 in 1933.

During the early 1930s, HERE membership hit its low point. Low wages and terrible working conditions existed throughout the hospitality industry. According to Matthew Josephson, "a one-dollar wage for a full day's employ-

ment was not unusual. Waiters, working a ten-hour day at certain clubs, were
provided with one meal which they had to eat while standing up." This set the
stage for a revival of organizing led by militant organizers using strikes, sit-ins,
and demonstrations. A key example of the union's new approach to organizing
during the late 1930s was provided by Local 705 in Detroit, where organizing
was spearheaded by two young, dynamic firebrands, Myra Wolfgang and Floyd
Loew. Their organizing techniques, as described by Jean Maddern Pitrone, were
aggressive. Among other actions, they staged what was probably the first sit-in
ever at a Woolworth's store.

> They walked into the main F. W. Woolworth store at Woodward and Grand River
> on a busy Saturday. "Striiiike!" The strident order rang out as Loew blew a shrill
> blast on a whistle. Shoppers looked about in confusion as cash-register drawers
> banged shut and clerks refused to make sales. Intimidated as they saw the doors of
> the store being taken over by union agents, shoppers meekly permitted themselves
> to be herded out of the store. "Tell 'em what to do, girls," Loew yelled. The girls
> obliged, clamoring for Woolworth managers to "get the hell out of here." . . .
> Local Woolworth executives were already on their way to Woodward and Grand
> River where they were confronted by union representatives, voicing their demands.
> The stakes rose as [union president] Koenig announced the union was consider-
> ing expanding the strike to include all 40 Woolworth stores in the Detroit area. He
> would participate shortly in a telephone conference with officers in Buffalo, New
> York, Koenig elaborated, at which time a decision would be made as to whether the
> strike would go nationwide, taking in Woolworth's 200 stores.
> . . . Myra moved about the store, offering encouragement and banter. . . . Myra
> also scheduled rounds of pep-talks, bringing in Frances Comfort, who represented
> the Detroit Federation of Teachers. Frances Comfort told the strikers, "Some peo-
> ple say you're lawbreakers, but I am here, a schoolteacher, proud to be among you.
> Many of you girls were in my classes in school and there you were trained to expect
> something from life. You find yourselves here behind a counter, working for a hope-
> less pay. You are fighting not only for yourselves, but for thousands of girls like your-
> selves all through the county. . . ."
> Three days of negotiations brought the Woolworth strike to a settlement before
> Koenig's announced deadline with a major concession from the company—pay-
> ment to striking employees for work-time lost during the sit-down. The union agreed
> to accept a 5 cent-an-hour raise and won its other objectives, including a 48-hour
> week and a 1-week vacation with pay after a year of employment, as 40 Woolworth
> stores were brought under union hiring policies.[10]

Local 705 followed up its victory with a series of direct-action organizing
drives. Similar actions took place around the country. New locals were formed,

existing locals regained their losses, and some defunct locals were reorganized. It was during this period that the union moved away from its focus on skilled craftspeople and began to organize on a "wall-to-wall" basis, including, for the first time, bellboys, porters, housemaids, and dishwashers.[11]

By the time of the union's 1936 convention, President Flore was able to announce to the cheering delegates that the union's membership was approaching 100,000. Among the delegates were many new members, including many women. But the high spirits of the convention were quickly dimmed by the gang murder of a leading local officer (who had connections to the Dutch Schultz mob) and the wounding of two other delegates. It was clear that the battle with criminal elements in the union was far from over. Between 1936 and 1938, a major effort was made by Chicago mobsters connected with Al Capone to elect George B. McLane, head of the Chicago local, as president of the national union. The effort was thwarted. A key moment occurred during the 1938 convention. President Flore gave an enthusiastic report pointing out that the union's membership was now over 200,000. In a direct challenge to McLane and the mob, he concluded his speech by stating, "We propose to keep our flag flying to the wind. There must and will be no surrender." When his speech concluded, Hugo Ernst "descended to the floor and promptly yelled for all Flore men to follow him. Many delegates jumped from their seats . . . and were led by Ernst back to the platform where they hoisted the President to their shoulders."[12]

Between 1935, when Congress passed the NLRA, and 1941, when the United States entered World War II, the union increased its already vigorous organizing efforts, reaching out to lower-paid workers—maids, doormen, bellhops, janitors, laundry attendants. Much of the organizing was done through strikes demanding union recognition. Women workers emerged from the strikes with a new reputation for being tough and steadfast. Myra Wolfgang, who was among other things an early fighter for women, civil rights, and racial equality, became the secretary-treasurer of Local 705 and the first female vice president of an international union.

In 1945 Flore died and was replaced as president by Hugo Ernst, who continued Flore's emphasis on organizing. The union added organizers and devoted much of its money to expansion. By the time of its 1947 convention, the union had over 300,000 members.

Ernst died in 1954 of a heart attack. He left the union with a large membership and many dedicated activists. Nevertheless, problems of racketeering, sexism, racism, and political division lay just beneath the surface. And they came to the fore quickly under his successor, Ed S. Miller of Kansas City. When he was selected, Miller seemed like a fine choice—young, energetic, and personable. He had organizing experience and was deemed independent and honest. Miller was reelected regularly at the union's conventions and remained president until 1973.

In many ways Miller typified the business model of leadership that came to dominate the labor movement during the late 1950s and 1960s. The union did little organizing. Key decisions were made without the membership's participation. The president had the final say on all decisions. Miller seemed to devote much of his time and energy to remaining in office. Internal union politics was his concern—not building the strength of existing locals. During his presidency, membership dropped and collective bargaining stagnated. Many committed unionists within HERE were dismayed by Miller's failures. But a significant opposition movement did not develop.

Among the fiercest critics of the union during the Miller period was Vincent (Vinnie) Sirabella, who, probably more than anyone else, helped guide, and revitalize, the union. Born in 1922 in Providence, Rhode Island, Vinnie Sirabella was the child of working-class immigrant parents. His family went from poor to abject misery during the Depression: "We had maybe ten sticks of furniture in the whole damn house including the table and chairs in the kitchen. We couldn't pay the rent; we were evicted at least fifteen different times. I would come home from school and see those sticks on the sidewalk. It was horrible."

His father was a cook—at that time among the most exploited workers in the city. His mother was a maid who contributed to the family income by cleaning the houses of rich Providence families. Late in his life, Sirabella still recalled with a mixture of shame and anger watching his mother "clean dirty toilets and dirty bathrooms, and clean up the vomit on the rugs [which made her] grow old in a hurry."

The great trauma of Sirabella's life was the early death of his mother during childbirth. Twelve-year-old Vincent was forced to drop out of school. His first full-time job was as a dishwasher during the height of the Depression. The experiences of poverty, degradation, and loss were never far from his mind. "I saw the unfairness of it. I saw my father as a very hard-working man who wanted to work, couldn't get a job. I saw my mother die on a charity bench. I held her hand in the hospital the night she died. My brother lived and she died. That was a devastating thing to lose a mother in those years. I was only about eleven and a half at the time. I just looked at the country as a system that gave the ordinary person no chance at all. My father wasn't a drinker, my mother was a good woman. . . . We weren't given the opportunity. . . . I just inherently saw that it was wrong and something had to be done about it. I was filled with anger and the desire to get even in some way."

Sirabella's anger was directed primarily at those whom he saw as the exploiters of workers and at those who talked about worker solidarity but failed to back up their words. During his teenage years, he spent much of his nonworking time listening to Anna B., "The Red Flame," orating in the Balbo Hill district of Providence, excoriating the bosses and the political system. Her message resonated with his feelings: "It's always them and us. It's always the haves versus the have-nots. It's never changed from time immemorial, and we have to combat that in whatever way we can." During the 1950s and 1960s, when union leaders felt important and accepted, they accused him of a having an outdated Depression mentality: "People tell me the thirties and forties are over and 'you still have a chip on your shoulder. You're a Depression kid.' That was true. I did have a chip on my shoulder, no question about it. But I always felt strongly and I still feel that way."

Sirabella believed that worker organization was the answer to class exploitation. Unionism became the central focus of his life—a channel for the expression of his anger and an outlet for idealism. The union movement also gave him the opportunity to use his intellect, focus his ambition, and exercise his passion for words. Sirabella was always ambitious for leadership, but his ambition did not lead him to curry favor with those in power. While he was still in his teens, an act of dissent almost ended his union career: "In 1940 some of the waiters approached me. They were all immigrants and said that they thought that Billy Gill, the incumbent, was not giving them a fair shake and they wanted that changed. I agreed with them. So I . . . made a two-sentence speech. I said . . . 'I think Billy Gill has had enough time to show what he could do and I don't think he's done very much. I think we ought to give someone else a chance. I nominate Brother Irving Cornstein.'"

The result was immediate retaliation: "I was working then at a little French hotel and the head waiter said to me, Sirabella, I'm sorry but I have to let you go. I said what do you mean? I don't understand, let me go for what? He said the orders come from Mr. Dreyfus upstairs. You're a good boy; I like you, but you have to go. What happened was the union president after the meeting . . . called Mr. Dreyfus at the hotel and told him I was under age to serve liquor. I was eighteen at that time and looked older, and so they fired me and that was my first union experience."

Sirabella spent the period from 1942 to 1945 in the navy. When he was discharged, he returned to the union and his work as a waiter. In 1951 he ran for the position of union business agent. He lost and suddenly found himself out of work: "I was blackballed, couldn't get a job, the union would not send me out, and employers didn't want me. I was known as an agitator and for two years I couldn't work, so I sold Fuller brushes and then I sold vacuum cleaners door to door."

For someone who had been making good money and who prided himself on his skill as a waiter, the situation was intolerable. And Sirabella was not one to passively accept injustice: "I walked into the hall one day in the union office and said, 'Let me tell you something. I have a wife and two kids, and you have blackballed me for two years. If I don't get a job pretty soon, I'm going to pick you up, carry you up to the second floor, and throw you right out in the middle of the street. I meant it.'"

A short while later Sirabella was offered and accepted a job in the black part of town in a nightclub called the Celebrity Club. He was warned that "in this place you're going to wait on niggers and chinks and pimps and whores." Vinnie took the job, which furthered his preparation for union leadership: "I got to understand something about the black people and culture and their history. I viewed them as just another group of immigrants who are being pissed on, who needed help, and more desperately than the other kinds of immigrants in many ways."

During this period Sirabella continued to learn as much as he could about the labor movement: "I spent an enormous amount of time with old-time labor leaders, progressive labor leaders, talking with them. That's one of the things my wife used to give me hell about. I would leave work or have a day off, and I'd be talking with these guys or going to other meetings. I recognized how low my base was. I had no education and I had to learn. I was soaking it up like a sponge, and I gravitated toward those from whom I could learn."

He continued to oppose the existing leadership, and sometime in the early 1950s Sirabella filed charges against the local's business agent: "I charged him with negotiating sweetheart contracts, with neglect of duty, with disgracing himself and demeaning us by coming in to the place he's working drunk. He did it everywhere. I brought him up on charges. His cousin conducted the hearing and tried to whitewash everything. I was booed rather heavily."

Shortly thereafter, Vinnie participated in a general strike by the Providence local, which a vice president of the union settled on his own terms, a settlement totally favorable to the employers. Sirabella openly expressed his outrage. When no changes were made, he led a group of dissatisfied members of the local into the then-rival Congress of Industrial Organizations (CIO).

He remained in the CIO until the AFL and CIO merged in 1957, at which point he returned to HERE full of ideas to achieve greater rank-and-file involvement in the running of the union. Both he and his ideas were quickly rejected by the conservative leadership of the local.

In 1957 he ran as an insurgent for business manager of the local and was attacked in a series of leaflets calling him a "Bolshevik." Till the day of his death, he believed that, had the ballots been honestly counted, he would have won: "Three days after the election, the international representative came to me, and he said, let me ask you something, Sirabella. Would you take a job for us out of town? I said absolutely, and he said, Does it make any difference where you go? I said no."

In 1958 Sirabella accepted the position of business agent for the nearly extinct Local 217 in New Haven, Connecticut. He knew that the offer was made to get him away from Providence. As one of the union's current officers explained, "They wanted him out of Providence, which at the time was 2,000 people. They didn't want him running against the officers in Providence. They wanted to get him the hell out of there, so they gave him little, broken-down Local 217, and it had 60 people at the time."

Sirabella focused much of his attention on forming coalitions with other unions, and within two years, he became the president of the Greater New Haven Central Labor Council (CLC), even though he held many positions that were unpopular[13] and many that were controversial.[14] But he was a charismatic leader—handsome, with a large, open face, flowing gray hair over a broad forehead, a Roman nose, a strong jaw, and a friendly smile.

Sirabella became a community activist and was ahead of his time in speaking of labor issues in terms of human and civil rights.[15] He developed a friendship with New Haven's charismatic mayor Richard Lee and used their friendship to organize city workers and restaurants. His organizing technique, which involved the use of political pressure, was unusual at the time. As described by Betsy Aron: "When he heard that a restaurant or a hotel was opening, he would call the owner and threaten to throw up a picket line, which 'his friend, the Mayor' would be loath to cross. Often, that was enough to get union recognition. In other cases, he used the hiring hall model: as restaurants opened, he went after them with a nucleus of workers. He told the owners: 'You open a new place like this, they're [the workers] naturally anxious to go there. You'd rather have them inside than outside on opening day!' He organized from the top down, 'on the assumption that the workers would have been pro-union if he had had the resources to organize them.'"[16]

It was in 1969 that the maintenance and food-service workers of Yale, who had lost a strike in 1968 in part because of poor leadership, asked Sirabella to become their full-time business manager. He agreed and set about uniting the union, which was split along race, craft, and ethnic lines. The Yale local (Local 35) required constant attention, and Sirabella realized that he needed to find a successor as business agent for Local 217. He decided to advertise the position. He placed an ad in the New Haven newspaper that has since become part of labor folklore: "Wanted: labor trainee, person willing to work long hours for low pay in order to learn to be a labor leader. Must be unmarried." The latter requirement was added to ensure that the person would be able to devote all his time to the demanding job. Among those who answered the ad was John Wilhelm, an honors graduate of Yale and a former leader of Students for a Democratic Society (SDS), who had been active in the anti-war and civil-rights movements. Wilhelm was working at the time as a community organizer but was frustrated with the job, which he decided did little to improve life for the poor people that he served. He concluded that their main needs were economic, not social: "What they needed were better jobs, with higher pay and decent working hours." Wilhelm agreed to work long hours and accept low pay. The problem was that he was recently married and wanted to stay that way. Sirabella liked everything else that he heard and finally agreed to take Wilhelm despite his being married. The fact that Wilhelm had once been a member of SDS would have made him anathema to most union leaders, but the passion of the student movement was what Sirabella was seeking. As Wilhelm explained many years later, "Vinnie had a theory that one of the things the labor movement needed to do to revitalize itself, to get out of its complacency and lack of organizing, was to tap into the energies of the civil-rights movement and the anti-war movement, and that's why he hired me." Wilhelm was hired in 1969 to be the sole staff member and business agent of Local 217.

Yale is an imposing place. Its officials are bright, articulate, and self-confident. Its alumni are rich, powerful, and distinguished; its faculty eminent, its students marked for success. Outsiders tend to admire it, and very few want to do battle with it. But Wilhelm, having graduated from Yale with high honors, had long lost that sense of inadequacy that almost all newcomers to the institution feel. In fact, he had never quite been comfortable with its affluent style and its lack of concern for the townspeople who worked in its offices, dormitories, and dining halls: "I was absolutely blown away by that. I literally never knew there was a place like this where people had those attitudes."[17]

Wilhelm had found his calling. He began his new job by reading the contracts that Sirabella had negotiated. He realized that they went beyond bread-and-butter issues to concerns over dignity and providing for adequate vacations: "I remember the vomit clause, for example. There's a clause that he had put in the contract that said that if a maid had to clean up a room in which someone had vomited, they got paid an extra dollar. It's not a big deal. But it showed he cared about more than bread-and-butter issues. And I later learned, which I had no way of knowing then, that in spite of the small size of this town and the small size of the local, those were among the best contracts in the United States."

Shortly after being hired, Wilhelm became Sirabella's driver: "On the second or third day, I'm eternally grateful for this, he lost his driver's license. He is the worst driver on the face of this earth. He got multiple speeding tickets, and they finally took his license away. It was the greatest thing that ever happened because I drove him everywhere for thirty days. I just followed him around. That was an experience. In the course of a month he did everything there is to do, negotiated grievances, met with some organized workers, did some organizing."

It was during his work with Sirabella that Wilhelm developed his philosophy of union leadership: "I'll tell you the things I think I learned from him right at the beginning. One was that you had to be militant in order to get anywhere. Even more important was to have faith in the members. I have never to this day met another person, including myself, who has such endless faith in the workers. He absolutely believes that as long as you provide the workers with the facts and as long as you give them some leadership, they'll always do the right thing, whatever that is."

Wilhelm believed that he was uniquely fortunate to have Sirabella as his union mentor:

I had the unparalleled opportunity to virtually live with Vinnie from 1969 [to 1973]. That was an education that could never be replicated, in particular because of the extraordinary range of his union, community, and political leadership, as well as his really remarkable abilities.

Everything we did basically was fun. One of the things he always lectured me on was that the day-to-day representation of servicing the workers had to be good. He always told me that while weak contracts were a problem, the lack of day-to-day servicing was a bigger problem. . . . His philosophy was that the business agents should do everything, including handling arbitrations, which he personally was very, very good at. He handled several in [Local] 217 and I watched several at Yale. A lot of lawyers and other arbitrators, people like that were dumbstruck. I think a lot of people who came to understand what an effective labor leader he is would still be surprised that he's so good at technical exercises like that. Again, one of the remarkable features about the guy is that while he thinks in very big terms, thinks about the big picture all the time from the day I met him, he also is insistent on excellence on nuts and bolts in the day-to-day stuff, and he always said you can't do one without the other; you cannot ignore the day-to-day needs of the members and pretend to think about the big picture.[18]

Some of Sirabella's friends in the labor movement thought that he was running a risk of being replaced by his new Yale-educated assistant. Sirabella, confident of his own ability, laughed them off.

Sirabella preached that all strikes and organizing are ultimately about dignity and that constant, aggressive organizing was crucial to the survival of the labor movement. He had developed his own approach to organizing, one that centered on using a committee of workers to play the key role in the effort. It was an approach that made Local 217 one of the most successful organizing locals in the country. The more Wilhelm learned about organizing, the more he was surprised at the lack of organizing commitment and skill in the labor movement generally. He came to the conclusion that a major reason for the failure of unions to organize effectively was the purge of anyone thought to be radical during the McCarthy years: "They chased out a lot of people who might have withstood the complacency that developed." That Miller and his cohorts failed to chase out Sirabella was not for lack of trying. As Wilhelm explained, "He only survived because he is the toughest person on earth."

Sirabella transformed Local 35 by establishing a leadership structure and creating a spirit of solidarity. The first task required time, patience, and a belief in the ability of the members: "I set up a shop-steward system. I trained them myself, trained functional illiterates. I tested them orally. I showed them alternative ways to fulfill those responsibilities. Fifty percent of the bargaining unit couldn't read very well; most of them couldn't write at all, especially in housekeeping and to a great extent in the kitchen."

The second task required toughness and vision, a perfect fit for Sirabella:

I had to pull the blacks and the whites together because there was an awful division between the groups here and between the skilled and the unskilled.

The snobs in the powerhouse and the building trade sector would say something about those nigger dishwashers, and I said, "Wait a minute, you can't win it without those niggers and without those dishwashers and don't you ever forget that, brother. . . . I don't care what you do after five [o'clock]. Do whatever you want, but between eight and five you better be together or I'm taking a walk."

The thing I pounded at, "It's your battle, not mine. You have to assume the burden, it's going to be your union." It didn't happen immediately. I had to work on it very hard. But finally, they began to come together.

By 1971, when negotiations for a new contract were scheduled, the union was still in the process of transformation. Wages and working conditions were poor. "Lower-wage workers, primarily women and minorities, earned only barely above the legal minimum wage. They were laid off at summertime, at Christmas, and at spring break. Fully a third of them were on welfare."[19] Wilhelm did not think that the union was ready to strike. He believes that the Yale negotiator was instructed to encourage a strike in order to crush the union. The time seemed ripe. As Sirabella noted in a report to the union's general executive board, "The Union's vulnerability was evident. We could strike on May 1. Five weeks later most of the students would be going home for the summer. Two weeks later graduation would be held. One week after that, Mr. Brewster [Yale's president] was going to London. . . . Other negatives were the 12% unemployment rate in New Haven, the past history of student scabbing, the always uncertainness of rank and file cohesion under the stress of a strike, especially a lengthy one, and the strength of our adversary Yale's awesome power."

Yale's chief negotiator told Sirabella that "what's required now by the union leaders is statesmanship as John L. Lewis demonstrated when he agreed to abolish the jobs of thousands of miners in order to protect the jobs of a fewer number of men."

It must have given Sirabella, the ninth-grade dropout and lifetime student of rhetoric, great pleasure to respond in elegant language paraphrasing Winston Churchill: "Our rejoinder was 'The mine workers' example is neither analogous nor germane to the issue at hand. Moreover, to paraphrase a political leader of the past, we wish to inform you that we did not become the leadership of this union to preside over its liquidation.'"[20]

Negotiations quickly reached an impasse. The strike that followed was bitter. It ended friendships that Sirabella had formed with Yale people in the antiwar movement, in which he had played an important role.[21] "They were nowhere to be found when the Yale workers had it on the line," he told me. "I remember in particular Sloan Coffin. . . . At one point I wanted to rip his head off."

Nor did he find much support during the negotiations from the Yale students, many of whom at that time considered themselves radicals. "New Left" students had, for the most part, little sympathy with old-line unions like HERE. They considered organized labor, at best, a movement whose time had come and gone. Sirabella was an anachronism: "My style bothered those kids, too. I guess I was an enigma to a lot of people around then. How can this guy be a liberal, how can this guy be really legitimate and genuine when he's wrapped up in the cause of the workers here? He's your institutional type, an old guy; he's this and that and the other thing. I think I had a major problem with every group on this campus."

When the strike occurred, Wilhelm thought it likely to be lost: "I think any rational person, including myself I'm embarrassed to say, would have never led that strike. Not only then but now, knowing what I know today, I would have been reluctant to lead that strike, and I'm embarrassed to say that. I didn't take him on about it at all."

According to Wilhelm, the strike that followed was kept alive only by Sirabella's toughness and determination: "He carried that goddamn thing on his back and there's no other way to look at it, and he particularly talked about the lower-paid people, especially the blacks. That strike really had very much of a civil rights theme to it."

The union had hoped to embarrass the university by getting Willy Brandt, the chancellor of West Germany, to refuse the honorary degree that Yale offered him. But despite requests from various senior officials in the labor movement, Brandt announced that he would attend and accept the honorary degree. Some urged calling off the strike at that point, but Sirabella refused. His report to the union's executive committee described the events leading up to the strike:

> On Thursday June 10th the Executive Board of Local 35 issued the following statement. . . . The Local 35 Executive Board . . . will recommend at the meeting that the members adopt a plan for massive non-violent demonstration to prevent business as usual at Yale's commencement ceremonies next Monday and at the other commencement and reunion festivities scheduled for the next 10 days.
>
> Brewster has left us with no choice but to say to Yale that it will not be allowed to celebrate its graduation as usual.
>
> On the next night, June 11, 800 members poured into the auditorium to participate in the non-violent demonstration on Monday June 14th. George Wiley had loaned us one of his key men, Bruce Thomas, who addressed our members.

Wilhelm considered Thomas's contribution particularly valuable: "He's the best street organizer I have ever seen in my entire life, a tall, handsome black guy, maybe thirty. The guy was a phenomenon—one of these people who could get people he never met before to do things that afterwards they would say, exactly how did I ever do that? There were about seven hundred people there. Vincent talked about the contract and the struggle, and Bruce got up and talked about the battle for human rights. And Bruce had that crowd of people, diverse as they were at Wilbur Cross High, all standing up holding hands, singing 'We Shall Overcome.' I've never seen anything like that in my entire life."

Sirabella later told me that Thomas's "speech was just so wonderful, tears were streaming down everyone's eyes in the whole auditorium, including mine. I finally wound up saying, 'You can rest assured Yale will not be permitted to have its traditional pompous ceremony in the streets on Monday. We will not permit them to have it.'"

Black and white workers locking hands and singing "We Shall Overcome" doesn't seem particularly inspiring or surprising by today's standards. But back in 1971, the antagonism in the North between white ethnic groups and civil-rights activists was fierce and often violent. It was a testament to Sirabella's effectiveness and Thomas's rhetoric that the Yale workers had overcome ethnic divisions in favor of class-based solidarity. Efforts to negotiate an agreement went on at a frantic pace over the weekend, but they failed.

On Monday morning, June 14 at 9 a.m., our members plus several hundred others (about 1500) assembled on the lower green adjacent to the University. Our objective was to confront Brewster during the graduation procession and demand that he enter the negotiations to help end the strike. Father James Groppi, the civil rights priest from Milwaukee, spoke about the justice and morality of our cause and his willingness to join in support of the union. His presence was especially uplifting for the many Irish, Italian, and Polish Catholics in our union. At 10 we began our march with one of our members leading, carrying the American flag. We stopped at a point two blocks away where the procession would pass. However, in an effort to avoid us, Yale for the first time in its history detoured its procession. When we spotted the rerouted procession we hurried there. A cordon of police with clubs raised had formed to block us. I was the first one arrested. Eleven others, including Father Groppi, would quickly follow. Some of the police panicked and swung their clubs at our members with recklessness. One member received an 18-inch head wound. The secretary of Local 217, John Wilhelm was viciously clubbed over the back by a berserk cop. Many others had an assortment of injuries and bruises. Three hours later I was released from jail and rejoined our members, who had been kept together in song by George Wiley. We publicly vowed to go to jail daily if necessary. We marched through the streets to Brewster's house, and demonstrated and then to the Lawn Club where Brandt was honored at a luncheon. After serenading the Chancellor, we marched back to our strike headquarters. The following Friday the class reunions were scheduled and we promised disruption of those activities. On Tuesday the mediators said that Yale would like to meet on Thursday. We reached agreement late Friday afternoon. The three-year contract was ratified on Saturday. Out of this struggle we built a union that will never be pushed around again.[22]

Sirabella thought that the attack on Wilhelm was particularly valuable to the union and embarrassing for the university: "What they did to John was something awful. We had films of that; we went to Channel 8. We were thinking of filing a brutality suit. It shows this cop whacking John with a club, and John is down on the ground. John was pulling away, trying to get away from this animal, and he drags himself about ten feet and tries to get up, and they keep hitting him. He did it a third time, and the same thing happened. When I heard all this shit, I really got angry, and I picked up a bullhorn and I said, 'Let me tell you something Brewster, you didn't beat us today. We beat you, and let me tell you something else. We're going to do this every day for the rest of the strike. We're going to get justice one way or another. They can start arresting us tomorrow and the day after, and when those old guys come this weekend, we're going to do a number on them.'"

The shared, emotionally powerful experience tightened the bond between Wilhelm and Sirabella. The sight of Wilhelm crawling to his feet after each beating was stirring to Sirabella, who might have seen in it a metaphor for his own career in the union. Wilhelm considered this victory one of Sirabella's greatest achievements: "If you compare the '68 contract with the '71 contract, you'd think you were on a different planet. I don't personally know of another achievement that can be compared to that. He did it with no staff, no stewards, no structure, no nothing. He probably succeeded because of his enormous personal strength. No matter what was going on, no matter which individual was opting out or losing their nerve, he never once thought that the workers were doing anything but the right thing, and that's one of the reasons why we won that. I could not have done that then and I'm not sure I could do it now, and I don't know anybody else who could either."

In the aftermath of Local 35's victory, Wilhelm was shocked to learn that Sirabella was treated with disdain by the union's national leadership. At one point, Sirabella drove to Cincinnati to meet with the national union president, Ed Miller. It was a depressing meeting. According to Wilhelm, "Vinnie told Miller that he wanted to do something more than what he was able to do in Connecticut. Miller said forget it, there's nothing for you to do and there's nothing to be done." Sirabella would regularly appear before the annual January meeting of the union's executive board,[23] preaching the need for rank-and-file involvement, greater militancy, and a greater focus on organizing. His comments were not merely ignored; they were treated with open contempt. As recalled by Wilhelm: "Ed S. Miller didn't just turn his back. I saw with my own eyes that when Miller was general president, he would get up from his chair when Vinnie sat down in the speaker's chair, and would return only when Vinnie had finished." Wilhelm witnessed this travesty of union democracy in 1971, 1972, and 1973.

Local 35 struck again in 1974 and 1977. After these strikes, the union had finally achieved a major goal of year-round employment and a livable wage for all Yale employees.

I was a visiting professor at Yale Law School during the 1977 strike. The strike had aroused a great deal of interest, especially—but by no means solely —among black students, who recognized that many of the lowest paid of the maintenance workers were black. I had the chance to watch Sirabella in a debate with Yale's chief labor negotiator. The debate was held in the packed auditorium of the law school. By then Sirabella had learned how to appeal to student opinion, and by the middle of the debate, outrage at Yale's refusal to make a decent proposal on wages and health care was widespread. With Sirabella sailing along and student support for the strike growing with almost each exchange, I saw a small knot of students huddling together. They seemed unhappy with the pro-union turn of events. Afterward, one of the group was recognized and said something like the following: "Mr. Sirabella, you've told us about the suffering of the strikers and their trying to get along without their pay and the indifference of management, but what about you? Aren't you still getting your pay while the workers you lead are struggling?"

The question was met with a loud chorus of boos and a small round of applause. Sirabella waved his hand to stop the boos. "That's a fair question," he said. He looked thoughtful. "The truth is that our situations are different. The strikers are seeking a decent wage and a fair contract. I have a contract with the union that guarantees me a decent wage. It is also the case that while the strike is on, the strikers are not working but my work increases. So I am now working eighty and ninety hours a week for the same basic wage." There was a smattering of applause and a few sarcastic laughs from the anti-union corner. "So it's entirely reasonable that I continue to get my pay during the strike." Sirabella paused as though finished. Then he leaned forward. His voice rose, filling the auditorium. "But as a matter of conscience, so long as the strike continues, I refuse to touch a single penny. Everything I earn goes to the strike fund." The auditorium erupted in cheers. It did not surprise me that the strike was settled, on terms favorable to the union, shortly thereafter.

In 1973, while Sirabella was focused on building Local 35, HERE's president, Ed S. Miller, died. His successor was Ed Hanley, who came from the ethically challenged Chicago Local 1. Hanley did not seem likely to be an improvement. He was a Chicago bartender often accused of having links to organized crime. The Department of Justice later alleged that Hanley's election as president of the union was assisted by the Chicago crime boss Joey Aiuppa. Although Hanley denied the accusation, he regularly refused to testify about mob connections when questioned by congressional committees. But Hanley recognized that the union, after twenty years of leadership by Miller, was in bad shape. It was losing members, and it was doing little organizing. He had been quietly listening to Sirabella's message of change while Miller was notably absenting himself. Fifteen years later, Wilhelm recalled his surprise at Hanley's commitment to change: "When he became the general president, the very first thing he said was, 'We have to get rid of these old ways of doing things like organizing. They don't work any more.'"

Hanley authorized Sirabella to hire four new organizers for Local 217. And once again, Vinnie ignored the traditional patronage system and appointed people of unusual talent, including Karl Lechow, who went on to become the organizing director and international vice president; Morty Miller, who became the director of the Service Trades Council, a multiunion bargaining coalition; Henry Tamarin, who was later elected president of Local 1 in Chicago; and Debbie Anderson, who is currently the coordinator of the union's airport program.

As Sirabella's status in the union improved, his unhappiness with the leadership of HERE, with the exception of Ed Hanley, continued: "I think that they get into these positions of authority, power, influence, comfort, large incomes, and all the other things, and they insulate themselves from any possibility of being deposed or even challenged."

The lack of respect was mutual. As Sherri Chiesa, a Sirabella protégé and now the union's secretary-treasurer, explained to me: "They hated him because he was pushing them. The labor movement had been resting on its laurels for a long time. And Vincent told them, 'We've gotta involve our members and we've gotta be militant.' Most of the leadership of the union had been around for thirty and forty years. And frankly, they weren't doing anything. Well, Edward saw that. And I think he realized that without a Vincent Sirabella bringing along new, aggressive, young union leaders, the union was gonna get its ass handed to it. And at the same time Edward had to balance the fact that the majority of the executive board of the union and people in leadership positions came from the old guard."

Chapter 5 The Rejuvenation
of HERE Local 2

In the mid-1970s San Francisco was the gathering place for radical groups formed in the late 1960s and early 1970s. Restaurant work, with its shifting schedules, was a job that fit easily into their lifestyle. They believed in unionism but thought that most unions, including HERE, were either corrupt or too accommodating to employers. By the early 1980s, self-styled revolutionists began showing up at Local 2 meetings and demanding fundamental changes. To control the situation, Hanley appointed an old-time union functionary, Joseph Belardi, who came out of the cooks' local to be president of Local 2. He was a poor choice, not well equipped to deal with the new, diverse makeup of the union. According to Marc Norton, who worked as a dishwasher at the time: "During the Belardi administration, the maids were, for all practical purposes, viewed merely as the ladies' auxiliary. All the important power brokers came from the better-off crafts— cooks, bartenders, waiters, and some waitresses. Back in those days, these crafts were also much more white and much less immigrant than today."[1] Those who were unhappy with Belardi and the conservative policies of the local formed an opposition group, the Alliance of Rank and File (ARF). They quickly became a powerful force. In 1978 the members voted Belardi out and selected, in his stead, David McDonald, an eloquent, well-educated ARF leader.

The new leadership could do little. The executive committee was split among the various factions of the union, which essentially immobilized the local. Negotiations with the major restaurant chains and hotels were about to begin, and the union had no coherent strategy. Members of the executive committee, including McDonald, asked Ed Hanley for help. Hanley called on Vinnie Sirabella: "Vince, we got a pack of trouble out there in San Francisco. A bunch of radicals have taken over the union. I want you to go out there. You know how to deal with the Left—you've dealt with them all your life." Hanley appointed Vinnie trustee of San Francisco Local 2.

The ARF radicals, who had little knowledge of the union's history, saw a gray-haired, ethnic union official and assumed him to be a conservative bureaucrat. "Vinnie the Bolshevik" became "Sirabella the fascist dictator."

Here I am a stranger, and I walked into town filled with Maoists and Trotskyites. The Soviet supporters were considered the right-wingers out there. Every gradation of the Left had their own caucus, their own newspaper, and they are all attacking me because I'm a "racket" guy that Hanley sent out there. All of the sudden, overnight, I'm a right-winger.

I arrived there September 18, 1978, my wife's birthday. and I checked into the Hyatt Regency the night before and I walked to the union from the Hyatt Hotel, and on the foundation of the building in red letters about two feet high was "Hanley and Sirabella keep your hands off Local 2." That was my salutation. Welcome to San Francisco.

Well, I walk in and I had arranged a meeting with the existing staff. I sat down with them and presented my credentials, my authority to take the union over. Within an hour I had a visit from three people from ARF. So I sat down and said, "Good morning, what can I do for you?"

They said, "We don't want you in this city."

I said, "You're not alone in that desire. However, I've been given an assignment and responsibility, which I'm going to carry out." I agreed to meet with their members.

An hour later I get a call from the gay caucus. They came in, and they said we want to know what your position is on gays. I said, "It's very simple. If any employer tries to take advantage of your gayness in any way at all, I'll go right for their jugular. I don't care what you do in your sex life. That's your business. I don't care what you do; I have enough problems worrying about my sex problems without worrying about yours." And I gave them a large donation for their political action committee.

But ARF stayed on the attack. The leafleted me in every hotel and restaurant, called me a racket guy, called me a fascist. Then they went to the *Examiner* and gave an interview to the *Examiner* and rapped the hell out of me.

The next day Sirabella had a press conference. The first question set the tone: "Mr. Sirabella, it has been speculated that you have been sent here by the international union to suppress the progressive elements in this union." There was no better way to rile Sirabella than to question his working-class credentials: "I said, 'Obviously you haven't checked my background.' I said, 'I don't think a labor leader, any labor leader, can be anywhere but on the left side of the spectrum. If you are on the right side, you really should be working for the Chamber of Commerce. However, I make a sharp distinction between the constructive Left and the destructive Left because the destructive Left has a hidden agenda that collides squarely with the interest of the workers of this country,' I said, 'and to the extent that there are destructive elements in Local 2, I will not only suppress them, I will extinguish them.'"

After the press conference, Sirabella, as he had promised, met with the radicals:

They went on the attack. "How dare you talk like you did?"

I said, "Let's get something straight. I didn't learn my stuff in any college campus like you did. I have a PhD that I picked up in the gutter, sleeping in Salvation Army shelters since I was thirteen. I talked to you guys on Monday with clean hands. You gave me no chance—you went right after me yesterday and I'm not complaining about that, but don't complain about me going after you today. I don't care whether you're a Maoist or an Albanian or whatever you are. You're free to express any idea you want, but I got to pull this whole union together. It's falling apart, and those employers are up on top of the hill laughing at all of us, licking their chops, anticipating how they're going to grind us all up next year. I believe there will be an inevitable citywide industry strike next year. I welcome you, in spite of what you did to me yesterday, to join the team, but if you keep attacking me publicly, I'll cut your fuckin' ears right off your head. You take your pick."

Sirabella began implementing his program of grassroots involvement immediately. Marc Norton recalled how different his operating style was from that of Belardi: "One of the key things he did was allow for an elected negotiating committee. That was brand new. We hadn't had anything remotely like that in anybody's memory. Those contracts had always been Belardi and company went behind some door with the boss, they hammered something out, they came out and if they bothered to tell us what it was and said take it or leave it to you. So having an elected negotiating committee changed the dynamic quite a bit. And when they had the elections the amazing thing is Sirabella's international backed slate took about 50 percent of the seats on the negotiating committee for hotel contract and the continuing divided rank and file movement also took about 50 percent. So the contract negotiations became fascinating to use one word."

During his period as trustee, Sirabella selected and trained shop stewards and called an election to select a citywide bargaining committee: "There was a strike going on against Zim's—twelve restaurants citywide. I put the new rank-and-file bargaining committee on it. Finally, I get the settlement. Now the committee, including one guy who was part of ARF, votes unanimously to support the settlement, a Cadillac settlement. They couldn't do anything other than that. So I call a ratification meeting two days later. And they [ARF] go after me again, calling me a crook and a gangster and all this bullshit."

When ARF tried to disrupt the meeting, Sirabella blew up at them. He announced to the membership: "You either hear me explain the terms and give you an opportunity to vote on this, or I'll go upstairs to my office and sign it. If you want to listen to these crazy lefties out here, it's all right with me. We've got a unanimous recommendation on this thing here including one of the guys from their group. If you want to stay on the street, go ahead, stay out there as long as you like. It's okay with me." Fortunately, "sensible people took control and put them down and passed it in a breeze."

Flo Douglas, who had been the head of the now-merged waitresses' union, told Sirabella that to cement his support, he needed to appoint a woman as business agent. She suggested a recently hired clerk, Sherri Chiesa.[2] Sirabella somewhat reluctantly agreed to interview her. Chiesa later recalled, "He was tough, very tough. It was one of the scariest job interviews I ever went through. But to his credit, he gave me a chance."

Just as Sirabella was gaining control, a federal judge dissolved the trusteeship and ordered new elections. By then, Sirabella had formed a highly favorable opinion of Chiesa. He suggested that she run for secretary-treasurer, the number-two position in the union. She ran on a slate with Charles Lamb, one of the ARF members originally elected to the union's executive board. He was by then out of favor with the leadership of ARF. They were both elected.

Citywide negotiations were scheduled to begin less than a year after the election. Neither Lamb nor Chiesa was an experienced negotiator. They knew they needed help, as Chiesa later recalled: "So we asked Vincent to stick around and help us. And it is during that period [that] I basically would follow him around like a puppy and sit next to him and just watch him. I learned about negotiating by watching Vincent very closely. I also learned from him that organizing was what it was all about. We had to put that first, we had to be serious about it, we had to sacrifice for it. He just pounded that message of organizing, organizing, organizing. If you were around him at all, you got to see the wisdom of that and how true it was."

They organized committees, including an elected bargaining committee, composed primarily of middle-of-the-road liberals, and asked Sirabella to stay on and negotiate their new contract with the hotel industry. He not only acted as principal negotiator but managed the predicted strike as well. The result was a major union victory—a 22 percent wage increase for the current year and substantial raises for the next three years. As Sirabella recounted:

> But the destructive Left can't allow us to have this, because this derails their whole program. I'm in their way. They have a larger program; they have the international scene to worry about and all their dialectical bullshit and cells and caucuses. So now comes the big ratification meeting in the stadium. I got a call from the police intelligence a couple days before the meeting—anticipate trouble. Charlie Paulsen was director of organization, and he said to me, "You need a bodyguard out there; that's a rough town right now."
>
> I said, "What am I going to do with a bodyguard? If somebody wants to kill you, how do you stop them?" I'll take my chances. I mean it was such a good contract— no one was going to turn it down. They [the radicals] were supposed to be the champions of the maids. I delivered for the maids. Hell, they got 35 percent in two months.
>
> I began to explain the terms of the contract, and I wanted to be as precise as I could. Charlie, the president of the union, and I were the only two on the platform and we both got bombarded with eggs. The second thing they did, they lit firecrackers in the hall. Hundreds of people were terrified—they thought some shooting was going on. Anyway, we got through that somehow, and I continued the explanation of the contract.

After further confrontations, the contract was ratified overwhelmingly. In the aftermath of the meeting and vote, Sirabella was interviewed by the press outside the stadium, "and then all of the sudden, I got hit in the eye. I was in shock, and then there was all this fluid on my face. I instinctively tried to brush it away and realized that I was bleeding. That was the lead story on the television that night. And that was the beginning of the end for the destructive Left. By the time I left, I had strong support from the rank and file."

Chiesa admits that the entire episode remains controversial within the still-radical San Francisco labor community: "It's a very controversial strike to this day, with lots of disagreement in our membership about whether we won or lost. I believe we won. We certainly got significant improvements in the contract. Where the dispute comes was how much improvement did we have prior to the strike as opposed to post strike. My view of this is that our membership was so angry that it didn't matter what the contract was, we had to have a strike. Because the workers were just up in arms about the way they were treated. So I view it as a very cathartic thing that had to happen, I think the strike was transforming for our membership."

Some of the Yale organizers, including John Wilhelm, Henry Tamarin, Karl Lechow, and Debbie Anderson, traveled to San Francisco to help out with the strike. They discovered, according to John Wilhelm, that the "sectarian left factions in Local 2 were more interested in fighting with each other and with the international union than they were in fighting the employers." It was the "housekeepers and kitchen workers who patrolled the picket lines."

The new, controversial agreement was signed in 1981 and expired in 1984. Controversy over the 1980 strike kept the union divided and its members angry. In 1984 new negotiations began with the restaurant industry. Another strike occurred, one that almost everyone agrees the union lost disastrously. In 1985, in the wake of the strike, Chiesa was elected president of Local 2. She explained how it happened:

> There were seven candidates for president and five full slates running. And I just determined that I was gonna be straightforward and not lie to people. Most candidates were running around saying vote for me and you won't have a strike. I was not saying that. I was saying vote for us. We're gonna get organized. We're gonna go back to grassroots. In fact, my campaign was called "Back to Basics." It was "Let's get organized." Then whether or not we strike, you guys are gonna make that decision. The members were receptive to that, and I won the election. So we organized the membership to win. That's how I won. So I become president, and I am facing this enormous challenge with the hotels because the hotels saw us on the brink of getting destroyed by the restaurants, and they figure they were going to put the nail in the coffin. And I decided that I'm [in] over my head. I don't have enough experience to deal with this. And I asked President Hanley to send me help. And he sent me, God bless him, John Wilhelm. And John worked with me through that whole thing. We won the greatest contract; it was spectacular. It was the greatest experience of my labor career.

It was Chiesa who conducted the negotiations, with strategic help from Wilhelm and Jeff Fiedler: "The hotels were appreciating in value hugely, so the hotels would come into negotiations and say occupancy is down and we're not making enough money, so we can't give you what you're asking for. So John and Jeff Fiedler came up with this idea in which we put a proposal on the table, which was all about 'Okay, we don't want a wage increase. All we want is our piece of the appreciation of the hotel.' And the press ate it up. I mean these hotels were appreciating by 200 percent in a year—it was just unbelievable. And so that was really one of the things that caught the hotels' eyes. But bottom line is, all the tactics and all that aside, the only reason we could carry it out is because we organized the members, and that was what was different from the 1984 strike."

Sirabella's impact on the union was well summed up by Marc Norton, one of his longtime opponents: "He made sure that the international remained in charge—that was his assigned task and that was Hanley and all he represented. On the other hand, he certainly had a more struggle-oriented view of what needed to happen here. It wasn't to the point that I thought we needed or could have done, but he was more interested in fighting with the bosses than Belardi was. He also understood, and this was really the beginning of the fundamental change in Local 2 in the period I've been around. He understood that the leadership of the union had to base itself not just on the most privileged members, the white guys in the fancy restaurants and the bartenders and such, but it had to root itself first and foremost among the room cleaners and the dishwashers and the stewards and the people in the back of the house."

Thereafter, Local 2 became one of the most active organizing locals in the union, using Sirabella's combination of worker activism and alliances with progressive forces. Chiesa herself advanced from leadership role to leadership role, becoming a member of the union's executive board, first as vice president and then as general secretary, once Jere Sullivan's position.

Sirabella's ability to achieve gains and focus the membership on union priorities led to his appointment in 1983 as director of organizing for the union.

Chapter 6 Organizing Yale's
Clerical and Technical Workers

When Ed Hanley appointed Vinnie Sirabella western regional director of HERE in 1980, it left a vacancy at Local 35, and Hanley, acting on Sirabella's enthusiastic recommendation, appointed John Wilhelm chief business agent. Soon after his appointment, Wilhelm, strongly supported by the members of Local 35, began an organizing campaign among Yale's clerical and technical workers, creating a new Local 34 to represent them.[1]

Organizing the clerical workers was bound to be a formidable task. The bargaining unit that the union sought was large, somewhere between 2,500 and 3,000 employees. It was diverse, including secretarial workers, librarians, journal editors, science technicians, and employees of Yale University Press. The workforce was dispersed throughout the many different schools, departments, bureaus, centers, and research groups. They had no history of solidarity; they were divided by skill level, salary, status, and job satisfaction. There had never been a successful organizing effort in a similar unit.

Wilhelm's organizing team was small, consisting only of four organizers at first and then two more.[2] The model for their previous organizing efforts was fairly simple. It was described to me by Ellen Thomson, one of the Local 217 organizers, as "find leaders, get a committee, have them understand what the union is about, prepare them for what an employer would say about union corruption, dues, and strikes, train them to talk, and organize."

The organizers of Local 34 quickly found that their previous tactics were not adequate to the task at Yale. As Thomson explained: "There was no model for organizing 2,700 people in two hundred separate buildings in offices of one and two and three and four. Our model was based on hotels where there are lots of people talking to each other, so the ratios were different. At Yale, if you got something exciting going in one building, it's not like it spread like wildfire across the campus. So the numbers and the ratios we contemplated were way off. Committees had to be much larger and stronger. There had to be this huge organizing committee. If there were four people in an office, there had to be someone on the committee."

The organizers reveled in the realization that they were breaking new ground. According to Thomson, "People used to joke about where's the book, what does the next page say? Well, there was no book. We were writing it."

The role assigned to the employee-activists went well beyond that common to members of internal organizing committees. Wilhelm explained: "We, out of necessity, developed the idea of a steering committee. We realized that we had to have people beyond the organizers who took greater responsibility and met every week, which they still do, and coordinated the organizing committee, which in turn would work with the workers, and that didn't turn out to be enough either. We eventually developed what we referred to as the rank-and-file staff, which meets every week or every two weeks, depending, and which now numbers sixty-five people who really are organizers."

Lee Berman was one of those early recruits: "I was brought on by one of the paid organizers. She pulled me forward. In fact, in this union one thing that happens is that you can be catapulted to great heights within a small amount of time. I came on in August, and in November I'm speaking at a big rally. It's crazy! There was a reason that I became involved then and didn't earlier, and that was because I realized that this was a very different organizing drive, and I have seen some of the others and they just weren't the same. They weren't built from the bottom up like this union was. I really liked the organizers, and I understood that what they were working for was something they could be proud of. And I loved organizing. I really enjoyed watching women, particularly, stand up for themselves."

One of the union's most effective tactics was comparing salaries of the union-ized maintenance workers (overwhelmingly male) with those of the nonunion-ized clerical and technical workers (overwhelmingly female). Berman told me, "It wasn't until we started looking at differences within the C&T [clerical and technical] unit that I realized that there was a real discrimination going on. I don't think I came into this whole thing thinking that there was any particu-lar discrimination against women. I thought it was against the group as a whole."

The drive did not become public until the union had secured authorization cards from more than a majority of the clerical and technical workers. The cards were hard won. Instead of stressing, as many unions did at the time, that a signed authorization card would be used only to get an election, Local 34 em-phasized its significance. Wilhelm told me, "We actually have a printed piece of paper that we gave out with the authorization cards that said 'Do not sign this card unless you've decided that you want to have a union.'"

When they had cards signed by a majority of the clerical and technical em-ployees, the union filed a petition with the NLRB seeking a representation election. Once the petition was filed, clerical workers all over campus showed up wearing union buttons, many of which announced their status as members of one or another union committee. Shortly thereafter, the university admin-istration hired the firm of Siegel and O'Connor to help defeat the union.[3]

Siegel and O'Connor began with a standard management tactic, raising nu-merous objections to the union's proposed unit. This commonly used tech-nique has two purposes: delay and disruption. Delay is known to help dissipate a union majority, and disruption weakens the union in the event of a strike. Local 34 countered by bringing members of the bargaining unit to the hearing and publicizing both the university counsel's tactics and the employees' reac-tions. For example, in February 1983 the union distributed a handout that in-cluded a transcript of the hearing and the following employee responses: "I found the hearing extremely degrading. . . . Watching the University stall our rights is disgraceful." "Yale was condescending, manipulative, devious, and out-right insulting to the clericals and technicals. . . . Not once would they meet our eyes. . . ." "It is increasingly evident that Yale is using every possible stalling technique. What the University may not realize, however, is that every day these hearings are prolonged, more and more support for the union is growing."

The effect of these statements, which were distributed campuswide, was dra-matic. It increased the feeling that many clerical workers had that they were dis-respected by the university administration. After a few weeks of constant attacks in union handouts, university counsel caved in and accepted the unit as described by the union. This turned out to be very helpful to the union.[4]

This tactic was used for the first time in the Yale campaign. Wilhelm was surprised by its success: "We sort of happened on it. It never occurred to us before to actually use the NLRB bullshit as an organizing device. It never crossed our minds, and we stumbled on to it by accident, and boy did that work."

Another innovation was the "Declaration of Independence Poster." Six days before the election, the union plastered the entire campus, during the night, with three-foot-tall cardboard posters designed to resemble the Declaration of Independence. The poster declared in bold letters "WE BELIEVE IN OURSELVES." Below was a paragraph in smaller type: "As Clerical and Technical employees at Yale we believe that our work is vital to the success of Yale's mission. . . . By joining together in our Union . . . we can achieve our rightful place as equal members of the Yale community."

To the side and below the text were over a thousand signatures. The care with which the signatures were written made clear that the signers believed they were doing something to be proud of. This technique, according to Wilhelm, came from another union: "I got that idea from someone who put out a much smaller version on a little sort of a scroll in a state organizing campaign here in Connecticut. I thought it was a really great idea."

With all its special tactics, the heart of the union campaign was the testimony of its members. From the start, the organizers undertook to inspire potential leaders to speak out publicly. This was a delicate task. Most of those recruited had never been activists of any kind and certainly not spokespeople for a controversial cause. They had previously worked in the shadows of their superiors. They demurred at first, but when they actually found themselves stepping forward, most of the activists found the experience exhilarating. As Andrea Ross, whose life was permanently changed by the experience, told me at the time, "There were times when they pushed me to do things that I felt were difficult or didn't want to do. . . . Like this building . . . where there's this group of anti-union people. They were extremely hostile, and it was much easier for me to ignore them and speak to people who were receptive, . . . but [an organizer] was pushing me and we went in there and had a couple of major arguments and afterwards I felt very good that I did it, and the next time it wasn't quite so difficult."

The union's rallies had a quasi-religious flavor. Members testified about their failures, temptations, and ultimate redemption through solidarity. When Local 34's president, the eloquent Lucille Dickess, described how she had fought unionism in the past and how she had become converted by realizing that university officials did not truly respect her, people wept, cheered, and stood up to applaud her. The sense of being inadequately respected was widespread, and it fueled the organizing drive: "Many of us felt that we were the invisible part of the Yale community: there to do the work without which the University couldn't function, but overlooked, ignored, voiceless."[5]

The emotion of the meetings affected the organizers, too. Paul Clifford, a Yale graduate who currently leads the union's Toronto local, told me that "I was moved to tears at every single big meeting we had." A feminist secretary wrote of similar reactions: "I was brought to tears more than once by the eloquence and fire of some of the women's speeches, and the feeling of massive support for making women's lives better. The enthusiasm for this struggle was evident from long rounds of cheers and applause and standing ovations from the crowds of women and men. I was inspired and filled with a sense of purpose that provided a kind of political renewal for me—the seasoned feminist."[6]

Both paid organizers and members of the inside organizing committee told me that the experience of working together changed them in a deep and lasting way. The change was most vividly described to me by Clifford: "I really think of it in very personal terms—how people changed personally and how I changed personally and how there's now an incredible intangible bond of solidarity. For me it was a changing of class. I grew up in an upper-middle-class professional family, and I've thrown my line in with working people, and that's where my identification is, and I don't identify with the students at Yale University, and I don't identify with the faculty. I can get along, and I know how people think and everything like that, but I really identify with the people who work for the university and the people who live in the city of New Haven, and not with the people who run Yale University or try to push around the city of New Haven. That's the change that I've gone through, and it's something that I'm not going to go back on."

In January 1983, just before the NLRB election, Yale University president A. Bartlett Giamatti issued a statement in which he claimed that unionization would disrupt "the structure of relationships created between the members of the staff and the University. It would be an additional threat to the collegial spirit that animates this place." At the union's urging, the noted labor historian David Montgomery and I prepared a response with the help of two law students, Cindy Estlund and Sam Issacharoff.[7] In our statement, we declared that "the administration's so-called 'fact books' are filled with distortions, misleading innuendo, and mischaracterizations about unions and collective bargaining. We are especially disappointed that the administration has acted as though the very idea of collective bargaining were a menace to . . . the collegiality of the University community." We concluded that it was "embarrassing to witness the University's use of its reputation for scholarly excellence for such an ignoble end." The union distributed our response to the voters.

The election was held in May 1983. Hundreds of union supporters attended the final vote count in one of Yale's auditoriums. The vote was close, and the count seesawed back and forth. When the union victory was ultimately signaled by John Wilhelm's putting his hands over his head, the workers cheered, cried, stamped their feet, and chanted "Union! Union! Union!" over and over.

It was a notable victory and received a great deal of favorable publicity. Clerical workers had never before been unionized at an elite academic institution. Wilhelm was portrayed as a master strategist in many articles. But he himself came away with a sense of how much he had learned and how little understanding there was in the ranks of organized labor about the relationship between workers and organizers.

> I think that we have a much better understanding of what the function of the organizer actually is, which is not to organize the workers at all but to train the rank-and-file leaders. It's a commentary on the movement's lack of focus on organizing that we had to learn. People should know that and pass it on. There have to be some isolated individuals who know these things, but nobody asks them.
>
> I'm proud of what we've done and I'm not trying to engage in false modesty here, but there are unquestionably people here and there who know some of these things. It raises an interesting historical question, why we don't know about them.
>
> One of the reasons for this is [that] the McCarthy period chased out a lot of people who might have withstood the complacency that developed.

Wilhelm was also slightly embarrassed by the fact that the organizing drive had taken far longer than any of the original planners had anticipated: "Clifford and Heyman originally came to work for us on the theory that it would take six months and they weren't doing anything else, so we paid them ten dollars a week and that was two or two and a half years ago. We made horrendous miscalculations with respect to how long this would take."

Despite the drive's success, there was an important warning signal in the closeness of the vote. The organizing drive had many things going for it that are absent during a typical NLRB representation campaign. University officials were restrained in opposing the union. They made no threats and fired no one on the organizing committee. The organizers assigned to the campaign were unusually talented and were able to make use of long-term town resentment against the university. The rank-and-file committees were made up of talented, articulate, and committed workers. The effort had the support of many faculty and feminist groups. Yet even with all of that, the union barely won.

Why, despite low wages and minimum benefits, did so many clerical workers vote no? The answer is not fear of university reprisal. I was there, and I spoke with enough clerical workers, both pro- and anti-union, to feel certain of that. Nor was the union hampered by lack of access to employees. They were able to conduct open meetings and take part in debates. The "no" votes were, I believe, based on a variety of attitudes often present among workers when an organizing drive takes place. Some workers were anti-union because of their own experience or that of relatives. Many were proud of working for Yale and did not want to do anything to damage its reputation or harm its mission. Some were content with their lives and jobs and were fearful of change. Some felt somehow ignored by the union. Some feared that their own status would be undermined by a union victory.

In the aftermath of the vote, the union carefully forged its bargaining proposals through one-on-one conversations and the "circulation of two rounds of surveys to all clerical and technical workers, union members and nonmembers alike, asking which issues they considered most important. Almost 2,000 employees responded, including many who were not yet union members. This open procedure for drawing up the contract produced a significant upsurge in membership."[8]

The administration's negotiating style with Local 34 was confrontational. During bargaining sessions, it treated the union not as a negotiating partner but rather as a naive entity that required education. As a result, the negotiations had less a sense of give and take than a sense of lecture and response. At one point, the union took the bold step of inviting members of the Yale faculty to attend the negotiations as adjuncts to the union's bargaining committee. I was one of those who took part. Like my colleagues, I was dismayed at the condescending and arrogant tone and style of argument used by administration's spokespeople. I was at the time the principal negotiator for the Connecticut State Police Union. I know something about rough-and-tumble negotiating, but none of the state negotiators that I dealt with would have used the tone of moral and intellectual superiority routinely used by Yale's spokespeople.

After a series of bargaining sessions failed to produce an agreement, a strike deadline was set for April 4, 1984. The union called a meeting for that afternoon. In the meantime, however, Wilhelm came up with a novel alternative, a partial contract that would contain all the terms already agreed to by the bar-gainers. The advantage to the union would be twofold. First, the new contract would lock in benefits already offered. Second, and most important, it would prevent a strike from happening at a time when the union's ability to apply economic pressure was limited because of the coming summer vacation—when many areas of the university basically shut down anyway. The union made the proposal, and the administration accepted.

Most observers expected that an agreement would be reached over the sum-mer, but the parties were deadlocked over wages. In September 1984, the strike began. The administration was in a strong position. The union did not attempt to shut down the university. Classes were taught, although some of us found ways to teach off campus so that we did not cross the picket line. Professors were free to go to their offices, students to classes and dorms. While the uni-versity went about its business, the union members were out in the increas-ingly cold Connecticut air waving their picket signs. These were poor people who needed their pay and weren't getting it. Inevitably, some of the clerical and technical workers began to cross the picket line—some because they dis-approved of the strike, some because they needed the money, and some be-cause they thought the situation hopeless. In the end, the greatest harm to the university's operations came from the Local 35 service and maintenance work-ers, who honored the picket line and did not show up for work.

The union's leaders had earlier come to the conclusion that winning the strike could not be accomplished merely through the withdrawal of services. As explained by senior organizer Karl Lechow: "After the election victory, I took a walk with John around the [New Haven] Green. The first thing that we dis-cussed was the fact that we were never going to be able to get an excellent con-tract based on the withdrawal of service alone." The key to success, they agreed, was to strike at Yale's reputation, which was one reason for the union's repeated claims of sex discrimination. The union distributed buttons that read "65¢" with a line through it. These buttons were meant to emphasize studies at the time showing that women on average earned thirty-five cents an hour less than men. The union also represented truck drivers, and all its spokespeople made clear that the appeal for pay equity was not an attack on the salaries of the men, whom the union insisted were "worth every penny they get." By the middle of the strike, if not earlier, the union's expressions of solidarity with the members of Local 35, whose members steadfastly refused to cross the picket line through-out the strike, were obviously heartfelt.

The union also made an effort to enlist support from members of the Yale

Corporation, the board that oversees the university. Two board members were feminists: Eleanor Holmes Norton, a former head of the Equal Employment Opportunity Commission and a member of the faculty of Georgetown Law School; and Deborah Rhode, a Yale Law School graduate and professor at Stanford Law School.[9] Norton, a prominent political figure, was the union's main target. Among those whom the union enlisted in this effort was Jeff Fiedler, a researcher and strategist for the Food and Allied Service Trades Department of the AFL-CIO. Fiedler, who had developed a reputation as a master tactician, tried to shame Norton into pressuring Giamatti to settle.

Lechow believed that Norton was getting ready to resign from the board when the strike was settled. This is not clear, but Fiedler's unorthodox tactics and his willingness to take on tough chores endeared him to Wilhelm. They became friends during the strike and have worked together effectively ever since.

The union extended the reach of the strike beyond Yale to wherever the trustees were. As described to me by Lechow at the time:

> We went down to Brown Brothers, which is Madden's [a member of the Yale Corporation] bank, the biggest investment bank in the United States, and we leafleted the investment bank. We leafleted all the secretaries. We went around the halls with a leaflet saying "You are in the same boat that we're in, Madden has stepped on both of us, call this number and we'll help you organize." And we got forty calls, and he went nuts. He was extremely upset.
>
>   There were some things we did on the investment level which were just a pain in the ass to them. We would hold up certain investments, transactions of ten million dollars or more, by having proxy votes. All this let them know that we were going to extend the fight beyond the walls of Yale. They would not be able to leave New Haven and leave their worries behind. We would call our locals in Cincinnati, in Los Angeles and New York and Chicago—everywhere—and we'd picket the Yale clubs. We followed Reverend Moore [another member of the Yale Corporation] out to Louisiana. He was giving a speech to the bishops down there, and we had a group of fifteen or twenty black workers leaflet all the bishops down there, and he was completely embarrassed.

The strike became the main topic of conversation on campus and a source of meetings, debates, rallies, and class discussion. Supportive faculty organized into a group that called itself "Faculty in Support of Local 34." It included some of Yale's ablest scholars. But Paul Clifford was not happy with the very modest level of support that came from the faculty, even those who thought of themselves as radicals. As he explained to me: "I got personally pissed off at people when the strike began. People who I would have expected to speak out or to do something more active were suddenly overcome by a sort of academic paralysis. I know their thinking was that they had done everything they liberally could in terms of writing letters and making polite noises, and so then when the strike began, folks said, 'It's not appropriate for us to do anything more, because, if we act in another manner, then we're changing the way this place runs, and we don't want to do that.'"

In accordance with the union's basic strategy, it was not the faculty and not Wilhelm or Lechow but Local 34 members Lucille Dickess, Deborah Chernoff, and Andrea Ross who were regularly quoted in the *New York Times*. It was Lucille Dickess who effectively debated President Giamatti on *The Phil Donahue Show*. This was a bit of theater that the union staff recognized could only help them. As explained to me by Lechow: "It was a plus, an unquestionable A-plus. It made no difference who won. Giamatti is up against a C&T [clerical and technical worker]. A well-known academic all-star with all sorts of degrees is debating Lucille Dickess, registrar in the geology and geophysics department at Yale, a fifty-year-old lady who worked at Yale for ten years, very nice spoken. She didn't beat him on the debate—no way did she beat him. But he lost hands down."

To attract publicity to the strike, the union regularly used celebrities—well-known feminist and civil-rights leaders. It employed civil disobedience, mass rallies, and candlelight vigils in addition to traditional picketing. On October 16, 190 strikers were arrested for blocking a public road during a silent protest outside the president's home. A week later, the union conducted an even larger protest action. Over 400 people, including students and some faculty, were arrested as a crowd of over 1,000 watched. This massive turnout would not have been possible without the organizers' earlier careful, painstaking work on developing a sense of ownership of the union and the strike among the clerical workers. The large-scale civil disobedience was the subject of a feature article in the *New York Times*.

The headline read "POLICE ARREST 430 AT YALE PROTEST IN SUPPORT OF STRIKING EMPLOYEES."[10] The participation of the civil-rights leaders Bayard Rustin and the Reverend Ralph Abernathy was featured in the *Times* story: "Bayard Rustin, who was granted an honorary degree by Yale last year for his activism in civil rights, led the silent protest. 'I believe that having been made a part of the Yale community by receiving an honorary degree, I am here not by choice but because I have a moral obligation,' Mr. Rustin said. The Rev. Ralph Abernathy addressed the protesters in New Haven's First Methodist Church before the demonstration."

Abernathy's participation, not expected by the union when the action was planned, was, according to Lechow, a key moment in the strike.

Despite the adverse publicity, the university continued to insist that it had made its final proposal. Some of the strikers began to fear for their jobs. With Christmas approaching, the union announced a return to work. They described the action as "home for the holidays." The union also announced its intention of resuming the strike after the holiday season. Wilhelm referred to the cessation as "bringing the strike inside. Many of us thought that the cessation was an act of weakness, a sign that the strike was lost." Yet it was during this period that the strike was settled on terms quite favorable to the union. University officials, I later learned, were very concerned with the threat of the workers returning but engaging in slowdowns and other job actions with no end in sight. They were aware that most of the strikers, who had stayed out for almost four months, had a deep commitment to the union.

University officials were right to be worried. Wilhelm was serious about the inside strike. What he wanted to achieve was the commitment and some of the effect of a strike without forcing the union's members to give up salary and to risk losing their jobs to strike replacements: "If you can get the rank-and-file membership of the union to do all the kinds of things that they did while on strike, and have the same level of commitment and urgency about it, but also report to work, I think you can achieve great power. Personally, I was in favor of guerilla warfare, intermittent strikes. That's one of the reasons I liked the partial contract."

Selling the idea of a return to work to the strikers was not easy, and Wilhelm would not have considered using the tactic if it had not been approved by the membership. The nature of the internal debate was captured in a *New York Times* article:

> Local 34 voted on Nov. 29 to return to work. The proposal had surfaced two weeks earlier. At first, rank-and-file picketers overwhelmingly opposed it, saying it represented a retreat. But, by the night of the meeting, enough members had changed their minds, after picket-line debates, to pass the proposal, 800 to 250.
>
> Many members said that the novelty of the proposal made it difficult to assess at first, but that they grew excited about forging new ground.
>
> "I cried when I first heard about it," an administrative assistant, Carol Johnson, said. "I screamed and kept my husband up all night. But by Wednesday, they convinced me of the logic of it."
>
> "Some people were still angry, but they'll be all right," Mrs. Johnson added. "That's how it is with our union."[11]

Because the union victory happened at Yale, because prominent people were involved and spoke out, and because the victory occurred at a time when union victories were few and far between, the strike and settlement received a great deal of publicity. And the victory helped propel a whole group of Sirabella's protégés into higher positions in the union.

Chapter 7 The Need for a New Organizing Model

In 1983 HERE president Ed Hanley named Vinnie Sirabella to the position of director of organizing of the international union. It was Sirabella's longtime dream come true.[1] He had since the 1960s preached the central importance of grassroots organizing to skeptical union officials. Now he would be able to put his ideas into action. Sirabella anticipated success. He had developed an approach to organizing that seemed foolproof. Between 1979 and 1985, relying on Sirabella's committee-centered strategy, Local 217 won eleven consecutive NLRB elections. In almost every case, the local won despite the efforts of a union-busting consultant to defeat it. John Wilhelm told me at the time that he welcomed campaigns against management consultants because he knew in almost every case exactly what they would do.

Sirabella immediately began planning a major national organizing drive. He offered Wilhelm the position of second in command of the drive, but Wilhelm declined because of family commitments. The position was then offered to Karl Lechow, whom both Sirabella and Wilhelm recognized as a superb field organizer. A number of the experienced Yale organizers were enlisted in the effort, among them Morty Miller, Paul Clifford, and Jo Marie Agrieste. Sirabella also placed ads in newspapers all over the country similar to the one that first attracted Wilhelm. An impressive group of young, liberal, mostly college-educated activists responded. Sirabella grilled the applicants and came away enthusiastic, convinced that those he chose were intelligent, committed to the rights of workers, and empathetic. He was right. Most were destined for important leadership roles in the union —among them D. Taylor, a waiter and student from Washington, D.C., who now leads the Culinary Workers Union in Las Vegas.

The newcomers were given a crash course in Sirabella's approach to organizing, which stressed the importance of the internal organizing committee. The motto "the organizer organizes the committee, and the committee organizes the workers" became as familiar to them as the Pledge of Allegiance. Actual field organizing began in early 1986 with great fanfare; however, by 1989, when I interviewed Sirabella on the status of the organizing program, he was quite depressed. The major goals of the drive were not being achieved. The union won a few elections, mainly for cafeteria workers at universities and federal buildings. But it had not won a single election at a hotel.

Vinnie initially accepted the blame for the failure: "I made a fundamental blunder, and that was relying on the model we developed in Connecticut over the years, particularly the Yale University white-collar drive." He also concluded that the young organizers were not prepared for the fierce employer resistance that they encountered: "When, for example, the organizers left there, they left with this feeling that they could organize anything, which was a good feeling, but nonetheless it wasn't realistic when carried to the arena of the real fights, the real battles." And he concluded that he had sent the organizers out too soon: "I can see there's no substitute for experience. I don't care how many colleges they went through or how many degrees, you got to go through it like anything else."

He also blamed union politics for the failure: "When these kids went out into the city, they learned some of the political facts of life, that not every one of these local union leaders welcomed us. Moreover, some of their staffs were uneasy about these kids being around for fear they might take their job in some unknown way. We had all kinds of political impediments that we ran into in these cities almost uniformly. Our guys come in and immediately the staff feels threatened before we even suggest anything because they have worked twice as hard, twice as long, at half or one-third the money. They say, 'What is this?' They call them Moonies, all kinds of things. Not in any pejorative sense, but nevertheless it is a criticism. So you have all of that to deal with. And we have had to take it from friend and foe alike."

One hotel, the Tremont in Chicago, was organized during the process. The comprehensive campaign that organized the Tremont was developed with the aid of Jeff Fiedler of the Food and Allied Service Trades (FAST) Department of the AFL-CIO, who worked with Sirabella during the national organizing drive. Fiedler came up with an unusual, situation-driven tactic that permitted Sirabella to organize the Tremont Hotel in Boston without an NLRB election. Fiedler discovered through intensive research that the owner of the hotel, John Coleman, had substantial debts that he could not easily pay.

> I said to Rich McCracken [a lawyer for both HERE and FAST], "I want to send letters to these four hundred people we know that he owes money to. Can I call this thing a creditors' committee even though we're not in bankruptcy?"
>
> McCracken said, yeah, sure. And I sent a letter out. I said, "Hey, look, he owes you, he owes us, why don't we get together and get our money?"
>
> My staff does these four hundred envelopes, and then a couple weeks later they say, "Jeff, did you get any answers?" I say no.
>
> "So it failed." I said no.
>
> "What do you mean?"
>
> I said, "You think anyone wants to settle on ten cents on the dollar with us? They are all going after him for 100 percent of their money."
>
> John Coleman then declared bankruptcy with $180 million in bills and $400 million of assets, none of which were liquid. He calls up Vincent, and says, "I'm fucking done."
>
> And Vincent and I go over to the Jockey Club in New York and negotiate the contract. And I'll never forget this as long as I live. Coleman turns to me and says to me—and says, "You're a goddamn terrorist!"
>
> I said, "No, John, you just thought we were stupid."

It was a notable victory that might have served as a model for future organizing. But Sirabella initially discounted its significance because of the young organizers' failure to establish a strong committee structure: "Although we organized the Tremont Hotel in Chicago, through a comprehensive campaign, we could never have won an election, even though we had somewhere in the neighborhood of the high 60 percent of the workers signed up. But at any event, we had no committee in the Tremont. And therefore we couldn't petition for an election. It would have been a loser. The workers would have caved in. Fortunately, we found a vulnerable area to attack the company. And we went at it, and he caved and he recognized us. But in terms of trying, for example, to follow what we did at Yale, it wasn't working."

Since Sirabella was committed to the central role of worker committees, he saw the Tremont victory as something of a fluke, a reaction that disappointed Fiedler: "Vincent never got the full implications." Fiedler also thought that Sirabella underestimated the importance of research. However, even toward the end of Sirabella's career, Fiedler recognized that "his instincts were extraordinary."

D. Taylor attributed the failure of the organizing campaign to Sirabella's failure to depart from the NLRB election model that Local 217 had employed so successfully and also to his rush to get the organizers out in the field: "I think he underestimated the length of time that it takes to get skilled organizers, and we did not do a comprehensive campaign in these. We did not use corporate campaigns. And we didn't use political power. In order to organize a whole company, you've got to use all the tools—which we didn't use. We just basically organized the workers to take on these gigantic companies, and that's not a fair fight."

Taylor's analysis would be accepted by most union-organizing experts today. It is surprising that Sirabella, who had worked so patiently with Wilhelm and Lechow, rushed this new cadre into action prematurely and that he failed, except on one occasion, to use the valuable comprehensive-campaign approach that he had pioneered. Perhaps, by then in his late sixties, he was feeling the pressure of aging—a desire to achieve something momentous before he became too old or too ill. Perhaps the early victories of Local 217 through Board elections and the victory at Yale made him imagine that the process was easier than it turned out to be. He later concluded that he was too focused on finding another Wilhelm from outside the ranks of organized labor. "This was against everything I stand for," he told me early in 1990.[2] By then, the drive was gradually moving away from its NLRB focus.

In the late summer of 1987, Sirabella gathered his team of organizers together in Las Vegas to discuss the state of the organizing drive and to come up with a series of organizing principles. Before the union could move forward, it would need to form a large internal organizing committee of at least 15 percent of the membership—within ninety days—and 20 percent would be even better. When the team tried to organize Washington's historic Willard Hotel, they were unable to put together an adequate committee within the ninety-day period. Sirabella scrapped the effort. And at that point, he became angry with his team of organizers: "The eighty-second day, and we're at 12 percent, then we're picking up garbage. These are superstars, so-called. Self-proclaimed superstars. I even said to them that our national program is in jeopardy because of their fucking egos. They were afraid to fail. They were afraid to lose their reputation for greatness."

In general, the late 1980s were not a good time for Sirabella. He was in ill health, suffering from diabetes and heart trouble that would soon kill him. His anger, once a weapon that he could use selectively, was now more generally aimed at anyone who troubled him, from hotel waiters to union officials to his handpicked organizers. He was furious with Wilhelm, who refused his entreaties to move to Washington as his primary assistant. He accused Lechow of betraying him and refused to shake hands with Taylor. His anger[3] saddened many of the union's leaders. I have found no one who believed that his anger was justified but, curiously, no one who lost admiration for him. Typical was Rich McCracken's comment: "I think that he was suffering from the illness that killed him when he became so angry at John."

Sirabella did eventually recognize that the Tremont success was an important first step toward a new approach to organizing, an approach that combined worker committees with comprehensive-campaign tactics.[4] But by then, the national organizing project was over. It is quite possible that the organizing drive, had it continued for much longer, would have shifted from NLRB-centered organizing to pressure for neutrality agreements and card-check recognition. Such a shift was evident in the final effort of the drive to organize a new Marriott hotel in San Francisco. The effort began when Sirabella was notified by the president of Local 2 in San Francisco that the union had leverage with Marriott. He came close but never succeeded in organizing it using a new approach that the union would later refine. Sirabella explained:

> He tells me there's a hotel site in the Moscone Center down in San Francisco, and Marriott is bidding for it. Marriott has hired Willie Brown, Speaker of the House in California, as their local counsel, and we have the juice on the redevelopment. They can't get it without Local 2's okay.
>
> And he said, "I'm willing to make a deal with this guy in a contract."
>
> I said, "Hold it Charlie, that's not enough."
>
> He said, "What do you mean it's not enough?"
>
> "Because you never get the cards, that's why. We need more than that." So I went out there and sat down with him, and they brought the senior vice president in from Bethesda, and they had to make a decision in forty-eight hours, so I said, "This isn't enough."

He said, "What do you need?"

I said, "Neutrality."

He said, "What's that?"

I said, "You pledge no interference because if you get involved, we can't win. You hire the people, you bring them in, you pound the shit out of them, we can't win, so where are we?"

One of the final acts in Sirabella's organizing campaign was a meeting in Washington, D.C., in which he asked the new organizers to submit a systematic plan for completing the organization of the Marriott Hotel in San Francisco. What the young organizers came up with indicated how much they had learned about the complex process of organizing. Their ideas were imaginative and involved both the workforce and the general community—a far cry from the traditional hot-shop model.

Taylor suggested "planting submarines in the workforce" and efforts to obtain a pledge of neutrality from Marriott. In support of this he suggested seeking mayoral support and a city council resolution regarding noninterference of the company. Morty Miller also suggested a broad neutrality agreement and that the union seek the company's cooperation through the Local 2 hiring hall. Warren Heyman suggested that the union recruit Local 2 members to apply for jobs in the hotel. Lisa Jaiks, an international-union organizer, called for an outreach program in which union members would contact the friends and families of other unions' members; Catholic churches in the Mission district; black churches; New College, San Francisco State University, and City College of San Francisco; and Democratic clubs like the Chinese American Democratic Club, Harvey Milk Lesbian & Gay Democratic Club, Alice B. Toklas LGBT Democratic Club, and the Latino & the Roots.[5] There were many more new ideas, and they were all thorough, thoughtful, and interesting. The union was now staffed with a cadre of organizing experts, and it was ready to employ a variety of tactics—some new and some old but rarely used.

It took many years for these ideas to come to fruition. But almost ten years after Sirabella's death, the hotel became unionized.

Sirabella continued to refine his thinking during this frustrating period. He became convinced that the union needed to expand its campaigns from one-on-one battles with particular hotels to broader battles with the major companies: "If we take on a Sheraton in City A, one-on-one, we can't win if they do what they normally do these days, but if they take us on—whether it's collective bargaining or an organizing drive or a strike—we've got to hit them in as many cities around the U.S. simultaneously as we can. We have to research those properties; we have to inform the coalition; we have to do a lot of things to bring that kind of pressure. Now, in addition to which, if we could hit ten countries abroad who have Sheratons, and connect the domestic linkage with the international, it's going to get their attention. There is no question about it."

Sirabella contacted unions in Europe and Asia with an idea of using international pressure to help win strikes and organizing campaigns. Sirabella was still developing new approaches to organizing when he died, bitter and angry, in 1993.

Chapter 8 The Culinary Union
and the Development of the
Comprehensive Campaign

NEW STRATEGIES AND PERSONALITIES

In the late 1970s the corporate campaign was developed as a tool for unions to augment the strike. The corporate campaign was given name and shape by Ray Rogers, a former student activist whose tactics were derived from the student movement. As Rogers told me, "No question Saul Alinsky played a role in my thinking and SDS [Students for a Democratic Society]. . . . They understood how you research companies." The basic idea of the corporate campaign was to discover and exploit corporate weaknesses other than those that could be exploited through striking. The corporate campaign required intense research into corporate policies, structure, and leadership. Rogers had his greatest early success helping the Amalgamated Clothing and Textile Workers Union (ACTWU) to win a contract with the bitterly anti-union J. P. Stevens Company.[1] His main contribution was the realization that unions needed to learn other techniques besides the strike for exerting pressure on companies.

Rogers became controversial within the ranks of organized labor fairly soon after the Stevens campaign. Rogers is charismatic and deeply committed to an egalitarian vision of social justice. His campaigns generally evoked fierce loyalty from rank-and-file workers. But he distrusted and was distrusted by union leaders who questioned both his tactics and his loyalty. By the late 1980s, Rogers had been largely isolated from the labor movement.[2]

It was during the late 1980s, in the aftermath of Vinnie Sirabella's failed organizing project, that HERE adopted a similar, but more flexible and effective, organizing technique, the comprehensive campaign. The development of this new organizing model took place over many years. The first major step occurred in 1981, when Jeff Fiedler, a former student activist and Vietnam combat veteran and then the director of corporate affairs for the Food and Allied Service Trades (FAST) Department of the AFL-CIO, developed a plan for the United Food and Commercial Workers (UFCW) and the Service Employees International Union (SEIU) to combat Beverly Health Enterprises, a notorious anti-union company. The power of Beverly was such that a strike at an individual unit was almost certain to fail. According to Fiedler, "They [the SEIU and the UFCW] won two-thirds of the elections they entered, but only 25 percent of those ever ended up in contracts."

Fiedler advised simultaneous organizing campaigns and bargaining strikes against Beverly throughout the country. "We were trying to get a contract at one of the Beverly homes in D.C., and I said, 'Wait a second, he's got about twelve hundred places; creating a problem for them in one home when they had twelve hundred was not going to help.' But then we recognized that . . . unions win two out of three nursing-home elections. 'You can use an idiot organizer and win because of the conditions. And hey, this is made to order. Let's just do it on scale. Put a thousand organizers on the streets to start.' We won every election in Arkansas by two to one. And we organized. We didn't lose anything in Mississippi, and eight months into the campaign, the company was talking to us."

Beverly was suddenly faced with the obligation to bargain at health facilities all over the country, and the two unions involved, the SEIU and the UFCW, at Fiedler's suggestion, applied economic pressure on Beverly largely by using nonlabor regulatory statutes. They reported health-code violations to authorities and in some cases opposed Beverly's applications for licenses. They issued a carefully documented patient-care report based on every inspection report for multiple years on every home in a number of states. The report was widely distributed. "We gave it to every regulator in the world. And we used it in the certificate hearings, used it in the newspaper, used it all over the place. It was a very solid piece of work." Fiedler and FAST lawyer Richard McCracken teamed up to instigate shareholder complaints and resolutions against Beverly. Fiedler noted that

> at the same time, we fought every one of the company's industrial revenue bonds. We went through every locale and gathered all the wrongful deaths and neglect cases —this is before real computers—and did a list of everybody suing the company and gave it to everybody else suing the company. We used political pressure in the certificate-of-need hearings. You know, every nursing home, when they want to build a new nursing home, you have to have a certificate of need. And they have rules, all right, about what the criteria were, but we would interject the patient-care information, which wasn't part of the criteria but became very difficult to ignore, and then you discover during the course of the fight, things like Mississippi, which doesn't like unions, hated the company. The regulators cooperated with us enormously because Beverly was driving up the reimbursement costs.

The campaign worked well enough that, thirteen months after it began, Beverly settled with the union. As Fiedler explained: "We reached an agreement that was sort of a neutrality pledge and a standard contract with wages and benefits to be negotiated locally."

The comprehensive campaign, almost by definition, is costly in time and money—and it is risky. Indeed, the SEIU's effort to follow up the Beverly victory with a broad-based campaign failed. As Fiedler recounted: "My great disappointment was that it wasn't followed. [John] Sweeney was president [of the SEIU], and after Beverly he misread all the lessons of the campaign, and his next one, which they wanted to do alone, although they talked to me about working with them on it, was Blue Cross Blue Shield. But it was eighty-seven companies; it wasn't one company. It's not the same thing. It's eighty-seven fights, not one. And first of all, he announced it like a big PR move so that everybody could get ready for them. And then it was a clerical campaign. It never came off."[3]

The comprehensive campaign can be used against any employer and for both organizing and collective bargaining. But it requires a broad-based attack. As explained by Jeff Fiedler: "It doesn't do any good to have 100 percent of the people in Marriott Hotel in downtown Washington if that's my only organizing piece when they got fifteen more around here. I mean, why would I fucking do that? What I tell people, 'You going to have one fight, or you going to have one a year for the next fifteen years?' That's the way the United States fought the war in Vietnam. As we used to say, once, fifteen times. If it's not 100 percent, it's some rational scale: all of a hotel chain, hotels in a particular city, the key ones in downtown, or whatever. Some critical mass that makes the fight worth doing."

It took a while for the SEIU's organizing department to learn how to use the technique effectively, but the SEIU continued to develop it during the 1980s. It is particularly useful for the low-wage workers whom they represent since the union can, through continual pressure over a long period of time, make the campaign more costly to the employer than the gains that the union is seeking.

Kirk Adams, the organizing director of the SEIU, explained to me how the technique of expanding costs in strikes and organizing campaigns works: "We've been able to get them to talk to us because we have been in several campaigns—almost foolhardy in how long we've been at it. We go at it—employers know that once they engage with us in a stick fight, it just keeps going. They know that it's not something that will go away. They can't wait it out. We sort of stay on them and stay on and stay on them—we have to have that reputation."

In 1984 McCracken, at Fiedler's urging, presented a paper at a meeting of FAST lawyers in which he described the advantages of unconventional pressure tactics over the NLRB election process.[4] McCracken pointed out that, as the Beverly campaign showed, unions had available a large number of pressure tactics, most of which had already been used successfully in specific instances:

> Unions have interfered in the process by which businesses obtain industrial development bonds, by appearing before issuing agencies and questioning whether the bond proceeds will actually be used to create new jobs or save existing ones. Unions have worked with success to deprive companies of government contracts, by presenting evidence to contracting agencies of such things as companies' involvement in financial or corruption scandals, or failure to meet contracting standards such as bonding. Food industry workers have put pressure on their employers by reporting to government authorities building and health code violations. Unions have sought representation on the board of directors of banks, by threatening to withdraw union funds and pension funds. . . . During the J. P. Stevens struggle, the same threat was used to force Stevens's directors off of bank boards of directors.
>
> What these examples have in common is that the pressure tactics do not depend upon the existence or use of any labor laws. In fact, they do not even have any content specifically related to labor relations. That is, the argument made or violation pointed out is not based in the nature of a company's labor relations, but rather in some other public policy—or in pure power, as in the case of the bank tactics.[5]

McCracken argued that nontraditional campaign tactics permit unions to bypass labor-relations officials and deal with high-level company officials: "We have also succumbed to dealing with people who are merely buffers . . . corporate labor relations people. Nothing has impressed me more in my work with FAST than how easy it is to leap over the labor relations people and walk right into the throne room."

There are two major advantages to unions in dealing with top officials. The most obvious is that the top executives have a greater ability to make concessions. The second has to do with job functions. It is the job of labor-relations people today to defeat unions. If they fail, they haven't done their job properly. But the job of the top officials is to keep the enterprise working efficiently to make sure that profits are maintained and customers satisfied. That may require recognizing or dealing with the union if refusal to do so is costly enough. McCracken argued that it would usually be easy for unions to make it costly if the officials refused: "There are, for example, many laws regulating company behavior. Every federal, state, territorial, municipal—and even international—law, ordinance, rule or regulation is a potential source of power for us. . . . Most of these laws are under-enforced, many of them ridiculously so. Underenforcement led to constant illegality. Violation of the law is a norm of business. The more we dig, the more we find. . . . What is instructive about the Beverly Enterprises campaign to those who will study it is that many different laws were used, and many different fronts were opened up against the company."

McCracken urged the unions that he represented to begin systematic planning of comprehensive campaigns[6] in organizing and strikes.[7] He also recommended that they avoid the Labor Board wherever possible. During the 1970s he had become disillusioned with the slowness of the Board's processes and the inadequacy of its remedies. "I swore in 1981 I would never file another NLRB election petition, because at that point I was convinced that you couldn't organize through the NLRB, period."[8]

Shortly thereafter, Fiedler and McCracken worked together to support a strike by HERE's Culinary Workers Union Local 226 in Las Vegas. The strike grew out of negotiations for a new master agreement between HERE and a consortium of Las Vegas hotels. In 1984, as reported by Dorothee Benz, "13 casinos, represented by the Nevada Resort Association, pressed for labor concessions and provoked a strike."[9] Most of the struck hotels quickly brought in replacement workers. They also quickly found an anti-labor judge who issued a very broad injunction against picketers. McCracken later recalled, "It speci-

fied that there were to be no more than two picketers every 35 feet. It also included various vague restrictions on behavior, like not 'annoying' people."[10]

The leadership of the Culinary was not ready for a mass strike and was not
sure how to respond.[11] Fiedler came up with a plan aimed at the Hilton Hotel,
which seemed to be leading the opposition. McCracken explained how it
worked: "One of the ways that we brought a conclusion to the strike was a
measure that Jeff and I executed after studying the finances of Hilton, the company that was really leading the strike. We traced their financial chain back to
England, and we, with cooperation from one of the English unions, made a big
splash at their bank's annual shareholder's meeting in Great Britain. Baron
Hilton actually publicly said that they decided to settle with us when we got
to their bank. And that's something the leadership of the union in Las Vegas
at that time really didn't see [the] importance [of]. Vinnie saw the importance
and so did John Wilhelm."

The new, more aggressive approach proved valuable in maintaining an agreement with Hilton. But overall, the strike was far from an unmitigated success.[12] According to Wilhelm: "The local's settlement of that strike was frustrating to the members as well as incomplete and messy; the union was
decertified by six casinos, four other casino hotels which had settled refused to
comply with the agreed-upon terms, and the local's only response was NLRB
and court proceedings with, of course, no result."

The status of the Culinary after these setbacks was shaky at best. Several employers including Harrah's and Boyd Gaming made clear that they were gear-
ing up for battle to decertify the union during the next round of negotiations.
In addition, there was the problem of Steve Wynn, who announced plans to
build what was to be the largest hotel in the world (the Mirage) and vowed
not to sign an agreement with the Culinary.

The local union, aware that it lacked the strength to take him on, appealed
to the international union for help. Ed Hanley responded by sending a team
led by John Wilhelm, whom he appointed western regional director. The team
included three of Vinnie Sirabella's organizing trainees, D. Taylor, Bill Granfield, and Joe Daugherty, and Rich McCracken was enlisted for both legal and
strategic advice. HERE organizers added to the comprehensive campaign formula, true to the teachings of Sirabella, the intensive use of employee committees. Wilhelm later recalled that the local union was ill prepared for a major
battle: "The local was so screwed up. It had not trained rank and filers to be organizers. A lot of people on the staff at the local were from the rank and file,
but they had never been trained in an organizing perspective nor in a militant

perspective." Wilhelm and his crew set about organizing worker committees. According to Wilhelm, the mobilization of the membership "succeeded in defusing decert campaigns by promising a new rank-and-file-oriented style of unionism, in contrast to what the workers saw in 1984."

D. Taylor, who now heads the Culinary, recently recognized the union's continuing debt to Sirabella in this regard: "Vinnie always said you have to build up a very good committee in order to win, and you have to use all the tools at your disposal to win. And he was right."

McCracken told me that the Wilhelm group "started a research department here, which was not the typical union research department, but actually doing corporate research. All this, coupled with mobilization of the members. So we started doing massive street actions, more high-tech things. So that's where we started calling these things 'comprehensive campaigns.'"

According to Taylor, who along with Wilhelm led HERE's battle to survive and then to grow in Las Vegas: "A comprehensive campaign involves many things. Obviously organizing the workforce is the core, the backbone, but you look at the financial vulnerabilities, you look at the political vulnerabilities, you look at community vulnerabilities, you look at their business plan, what is helpful or not. So you are looking at an entire body of information." Wilhelm coordinated the effort, mixing worker mobilization and research on the structure of the hotels they were attempting to organize. He also added the strategy of demonstrating to the hotels that good relations with the union could be helpful to them. Bill Granfield described the aspects of the campaign:

> While the organizers, D. Taylor and myself and the others, were working on [forming committees], [Wilhelm] really worked at understanding who the leaders of the gaming industry were at that time in Nevada and how he could deal with them. The gaming industry was very worried about certain federal tax initiatives that were being talked about, and they didn't have a prayer about doing anything about it because they were in two states at that time, Nevada and New Jersey. So here's a federal tax thing and they've got a maximum of four senators. So John gets together with Ed Hanley. Maybe HERE could be helpful on this tax question. And that might open the doors to real communications with the industry. And no one else was speaking about that. It emerged that we had a way of both applying pressure and being helpful to the industry.

The union's tactics proved successful. Steve Wynn's Golden Nugget Inc. became the first company to settle with the union in 1989. In return, the union offered work-rule changes. The union also agreed that it would refrain from economic action against the company's new casinos. The company in turn agreed not to oppose unionization in those new casinos and to recognize the union on the basis of a majority of signed authorization cards. The "Big Six," an informal grouping of some of the city's biggest corporate gaming establishments, were the next to settle, and a majority of the city's casinos followed.

It was at this point that the Las Vegas union leadership recognized that it had developed an entirely new approach to organizing. It was based on labor-movement precedents, but it was the union's own elaborate protocol. According to McCracken: "In 1989 we decided we would expand the idea of voluntary card-check recognition, and it evolved into a pretty elaborate set of ground rules for organizing. The old UFCW model was—and this goes back to the Kroger cases—the contract would be extended to any new facility. That's all it said. There was nothing in that about union organizers' access to the new facility or getting the names and addresses of the employees there. There wasn't even anything about card check. So we took all those things and made them into an elaborate set of ground rules in 1989, which became part of the Las Vegas contract, and it has become the foundation for all our card-check neutrality agreements."

A major test of the new internal organizing occurred during a ten-month strike at the Horseshoe Hotel. The strike was bitter and involved marches, replacement workers, court injunctions, and acts of civil disobedience. Over nine hundred workers were arrested during the strike. Joe Daugherty, who had primary responsibility for running the strike, was arrested thirty-six times in the ten months. According to eyewitnesses, it was not that Daugherty was violent but that he refused to be intimidated. He later recalled in an interview with me, "I think it is now illegal, but they used to have this charge called 'provoking a breach of the peace,' so if you were picketing and some scuffle broke out, they could use that to arrest you." Daugherty said that he was determined to show that the union leaders could not be intimidated: "I think it was more for the membership to see that the union was not going to allow them to get pushed around and would do what was necessary to win." Wilhelm described Daugherty's actions as "a display of leadership that should be at the top of the annals of labor history."

Daugherty, like Bill Granfield, credits the union's ultimate victory to the combination of union militancy and its willingness to help the industry stave off new federal taxes: "At the same time, John and Vincent and President Hanley demonstrated that while we could be adversaries, we could also be a strong partner in the gaming industry. The corporations saw that the union could be very powerful, be very militant, but at the same time be a good partner. I think

they chose the partnership model and I think it took both things kind of simultaneously."

THE FRONTIER STRIKE

The Horseshoe strike was only a minor skirmish compared with the six-year
Frontier strike, which followed soon after. The strike began in 1991, when the
contract between the Frontier Hotel and the union expired and Margaret Elardi
and her sons took over the hotel. Their approach to the union was described
in a *New Yorker* article:

> They bought the place in 1988, just a few months before its Culinary Union contract
> expired. By law, the Elardis were required to bargain "in good faith" with the union
> to reach a new settlement, but after months of stalling the family hired Joel Keller,
> a notorious union-busting lawyer. (Keller, whom the National Labor Relations Board
> later suspended for a year from handling labor cases before it, no longer represents
> the Frontier.) After a confrontation with the unions staged by Keller, the Elardis
> unilaterally declared an impasse and imposed their own work rules. Salaries for new
> employees were drastically reduced; workers were fired without cause; seniority rules
> were essentially abandoned. Women who had worked days suddenly found them-
> selves on the graveyard shift. A forty-hour work week, on which paid vacations and
> holidays depended, was no longer guaranteed.[13]

Almost immediately after the strike began, the hotel management permanently replaced the strikers. This was the beginning of one of the longest strikes
in labor history. The workers stood fast. In a remarkable display of solidarity,
not a single worker crossed the picket line despite the anguish of watching for
more than six years, day after day, as replacement workers and customers entered the hotel. The Frontier workers withstood hours of boredom, the taunts
of anti-union hecklers, physical attacks, and the inevitable moments of doubt
about the outcome. They received support from their union brothers and sisters in Las Vegas, who voted to double their dues to give them financial support. Unions from around the country came to Las Vegas to show support.
The strike was the subject of an excellent film,[14] which pointed out, among
other things, that seven languages were spoken on the picket line.[15] Tom Snyder, the newly appointed political director of HERE, joined the staff just as
the strike was ending. He told me that was struck by the diversity of the strike's
leadership: "I mean there the leadership was white, black, and brown on that
strike, on the picket line, and at every level."

In an attempt to obtain political support, the union undertook a campaign to elect Maggie Carlton, one of its shop stewards, to the state senate. She won and was able to use her position to pressure the governor to try to mediate the dispute. When the governor failed to get a settlement, he appointed a fact finder, who reported that the Elardis had bargained in bad faith. Union investigators were able to discover a variety of likely illegal behavior by the Elardis, which put their casino license in jeopardy. The continued pressure finally forced the Elardis to sell to a new owner, who was eager for a good relationship with the Culinary. Under the new, quickly negotiated contract, all strikers were rewarded with substantial raises and seniority credit for their time on strike, something rarely achieved in strike settlements.

According to Wilhelm, the battle-tested Frontier strikers provided the Culinary with a new generation of leaders:

> Many key leaders of our union in Las Vegas emerged from the early struggles, including Geoconda Arguello Kline, an immigrant from Nicaragua who was a room cleaner, later a member of the Frontier strike team (now the president [the number-two position] in Local 226; Ted Pappageorge, a Horseshoe striker who was a bartender, now the internal staff director of Local 226 and clearly a key leader for the future; Jim Bonaventure, a staff member at the local when we got there, a former showroom waiter, now the head of the Local 226 grievance department; Chris Walker (female Chris), a former cocktail server at the Dunes who was on the original team that organized and serviced the Mirage Hotel when it opened in 1989, a critical turning point for the rebuilding, now the staff director of Local 54 in Atlantic City leading the rebuilding of that union and a key leader of the successful 2004 casino strike in that city; and many others, including several Frontier strikers who now lead organizing in Las Vegas.

After crediting the strikers for their great display of courage, Wilhelm gave credit to the staff:

> Joe Daugherty ran the Horseshoe strike (he was one of the young organizers Vinnie hired for the 1985 organizing projects, and was part of the original team that came to Las Vegas with D. [Taylor] in 1987). Our strategic research department, which is now a crown jewel of our union and of the labor movement, began in Las Vegas when President Hanley let me hire Mark Atkinson. Another key organizer who came to Las Vegas in January 1987 with D. and me was Kevin Kline, also one of Vinnie's 1985 hires, who is now the Organizing Director for our union nationally in gaming under D.'s direction. Glen Arnodo, who came to our union from the United Electrical Workers in the 1980s, was the first Local 226 political director, and laid the foundation for what is today an extraordinary rank-and-file-driven political program, including among other things the election of a shop steward, Maggie Carlton,

to the Nevada State Senate (where she still serves, and has become one of the most influential state legislators, and since the Nevada legislature is part-time, she also still works at Treasure Island as a coffee shop food server).

While the Frontier strike was in progress, the Culinary became involved in another major dispute. In 1993 MGM opened the MGM Grand Hotel & Casino. MGM signaled its intention to remain nonunion by hiring Robert Maxey as its president and CEO. According to a knowledgeable commentator, Maxey "had a history of antagonism to the union"; he was "a man on a crusade, a jihad against the union" at the MGM.[16]

The union responded to the announcement of Maxey's first moves with all the techniques suggested by McCracken, who was one of the chief strategists involved in the struggle.

> The union produced literature that prominently highlighted operating losses in the millions at three separate casinos which Maxey had previously headed. . . . The report was circulated among stockholders, potential investors, lenders. . . . The union also intervened in the MGM's efforts to expand. . . . The union used its institutional relationships with central labor councils, state federations and other union bodies to help mount opposition to MGM expansion.
>
> Maxey resigned in June of 1995. J. Terrance Lanni, a former CEO of the unionized Caesar's Palace, became the new chairman, and within months the MGM and Culinary had negotiated a card check agreement that ended the labor war. The company returned to profitability in 1996.[17]

Thereafter, the union continued to organize successfully. Today, all but one casino hotel on the Strip is unionized. The union's continued success in Las Vegas was in large part the result of its victories in battle, but it was also facilitated by the union's willingness to work cooperatively with organized hotels. The Culinary offered employers who signed on support in dealing with government regulations and a way of obtaining qualified workers through the union's Culinary Training Institute. The institute, union run and employer funded, is modeled on the hiring hall and training programs used by building-trades unions. It offers workers a chance to learn both basic hotel jobs and new skills. It teaches every type of hospitality job, from room attendant to chef. Its teachers come from the industry. It is free to employees of contributing employers and to those out of work. As D. Taylor explained, "Based on your economic status, it charges you or you get basically grants."

The program works well for both employers and workers. It is an important part of the union's success, according to Taylor: "We have made it a priority value plus. You are going to pay our folks more, but you are going to get a better quality."[18] As a result of the institute, according to D. Taylor, "We [the union] are now the largest movers of welfare to work in Las Vegas."

The Culinary is today one of the largest and most powerful local unions in the country and a major political force in Las Vegas. It helps train hotel workers, and it provides them with good wages and benefits. Its success was reported by Steven Greenhouse of the *New York Times*:

> Culinary Local 226, also called the Culinary, the city's largest labor union, an unusual —and unusually successful—union . . . has done a spectacular job catapulting thousands of dishwashers, hotel maids and other unskilled workers into the middle class.
>
> In most other cities, these workers live near the poverty line. But thanks in large part to the Culinary, in Las Vegas these workers often own homes and have Rolls-Royce health coverage, a solid pension plan, and three weeks of vacation a year.
>
> The Culinary's extraordinary success at delivering for its 48,000 members beckons newcomers from far and wide. By many measures, the Culinary is the nation's most successful union local; its membership has nearly tripled from 18,000 in the late 1980s, even as the rest of the labor movement has shrunk. The Culinary is such a force that one in 10 people here is covered by its health plan, and more than 90 percent of the hotel workers on the Strip belong to the union. The union is also unusual because it is a rainbow coalition, 65 percent nonwhite and 70 percent female. It includes immigrants from Central America, refugees from the Balkan wars, and blacks from the Deep South.[19]

Taylor, who is now the head of both the Culinary and UNITE HERE's gaming division, believes that a great many factors account for the union's success: "First and foremost, we had John guide us, and there's no better strategic mind I know of than John Wilhelm. And he taught us how to be strategic thinkers. We spend an enormous amount of time on staff development; we build very big committees; we have a very good research department; we use political power in order to help us organize. We obviously have shown to the industry that when we get in a fight, we're in there for the long haul. The Frontier strike was key to that. But we also devote an enormous amount of resources to organizing. I mean, we spend a lot of money on organizing. And also we view our contracts as just another tool to organize new members, so it's a lot of different things."

The success of the Culinary offers many lessons to the labor movement, most of which have not yet been adequately understood. First, it is important to realize that the union's far-from-inevitable victory was not simply a function of the special nature of Las Vegas. The Culinary was on the verge of being rendered impotent when John Wilhelm arrived along with D. Taylor, Bill Gran-field, Rich McCracken, Joe Daugherty, and other activists. Their ultimate success is a reminder of the importance of cohesive leadership and mobilization of the union rank and file.

For all its success, the Culinary has not been able to organize every casino or gambling hotel in Las Vegas. Its single Strip failure is the Venetian, owned by right-wing billionaire Sheldon Adelson. Adelson has battled the union in a variety of forums. One of his main techniques has been to match or exceed union wages and benefits. The Culinary has also failed to organize the "station casinos," which are casinos located in local Las Vegas neighborhoods—neither on the Strip nor downtown. According to Wilhelm, "They have been wildly successful." They have thus far held off the union, according to Wilhelm, "by running an extreme carrot anti-union program. . . . They went to some lengths to match our union wages; they went to some lengths to give at least a cosmetic appearance of matching our health plan and our pension. They ran citizenship programs for noncitizen workers. They had a very sophisticated carrot-style anti-union program." These two failures indicate that a combination of determined ownership and basically satisfied workers can resist comprehensive campaigns.

Chapter 9 From Hanley
to Wilhelm

While HERE's young leaders and organizers were changing the focus and tactics of the union, its leadership and many of its locals were being investigated by the President's Commission on Organized Crime, which in 1986 issued a report critical of the union's top leadership and its Chicago locals:

> For 40 years Joseph Aiuppa, now the underboss of the Chicago Outfit, and boss Tony Accardo wielded power in the Chicago area locals and the HEREIU joint executive board. Their actions took on national proportions when Edward Hanley, who began his career in Local 450 as a business agent in 1957, was elected to the HEREIU presidency in 1973. . . . According to the Senate Report, the reign of Hanley has been surrounded by allegations of organized crime's influence in the choice of international union organizers, operation of benefit funds, and conduct of union affairs.
>
> Since Hanley took office in 1973, union assets dropped from $21.4 million to less than $14 million in 1982. Nearly $6 million of this money went into three loans executed with private developers, one of whom was Morris Shenker, an associate of the late Kansas City organized crime leader Nicholas Civella.

The Subcommittee found that the union's assets have been used to enrich the top officers of HEREIU's hierarchy. Base salaries augmented by expense accounts and "allowances," lifetime employment contracts, and increased expenditures of tangible items have resulted in expenditures for HEREIU officers skyrocketing from $229,051 in fiscal year 1973 to $1,689,370 in fiscal year 1983. Former HEREIU general secretary-treasurer John Gibson was found guilty in May 1980 of misusing the union's airplane and of conspiring to embezzle union funds. Gibson received concurrent four-month sentences, which he served in 1983, while receiving his lifetime contract checks from the union. The list of employees and organizers hired after Hanley became HEREIU president includes organized crime associates and numerous patronage jobs. Most troubling to the Subcommittee was the unprecedented degree to which Hanley has been able to centralize authority within HEREIU and to control local chapters through the use of mergers, trusteeships, and personnel transfers, an action which mocks the goals of local autonomy and members' rights.[1]

The report was followed by a series of civil suits by the Department of Justice and federal prosecutors under the Racketeer Influenced and Corrupt Organizations Act (RICO). In December 1990 the U.S. attorney for the Northern District of New Jersey filed a civil RICO suit against Hanley, Philadelphia Local 54, and officials of the local.[2] Under a consent decree, various officials and former officials were ousted from the union and a court-appointed monitor was installed.

Five years later, in September 1995, the Department of Justice brought a civil RICO suit against the international union alleging a long history of mob control. The parties entered into a previously negotiated consent decree, which resulted in the appointment of the former federal prosecutor Kurt Muellenberg as monitor. He had broad powers, including the ability to appoint or discharge employees and to reject both candidates for office and collective-bargaining agreements. The consent decree also directed the international union's general executive board to create a public review board and to adopt an ethical-practices code, which were approved at the international union's convention in 1996 and adopted as part of its constitution, effective September 9, 1996.[3] At the convention, Hanley was reelected president and John Wilhelm was elected general secretary-treasurer, the number-two position in the union.

With cooperation from the union, Muellenberg started a major review of HERE's operations. In February 1998, Hanley stepped down as president. His resignation was part of a deal whereby further investigation was halted and he was guaranteed his retirement salary of $350,000 per year. At the same time, his son Tom Hanley, the director of organizing, agreed to resign for one year. In exchange for these actions, it was agreed that neither father nor son would be indicted. In May 1998, the union's general executive board selected Wilhelm to succeed Hanley as president, a decision ratified at the union's 2001 convention.

In August 1998, roughly three years after his initial appointment, Muellenberg issued his final report. It contains a powerful indictment of the union's business practices: its lack of set procedures, its lack of audits and controls, its lack of membership involvement. It is particularly scathing in its discussion of the organizing department under Ed Hanley's son Tom, who had succeeded Vinnie Sirabella: "In 1995, the Teamsters had a membership of 1,437,000 served by 35 international organizers. In a comparable period, 1994–1995, the International Union had a membership of 243,467 served by 105 international organizers. Thus the International Union, with a membership of only 17 percent of that of the Teamsters, had three times as many organizers. The fact is that most of the international organizers are not engaged in organizing activities."[4]

Muellenberg also charged the organizing department with carelessness with the members' money, a constant theme of the report: "While salaries of most employees seem to be very generous, there were no uniform standards for selection of appointees, no uniform compensation standards, no performance review process, and no established criteria for promotion or pay increases." Muellenberg's report was particularly pointed in its discussion of credit-card abuses, which can be summed up as large expenditures with little or no backup: "Personal expenses are placed on union credit cards, including personal meal and beverage expenses." He was equally displeased with the union's policies of leasing automobiles for its staff: "Despite the fact that the International Union's outlay for automobile-related expenses are well over one-half million dollars per year, there is no budget for vehicle leases and related costs, nor are there any administrative controls to provide management with timely information pertinent to controlling costs throughout the fiscal year."

Another area of great expenditure for little result was in the hiring and payment of consultants. The monitor detailed a series of questionable expenses; for example: "Paul Burke, a retired actor and neighbor of Mr. Hanley's in Palm Springs, California, has been a consultant since 1980. He was paid $25,000 per year, received health insurance and a union-leased Cadillac Seville. Mr. Burke's job was to provide a 'celebrity presence' to the International Union's General Executive Board and fund meetings. His contract was terminated in February 1997 after an inquiry by my office. He now receives a $600 monthly pension from the union. There are no reports of Mr. Burke's activities." The monitor was also critical of the way the union used its private airplane. Although he found that it was not used to ferry organized crime figures, it was frequently sent from Washington, D.C., to pick up President Hanley in Chicago and fly him to Washington. The cost was enormous. The monitor was critical of the president's unlimited authority to hire, promote, and set salaries.

The report also contains the monitor's conclusion with respect to some twenty locals that were investigated. None were found blameless, and some reviews resulted in disciplinary charges. The monitor reported that "five local unions have been placed in trusteeship at my request. These trusteeships were imposed in order to restore democracy to the local unions following charges being filed against the officers for violations, such as association with organized crime figures, embezzlement, and filing false reports with the U.S. Department of Labor, etc." He made a series of recommendations—forty-seven in all—for correcting the union's operations.[5]

What the monitor did not report was criminal or mob activity at the international level. He concluded: "There was no credible evidence to support any finding that Mr. Hanley was associated with or indeed controlled by organized crime." His only recommendation in that regard was that the international union carefully monitor the situation. The fact that the final report did not find criminal influence and that it left HERE's election procedures intact was worrisome to some labor reformers. "Whether HEREIU has been purged of LCN [La Cosa Nostra] influence is an open question," according to Professor James Jacobs, who was skeptical of Muellenberg's report:

> The trusteeship in the HEREIU case is by far the least intensive and comprehensive of those imposed on the four international unions. Compared to the others, that trusteeship was brief in duration, scantily staffed, and minimally intrusive. . . . It is hard to believe that the relatively minimalist effort in the HEREIU case could have been sufficient (assuming, of course, some rough parity in the extent of racketeering). Nevertheless, there are several important achievements. Ed Hanley was removed from office. . . . The new president has better credentials than the presidents of the other three international unions, but even he has not repudiated the old regime. Investigations of labor racketeering in HEREIU . . . have more or less ceased. . . . We do not know whether HEREIU has been substantially liberated. If so, it is crucial to determine how this could have been accomplished with such a comparatively inexpensive and short-term effort.[6]

Jacobs's discussion raises several questions. First, what is his basis for assuming "some rough parity" in the extent of racketeering since the monitor, a former prosecutor operating with the support of both the Department of Justice and the Department of Labor, did not find evidence of mob infiltration or racketeering at the international level? But what of Hanley and the conclusion of the President's Commission on Organized Crime that he was brought to power with the help of Tony Accardo and Joey Aiuppa? What of Hanley's regular use of the Fifth Amendment? His willingness to step down rather than face the likelihood of indictment? Jacobs seems to have no doubt that Hanley was mob connected during his presidency, although Jacobs gives no evidence. Jacobs considers Wilhelm's refusal to disavow Hanley as a basis for doubting Wilhelm's devotion to reform. He points out that Wilhelm's position goes beyond refusal to condemn, darkly noting that "in 1999 Wilhelm named the HERE International headquarters building in Washington, D.C., for Edward Hanley."

Wilhelm has remained steadfast and unrepentant in his support of Hanley's basic honesty and devotion to the union. He goes beyond that and credits Hanley with playing a key role in the transformation of the union.[7] He points out that it was Hanley who first recognized Vinnie Sirabella's contribution to the union and who gave full support to the Yale organizing drive: "I mean he literally said first to Vinnie and then me, 'As many of the places as you guys can staff and improve, go for it.'" It was Hanley who brought Sirabella to the West Coast in the late 1970s, when political turmoil threatened to destroy the union. It is Hanley whom Wilhelm credits with the transformation of the Culinary:

> Somebody else could not have done it. The idea of sending D. Taylor and me and a squad of similar people to Las Vegas, of all places, was regarded as complete apostasy in our union, and a different kind of a leader never could have got away with it. I liken it to Nixon going to China, you know. They used to also say it took a conservative Republican to go to China because a Democrat would have been skewered had he done it. I have the same point of view of Edward [Hanley]—he was a bartender's bartender. He was out of the traditional heart of our old union. . . . Had I become president of our union or had Vinnie become president of our union in 1973, when Edward became president, we would have failed, in my opinion, because we would have had too many internal and political obstacles in our way. He was able to do these things partly because he was extremely smart but partly because he was unassailable by the traditional wing of the union.

Wilhelm agrees that there was a corruption problem in the union when he became president, although he does not blame Hanley: "There's no question that there were a number of local unions that were either corrupt or mob influenced or both. But bear in mind, that was a time when there was a very high degree of local autonomy." He also somewhat reluctantly acknowledges that Hanley's spending practices were unnecessarily lavish, although he insists that they were not out of line by the standards of the time: "I think it would be fair to say of the Hanley administration that he spent money on some things that I wouldn't have spent money on, but he was certainly not out of sync with the labor movement of that era. Just by way of illustration, the union owned an airplane under Edward's administration, and I sold it literally on my first day in office. Now having said that, he was hardly alone. There was a bunch of unions in those days that had airplanes. So I would say that his administration spent some money on things that I would not have spent it on and didn't spend it on when I became president. I don't think those were in the category of outrageous, and I think they were very consistent with the standards of a lot of the labor movement at that time."

Wilhelm's comment is as much an indictment of the standards of the labor movement at the time as it is a defense of Hanley. Hanley's lavish use of the members' money was not lost on activist rank-and-file members. As one who asked not to be quoted told me: "From everything that we understood at the time, there was tons and tons of money—that's our dues money—spent on all sorts of hangers on, gross mismanagement of our money. I haven't read his full report, but my expectation is that the monitor's report is a cleaned-up version of what Hanley was about. When I showed up here, there was a reporter whose name I don't remember off the top of my head, but he was running a series of articles about Belardi and Hanley, and one of the symbols of Belardi was some diamond-encrusted gavel that Hanley had presented to Belardi. It just felt like that's what they are spending our money on—diamond-encrusted gavels. And I remember the airplanes were a big thing the people always talked about."

Despite his admiration for Hanley, Wilhelm took steps to make sure that his lavish spending was not repeated: "Local 1 had spending practices I would not have approved of and that we changed after we trusteed Local 1 in 1999 and sent Henry Tamarin there as the trustee. But there was no evidence of any kind of any corruption there."

Despite Hanley's loose ways with money, Wilhelm's regard for him is shared by every progressive leader of the union I have interviewed. Paul Clifford, the Yale-educated architect's son from Canada, and now head of the Toronto local, worked with Hanley when he was dispatched to Chicago to work on the organizing drive led by Sirabella. It was not an easy task to accommodate the new, idealistic organizers with the old-line union staff. As Clifford told me, "At the level of the staff of Local 1 and the organizers, it was kind of oil and water. I think he was really dedicated to seeing the union change and both encouraging our whole group and also kind of greasing the wheels and making room for all of us."

Clifford's relationship with Hanley illustrates Hanley's remarkable willingness to accommodate the major changes that were taking place in the union through the efforts of Wilhelm and his new breed of organizers, as the following story, told to me by Clifford, about a longtime major goal—organizing the Marriott—reveals:

> There was a meeting where Host Marriott had wanted to meet with me and Hanley, or wanted to meet with Hanley and he brought me to the meeting. So we had a meeting in a hotel in Chicago, and Host Marriott said, "Look, we'll recognize the union, but we actually want to bargain the contract like right now."
>
> And so Hanley looked at me and said, "What do you think?"
>
> And I said, "Can I speak with you?" So privately, I said, "Look, Edward, I think it's great we are getting recognized, but through the organizing I promised workers that we'd have a rank-and-file negotiation committee. The union is their voice, you know."
>
> And Hanley's like, "Paul, this is the Marriott—can you believe, we just beat Marriott. Come on, we can get it done right now."
>
> And I said, "I'm sorry, Edward, I can't do it. I can't do that as an organizer. I can't do that, I promised them, I gave them my word."
>
> He kind of takes a big sigh and, "Okay, we'll go through the bargaining process."
>
> You know it's remarkable. And the reason he did that was that he knew what I had promised and also what I had put into it and didn't want to crush my spirit.

This story illustrates HERE in transition. A young, committed organizer takes on the president of the international union to show support for rank-and-file power. The president supports him, risking an important union goal. There are not many unions in which young organizers would be willing to take on the president in support of the rank and file, and not many in which the president would listen and be swayed.

What would surprise those who knew him in his early "workers need to hate the boss" days is that Karl Lechow, an international vice president of the union, thinks of Hanley, along with Vinnie and John, as a mentor—a mentor who taught him the value of cooperating with management in the interests of the workers. As Lechow told me: "Ed Hanley, you know, I say surprisingly, was very instrumental. He came out of a different culture than either Vinnie or . . . certainly John, and his approach to stuff was initially very perplexing to me. But he was actually over a course of ten or fifteen years very, very helpful in showing us how to gain by being cooperative as well as by being oppositional. He introduced some tools to us. . . . 'Look guys, there are a number of ways of skinning a cat and you know these people we're dealing with are very powerful. It may be worthwhile not only to have some struggle but also to have some cooperation.'"

None of my informants in the union was in a position to say whether Hanley had ever been mob connected, but Clifford made clear to me that he never saw signs of it: "I was in Chicago quite a bit. I've no reason to think anything other than good things about Ed Hanley."

Sherri Chiesa, now UNITE HERE's secretary treasurer, believes that those aspects of Hanley's career that made him distrusted by labor reformers also permitted him to initiate the most thorough reforms in the union's history. As she told me, "Edward was brilliant because he saw that change needed to happen but he knew that only he could carry it out, 'cause the old guard trusted him."

Hanley played a similar role in the transition of the Los Angles Local 11 from a bastion of Anglo domination to a center of Hispanic pride. Maria Elena Durazo, now the leader of the Los Angles County Federation of Labor and a major force in the battle for immigrant-workers' rights, remains a staunch defender. She recalls that, among other things, Hanley provided money to help process citizenship and green-card applications under the Immigration Reform and Control Act: "The international gave us $100,000 to do amnesty processing. And it was Hanley who gave us the $100,000, so we hired a team of paralegals and lawyers."

Professor Jacobs expressed concern about the softness of the monitor's recommendations. However, it is clear from a report that Muellenberg had faith in the ability of John Wilhelm to rectify the abuses that the monitor uncovered. For example, a major criticism by the monitor had to do with the haphazard nature of the union's operating style. Muellenberg wrote in his final report: "Interviews of officials, employees, and some consultants confirmed that the International Union has traditionally operated without some absolute basics. There is no budget, no organization chart, no job description for employees, and no policy manual." But he pointed out that "General President Wilhelm has implemented a computer accounting program which will be the basis of a HEREIU budget. He hopes that all departments of the HEREIU will be operating on a budget within a year or two. He, in his capacity as Secretary-Treasurer, took the initiative to implement a budget procedure for the International Union's overall operations." The monitor also pointed out that although Tom Hanley was the director of organization, "in fact, the most significant increase in membership for the International Union in decades has come from organizing drives in Las Vegas, Nevada, directed by John Wilhelm. While Mr. Wilhelm's activities could be characterized as those of a local union, their size and scope argue that they be considered in a national context."[8]

The monitor's trust in Wilhelm has turned out to be well deserved. It is notable that, despite his fondness for Hanley, shortly after becoming president, Wilhelm put Local 1 in trusteeship. The person he appointed was his old friend, union militant Henry Tamarin, who had been hired by Vinnie Sirabella in 1973 for Local 217. When the union struck the Congress Hotel, Tamarin mobilized the rank and file, many of whom believe that the local has been revitalized under Tamarin. According to Ricky Baldwin:

> The contrast between HERE Local 1 of today and the same local of a few short years ago could not be starker. Corrupt leadership and a knack for inactivity characterized the local for years. "It was like [the union] was non-existent," says [Sharon] Williams [a phone operator at the Congress Hotel].
>
> But after trusteeship, a reformer named Henry Tamarin became president, and the local reversed course. "After Henry came," says Williams, "it was like, this is about you guys. We're here for you. Now it's our union."[9]

That the union has remained vigilant with regard to issues of corruption is revealed in its treatment of a case in Florida involving the misuse of union funds:

> A theft in the four figures might not seem worth a year-long investigation. But UNITE HERE is a union unlikely to leave things to chance—especially given its recent history of federal supervision. On May 1, the union's ethics board took disciplinary action against two top officials of Local 355, representing 2,700 hotel, restaurant and catering workers in the Miami-Ft. Lauderdale area. Jorge Santiesteban and Andre J. Balash, respectively the local's president and secretary-treasurer, were forced out of their positions after a UNITE HERE internal probe concluded the pair had diverted union funds toward personal expenses, among other violations. The New York City–based international union also recommended placing the local under trusteeship. . . .
>
> Santiesteban and Balash, charged the review board, each misused between $3,000 and $4,000 in union funds for meals and hotel stays. Additionally, Balash knowingly associated with Rocco J. Panaro, who had been barred from contact with union officials as part of a 1992 consent decree that settled a racketeering charge against a HERE local in New York. In the wake of the probe, Santiesteban resigned from his post, while Balash agreed to a two-year ban on holding union office. UNITE HERE named William Granfield, president of New York City's powerful Local 100, as trustee of Local 355 for an indefinite period.[10]

Chapter 10 Refining the Comprehensive Campaign

Shortly after John Wilhelm became president of HERE, the union abandoned the NLRB election process entirely. It was the Las Vegas experience that convinced him: "Our shift from NLRB elections to card check evolved over a period of time. As we moved toward true comprehensive campaigns and the conviction that workers should never be left to go one-on-one against their employers, we realized that we should leave NLRB elections behind altogether. We pioneered card checks in Las Vegas. I believe the best reading of the history is that card checks became more prevalent in the labor movement because of our extraordinary success in Las Vegas."

Card-check campaigns have since become widely used by unions. However, Jeff Fiedler, whom Wilhelm describes as "the guru of comprehensive corporate campaigns," believes that most unions do not know how to execute them effectively. "These actually are more complicated and difficult campaigns than are traditional campaigns," he says. "More work, not less. Everybody is looking for less, not more. That's one problem. The key part of the work is convincing the members that they have a vital stake in the organizing process so that they will take part in job actions."

According to Mike Casey, the president of San Francisco's famous Local 2: "If you organize the members and really take the time to talk to them about how organizing is the future, they will understand. The way we run our campaigns, our members are out on the streets because a lot of time the people working at the hotel you are organizing are too afraid to be out on the streets. You might have three hundred workers in a hotel, and maybe only fifty will get out in the streets. Well, you can't win with just fifty people out on the streets. You've got to have hundreds or thousands of people coming into actions and that happens because the rest of the local gets out on the streets."

Casey is aware that the existing members must be pleased with the quality of the union's representation in order for them to participate enthusiastically in the organizing effort. As he explained, "We've got to always be paying attention to the representation so we have the credibility with our members to get them out on the streets."

Comprehensive campaigns are more costly and time consuming than traditional hot-shop organizing. But Casey finds that well-motivated members will participate enthusiastically as long as they believe that leadership understands what it is doing: "We were in a four-year campaign against the Park 55, a seven-year fight against the Marriott. It's grueling. But as long as you keep it fresh and keep making progress every step of the way and showing people that this is how we're winning, you can do it. I'm sometimes troubled by the lack of belief that workers, members will do anything—I mean, part of it is leadership and staff, not believing that their members will actually do something. It's like they are not going to do it, we shouldn't even ask. Sometimes, of course, people are not going to get involved if you don't inspire them and ask them and show them that it's expected. Paying their dues is only the start; it's the least obligation of a union member."

Before beginning a comprehensive campaign, a union must do considerable work to locate corporate vulnerabilities, which it will exploit during the campaign. The exploitation of company vulnerabilities is one difference between a comprehensive campaign and an NLRB campaign. According to Fiedler, "You don't want to damage the business during an election. But you certainly can for a card-check agreement fight. It's no holds barred."

To be able to exploit weaknesses, the union must contact potential allies, other unions, politicians, immigrant groups, environmental groups, progressive interest groups, and community leaders. HERE also increasingly makes sure that, before it begins its actual campaign, it has placed pro-union workers at the target facility. These union sympathizers—typically college graduates—are referred to as "interns" by HERE and "salts" by construction unions. The union maintains a continuing relationship with them during their time on the job. As Karl Lechow explained to me: "We really work with all the kids that are in there. We have an organizer that meets with them every week. If the kids are interested in becoming organizers, we yank them out. Now it may be a little odd to say this, but in a way, since they have been working on the property, to us they are rank-and-file waiters or maids or cooks or front-desk people, so even though many of them have a college degree, they have become rank and filers."

Fiedler also believes that very few other unions, even those heavily engaged in organizing, recognize the importance of the workforce as a necessary part of the campaign: "They think you do this stuff top down and the workers don't matter. These kids don't get out there in organizing campaigns, don't go out there on strikes. They think they can look up on the Internet, get a little bit of fucking information, and collapse the company. And I've met organizers who allegedly organized nurses—never met a nurse—just doing it over the phone. And this is sort of really stupid. And there's a lot of elitism. It's scary to me because it's not what I intended. Comprehensive is at every level."

The greatest advantage to a union of organizing on the basis of worker committees is that when it succeeds, the newly recognized union is in a powerful bargaining position; it has enlisted and trained a large group of activists who understand the priorities of their coworkers.

The strong bargaining position enables the union to bargain for neutrality and card check at other facilities. In San Francisco, Local 2, led first by Sherri Chiesa and then by Mike Casey, convinced hotel owners and managers that there would be continual union opposition to their efforts to get government approval or permits and no let-up in demonstrations until an agreement was signed. They succeeded so well that by the mid-1990s hotels began to approach the union, offering card-check recognition before the union even requested it. The *Wall Street Journal* noted this unusual development:

> The biggest thing fostering closer collaboration is the realization that the union can muck up a big hotel project unless it is made part of the process from the start. In particular, hoteliers worry that union opposition could lead to extensive delays in getting necessary permits and approvals from the city, which has long had a reputation for being friendly to labor. And once a hotel's doors open, nobody wants to see picket lines outside—something that has happened in the recent past.
>
> "Most developers don't want the risk of fighting the union during the construction or opening of a property," says Bob Murphy, a San Diego lawyer who represents

hotel operators here. "So they're trying to hammer out a deal with the union that makes sense."

Take developer Chip Conley. Even before he won a bid to exclusively negotiate with the city of San Francisco to build a 170-room hotel on property owned by the Public Transportation Commission, he asked Local 2 of the Hotel Employees and Restaurant Employees Union for its support. The union, in turn, agreed to write a letter backing the project.

The open dialogue marks a big change for Local 2, which has prevailed in six bruising organizing and contract campaigns since 1990 and now represents about 80 percent of the workers at San Francisco's full-service hotels.

"Operators and developers are beginning to recognize that if they work with the union, they can avoid punishment and may actually get some competitive advantages," says Mike Casey, President of Local 2, which represents about 7,000 workers. Stuart Korshak, a Los Angeles labor lawyer, notes that he represents a group of 12 hotel managers in San Francisco who have partnered with Local 2 during the past few years. The effort is designed to make the hotels more competitive by implementing flexible work rules and joint worker training programs.

The "new generation of union leaders" are "better able to work with businesses that want to work with them," Mr. Korshak says. At the same time, they are "more effective in fighting businesses that don't."[1]

A similar situation occurred when the Staples Center was built, when Maria Elena Durazo was the head of Local 11 in Los Angeles. As Rich McCracken later told me, "The Staples Center group came to us and said, 'Let's not fight. Let's work together and get this done without any labor disputes.' And sure enough, we did. And it's an all-union facility in L.A. with no NLRB charges, no NLRB representation litigation, no strikes, no boycotts, no picketing. Just everybody making money. How about that for an idea?"

After a seven-year struggle, Local 2 succeeded in organizing the Marriott Hotel in San Francisco, which Vinnie Sirabella had targeted in his organizing campaign. The Marriott had opened in 1989, and the union's initial efforts to organize it on the basis of a weak card-check agreement failed. The union had depended on a weak neutrality agreement obtained by Sirabella. The union made no further efforts until 1995, when Mike Casey had been Local 2 president for three years. He later described how the goal was fully reached:

> We won a great contract in '94. Had a strike at the Mark Hopkins Hotel, and then in 1995 finished up the rest of the contracts. John said, "So, what are you going to do about the Marriott? Now that you guys have had this great contract fight, you've got to turn your attention to organizing." We were at 73 percent unionization at that time in the city, which is pretty high. We didn't really have the money. And he

suggested, "Well, you have a strike fund. So why don't you see if you can use that money from the strike fund?" The strike fund is pretty restricted, so we had to go to our membership for a vote to take a couple of hundred thousand dollars out of the strike fund.

There was some opposition—"Keep your hands off our strike fund!" But we passed it pretty overwhelmingly, and we started the organizing again, and this was '95. [After a lawsuit] Marriott renegotiated the card-check agreement with us. And it took us several months. They were very arrogant. They thought that even with the card check we wouldn't organize the place, and we set about in early '96 to begin the work of organizing and built a very strong committee. We did that for about eight months, from January to August of 1996. And [in] August of '96 over a period of about two weeks, thanks to the committee that the organizers had built, we drove to a majority and we did the card check, and the arbitrator counted the cards, and we won recognition. And so that was pretty remarkable because that was the first time that any local, any union, had ever organized a Marriott.

We won that, but when we started bargaining, the company said, "You can't have the citywide deal." We ended up in a six-year war with them, which included a boycott and a couple of two-day strikes and a number of weekly actions at the place and just finally wore them out. We ran a very comprehensive campaign.

We did a two-day strike. And by this time, the boycott was really pretty effective; there were several developments that we prevented Marriott from building—new hotels in Boston, in Houston, in Denver, in Sacramento, in Monterrey. There were a number of different hotel developments that they were trying to get the development rights to. We roll in and get the local there or, if they didn't have a local, send our own folks. Jeff Fiedler was involved in all that.

We got a sense that we could screw them up at the entitlement level, planning department, or whenever. They saw this fight going on, and they said, "These guys never let up. They just keep on going. If we work something out, maybe they'll give us some breaks to start the thing up."

So we had a carrot and a stick. We said, "Look, if you want to work with us, we'll give you some start-up breaks, you know, so you don't have to go up to the full standard right off the bat."

By 2008 only a handful of nonunion hotels remained in the San Francisco area; this achievement would be remarkable for any local. It is astounding for a union that seemed on the verge of collapse in 1984.

Comprehensive campaigns were equally successful in New York, where Local 6, once put under a trusteeship because of its radical leadership, spearheaded the successful organizing effort of the Hotel Trades Council.[2] Local 6 is one of the few locals that do not trace their rank-and-file orientation to Vinnie Sirabella or one of his disciples, as its president Peter Ward insistently made clear to me: "The stuff that you are talking about [rank-and-file mobilization] has been going on here when Vinnie was in diapers. The way that Vinnie ran his union has absolutely no influence on the way this organization became organized or was run. And a lot of the things that we are talking about have been institutional parts of this union since the thirties."

John Wilhelm seems to relish the independent, somewhat cantankerous, approach of Local 6. He agrees with Ward that its contracts are outstanding, and he attributes its current success in part to its radical past:

> The story of Local 6 is fascinating. It was organized industrially, rather than on craft lines, by Communists led by Jay Rubin during the thirties; the Communists prevailed over the Socialists and the gangsters, according to legend, because they were, unlike the Socialists, tough enough to fight the gangsters. Local 6 inherited from that prewar period of organization and struggle a legacy of militant unionism, great contracts, and progressive civil-rights and political positions. Peter Ward, only the third leader in the history of Local 6 and the Hotel Trades Council, has modernized and improved the union, but that legacy shines brightly. The Local 6 contract is the best hotel contract on the planet, and in 1985, under the leadership of Vito Pitta, Local 6 became the first local in our union to negotiate card check for all future hotels owned or managed by any union hotel. Density is 90 percent or greater for full-service hotels in New York City.

Although neither Local 2 nor Local 6 is committed to a single organizing technique, both share the worker-centered approach so powerfully advocated by Vinnie Sirabella. It is the constant use of the rank and file as part of the organizing process that is the hallmark of a HERE campaign.

HERE is not the only union using comprehensive-campaign tactics for organizational purposes. The United Food and Commercial Workers International Union (UFCW), the Service Employees International Union (SEIU), and the Communications Workers of America (CWA) do so as well, in a significant way. Each union has its own nontraditional campaign style. But the UNITE HERE model is the most comprehensive because it involves continued rank-and-file mobilization.

The SEIU, which is larger than HERE, relies more on its bargaining power to facilitate organizing. For example, in 2006 it obtained a great deal of publicity for organizing janitors in Houston, one of the first successful major organizing campaigns in the South in many years. At the heart of its campaign was pressure on national companies doing business in Houston. The process was described to me by Kirk Adams.

In Houston there was a real-estate interest that we were dealing with, and Boston and New York, D.C., Chicago, L.A., and San Francisco basically owned 75 percent of the market. And cleaning companies who we're dealing with in the North, Northeast, Midwest, and West Coast had about 70 percent of the market. So we thought from the very beginning we had a way to win this thing because we had significant leverage not in Texas, not in Houston, but in San Francisco, New York, Chicago, and other places based on the relationships we had both with the real-estate interests and the cleaning companies. And so that was really the essence of the strategy. Even with this head start, the union put in considerable time in preparing the grounds. We spent a good two years developing political relationships, religious relationships, community relationships, in the Latino community to make sure we weren't run out of town as outsiders, although certain folks tried to do that. Bishop Fuentes was incredibly important.

It was the same type of leverage that permitted the janitors to win a strike against their employers:

The folks who helped us settle that were the oil companies. That was at a time when the price of oil was incredibly high; the price of gas was going up like crazy. Their quarterly profits were in the $25 billion range—they were just very nervous about it. At first they said, "We're not the employer." But we started to come after them using the press and then their European markets, their stockholders, and their board. They have a fairly diverse board with some people on it that are central to left politically. So it was just a way of saying, "You are really running a risk here of beating up on these poor janitors when you've got this gazillion dollars coming back. There's no reason for you to get into that fight." The Chevron guy in particular, he was very helpful. He went to the partnership down there, he went to the chamber, he said, "Listen, I'm settling."

The SEIU assures the employers from whom it is seeking a neutrality agreement that they will not suffer economically as a result. As explained to me by Adams:

I think our one additional thing in both property service and health care is we don't want to put you at a competitive disadvantage.

I think most employers say, "Well, you are going to put me in a bad place amongst my peers personally, but also economically."

And we say, "No, we are going to organize the market. You will not be disadvantaged. We will not just organize one hospital in Vegas, we will organize all hospitals in Vegas."

This approach is somewhat controversial. Reassuring employers is a common aspect of "top-down organizing," a term with a bad reputation among unionists and pro-labor academics. Top-down organizing has on occasion been used by unions as a way of padding their membership rolls without working for the welfare of those organized. Management lawyer Katherine Lev told me of a negotiation in which she represented a janitorial-services employer whose employees were organized by the SEIU as a result of pressure on the president of an institution that had contracted with the employer for services:

> I met with the local in order to negotiate a contract, and I put together my list of proposals in the form of the first contract, so I had every section, every article laid off. And I said, "This is what I'm going to be asking for."
>
> And they flipped through it and they said, "You know, this looks good. We want to wrap this up; we want this done as soon as possible. Just do me a favor, give this to me and let me present it across the table to use as our proposals."
>
> I sat across the table from them, and they presented my proposals to me as their own. Every one of his proposals were mine, and they just presented them across the table in front of their committee as if they had worked them out. It was everything I ever wanted in a contract. And they handed it right back over to me. They didn't have one proposal throughout. They just wanted to get the contract done so they could start collecting dues. They wanted it signed and done.

Lev said that this performance was not typical of the SEIU, which is often accused of creating company unions because of its willingness to enter into initially soft agreements. SEIU president Andy Stern is willing to organize without rank-and-file commitment because he believes that the key to strength is numbers and that units organized top down can develop into militant unions.

The CWA also effectively adopted the comprehensive-campaign model in their struggle to survive the breakup of AT&T. For many years before the breakup, the CWA did not have to do much organizing. The union had a stable base of 650,000 members. But the 1983 court-ordered divestiture, which broke up the Bell system, "undermined the union's power, in terms of both membership levels and bargaining leverage." The losses were severe. Nonunion companies entered the field, and "Bell companies downsized the traditional core union work force and set up non-union subsidiaries for their growth businesses."[3]

The union lost more than half its membership. The situation was grim:

> The CWA also lost bargaining leverage . . . because the break-up of the Bell system destroyed the centralized system of collective bargaining and stable union-management relationships that existed at the national level. . . . Also, deregulation led to ongoing corporate restructuring and downsizing, so that the union faced a parade of new managers at the bargaining table and in line positions. . . .

. . . With a history of predictable and paternalistic . . . labor relations in the old Bell system, the CWA needed to learn how to mobilize a membership accustomed to relatively easy contract victories.

Suddenly, the union was faced with massive adversaries as the Bell spin-offs merged and new companies grew into "global behemoths." The union coped by adopting strategies very similar to those used by HERE to stave off its destruction in Las Vegas, San Francisco, and Los Angeles. The first thing the union did was mobilize its membership:

> Mobilization tactics include petitions, one-on-one postcard messages, work-to-rule campaigns wearing common colors . . . expressing solidarity through coordinated workplace stand-ups, picket lines, electronic picket lines and strikes. Mobilization also includes . . . linkages with community and consumer organizations to support union demands, as well as external political action in the form of public rallies and campaigns of writing to state and local political officials. . . .
>   . . . The CWA developed a new strategy and capability—the linking of collective bargaining organizing and political activities.[4]

The CWA did not achieve organizing success until the telecommunications companies needed the union's support for legislative and regulatory action. In exchange for its support, CWA was able to obtain neutrality agreements and expedited or card check elections. Through these agreements and mergers, the union grew so that today it represents over 700,000 workers of whom over 550,000 are members.[5]

REJECTING THE NLRB

HERE is unique among the unions that use comprehensive campaigns because of its total rejection of NLRB elections. The other comprehensive-campaign unions recognize the advantages that come with selective use of the NLRB. The Board's processes can be speedier than a comprehensive campaign. And Board certification requires the employer to bargain and provides protection against decertification, which card-check recognition does not.[6] Since the HERE model requires winning the allegiance of the workers and their public declarations of support, a local union capable of carrying out an effective comprehensive campaign should be in a position to win NLRB elections conducted by secret ballot. Bill Granfield, the president of Local 100 in New York, explained to me the reasoning behind forgoing NLRB election victories in terms of follow up: "This approach of building a strong majority of workers to fight for a fair process or card check wasn't developed in HERE by organizers who couldn't win elections. It was developed by organizers who had won too many elections and had to sit around afterwards for years attempting to negotiate contracts. . . . So it's like we know we're going to have to have the battle sooner or later, so why not get right into it—let's change the rules and remove the comfort of the NLRB timeline from the opponent."

D. Taylor too sees the major advantage of the comprehensive campaign in the fact that when successful "it leads almost inevitably to contracts while Board elections do not." Other apparent drawbacks also turn into advantages in a well-run campaign. For example, the fact that comprehensive campaigns are often quite lengthy will prove to be more troublesome for the employer than for the union. Very few employers are willing to live with long periods of workplace turmoil and public attack. That turmoil is likely to hurt the employer's image and reduce productivity. There are considerable costs for the union, too, but these are costs that arise from the union's primary function—organizing.

In an NLRB election campaign, the employer can generally anticipate an end to major agitation after it wins an election, but in a comprehensive campaign the union can continue to agitate until the company agrees to card-check recognition. Katherine Lev represented a company that provided janitorial services to the University of Miami. When the SEIU began a comprehensive campaign aimed at persuading the president of the university to pressure UNICO into agreeing to neutrality and card check, the company petitioned for an election, which it thought it might win. But the union filed a series of what are called "blocking charges" to postpone the election for as long as possible. The university administration, eager to end the turmoil and personal attacks that were part of the campaign, finally put pressure on UNICO to sign up.

As Taylor points out, the Culinary Workers Union in Las Vegas was able to organize successfully after the Frontier strike because "it was very clear that once the union dug in we weren't going anywhere, and most employers think you can outlast the union, and I think the Frontier strike proved that completely contrary." And when the comprehensive campaign shifts the time pressure or the power balance so that the company is the party seeking to end the turmoil, the company will not be motivated or able to manipulate the unit to remove workers who have a common interest with those in the unit. Indeed, where the union has demonstrated power and the employer is eager for peace, the union may well be in a position to dictate the unit. Lev described dealing with the SEIU in Boston after a corporate campaign and having the union demand a unit covering three states: "The SEIU said as part of this contract, we'd like to recognize all of Providence and all of southern New Hampshire and have them brought in under this contract. I mean, there's no shared working conditions between those employees in Providence and those employees in Boston. To demand that as part of a Boston contract—and then agree ahead of time to put those employees under the Boston contract—that violates the Act. When I pointed that out to them they said, 'Oh, well, the companies have already agreed to it.' No one seemed to really care that this violated the rights of the employees that weren't at the table that they were trying to bring into this contract."

Lev had to battle her own client to get them to refuse. They did, however, agree to a broad neutrality and card-check agreement covering much of New England. Once the union has won a major battle seeking neutrality and card check, other employers will begin to anticipate unionization and often decide not to engage in battle. As Bill Granfield, of Local 100, explained to me: "Here in New York, where we got big public battles for a year or so with the company at one place, and then when we appeared at the next one, it was a lot quicker and sometimes there was practically no battle at all. For example, when we first started organizing Aramark with this method among cafeteria workers in New York, the first one that we really mobilized against was Smith Barney. And that took a protracted fight, and we had our allies sitting in at the doors by Smith Barney, and finally Smith Barney paid attention and directed Aramark to do a card check. After that, we moved on to Solomon Brothers, and after that, J. P. Morgan Chase. We got the workers up there, and it just took a threat. We posted up notices that we were going to have a rally and stuff. They called us up before the first rally, even."

EMPLOYEE ATTITUDES

The fact that comprehensive campaigns require employee activism means that the workers in a newly unionized facility will be committed and active in its affairs. They are more likely to try to resolve problems on their own than to call in union officials. When Sarah Julian joined the staff of Local 19, her first task was to organize the already-represented workers. She noticed differences in employee attitudes depending on whether they were organized during the NLRB period or during the comprehensive-campaign period. She told me: "The people in the newly organized places or the places that were recently built, they are much more open to being leaders in their workplace and resolving problems themselves and learning to stand up for themselves."

Comprehensive campaigns also make employers less prone to retaliate against union members. In a comprehensive campaign by HERE, by the time the union goes public it has enlisted clergy, politicians, and interest groups to work with it. A discriminatory discharge will not get buried in the legal process but will likely be met with marches and protests and political and often nontraditional pressure. An example from an incident in Las Vegas in the mid-1990s is described by Vanessa Tait: "When the antiunion Ark Restaurants Corporation fired eight activists for organizing their coworkers, HERE held a 'sip in' at the restaurant, in which hundreds of union members clogged business by ordering only water and staying to drink it for hours. . . . Some 10,000 unionists and their supporters then marched on the hotel to demand union recognition."[7] The ability of the comprehensive campaign to counteract discharges was also demonstrated during the first Beverly Enterprise campaign. Jeff Fiedler recalls, "UFCW had organized or had campaigns at a number of Jackson, Mississippi–area Beverly homes, and the company had fired twenty-six people. . . . It reinstated them in return for us backing off an Ohio industrial revenue bond. So in that case we were not relying on the Board to get those people back, and reinstatement gooses a campaign."

SECONDARY TARGETS

The comprehensive campaign also frequently succeeds by targeting companies that do business with the company being organized. That is often effective because the new target company is likely to prefer peace and to urge the company being organized to settle. That technique was a key part of the SEIU's success in organizing the janitors at the University of Miami. The process was described to me by Katherine Lev:

> CalPERS is a California pension group. A lot of CalPERS's money was invested in real estate trusts. REACH, the real-estate investment-trust group, was dependent on money from CalPERS. At the bidding of the SEIU, CalPERS said to REACH, "We're going to pull our money from you if you don't sign responsible-contractor agreements saying that you are only going to hire what we deem to be responsible contractors." So companies like REACH sign these agreements because they don't want to lose their CalPERS money.
>
> The real-estate companies turn to the people providing their maintenance and facility services, and say, "Look, you got to get on this responsible contractors list."
>
> So the company says, "How do you get on that list?"
>
> "You sign a national agreement agreeing to recognize the union at whatever site the union gets cards signed for and you have to be neutral."

Use of the comprehensive-campaign model does not guarantee victory—as demonstrated by the failure thus far of the United Mine Workers of America (UMWA) campaign to obtain card-check recognition from Peabody Energy. The UMWA is a union with a great organizing history and admirable leadership.[8] It was involved in a major comprehensive campaign against Peabody (the largest coal company in the world) for over three years. Peabody was once 70 percent organized, but in recent years it has closed unionized mines and opened new mines in which it has successfully fought off the union. The union sought to fight through NLRB elections. They were unsuccessful. When Mine Workers president Cecil Roberts, who had used comprehensive-campaign tactics in the famous strike against Pittston Coal Company in 1989, concluded that the NLRB process was fatally flawed from the union prospective, the union decided to engage in a major campaign seeking neutrality and card-check recognition. The UMWA's campaign has been carefully planned and broadly comprehensive—and costly, costing the union over $4 million during the first three years. According to Roberts, the campaign received significant help from the national AFL-CIO, which provided experienced organizers. The UMWA also used a large number of rank-and-file organizers who didn't do anything but this specific campaign. It also made use of Voice@Work organizers as well as "young folks from the organizing institute."

I interviewed Roberts concerning this effort in 2007:

We decided three years ago that we are going to start this campaign. So we have started this campaign of trying to convince not only the workers to support the union that work nonunion for Peabody, but also trying to convince Peabody through a variety of means in the communities where they operate—through the religious community, through whatever means possible to convince them to recognize the card-check majority. We just started talking to our own people by house calls, saying, "We need your help. We need you to be supportive on a community level. We need you to be at various meetings and rallies that we may be conducting in the future." That was literally thousands of people we visited, old members in the community, not people working currently.

Then we went to the various county commissions—people who had the power to make decisions about whether to give tax breaks to these companies. And many of these county commissions have been very supportive, passing resolutions in support of the employees—just a huge number of those kinds of resolutions passed on a local level urging that Peabody workers have a right to a real voice at work.

Then we started enlisting the churches of various denominations—whether it be Catholic, Methodist, Baptist—trying to get them on board, convincing them that this is a religious issue here that people should have the freedom to make these kinds of decisions about their lives, and getting many of the religious leaders within the coalfield communities where these mines operate on our side.

We pretty much followed the CEO and the other corporate officers of Peabody wherever they've gone to, whether it's New York City to make presentations to the investment communities, or whether it's somewhere else in the United States or the world to speak.

The campaign produced only limited success. Roberts conceded in late 2007, "We haven't organized one single nonunion worker." Since then, there have been some small signs of success. Peabody has spun off its West Virginia operations that are unionized into a new corporation called Patriot Coal Corporation. The union has successfully organized Patriot's new facilities. Nevertheless, the entire campaign has not come close to achieving its original goals.

The failure to date of the Peabody campaign, given the careful planning devoted to it, as well as the dedicated and well-trained personnel and the considerable financial resources, suggests limitations on the effectiveness of the comprehensive campaign. If we contrast mining with hotels, what is immediately obvious is that hotels are dependent for success on public patronage but mining companies are not. The key customers of Peabody are unlikely to withdraw patronage because of union leaflets or local resolutions. And Peabody was not looking for new permits. The campaign is undoubtedly a nuisance, but it is doubtful that it has had a major financial impact on Peabody. Absent the union's ability to affect business in a substantial way, a determined corporate entity can withstand a comprehensive campaign. Even in Las Vegas this is true —witness the Culinary union's failure to organize the rabidly anti-union Venetian Hotel and the neighborhood casinos.

It is thus understandable that many unions in the manufacturing sector, where employers are less vulnerable to the public and where customers are not easily reached, have hesitated to employ a version of the corporate campaign. These unions may continue to use the NLRB procedures in organizing simply because they are less expensive than a comprehensive campaign.

Chapter 11 The Immigration Issue

When the issue of illegal immigration became politically charged in the early 1980s, HERE's leadership was overwhelmingly white male. The attitudes of its leaders were mixed. Some thought of immigrants as a threat to union standards. Others, including Vinnie Sirabella and John Wilhelm, considered them to be the future of the labor movement.

The struggle was particularly heated during the early 1980s in Los Angeles, an area of constant immigration from Latin America. Los Angeles Local 11 was one of the largest in the union. For many years, its leadership had resisted any serious effort to incorporate immigrants into its ranks. Local 11's longtime president Scotty Allen refused to translate proceedings or key documents into Spanish even though a large percentage of its membership could not otherwise understand union policies or activities. He used a variety of other techniques, such as closing the office at 4:30 each day, to keep the largely female Hispanic membership separated from the union's leadership.

In 1985 Local 11 hired Maria Elena Durazo to be an organizer. An immigrant-rights activist, Durazo had been an organizer for the International Ladies' Garment Workers' Union (ILGWU). As she explained to me: "They [the ILGWU] were pretty much the only union that was not blaming immigrants for all the failures. They had a very aggressive legal strategy, which was to challenge the general search warrants that INS was using. I was in heaven because it merged the rights of immigrants with the rights of workers."

The ILGWU offered to make her a business agent, but she declined and went to the People's College of Law. She was working as a clerk at a union-side law firm when Allen hired her. No one quite knows why he did. One theory is that he was under pressure to hire a Hispanic staff member and mistakenly thought that the law clerk that he dealt with would be easy to control.

Once on the job, Durazo was appalled by what she discovered: "Everything I could see at the local level was very, very undemocratic. They had no negotiating committees. Their monthly meetings were deliberately set up in such a way that members couldn't participate. The executive board repeatedly voted to not translate the materials into Spanish."

Shortly after her arrival, a group of Hispanic activists, led by Durazo, brought a lawsuit against the local charging discrimination. The leadership was ordered by the trial judge to translate documents and provide for translation at meetings. Allen and his supporters fought the decree on appeal, spending a great deal of the members' money in the process. This led to the formation of an internal opposition movement. As Durazo recalled, "We ran a slate against Scotty and we shook things up and we challenged and we did actions around the union." Durazo was fired during the resulting turmoil. Shortly thereafter, an election was held and was apparently won by the dissidents, but the local leadership once again went to court, and the ballots were impounded. The local's leadership appealed to the international president, urging him to establish a trusteeship. Ed Hanley, whose views on the topic were not widely known, agreed, and for a brief time Allen and his followers thought that they had won the battle. But to their dismay, Hanley appointed Herman Levitt, the secretary-treasurer of the international union and a longtime immigrant supporter, as trustee. To make his position clearer, Hanley assigned Bill Granfield and Miguel Contreras to work with Levitt. This was a clear sign of Hanley's support for the dissidents. Durazo knew that. As she explained to me, "Both Bill and Miguel came out of the farmworker movement. All their roots, their organizing experience, came out of the farmworkers' union [the United Farm Workers of America]." Granfield told me that he took his appointment to signify that "it was time for a big change there." It was the start of a new immigrant-friendly policy by Local 11. According to Durazo, "They were assistant trustees who actually ran the program to rebuild the local—Scotty had fired me many months before—and Miguel asked me to come back and then we started the whole rebuilding process, and then we got married."

Although the battle within the labor movement concerning immigration was sometimes heated, a compromise of sorts was reached in 1986 to support the Immigration Reform and Control Act (IRCA). Pro-immigration forces were pleased that the Act provided a path for amnesty for immigrants in the country before 1982. Anti-immigration forces were pleased that it provided for stricter enforcement and that it included harsh penalties for employers who hired illegals. Both sides hoped that it would end the problem of illegal immigration by providing amnesty for some, inducing others to return, and stopping the flow of new illegals.[1] Hanley provided funds to Local 11 to aid its members in obtaining amnesty.

In 1987 Durazo became president of Local 11 and then international vice president, with a significant voice in the union. Like so many of the progressive leaders of the union, she remains steadfast in her support of Hanley: "I credit him. He had a choice when this trusteeship was established. He had a choice of who he was going to put as a trustee, and without a doubt, he wanted this local to be rebuilt. If he had put somebody that was friendly to Scotty Allen, it would have gone on the same that it had always been. And he knew that. And instead he put in a team of people that was going to truly rebuild the local and involve the members. That was a very deliberate political decision on his part. And from then on, he supplied us with the organizers, the team, everything that we needed. . . . We would have never been able to do it without that political and financial support."

John Wilhelm was then the western regional director. He made a special effort to aid Local 11. According to Durazo, "He came in to help to negotiate the citywide hotel contract, and that was the first time we put a committee together. President Wilhelm taught us to work hard to establish partnerships with employers, and we succeeded. We also learned that we must fight back if that partnership is rejected and if our members' livelihood is threatened."

Wilhelm brought in his longtime ally Karl Lechow, who helped establish an organizing program for Local 11. According to Durazo, "Karl was one of my mentors. He kept me and the local on a real organizing program. He also helped to identify and train staff, to rebuild the local and train rank and file, to be in a position to take on the bosses."

When Wilhelm became president of HERE, he moved the issue of immi-

grant-workers' rights to the top of the union's agenda: "I think the twin problems of immigrant rights and the economic plight of African Americans (which
I see as indivisible, meaning to deal successfully with either one we need to
deal with both) are the most important human-rights, political, and organizing issue[s] we face."

Early in his presidency, he declared that the AFL-CIO policy backing the
IRCA was misguided. He argued that illegal immigration would continue despite the enhanced border security, deportation, and harsher penalties, and that
the new immigrants, regardless of status, whether legal or illegal, were the rightful heirs of the immigrant workers of the 1920s and 1930s who first built the
labor movement: "To me it's the same as all the earlier generations. They come
here because it's 'The Dream.' They get here and they find out that reality is
much more harsh than the dream. So when somebody comes along and says
there's a way to fix that, [they] say oh, ok-ay, I came here to do better, and goddamn it, I'm going to do better. I mean that's how we organized the factories,
right?"

In this position he was allied with key service-industry unions, including
the SEIU, UNITE, and the Farm Workers. At the 1999 convention, the pro-
immigration forces offered an amendment from the floor advocating repeal of
the 1986 Act. After a period of intense debate with no agreement, the matter
was deferred and AFL-CIO president John Sweeney appointed a committee
headed by Wilhelm to study the matter. The committee recommended general
amnesty for illegal immigrants currently in the United States and repeal of the
IRCA. The new pro-immigrant policy, which was adopted by the AFL-CIO's
executive committee in February 2000, contains sweeping language: "The
AFL-CIO proudly stands on the side of immigrant workers. The AFL-CIO
believes the current system of immigration enforcement in the United States
is broken and needs to be fixed. Our starting points are simple: Undocumented
workers and their families make enormous contributions to their communities and workplaces and should be provided permanent legal status through a
new amnesty program. Regulated legal immigration is better than unregulated
illegal immigration. Immigrant workers should have full workplace rights in
order to protect their own interests as well as the labor rights of all American
workers."

At the convention, with Maria Elena Durazo at his side, John Wilhelm spoke
forcefully for adoption of the policy. As reported by the labor reporter David
Bacon: "He declared [that] his own union's support for [sanctions] in 1986 was
a big mistake: 'Those who came before us, who built this labor movement in

the Great Depression, in strikes in rubber and steel and hotels, they did not say, "Let me see your papers" to the workers in those industries. They said, "Which side are you on?" And immigrant workers today have the right to ask of us the same question. "Which side are we on?"' The convention erupted in applause."[2]

The committee's recommendations were adopted overwhelmingly.

The AFL-CIO immediately set about to explain and implement its new policy. In the summer of 2000, the AFL-CIO held a series of "town hall" meetings to announce the change in immigration policy and to reach out to immigrant workers to share their stories. The most impressive of these meetings was held in Los Angeles, where 20,000 immigrant workers turned out.[3]

Chapter 12 HERE in the Twenty-first Century

THE IMPACT OF 9/11

By the fall of 2001, using the comprehensive-campaign method to obtain card-check agreements, HERE had made up the losses suffered during the Miller and Hanley presidencies. Then came 9/11, a compound tragedy for the union. Many of its members working at the Windows on the World restaurant in the North Tower were killed. Bill Granfield—the secretary-treasurer of New York Local 100[1]—had the grim task of searching morgues and hospitals to discover the extent of the devastation. He found out that forty-three members had been killed. The physical destruction was followed by economic devastation.

As John Wilhelm later recalled: "In the aftermath of that day, as travel to and within the U.S. collapsed, as many as half our members were laid off for periods of time, many of them laid off for many months. The union was severely threatened: simultaneously our income collapsed because so many of our members were laid off and not able to pay dues, the demands on our union to help our members increased substantially, and collective bargaining became incredibly complex and challenging."

The problems were exacerbated by the fact that many of the members of key locals, including Local 100 in New York, were undocumented.

Bill Granfield turned to the restaurant owners in hopes of providing help for those who lost their jobs because of the downturn in the hospitality industry. As he explained to me: "We had a plan to go to employers and ask them, 'Hey, could you put on an extra guy over the holidays?' or something like that. We had a meeting with a bunch of our employers in late September. But they turned the agenda around and said, 'We need relief from having to make contributions on pension and welfare because business is so bad that we are not making it.' So that blew our idea out the door. What we learned was that the whole hospitality industry all around the country went into a nosedive after September 11."

HERE's organizing efforts were put on hold in the aftermath of 9/11 while the union struggled to survive the general hospitality-industry recession. According to John Wilhelm, help from other unions was crucial to HERE: "Many unions rallied to our support, first and foremost the UFCW, led by its then-secretary-treasurer Joe Hansen, now UFCW president. SEIU was helpful financially and morally. For many weeks Andy [Stern (the president of the SEIU)] called me once a week just to see how we were doing. HERE International Union laid off many employees, cut the salaries of those of us who remained (for the general officers, the cut was largest on a percentage basis, 20 percent initially, then 10 percent permanently; for other IU employees other than the lowest-paid, the cut was 10 percent, which was eventually restored), and many local unions had to lay off employees or go without pay for periods of time. We came through it all stronger in many ways, but also mindful that the union was vulnerable."

The 9/11 attacks were also a huge blow to the campaign for the rights of immigrant workers. The national mood immediately focused on security. Immigrants were seen as a threat. New immigration raids were staged, including "Operation Tarmac," which rounded up suspected undocumented immigrants at the airports, including food-service workers. Many immigrant workers, including documented residents who had lived legally in this country for decades, were thrown out of their jobs.

HERE leaders remained active in the effort to achieve immigration reform, working behind the scenes with legislators, politicians, and immigrant groups. By 2003 they decided the time had come to go public once again. Esperanza

Ross, then working with Local 11 in Los Angeles, proposed the Immigrant Workers Freedom Ride—a bus trip by immigrant workers intended to parallel the Freedom Rides of forty years earlier. Wilhelm quickly agreed. As he later explained, "The Immigrant Workers Freedom Ride was intended to revive the movement for immigrant rights[2] in the wake of the terrible regression on the issue caused by 9/11 and its aftermath."

Wilhelm enlisted the support of other unions and the leadership of the AFL-CIO. The plan went into effect in September 2003 when a group of nine hundred immigrant workers and supporters boarded buses in ten cities. HERE officials, led by Maria Elena Durazo, who was the general chair of the project, enlisted the support of civil-rights activists. As Wilhelm later noted: "We worked hard to make sure that there was significant African American leadership, and that the linkage to the earlier civil-rights freedom rides was a positive one, not perceived as being an inappropriate rip-off; Rep. John Lewis was very active and helpful in that regard, along with others including [the] Rev. James Lawson, an original leader and philosopher of the civil-rights freedom rides, and Rev. James Orange."

According to HERE's political director, Tom Snyder, Lewis's role was critical: "He was essential because there were some in the traditional civil-rights community who balked at what they viewed as our improper appropriation of the Freedom Ride icon. And Lewis was huge in establishing our street credibility, if you will."

The immigrant workers came from ten cities. In Los Angeles, Durazo set up a broad-based coalition that included community, student, and civil-rights organizations. The *Daily Bruin* reported that three UCLA students of varying backgrounds took part: Daniela Conde, the daughter of Mexican immigrants; Emily Kane, copresident of UCLA Hillel; and Angela Jamison, a doctoral student in sociology.[3]

Beginning on September 23, the students, along with nine hundred immigrant-worker activists from all parts of the country, traveled across the United States attending rallies, church services, and marches—all to support more worker friendly immigration laws. As reported by Kent Wong and Carolyn Bank Munoz, "At every stop along the way, supporters greeted the buses, shared stories, and encouraged the riders to take their message to Washington, D.C. At every stop the immigrants were greeted by local supporters and veterans of the Civil Rights movement and the labor movement."[4]

There were also numerous hecklers and protesters, many overtly racist. In Sierra Blanca, Texas, the riders were interrogated by Border Patrol agents. When the agents boarded the buses and asked the riders to produce evidence of citizenship or permits, the riders held up signs announcing their refusal under the Fifth Amendment to answer. They began instead to sing "We Shall Overcome," taught to them by organizers before the ride began. For four hours, the riders held firm until the Justice Department ordered them released. They resumed the ride with a sense of triumph and a greater feeling of unity. As UCLA student Angela Jamison told the *Daily Bruin,* "I felt that, ironically, it was a very positive thing to have happened because it brought solidarity to our group."

The buses went to Washington, where the workers met with members of Congress and other government officials. The final stop was New York, where they took part in a massive rally for immigrant rights, with over 100,000 people in attendance.

The ride received lots of media attention. Many articles, mostly favorable, were written about it. Typical was a column by John McCann in the Durham, North Carolina, *Herald Sun:*

> A two-week, 100-city rally for immigration rights brought two buses from the Immigrant Workers Freedom Ride to downtown Durham last week, where some 250 people stood in support of legalizing the many undocumented workers who comprise a vast pool of productivity.
>
> Immigrants are a financial burden during their first years in the United States, according to the NIF [National Immigration Forum]. But give them 10 to 15 years to make some moves, the NIF said, and immigrants become contributors, from paying taxes that help shore up the Social Security system to being part of the American military fighting terrorism in Iraq.[5]

The ride inspired a number of columnists, themselves immigrants or the children of immigrants, to put a human face on the issue. One of the most eloquent was Ricardo Pimentel, writing in the *Arizona Republic,* who described the fear that shadowed his mother's life in the United States:

> My mother, a Mexican immigrant, probably wouldn't have been on the Immigrant Workers Freedom Ride, which just concluded its cross-country trip to Washington, D.C. She would have been afraid.
>
> I'm not sure you get the significance of the phrase. Let me repeat it. She would have been afraid.
>
> Many folks, of course, view this as mere political theater. It was really the present-day Freedom Riders making the argument that immigrants who give more than they take have a right to freedom of travel. Mostly, however, they have the right to be free from fear.
>
> I'm not sure my mother ever was.[6]

For those who took part, the trip was exhilarating; it expanded their sense of community, convinced them of the union's commitment to their cause, and put them in contact with supporters all over the country.[7] As D. Taylor told me, "I think they got a larger sense of struggle in this country."

During Wilhelm's presidency, the union has maintained close relations with the United Farm Workers. HERE leadership made sure that Hispanics and other immigrants were in positions of leadership. Durazo now heads the Los Angeles County Federation of Labor, which has over 800,000 members. Wilhelm considers her to be the most eloquent voice of the new labor movement —"a charismatic, inspiring woman." He has mixed but mostly positive feelings about her moving on to this new position: "We made a gut-wrenching decision for her to run for the top position at the L.A. County Federation of Labor after the untimely passing of her husband, Miguel Contreras, who had previously led that council. Beginning with his leadership, and growing significantly under hers, the L.A. labor council is by far the most effective in the country, politically and otherwise."

The costs of new programs and the repercussions from the crisis of 9/11 made Wilhelm and other key officers of HERE aware that the union's precarious financial position had to be fixed if the union was to undertake the types of organizing and political programs that they contemplated. This concern, as Wilhelm explained, "was no doubt one of the many strands that led to our merger with UNITE in 2004."

UNITE (the Union of Needletrades, Industrial and Textile Employees) was formed in 1995 through the merger of two unions with storied pasts: the International Ladies' Garment Workers' Union (ILGWU) and the Amalgamated Clothing and Textile Workers Union (ACTWU). The ILGWU was once one of the largest labor unions in the United States. It was one of the first U.S. unions to have a primarily immigrant female membership. Throughout its history it was known as an activist liberal union. It was the union of Clara Lemlich, the shirtwaist strikers, and "the great revolt." It was the union that "defied the preconceptions of more conservative labor leaders, who thought that immigrants and women could not be organized."[8]

ACTWU was probably best known for its long, semi-successful struggle to organize the J. P. Stevens Company. It was during this struggle that a young, onetime student activist named Ray Rogers developed the concept of the "corporate campaign." The Stevens battle was the setting for one of the great acts of defiance in labor union history when Crystal Lee Jordan, "a 33-year-old mother of three who earned $2.65 per hour folding towels at the J.P. Stevens textile plant, was fired in 1973 for her pro-union activity. Before the police hauled her off the factory floor, the 16-year veteran of the job wrote 'UNION' on a piece of cardboard, climbed on to a table and slowly rotated so her fellow workers could see her protest."[9] This action was later made a part of America's cultural history when Sally Field reenacted it in the movie *Norma Rae.*

Both the ILGWU and ACTWU were wealthy unions with few members when they merged. They continued to lose members during the late 1990s and early part of the twenty-first century as the garment industry continued its relentless movement overseas. For Wilhelm, the decision to merge with UNITE seemed obvious: "We have similar philosophies. We represent similar kinds of workers. We had an industry that can't move overseas, and no money, and they had an industry that was rapidly disappearing, and piles of money."[10] When UNITE HERE was formed, Bruce Raynor, the president of UNITE, was made general president of the new union. Wilhelm became copresident of the union and president of the hospitality division.

UNITE HERE had the funds to undertake organizing drives that HERE alone would have been incapable of. In early 2007, Wilhelm declared the merger a success: "We have bottom-up hotel organizing going on now in somewhere close to forty hotels, which is far more than we ever had at any one time in the former HERE. Of course, there are the kind of predictable bumps in the road that you would expect, but a far greater volume of organizing going on."

The way in which the hospitality division of UNITE HERE used its new resources is demonstrated in the experiences of Sarah Julian, a young West Coast hotel-worker organizer recruited into the union shortly after the merger, in 2004. Julian graduated from Smith College in 2003. She wasn't sure that unions were for her. But a HERE recruiter convinced her that it was worth a try: "I wanted to work with immigrant rights or economic and social justice. But my experience with unions before was like white guys from the Midwest, and that's just not who I am. I am a woman, and after college I worked a lot with immigrants and spent time in Latin America and spoke Spanish, and so when I heard about UNITE HERE, it was like a union, but it wasn't. It was a lot of women and a lot of immigrant women and it fit kind of with a lot of my life experiences. It wasn't my stereotypical idea of unions."

She signed on, anticipating a few years of union experience to broaden her understanding of workers and unions. After a brief training course, she was assigned to develop worker committees at unionized hotels in anticipation of negotiations. She found the interaction with the workers stirring: "They were patient with me because they had something to teach me. That was how I approached it, especially as a twenty-three-year-old starting out organizing in an industry that I hadn't worked in. That was my whole approach, trying to be humble and learn from the workers about the industry. They taught me Spanish and they taught me about themselves and they were happy to be respected."

When the new contract was negotiated, Julian was assigned to work on organizing the Doubletree Hotel in San Jose, a task made easier by virtue of a broad neutrality pledge signed by Doubletree in 2006: "We organized underground for about three years through 2004, 2005, and 2006, and the card-check agreement nationally was signed in August of 2006. We already had a very strong committee by that point, and so basically a few weeks after the card-check neutrality agreement was signed, we dropped cards, we got people signed up at 80 percent within two or three weeks, and we had the actual card check about a month after the national neutrality agreement was signed. The company agreed to recognize us, and we began bargaining in October of 2006."

With the Doubletree signed up, the union had achieved 90 percent density in San Jose. It then began an organizing drive at the Hyatt in Santa Clara. The first effort was to form an inside organizing committee. The process by which this was done was painstaking:

> We go through a clearing process. We have a couple of contacts inside. We start with people who worked in our union hotels that we already know. First, they agree to confidentiality, to not talk to anybody about our conversations. Secondly, they give us information about their coworkers, and so through the contacts that we have we go through a clearing process: we make sure that we know what that person gets mad about, we know their relationship to management and hopefully if they are a leader or not. And then, we want to know if they are positive or negative towards the union. Once those criteria are met, we are ready to start house calls to form the committee. It goes kind of slowly at first because we only visit people that have been cleared, that have met all those criteria.
>
> It took us about 9 or 10 months to build a good cross section of leaders from the different departments, and we began having committee meetings in May of this year. Then we had about a month and a half of secret committee meetings, and then the committee went out and solicited support from their coworkers to have a card-check agreement. They went public through the leaflet with their faces on it saying "We're the union committee and we want a fair process to choose the union through card check agreement."
>
> The same week that we went public, the company began captive-audience meetings department by department. And the manager basically would just go in and lie about the union.

The management campaign brought employee fear of reprisals to the surface. The organizers pointed out that retaliation was against the law, but they focused primarily on worker solidarity and community support. Julian described the union's approach:

> If they try to discipline you or fire you, yes, we will utilize the law to protect you, but more importantly that's why we have a committee, that's why the union workers are organized to support you, that's why the community and religious leaders are there to support you, as part of the comprehensive campaign.
>
> At the same time they are organizing the workers, we have a community organizing program through the South Bay. There is a religious organizer that organizes the religious community. We do this thing called "labor in the pulpit." [On] Labor Day we are going to have about thirty workers from the hotel speak to congregations. The church alliances were developed by a community organizer sent by the union. There was also a research component going on simultaneously and a political organizer involved trying to enlist city and state officials to support the campaign to achieve a card-check agreement.

When a group of anti-union employees was formed, organizers encouraged workers from the newly organized Doubletree to describe their experiences: "Banquet has been a difficult department. That's where some of the most outspoken anti-union workers have been coming from. There's a banquet server that came out and worked with us for two weeks to do house visits to all the banquet workers. She told about their negotiations and how they were able to improve conditions. That's the most effective thing that we find in terms of being able to show that the union is not a third party—by having workers come out and talk about their experiences being leaders in the union."

The HERE process described by Sarah Julian is far more deliberate and costly than the hot-shop approach. But it demonstrates how a movement, as opposed to an organization of dues payers, is created. Julian described the impact of the organizing approach on the membership:

> There's the workplaces where they have been union for over twenty years and the members there are not used to being involved. They are used to the leadership coming in and solving their problems for them. Then there is the other kind of workplace where they are recently organized and know about committees and depend on their own leadership. So in the houses where they have been union for a long time, or the workplaces where they have been union for a long time, the workers are used to other people doing the work. They are proud of the leadership and they are proud of the heads of the locals, but they don't necessarily see themselves as the union. The union is very much the people in the office. Whereas the newly organized

places or the places that were recently built are much more open to being leaders in their workplace and resolving problems themselves and learning to stand up for themselves.

For Julian, the experience of working closely with the hotel workers was so gratifying that she stopped thinking of organizing as a temporary experience on her way to something more rewarding. Asked "What is the greatest source of satisfaction?" she responded quickly: "Connecting with workers—especially at Local 19. We basically doubled the membership since I started here. Being part of a small local that's growing and being connected with the community of workers is very satisfying, as is being able to see that community change and get stronger and being part of a growing local."

The type of organizing Julian described was far different from that used by UNITE and was from the beginning a cause of disagreement between the two unions. Some of the UNITE staff argued that HERE's approach to organizing is too costly and that more money should be spent organizing laundries and food-service establishments. High-level staff from HERE concluded that UNITE leaders did not involve the members enough in key decisions and actions. As Joe Daugherty told me: "Those of us who have kind of come up through HERE have been taught to put a greater emphasis on organizing committees."

At the time of the merger, although both had supported John Sweeney when he ran for president of the AFL-CIO in 1995, neither Wilhelm nor Raynor was happy with the federation. They were joined in their disappointment by Andy Stern, the president of the SEIU. All believed that Sweeney had not lived up to his pledge to make organizing the AFL-CIO's top priority.[11]

By 2003 disappointment with the AFL-CIO had grown stronger. Wilhelm's dissatisfaction was based on the federation's failure to provide an atmosphere of consultation and joint decision making: "The AFL-CIO executive council is a show; it's not a forum for discussion or debate. It's a show. It's dominated by innumerable staff reports; the group is too big to have any debate and discussion even if anybody wanted any; everything is scripted—President Sweeney's comments are scripted literally from the moment the meeting opens starting with 'good morning.' So they are both sterile and frustrating. There isn't any other organized leadership forum in the AFL-CIO and the consequence of that is that the whole thing is very much staff driven, it's very much Washington, D.C., driven."

The dissidents included—in addition to Wilhelm, Stern, and Bruce Raynor —Terence O'Sullivan, the president of the Laborers' International Union of

North America; Doug McCarron, the president of the United Brotherhood of Carpenters; and James P. Hoffa, the general president of the International Brotherhood of Teamsters. They called themselves the New Unity Partnership and met regularly to formulate plans to significantly change the AFL-CIO. In 2005 they proposed a plan by which unions would reduce their contribution to the AFL-CIO by half and use the money retained to organize. Since the proposal would mean the elimination of many important departments and services, it was certain to be controversial, and in March 2005 the proposal was rejected by John Sweeney and the AFL-CIO's executive committee. In July 2005 the dissident unions left the AFL-CIO and formed their own competing organization, Change to Win, and were soon joined by Arturo Rodriguez of the Farm Workers. The new group represented over six million members. For reasons discussed in the next chapter, the future of Change to Win is bleak. UNITE HERE has returned to the AFL-CIO.

After it left the AFL-CIO, the hospitality division of UNITE HERE reshaped its organizing efforts. An innovative part of the new approach involves setting up ongoing community-union alliances. Andrea van den Heever, once a Yale clerical worker (Andrea Ross at the time) and a HERE employee ever since, is the president of one such group, called the Connecticut Center for a New Economy. It was created to develop a permanent alliance between the union and progressive community groups. As she explained to me:

> We went into negotiations in 1995. I did what I normally do and went out and met with African American clergy and white clergy and talked about the fact that we were going into negotiations and needed support, and met with resistance. The response, particularly from the African American clergy was, "Where have you been? We have been out here. Our children have been dying on the streets, and now when you come to us we've got to just get up and jump, right?" And it was during those contract negotiations that the university proposed subcontracting all of the dining-hall jobs as well as getting rid of retiree health, or severely restricting retiree health benefits. So we decided to frame the issues in basic economic terms for the community, which was there are three hundred dining-hall workers who live in the community, and if those jobs get turned into contingency jobs or part-time subcontracted jobs, it's going to have a serious economic impact, especially on the black neighborhoods immediately surrounding Yale. And so all through that summer we had neighborhood meetings; we got people, neighbors, together; we got shop owners together; we did all kinds of community organizing that we had not done before; and people rose to the occasion. There was a general consensus in the wake of that particular contract fight that it was the community that had saved the day. It was that particular contract that then led us with Wilhelm's leadership to decide that we could

no longer practice the same thing that we had been doing before. We needed to have an ongoing presence in the community, so the result of that was that I moved from out of my elected position in the union to become the first community organizer for the Yale locals.

The Connecticut Center for a New Economy was the result, and it quickly proved valuable to both the community and the union: "That first year, we passed the state's first living-wage ordinance in New Haven. We ran a campaign against the Omni Hotel not only for card-check neutrality for the workers but also for a very aggressive training and hiring component for local residents."

HOTEL WORKERS RISING

Historically, organizing has been handled primarily by local unions. This made sense when the employers being organized were local or essentially autonomous divisions of larger corporations. But locally controlled organizing no longer makes as much sense as it once did. Tom Woodruff, the director of the Change to Win organizing program, told me that this is a major problem: "Now that the local employer is a global conglomerate, it's impossible for a local union to effectively take that employer on—which goes to one of the problems that we have in the labor movement, which is restructuring ourselves. We are basically structured as the economy was structured in the 1950s, and the whole economy has a different structure now." Woodruff acknowledged that this issue has caused problems for his home union: "No question. In [the] SEIU, over the last ten years, we've gone through a real revolution between the national unions and locals. That's a work in progress that's still going on."[12]

At HERE's 2001 convention, the union decided that it needed to change its approach to organizing. As Wilhelm explained to me: "We've become a globalized industry, so the old approach of our union in each city, standing on its own, didn't work anymore, and people were having increasing trouble bargaining and increasing trouble organizing. We had a balance between local ownership or local direction and local unions. But, of course, that all changed. We, as usual, lagged in the union in changing our structure. So, at the convention we decided that we had to figure how to join together and address these companies in a more unified fashion."

The new approach was to be at the heart of a major organizing effort called Hotel Workers Rising. The program was delayed but not stopped by the catastrophe of 9/11 and the ensuing drastic downturn in the hospitality industry.

The program finally began in February 2006. Before then, a great deal of preparatory work was done getting HERE's members to understand the importance to each local of a broad-based organizing effort. A key part of the program was to use a coordinated collective-bargaining process as a way of obtaining card-check neutrality. To achieve coordination, the union attempted to arrange for local hotel agreements to terminate around the same time. Wilhelm explained that "we formally resolved that we ought to try to get as many big hotel city contracts as possible to expire in the year 2006. And the reason we picked 2006 was, just before the convention, the New York City Hotel Union, which is our biggest nongambling hotel local, had negotiated a contract which expired June 30, '06."

Union contracts were nonuniform in terms of expiration dates before this resolution. HERE set about coordinating them as unobtrusively as possible during the next few years. The hotel industry seemed not to notice, which Wilhelm found almost insulting: "It was symbolic of the lack of respect with which we had permitted the hotel industry to treat us. For quite some time, they didn't understand what we were doing even though we announced it in our convention."

It wasn't until Chicago Local 1 (Ed Hanley's old local, now led by Henry Tamarin, another former student activist and Vincent Sirabella hire), whose contract expired in 2002, insisted on a four-year contract, something unusual in the industry, that the Hilton negotiators even suspected that the union was seeking coordination. Wilhelm recalled that "Henry called me up just laughing one night, shortly before they settled. He said that the labor relations guy from Hilton had blown up . . . that very day, and suddenly expostulated, 'Wait a minute! Are you trying to get a 2006 expiration because of New York?' Henry said, 'Certainly not! That's ridiculous.'"

The mobilization campaign directed at the membership worked well enough for several major unions to make the expiration date a critical part of their bargaining. The San Francisco local led by Mike Casey worked without a contract and braved a lockout[13] for over two years to achieve this result. This was a remarkable achievement that awed Jeff Fiedler: "Let me tell you, you don't leave contracts open for long periods of time without having a deep relationship with the members." Other local unions were similarly determined, and as a result the union was able to achieve its goal of having a large share of its contracts expire in 2006. Local 11, then led by Maria Elena Durazo, played a key role: "In '04 in L.A. we fought in our negotiations to have a two-year agreement, so that in '06 we would align our expiration with the major cities across the country and Canada. 'Cause that put us into the picture as far as all our different cities working together."

The negotiations that followed provided the foundation for the Hotel Workers Rising campaign. As explained by Wilhelm:

> In those varying ways, we arrived at 2006 with the largest concentration of collective bargaining in the history of the hotel industry in the U.S. We had expiration some time in '06 in Toronto, Boston, New York, Chicago, Honolulu, San Francisco, Los Angeles, Monterey, San Jose, Seattle. And then we had some individual hotel contracts, so that we had 60,000 hotel workers with contracts expiring in all of those major cities. At the negotiations we said we want new contracts with good wages and benefits and working conditions, but we also want card-check neutrality going forward. We said to the union companies, anything you build, buy, or develop in this city, in the future, we want card check. We had it in only two places, Boston and New York, but as a result of this whole campaign, we added card-check neutrality going forward with the union companies in Washington, Chicago, San Francisco, Los Angeles, Honolulu, Monterey.

Durazo was delighted with the result: "I know that the coordination led to our best contracts, including what we called growth clauses—our card-check neutrality agreements—with owners and operators in L.A. I know on the national level there was success on that as well. At the local level we adopted the same approach, which is we wanted local owners and operators functioning here doing business in L.A. to also give us card-check neutrality for future hotels, and we won it in the overwhelming majority of hotels."

She believes that the victory of the 2006 negotiations was the result of the comprehensive nature of the union's strategy: "It wasn't any one thing. We had a very comprehensive campaign. We had everything from a boycott that was gradually instituted targeting certain hotels. We just didn't do it to everybody willy-nilly; we had very focused actions. Our political allies came into the picture to publicly support and denounce. We had a legal strategy; we had a negotiating strategy. I think it was a lot of things plus the fact that we were able to coordinate actions across the country. So workers saw themselves not only in L.A., but we did a lot of actions to connect us. Workers from L.A. went to Toronto, Chicago workers came here, our workers, our rank and file, were all mixed up."

Another theme of the Hotel Workers Rising initiative was the community's stake in its organizing success. When the program formally began in February 2006 at a union rally, John Edwards declared that the success of the program would shape the nature of America's future. The kickoff was followed by a tour of large cities in which mass meetings were held. At every meeting, the speakers were a mix of politicians (John Edwards; the mayors of Boston, San Francisco, and Los Angeles), celebrities, and workers.

As part of Hotel Workers Rising, the union has underwritten a series of documentary films, which have been transferred to DVDs for use by organizers. One of the documentaries, *Sharing the Banquet*, tells of a series of meals involving over four hundred clergy in August 2006 in Chicago, under the auspices of Local 1. Ministers, rabbis, priests, and imams were involved and all signed a statement of hospitality and human dignity calling for decent treatment of hotel workers. The night before the banquet, they met with hotel workers, who described the pains and strains of their work. Baptist minister Stephen Greer responded, "I feel challenged to go back to the West Side and tell the African American congregation that this is a serious issue that we need to embrace." After the banquet, the clergy were "sent out" to various hotels to speak with workers. Many, like Father Dowling, declared it a moving experience that would encourage them to give further support to the union. And, not surprisingly, contact with clergy was exciting for the hotel workers. Rosa Patina declared in Spanish how good it felt to realize that the workers were not struggling alone.[14]

The organizers of UNITE HERE have relearned some of the lessons of the civil-rights movement and the labor movement of the 1920s and 1930s. The events that they sponsor are filled with ceremony and emotion. People laugh, cry, cheer, and raise their voices in song. There is dancing and laughter along with the terrible stories of oppression. This was true throughout the Immigrant Workers Freedom Ride. It was this sharing of emotion that made many of the riders sad when their long trip ended. The Hotel Workers Rising campaign represents a remarkable blending of people not only by race and ethnicity but also by class and status. There are very few times in our society when undocumented workers, movie stars, and presidential candidates meet and hug.

Although Wilhelm leads the Hotel Workers Rising campaign, it is difficult to find him in the videos that are used to sell the program, videos that are filled with workers: male and female, Hispanic, Anglo, black, and Asian. The policy of stressing the role of workers and not that of union officials applies with equal force to the union's other key leaders, like D. Taylor and Karl Lechow. This is a matter of basic organizational philosophy for Wilhelm: "Unfailingly, workers are better faces and voices for the labor movement than union leaders, myself included."

Decisions about targets and methods are made collaboratively. Mike Casey explained to me how it works.

> Shortly after the 2006 campaign, when we managed to take Hotel Workers Rising to the next step, John [Wilhelm] kind of divided up the country. The Midwest and East under Henry Tamarin. He asked me to work with the locals in the West. And Courtney went around, examined, researched, and looked at what the different targeting was and came up with what amounted to basically three corporate targets. This is all new—we're just making this up as we go along. That's the other thing. People mention the UNITE HERE model of organizing; there isn't a UNITE HERE model of organizing other than we are committed to building committees. I think what connects people most is involving the members in all aspects of the campaign, whether it happens to be your existing union members as well as the nonunion workers that you are organizing. The so-called model is emerging and evolving week in and week out. There isn't one size fits all.

In September 2007 UNITE HERE organized forty-four new hotels outside the gaming industry and had active campaigns underway in forty more. Its success was described to me by Wilhelm in late 2007 as follows: "It would be fair to say, going back fifteen years, that the only local unions in major cities that were focused on hotels and that really had the capacity were New York City and San Francisco. Because President Hanley supported rebuilding efforts in major locals when the situation made it possible, and because those efforts continued and expanded after I became president, and have continued since the UNITE-HERE merger, I now include several more significant locals focused on hotels: in no particular order, Boston, Toronto, Washington D.C., Chicago, Los Angeles, San Jose, Detroit, and Honolulu are pretty much there, and on the way are San Diego and Seattle, with Minneapolis and Vancouver a bit behind those two."

By the end of 2008, the union had added roughly 11,000 new members in the nongaming hotels. Membership increased each year of the campaign: by 3,000 in 2006, 3,500 in 2007, and 4,000 in 2008.

The union has used both a carrot and a stick. The stick was opposing permits and taxpayer support. It has been most effective with new hotels. Karl Lechow explained the strategy to me: "If a hotel is being developed somewhere, before it ever gets built, we try to look at what leverage might exist, if the hotel is seeking some sort of taxpayer subsidy. That's one possibility. If it's seeking an indirect taxpayer subsidy, like infrastructure improvements, that's another possibility. If it needs zoning permits, if there are arguments against the notion that a hotel can be built in that place, you know, either environmental or whatever, we'll use it if we need to."

On the other hand, the union has been eager to form alliances with the hotels it organizes, and it is in a position to provide all kinds of help to unionized hotels. This is something that Wilhelm has strongly supported:

> It could be political help in getting the approvals they need. It could be helping them attract capital from pension funds or something. Take a place like Austin. I've been trying to persuade a couple of the large hotel companies that if they develop a hotel in Austin, and agreed to a card check, that they can get Democrat business, labor business, various kinds of business 'cause they know Austin. One of our developing tools is this thing called INMEX, which stands for Informed Meetings Exchange, which, you can go on the Web site and look at it. We have a huge number of subscriber organizations, most unions, Sierra Club, National Organization of Women, the NAACP, the Urban League, the National Council of La Raza, all kinds of people, and the proposition is that these organizations prefer to patronize union hotels because it's consistent with their values.

Demonstrating that community support works both ways, the Toronto local led by Paul Clifford has followed the pattern exemplified by the Connecticut Center for a New Economy and has won allies and public support by demonstrating concern for other causes as well as its own. As described in a news report, in August 2006, 2,000 workers at seven hotels in Toronto voted to authorize a strike, but they put the strike on hold during the XVI International AIDS Conference. "'We know the fight against HIV/AIDS is a fight against many issues including poverty. That is a struggle that we share, identify with and support,' said Sheraton worker Habtom Ogbamichael."[15]

UNITE HERE has been targeting hotels in the South and the Southwest. Texas is a particularly tempting target. Its four major cities, Houston, Dallas, San Antonio, and Austin, are filled with hotels and staffed by poorly paid, largely immigrant workers. The first three are among the ten largest cities in the country. Austin is one of the country's fastest-growing cities. In both San Antonio and Austin there are well-organized, progressive groups that would be eager to work with the union. Before the great economic recession began, HERE was readying itself for a major effort to organize the hotels of San Antonio and then Austin. It was also preparing for a major struggle to organize the Hyatt chain. It had put the two together in a major organizing effort at the San Antonio Hyatt—an effort led by former UNITE organizer Willie Gonzalez and a key HERE organizer, Yale graduate Danna Schneider. By the fall of

2009, the effort was ongoing, but it had run into problems described in the next chapter.

It is still too early to tell what the long-term effect of the recession will be on membership and organizing. I interviewed Wilhelm on this topic in November 2008. He was concerned but far from depressed. He even pointed out that, bad as it was, the recession offered some opportunities since employers were themselves more vulnerable in several ways:

> It's a double-edged sword. On the one hand, first and foremost, it's a negative impact on the members because we have a lot of members laid off or [who] have their hours cut. It's also a negative impact on the union's treasury, which means that there is less money available to organize. A significant number of hotels and casinos that were planned, including a bunch for which we have card-check agreements, either are being delayed or may never be built at all. On the other side of the coin, though, nonunion employers are doing really draconian things to workers, and we believe that will significantly increase the interest in workers seeking out the union even if we haven't targeted a particular company. Then the second part of the other side of the coin is that the debt load that so many of these companies have taken on, particularly those that have experienced private-equity buyouts but also others that simply borrowed tons of money to expand rapidly—the debt load they have taken on is something they could handle when the economy was booming and they had good cash flow. But a lot of them are really extremely shaky right now because the debt load is so huge and the cash flows are decreasing. It showed up first in gaming and now it's showing up in hotels, and so that makes bargaining for a first contract more difficult, but it also means that the companies don't have the strength they had to resist our organizing drives or to take a strike.

He gave as an example of an organizing opportunity created by the downturn the Station casinos in Las Vegas, which had managed to remain nonunion through a combination of maintaining a low profile and giving high wages and good benefits to their workers:

> They have about 14,000 workers in the classifications that we traditionally represent in Las Vegas: they are all nonunion; they are aggressively anti-union. So two things happened. One, they were bought out. There was a private-equity buyout by a company called Colony Capital, which is a Los Angeles–based private-equity firm which has been especially interested in the hospitality industry. And as is typical with those transactions, they loaded the company up with an extraordinary amount of debt. Had the business continued to boom, they could pay that debt, but the intersection of the enormous debt load and the resulting interest requirement and the collapse of the economy—the local casino business has been way down in Las Vegas

just because of the overall economic crisis there—and so they now have come after the workforce with a vengeance. They have reduced benefits; they basically totally abandoned the carrot program. And if an employer never had a carrot program, no one ever noticed, but if you built a whole identity with your workforce on the carrot, and then you take the carrot away, that produces quite a reaction. The workforce is now very disillusioned with the company, and the company's debt load is staggering in relation to their business, and they are not as strong as they were. Now I don't underestimate them, I don't mean to sound cocky about this, but that is the flip side of the negatives of the economic crisis in my view in respect to organizing prospects.

Chapter 13 Solidarity Rebuffed

During its first years, the UNITE HERE merger helped both unions, providing a strong membership base for UNITE and needed financial resources for HERE. It was not, however, a perfect marriage. The two unions entered the alliance with different approaches to organizing and collective bargaining. UNITE did mostly top-down and hot-shop organizing. Its leaders often cut deals with employers offering low-cost contracts and the promise of labor peace in exchange for recognition. They regularly controlled contract negotiation. HERE organized through comprehensive campaigns using worker committees, job actions, and alliances with progressive groups. Its negotiations depended on rank-and-file involvement. HERE leaders conceded that their method took longer but insisted that it produced better contracts.[1]

The ideological differences between the different parts of UNITE HERE were summed up in an article in the *American Prospect:* "The HERE worker-committee bottom-up model of organizing, its leaders argue, produces a membership better able to win a good contract. It can take a long time—"sometimes, too long," one leader concedes—

but the contracts justify the sometimes tortuous means. UNITE leaders, by contrast, share a vision of union growth that can be more top-down, that is more wholesale than retail. The growth—organizing previously unorganized workers—justifies what may be less than stellar contracts. HERE leaders couldn't disagree more. "'If I have to spend the next phase of my life fighting top-down organizing,' says one, 'that's fine with me.'"[2]

Young HERE-trained organizer Trent Leon-Lierman explained the value of the HERE approach:

> I enjoy how we organize. It's intensive and very community based and very worker led. I've enjoyed how we focus on building strong committees and pushing workers to attend rallies and take leadership. . . . I really agree with the model.
>
> I mean, it's a lot easier to go to the hotel and say, hey, we're going to be outside marching so grant us recognition, rather than going to the leaders inside the hotel and pushing them to get people out there marching. It's easier to have union staff go out and picket in front of the hotel and not have a whole lot of workers doing it. But the strength comes from the workers, and worker-leaders are the ones that ultimately make the change. Once you have those leaders—I'm thinking of the Sheraton City Center—once we win there, then those leaders can help us fight in the next hotel in Baltimore, so it is a movement when you think of it like that.

Another major source of tension was the different leadership styles of the copresidents. Wilhelm leads through discussion and consensus. According to Jeff Fiedler, "John [Wilhelm] is much more of a consensual leader than you will meet anywhere else."[3] According to D. Taylor: "John never orders you to do something. He allows you to make the decision after discussion, thought, and deliberation." Wilhelm is viewed affectionately by those who have worked with him. If there is lurking unhappiness with his leadership among organizers or local presidents, it is not easy to find. Mike Casey, the dynamic leader of Local 2 in San Francisco, described Wilhelm's leadership in a phrase he borrowed from another HERE organizer: "A lot of union leaders develop followers, whereas John Wilhelm develops leaders. That's the type of leader he is."

Bruce Raynor operates very differently. He is tempestuous and demanding, given to unilateral actions and no-debate command decisions. He does not take advice from subordinates. One longtime organizer told me that "Bruce Raynor is a hot-shop and top-down organizer with a big mouth—that's about it." Former HERE leaders who worked with Raynor found the experience unsettling and often unpleasant. One of the first to experience firsthand the change in leadership style was Jim Dupont, a HERE vice president who had directed the food-services division of the union. He had worked closely with

Wilhelm for many years before the merger and with Raynor, who became head of the division, after the merger. Almost from the beginning, he found the new arrangement troubling: "Raynor made up his mind, and that was it. Sometimes he would ask you what you thought, but it was only to make sure that you agreed with what he had already decided. He was the polar opposite of John, who would ask my opinion to help make up his mind." Dupont was dismayed by the relationship between Raynor and his staff: "He's despicable—he would talk about staff like they were dogs."[4] Top leaders from the UNITE side instructed Dupont to pretend to agree with Raynor and then ignore his instructions: "The people I worked with closely from the UNITE side would tell me we got to 'Bruce-proof' our operations. There was just an incredible culture of dishonesty that I got uneasy with very quickly. My head was spinning because I come from a culture where people say what they are going to do and they do it and if they can't they let you know."

Dupont concluded that Raynor was "a horrible trade unionist." As an example he cites Raynor's unilateral deal with ARAMARK management in which he gave up a unit of twenty workers at Citibank, a group that had fought tirelessly for the union, signed cards, demonstrated, and picketed for card-check recognition. Both Dupont and Bill Granfield, whose Local 100 would have been the group's home, bitterly opposed Raynor's decision, but Raynor ignored their protests.

In his frustration, Dupont on several occasions complained about Raynor's actions to Wilhelm, who refused to intervene, insisting that under the terms of the merger food services was Raynor's jurisdiction. Dupont was not the only HERE leader who complained about Raynor's actions. Some in the hotel division (officially led by Wilhelm) reported that Raynor was attempting to negotiate private deals with hotel management. By 2008, unhappiness with Raynor was widespread among former HERE leaders. As Wilhelm told me: "Bruce is an enormously smart, talented guy, but he's used to making decisions and telling the other leaders of the union later what those decisions were. Not only are the former HERE leaders not used to that approach, they won't accept it. The next generation of HERE leaders behind me, Mike Casey and Tom Walsh and Peter Ward and Maria Elena Durazo and D. Taylor and Paul Clifford, simply won't accept that style. I don't think it's an appropriate way to run a far-flung, dispersed organization, because I think it fails to take advantage of the wealth of leadership that we have in the union at various levels."

By the fall of 2008, HERE leaders asked Wilhelm to forgo any plans for retirement and oppose Raynor for the presidency at the upcoming June 2009 convention. Jeff Fiedler believes that Wilhelm agreed "as an act of loyalty." Since former HERE leaders would be in the majority at the convention, Wilhelm's election was guaranteed. Raynor reacted furiously to Wilhelm's decision, demanding that the merger be undone. But neither Raynor nor his followers had the power to insist on such a result. Article 1, section 7 of UNITE HERE's constitution provides that "this international union may not be dissolved as long as three local unions or more oppose such dissolution." Article 5, section 7 provides that "a local may not withdraw from UNITE HERE, go out of existence, dissolve, or join or amalgamate with a non–UNITE HERE union without the prior consent of the GEB [general executive board]." And the general executive board was controlled by former HERE leaders, who rejected Raynor's demands. They considered the merger a success. D. Taylor argued that the merger had helped the workers of both unions obtain first-rate contracts and had strengthened UNITE's joint boards: "Let's take their old Midwest. About 60 percent of their entire membership now is former HERE locals. That's just one example this merger's working both ways. Take the laundry workers here in Las Vegas. Former UNITE. We took them over. Now we have by far the best laundry contract in the country, free health care, etcetera. They never could achieve that in isolation."

Sometime in the winter of 2008, after it became clear that he would not be elected president of the union at its 2009 convention, Raynor, together with other former UNITE leaders, formed a plan to force dissolution of the merged unions. Warren Pepicelli, formerly a UNITE vice president and the head of the New England Joint Board, described the plan:

> In December a group of leaders from former UNITE met in a small room and hatched a plan to secede from UNITE HERE by April. The strategy was a three-prong strategy, described as creating chaos and confusion.
>
> The first part of that strategy was to jump ahead and go into the courts and sue UNITE HERE for corruption and to attack leaders of UNITE HERE personally. If you get into court early, you can set the tone, it was said.
>
> The second leg of this strategy was to bring in SEIU, who attended those meetings, and tell UNITE HERE that SEIU is going to go after the hotel jurisdiction and organized hotels, to put the fear of God into the leaders of UNITE HERE.
>
> The third leg of this stool is for me the most troublesome. It was a strategy of collecting dues money, money from the joint boards and from our International and to hire a consulting firm who is first going to send you letters about Obama, about the hope for Employees Free Choice and then do a 180, as they would say, and to call you with lowball calls. To create dissension . . . and pit worker against worker.

When I reported this back to my Executive Board, we said, we will not go along with this strategy.[5]

In subsequent litigation, UNITE HERE obtained copies of two documents that set forth the basic strategy of the Raynor group. Document 66-2 included the following:

Need a "game changer" so other side realizes that when they wake up in control of the union on July 3, 2009 that they in fact have won nothing—no assets to control, affiliates who won't roll over, leader of the UNITE forces in exile, polarized union. . . .

3. Increasingly put the squeeze on them to make it harder for them to fight back—financially and through destabilization.
4. Increasingly embarrass them and make them look bad for the union.
5. Isolation—turn key allies against them.

Document 66-3 included plans for "convincing the Wilhelm faction" that "we will either take our resources with us or tie them up in a way that they will not be able to get at them for a long time."

Starting in the winter of 2008, in accordance with the plan, Raynor bombarded the membership and labor activists with a series of e-mails, letters, and public statements attacking Wilhelm and "his small clique of zealots." A staff person who received the e-mails told me that "the beginning e-mails were defamation e-mails. Then, they transitioned into splitting e-mails, insisting that the merger be undone."

As 2008 ended, the battle heated up. On January 5, 2009, agents of the Chicago and Midwest Regional Joint Board physically took over the union hall of HERE's Local 24. They tried to remove Joe Daugherty, the local's elected president and the Michigan director of the union, from the union's office. Daugherty resisted. The events of the confrontation were described in an article in *Labor Notes:*

Detroit's UNITE HERE Local 24 was padlocked in January after the union's regional board took over the local's office and removed the appointed state director. . . .

Officials of the Chicago Midwest Regional Joint Board say ejecting Michigan State Director Joe Daugherty was a necessary response to member complaints about the local's failure to process grievances. . . .

Many of Local 24's sidelined leaders—including Daugherty—were elected to local positions in December. . . .

After learning he was fired, Daugherty staked out an overnight watch inside the union's office. He said staffers from Chicago and Canada, flown in by the Joint

Board for the takeover, kept him from placing phone calls and blared recordings of UNITE HERE President Bruce Raynor's speeches at full volume.[6]

The claim that Daugherty was ousted after an investigation, because of faulty grievance handling, was contradicted by Local 24 shop stewards, who pointed out that they were not consulted. One shop steward said, "No one ever called me up. No one ever called any of the shop stewards and the elected officers that I know."[7] A majority of the members of Local 24 signed a petition urging Local 24 to end its affiliation with the regional joint board.

On January 22, 2009, in accordance with the plan described by Pepicelli, Raynor brought suit against Wilhelm and the HERE members of the executive committee of the union's executive board, charging that the executive committee infringed on his prerogatives as general president. He also accused Wilhelm of plotting to "take control of the union's financial resources . . . including, in particular, the Amalgamated Bank." He sought a declaration that specific unconstitutional acts of the defendants were "null and void."[8] Raynor voluntarily withdrew the suit in February.

In February 2009 Raynor entered into a client-services agreement with The Organizing Group, Inc., led by Steve Rosenthal, who agreed "to provide strategic advice on an ongoing basis." Rosenthal, who had been a major union political organizer, is a close personal friend of SEIU president Andy Stern.[9] UNITE HERE officials are certain that Rosenthal's subsequent actions were taken with the active support of Stern.[10] This is disputed by some SEIU officials.

Shortly thereafter, Rosenthal launched a Web site, www.fixourunion.org. It contained a series of personal attacks on HERE leaders—for example, under the headline "STORIES OF GREED," it states, "President John Wilhelm is focused on himself, not UNITE HERE members. He funds locals and campaigns that increase his power and financial control. He even uses his power to help 'organizers' invade your personal privacy." This was followed by an attack on the Canadian director of UNITE HERE, Nick Worhaug, who, it was claimed, "is getting rich by wasting our dues dollars." Karl Lechow was charged with spending union money on himself and friends: "In September of 2008, he took 15 of his friends to dinner and billed the union $2,395." Under the heading "DISASTER AT LOCAL 11," the following charge was made: "The leaders at Local 11 are sending their organizers all over the country in an attempt to consolidate their own power. Meanwhile, Local 11's dues-paying members are completely neglected." The final segment was an attack on the Culinary: "The casinos are

empty and so are the union offices. With the gaming industry in distress, culinary and casino workers need their union more than ever to protect their jobs,
benefits and working conditions. But your organizers are off in Detroit,
Phoenix and Pennsylvania focused on union infighting, instead of you."[11]

Although the Web site suggested the existence of factual evidence in support
of its charges, clicking on the link "LEARN MORE" provided no additional relevant facts.

Rosenthal claimed to be motivated by the Judaic tradition of "*tikkun olam*,"
which translates as "repair the world."[12] It is difficult to understand how something positive for the world, or the cause of labor, could be achieved by writing the script for future management campaigns against the union. His in-
flammatory rhetoric seemed calculated to disturb the membership and to
provide material for anti-labor blogs. It was not surprising when hotel management—battling unionization in Texas and California—began to distribute
flyers copied verbatim from the Web site.[13]

The rhetorical overkill of the Web site was matched by Raynor's comments
to *New York Times* reporter Steven Greenhouse: "'We're not going to allow
them to hijack the resources that were put aside by generations of ladies' and
men's garment workers,' Mr. Raynor said. 'We'll do whatever we have to do
to show that we can't be held captive by a bunch of thugs.'"[14] Thugs? John
Wilhelm? D. Taylor? Maria Elena Durazo? Sherri Chiesa? It might have been
possible to find a more inappropriate way to describe the HERE leadership. But
it would not have been easy.

HERE leaders in the combined union consistently made clear that they
would not voluntarily split the union. In a statement to the membership issued
on February 4, 2009, a majority of the UNITE HERE executive board (nearly
all from the former HERE) rejected the idea:[15]

> We believe the merger that created UNITE HERE made sense in 2004 and we be-
> lieve it makes sense today. Combining our two unions helped us win a long strike
> in Atlantic City [and] helped many Joint Boards gain membership and organize in
> new industries. . . .
>
> Bruce Raynor has told us that he wants to throw all that out and break the union
> apart. He has told numerous people that he intends to create chaos and strife inside
> the union to achieve that goal. In fact, more than once, he has said to us either you
> agree to a divorce or we will destroy the union.[16]

On February 9, 2009, Raynor distributed an e-mail statement maintaining
that the merger had failed to produce results and once again attacking John
Wilhelm:

John Wilhelm and his small band of zealots . . . want to seize control of the union and UNITE's assets that were built through 100 years of hard work by low-income, largely immigrant men and women so he can then redirect them to the failed programs of a few of his favorite locals. We will not let that happen.

Wilhelm and HERE have a history of spending recklessly and squandering resources. At the time of the merger, HERE was nearly bankrupt. They had mismanaged their money, including their national pension fund and some of their welfare funds. We bailed out these funds so their members could have their health care and pensions. We will not allow them to run this great union into the ground.[17]

Like much that was to follow, Raynor's statement was misleading and factually inaccurate in places. It is true that HERE was in financial difficulty at the time of the merger. But as the monitor's report made clear, this was a situation that Wilhelm inherited in 1999 and that was exacerbated by the economic fallout following 9/11. Wilhelm, who sold the union's plane (regularly used by his predecessor) on his first day in office, has no record of spending recklessly or squandering resources. Indeed, it was Wilhelm who, as the monitor noted in his report, imposed financial discipline on the union after he became president.

The theme that Wilhelm and his followers have failed to properly respect the sacrifices of low-wage immigrant garment workers has been sounded repeatedly by Raynor and his allies. It is a particularly curious claim to use against someone with Wilhelm's long record of organizing and supporting immigrant workers.[18]

The theme runs counter to the basic idea of labor solidarity. It suggests that immigrant garment workers would be dishonored by sharing the fruits of their labor with hotel workers. This position implicit in Raynor's statement and similar statements by his followers was rejected by a group of retired officers of the International Ladies' Garment Workers' Union (ILGWU): "Our focus, historically, has always been to benefit the workers, without regard to craft or industry. A hotel worker is as much a member of the working class as a garment worker in our day. We are more concerned with the principles which guide the union than with the members' trade."[19]

On February 10, 2009, a group of UNITE officials made up of fourteen joint-board managers and one local president filed a lawsuit against Wilhelm and other HERE leaders seeking dissolution of the combined union.[20] They alleged that the "defendants have engaged in conduct that destroys the basis for the merger of these unions." The plaintiffs sought "a declaration that they are free to disaffiliate from UNITE HERE with their property and assets intact

[and] a declaration that the Constitution of UNITE HERE is invalid and un-enforceable." This suit, discussed more fully below, had not been settled at the time this book was written.

While the increasingly bitter struggle between UNITE and HERE forces continued unabated, Andy Stern of the SEIU became an open participant in the battle. In a letter dated January 30, 2009, and addressed "Dear Bruce and John," Stern said that "it is apparent to us that the merger of UNITE and HERE has failed." He suggested that it was time for "both unions to reconsider their future." He argued that either separately or together, their future could be best assured by becoming part of the SEIU. Although Stern's letter was addressed to both Wilhelm and Raynor, and was carefully neutral in tone, it was in fact supportive of Raynor because it took the position that "the merger has failed."[21]

Stern initially attempted to portray himself as a neutral outsider seeking only to help. In a memorandum dated March 10, Stern announced that the SEIU would abide by the decision of UNITE HERE on the merger. Whatever force this understanding might have, it was undercut by Stern's refusal to recognize that the decision had to be made in accordance with UNITE HERE's constitution. Indeed, throughout his memo, as in other statements, Stern seemed to assume the legal right of former UNITE affiliates to end the merger. He acknowledged that "upon the request of Joint Board leadership, SEIU has provided staff assistance to defend against an attempt by some HERE officials to interfere with the established representation rights of the Joint Boards."[22] But the idea that joint boards have established representative rights separate from UNITE HERE was directly contrary to the position taken by the majority of the UNITE HERE executive board. This statement, far from testifying to Stern's impartiality, demonstrated that he was supporting those trying to break away from UNITE HERE. Stern's message also assumed that the former UNITE was an independent entity that could choose to affiliate with the SEIU and bring the Amalgamated Bank with it. This assumption, directly contrary to UNITE HERE's constitution, negates any claim of neutrality on Stern's part. A smattering of neutral prose aside, there was no doubt which side the SEIU supported.

A *New York Daily News* article provided a knowledgeable summary of the battle as of the end of February 2009 and Stern's role in it:

> [Andy] Stern . . . is forever on the prowl for new workers to absorb into his empire and he doesn't much care how he does it.

"We are not shy in saying that their members would be better off if they were all in SEIU," Stern said yesterday.

It is not an idle offer. Stern acknowledged he has assigned teams of lawyers and staff members to study legal documents and prepare proposals for such a merger.

Meanwhile, labor strategist Steve Rosenthal, Stern's best friend and the husband of an SEIU vice president, is coordinating a campaign on behalf of Raynor to force the breakup of UNITE HERE and keep the bank away from Wilhelm. . . .

In late December, Raynor, who controls a majority of the bank's directors, amended the rules to ensure he stays in control of the bank when Wilhelm becomes union president in July.[23]

On March 19, 2009, Wilhelm and the executive-board majority filed a counterclaim against Raynor and the joint-board presidents, charging them with breaching their obligations as officers of UNITE HERE by using union money for their own benefit rather than that of the members.[24]

The charges were serious. Both federal law and UNITE HERE's constitution prohibit using union funds or property for reasons other than the advancement of the union. Section 501 of the Labor-Management Reporting and Disclosure Act provides that union officers must use union funds or property "solely for the benefit of the organization and its members." Article 21, section 2(b) of the union's constitution provides: "The funds and property in the possession of an affiliate shall be exclusively devoted to the fulfillment of the organizational purposes set forth in this Constitution. . . . The International Union's Presidents shall take all necessary steps to protect the Union's property."

The counterclaim alleged that once it became clear that Raynor would not be elected president at the July 2009 convention, he and other former UNITE officials used UNITE HERE's property in a manner hostile to the union's overall interests. A significant claim concerned the effort to diminish UNITE HERE's control over the Amalgamated Bank: "Bruce Raynor used his position as General President of UNITE HERE—which gave him the authority to vote the Union-owned shares of the Bank—to orchestrate amendments to the bylaws of Amalgamated Bank which entrench him and other counterclaim-defendants as Bank Directors in perpetuity, regardless of whether they retain their elected UNITE HERE offices." The counterclaim defendants were also charged with generally fostering secession from the union and using union funds for that purpose in direct violation of UNITE HERE's constitution.

On the weekend of March 21 and 22, 2009, UNITE-led dissidents announced the formation of a new union, "Workers United," which was immediately incorporated into the SEIU. "Workers United" is a shrewd choice of name. It conveys class solidarity, perhaps to obscure the fact that the organization represents a hostile effort to break up an established union. The breadth of the name suggests unlimited jurisdiction—broad enough to claim locals and joint boards of the former UNITE and to challenge hospitality-industry locals that were part of HERE. The breadth of the name also hides the absence of an obvious core jurisdiction. Workers United could not survive as a successful garment-workers union. The garment industry in the United States was by then almost nonexistent, and it has continued to shrink.

UNITE had done some effective organizing among laundry workers (some with the aid of former HERE personnel). But they then were too small a group to constitute a core union jurisdiction. It seemed clear from the start that the best chance for the new union to thrive was by establishing itself in the large and growing hospitality industry traditionally organized by UNITE HERE.

And almost as soon as Workers United was formed, its president, Edgar Romney, a former vice president of UNITE, indicated the union's intention to organize broadly and to take on UNITE HERE. His initial statement bristled with a challenge to compete for hospitality workers:

> With this affiliation we will have the support of SEIU, and there is no question that we will be stronger together. . . .
>
> . . . SEIU has transformed the property services industry through incredible international campaigns for janitorial and security workers.
>
> Unfortunately, hospitality workers have not witnessed a similar transformation of their industries outside of a few metropolitan areas. . . . Millions of hotel, hospitality and gaming workers in other geographic areas and types of properties have been left to fend for themselves.[25]

The assumption behind Romney's remarks, that the SEIU had been more successful in private-sector organizing than HERE, is incorrect. HERE had organized roughly 19 percent of hotel workers and close to 50 percent of gaming workers. It had repeated its Las Vegas success in Atlantic City and was in the process of organizing gaming workers in the Gulf Coast casinos and in the Midwest. Wilhelm had overseen the original organizing effort in Las Vegas, and D. Taylor, another of the defendants in Raynor's lawsuits, had taken the lead thereafter. By contrast, the SEIU had organized less than 10 percent of private-sector health-care workers.

Nevertheless, Romney's claim that the remnants of UNITE combined with the SEIU would be able to out-organize and overpower UNITE HERE, although questionable, was not without basis. The SEIU had millions of members, lots of money, and first-rate organizing leadership. It was bigger and stronger than UNITE HERE. In addition, the recession, then in full throttle, was bound to weaken UNITE HERE. Jobs were lost. Planned hotels were delayed or canceled. Workers were edgy.

Immediately after the Workers United convention, Stern wrote another letter to Wilhelm and Raynor in which he seemed to promise that the SEIU would not attempt to raid HERE locals: "SEIU including the Workers United Conference will only defend those bargaining units and locals that have been part of UNITE and its Joint Boards and/or have voluntarily disaffiliated from UNITE HERE as part of the Workers United Movement."[26] Read carefully, the letter offered little comfort to Wilhelm and others who were intent on keeping UNITE HERE together. For one thing, it assumed the ability of locals and joint boards to disaffiliate from UNITE HERE. With the carefully placed "or," Stern's letter also suggested the willingness of the SEIU to defend former HERE locals that have or will "voluntarily disaffiliate from UNITE HERE." And in the days following, a variety of attempts were made to persuade HERE members to quit the union and join Workers United. The tactics used included robo-calls attacking the union's leadership and false claims made during the calls.

On April 21, 2009, by a 32–0 vote with three abstentions, the general executive board of UNITE HERE voted to suspend Raynor, the union's general president, for "attempts to divide the union as well as promote SEIU."[27] Raynor resigned from the union on May 29 and was quickly made president of Workers United. By the time Raynor resigned, UNITE HERE was engaged in a series of battles with the SEIU and Workers United. There were three main fronts—the law, the labor community, and battles for the allegiance of workers.

Gillis v. Wilhelm, the case brought by Raynor and UNITE vice presidents to dissolve the merger of the two unions, is likely to cost both sides lots of money. But the Raynor camp's chances to use the law to force a breakup of UNITE HERE seem bleak. They made three basic claims. Their first claim was that "the Joint Boards are independent trade unions"[28] entitled to leave at their option. Their second claim was that the HERE faction of the union entered into the merger in bad faith: "The huge budget deficits demanded by the HERE Faction to fund its goals and program demonstrate that the merger was viewed as an opportunity to exploit UNITE and plunder its assets." The third claim was that "the fundamental merger purpose of organizing hundreds of thousands of new workers in the hospitality industry has simply not been met."

It is difficult to imagine the plaintiffs winning on any of these theories. Joint boards are not independent labor organizations. They are traditional union intermediate administrative units that were governed by UNITE officials before the merger and by the national officers and the constitution of UNITE HERE afterward. It is noteworthy that the Labor-Management Reporting and Disclosure Act specifically refers to "intermediate bodies, such as . . . joint boards."

There seems equally little to the plaintiffs' second argument that HERE leaders were attempting improperly to gain access to UNITE's resources. Absent the word "plunder," it would be difficult to claim that there was anything either illegal or hidden in HERE's desire to take advantage of UNITE's assets. Wilhelm never denied that he was interested in the merger in part because the new union would have access to UNITE's assets. Both groups entered into the merger because they hoped to profit from it. UNITE leaders, faced with a dying core industry, were seeking to take advantage of the growing membership and potential for growth provided by the former HERE.

The claim that the merger failed because the combined union did not organize hundreds of thousands of new members in its first four years is absurd. The fundamental goal of the merger, to combine the assets of the two groups for the purpose of organizing the unorganized, was fulfilled. There was no promise of immediate success contained in the merger agreement, which the plaintiffs attached to their complaint.[29]

Another legal issue that could take some time to resolve involves control of the Amalgamated Bank. The bank stock belongs to UNITE HERE under section 10 of the affiliation agreement, which provides that "all property, real, personal and mixed . . . tangible and intangible, of UNITE and HERE . . . of whatever kind or nature whatsoever shall . . . be transferred to and vested in UNITE HERE." The significance of the clause seems plain enough. However, serious questions of bank governance arose because of actions taken by Raynor during his final days as general president of UNITE HERE to increase his own authority and diminish that of the union. According to the counterclaim in the *Gillis* case: "Bruce Raynor used his position as General President of UNITE HERE—which gave him the authority to vote the Union-owned shares of the Bank—to orchestrate amendments to the bylaws of Amalgamated Bank which entrench him and other counterclaim defendants as Bank Directors in perpetuity, regardless of whether they retain their elected UNITE HERE offices." This issue, whether Raynor exceeded his authority and, if so, what remedy to impose, is not likely to be resolved for some time.

UNITE HERE's constitution makes clear that local unions cannot disaffiliate, but it is silent as to joint boards. It is difficult, however, to understand why joint boards would be permitted to disaffiliate when their constituent locals cannot.[30] Even if the courts ultimately decide that joint boards are free to disaffiliate, it will still leave open the question of ownership of their property. Article 21, section 2 of UNITE HERE's constitution provides that "all initiation fees, dues . . . and all other funds and property in the possession of . . . any affiliate shall be and remain the property of UNITE HERE."

The counterclaim brought by Wilhelm and the other former HERE leaders charging that Raynor mishandled union funds seems quite likely to succeed on the merits if it is actually tried. Part of the original plan announced by Raynor's group was ensuring that "when they [Wilhelm and other HERE leaders] wake up in control of the union on July 3, 2009 that they in fact have won nothing—no assets to control. . . ." It is difficult to understand how this was to be achieved if Raynor, who was still general president of UNITE HERE, acted in accordance with his fiduciary obligation under the law. There is plenty of evidence to indicate that he did not do so.

The most drastic action to deprive UNITE HERE of resources involved depleting the union's strike fund. At the 2009 UNITE HERE convention, Wilhelm described the actions taken by Raynor:

> In the merger Convention five years ago, we started building up a Strike Fund. That Strike Fund has the value of slightly over $20 million American. The nature of a Strike Fund is that when there is a strike, you need to write checks to the strikers. The Strike Fund needs to be liquid money readily available. Of that $20 and a half million, we learned in the last few days that at least 19 and a half million and probably closer to 20 million, that is all about a few hundred thousand dollars, has been converted from cash money into stock in the Amalgamated Bank.
>
> Now, stock in the Amalgamated Bank is not like some other kind of stock that you can sell. Stock in the Amalgamated Bank cannot be sold except to the bank. There is no way—and the bank, by the way, doesn't have the money to buy it in the current crisis—there is no way to reconvert that Strike Fund into cash that would be available for members who stand up and fight and go on strike if they need to or get locked out by their employer. Of all of the things that have been done, that one is the most unconscionable.[31]

Other charges of mishandling union funds were spelled out in an article by Juan Gonzalez in the *New York Daily News:*

> In the weeks before a bitter power struggle at one of the country's biggest unions, UNITE HERE, erupted into an open split, the union's general president ordered

more than $12 million be transferred to local affiliates loyal to him and to outside groups, documents obtained by the *Daily News* show.

Bruce Raynor disbursed the money without the knowledge or required approval of the union's co-president, John Wilhelm, UNITE HERE leaders said this week. Those funds, they claim, were then used to finance a breakaway group from the union. . . .

. . . Internal documents obtained by The News show that in the weeks leading up to the split Raynor ordered several sizable wire transfers without any approval from Wilhelm.

On Jan. 31, for example, he directed that $457,981 be paid from UNITE HERE to The Organizing Group, a political consulting firm with close ties to SEIU.

The head of The Organizing Group, Steve Rosenthal, then organized mailings and robo calls to union members that promoted the secession campaign of Workers United. He also organized a Web site for the group. Rosenthal did not respond to calls for comment.

Between Jan. 26 and Jan. 31, Raynor ordered another dozen transfers totaling $11.2 million for various UNITE HERE locals around the country. . . .

On March 6, the day before those locals officially voted to secede, Raynor ordered more [than] a dozen wire transfers sent to them, totaling another $500,000, for "reimbursement of expenditures."[32]

Raynor's precarious legal position is undoubtedly one reason why recent public statements from Workers United and the SEIU during the spring and summer of 2009 focused on the need for a settlement of outstanding issues with Wilhelm and UNITE HERE—always put in terms of the needs of workers and regularly claiming that Wilhelm does not appreciate the harm he is causing them.

Despite a barrage of propaganda portraying the SEIU and Workers United as helpless victims of Wilhelm's ego, by late summer of 2009, UNITE HERE was winning the battle for support from the labor community. The SEIU's intervention in particular drew considerable criticism. On March 2, 2009, Mark Ayers, the president of the Building and Construction Trades Department of the AFL-CIO, issued a memorandum to leaders of the AFL-CIO titled "Interference into Internal Union Affairs." In it he said:

The fact that one large international union has chosen to insert itself into the affairs of UNITE HERE is deplorable and arrogant.

We believe and hereby reassert our firm support for the leaders and members of UNITE HERE, and trust, through this union's own democratic process, it will self-determine its course for the future.

We stand in solidarity with the members of UNITE HERE as their union re-
solves its internal differences.[33]

Terry O'Sullivan, the president of the Laborers' International Union of
North America, wrote on two occasions to Andy Stern expressing his disap-
proval of the course the SEIU was following and politely disagreeing with
Stern's version of the facts surrounding the dispute.

During the spring of 2009, twenty-four labor federations formally condemned the SEIU's actions. Typical was the resolution of the San Diego and
Imperial Counties Labor Council, which noted that the "SEIU's reprehensible
behavior not only undermines UNITE HERE's local unions, but will also be
exploited by anti-union corporations and interest groups . . . and is contrary to
the basic principle of solidarity." It concluded: "Resolved that the San Diego
and Imperial Counties Labor Council condemns the intervention in the internal concerns of UNITE HERE by President Andy Stern and top SEIU leadership, and their actions designed to attack, disparage and weaken UNITE
HERE; and Condemns the campaign being waged against UNITE HERE and
its locals with the reliance on corporate-style anti-union tactics; and Condemns
SEIU's disrespect for union democracy and the ability of UNITE HERE members to elect their own leaders and participate meaningfully in the functioning
of their own unions."[34]

Stern and Raynor, beginning in the spring of 2009, took a new tack, portraying themselves as eager for a fair resolution of the dispute. On May 1 Stern,
Raynor, and Edgar Romney released a statement urging arbitration of outstanding issues if the parties were unable to negotiate a settlement. According
to their statement: "All three leaders who submitted the proposal want an end
to the name calling, accusations and public attacks against each union's leaders and members, and are willing and eager to put this dispute behind them
through an expedited dispute resolution arbitration process."[35]

Wilhelm quickly rejected the proposals. In a letter dated May 1 to Stern, he
pointed to what was excluded from the nonintervention pledge.[36] Wilhelm
was highly critical of the SEIU's arbitration proposal, pointing out first that
"UNITE HERE would have all the risk in such an arbitration, and SEIU
would have no risk at all, because UNITE HERE has not tried to hijack SEIU
membership, jurisdiction, and resources."

On June 15, Wilhelm once again rejected Stern's offer to arbitrate:

First, let's recap.
. . . You and other top SEIU officers conspired to split UNITE HERE, promote

secession of thousands of members, remove assets, and organize in UNITE HERE's core hotel, gaming, and food service jurisdictions. You enlisted your long time confidant Steve Rosenthal, who was paid by Bruce Raynor $500,000 in UNITE HERE dues money to conduct a months long massive communications program that directed hundreds of thousands of mailers and phone calls into our members' homes all across North America. . . . You used a private investigator to pry into my family's personal affairs as well as the personal affairs of other key leaders of UNITE HERE. . . .

No International Union would agree to put its future members, its jurisdiction, and assets in the hands of an arbitrator.[37]

Wilhelm's rejection of arbitration has confused many who sincerely want the internal union struggle to end and these formerly well-regarded unions to live in peace with each other. But the problem with binding arbitration arises because there is no natural jurisdiction for Workers United. It cannot survive as a garment-workers union because of the lack of garment-industry jobs. That is why Raynor agreed to a merger first with HERE and then with the SEIU. In his effort to mediate the dispute, Joe Hansen suggested that food-service organizing jurisdiction should be shared between UNITE HERE and Workers United. But to the extent that food services was organized historically, it has mainly been through HERE. UNITE HERE has many more food-service workers in its ranks than does Workers United. If Hansen's recommendations were cast in the form of an arbitral award, the result would be to transfer jurisdiction over some food-service workers from HERE to Workers United. That is why Stern and Raynor are so eager for arbitration and Wilhelm is so reluctant. There is no chance of UNITE HERE benefiting from an arbitration award because Workers United has no core membership outside the disappearing garment industry. Thus, as Wilhelm has pointed out, in an arbitration UNITE HERE would bear the risk and would have nothing to gain. This point seems to be missed by the well-meaning commentators who have embraced the arbitration suggestion.

The problem of finding an appropriate jurisdiction for Workers United is also a key problem for mediation. Although Wilhelm has praised Hansen's efforts and generally said that his recommendations have suggested a path to resolution, Wilhelm would probably resist suggestions that would give Workers United significant access to a traditional HERE constituency.

Wilhelm's rejection of arbitration permitted Stern and Raynor to portray themselves as responsible leaders seeking a reasonable solution and Wilhelm as the person intent on keeping the dispute going. By June 2009, both Raynor and Stern were piously condemning interunion infighting and name-calling. On June 3 Raynor, Stern, and Edgar Romney sent an open letter to the labor movement emphasizing their desire to resolve the dispute amicably and denying any responsibility for its existence:

> The conflict between UNITE HERE and Workers United/SEIU must end. All of the workers affected by this dispute deserve nothing less.
>
> . . . A few weeks ago we put forward a comprehensive proposal that provides a clear path to resolution. . . . We expressed a willingness to submit any outstanding issues to binding arbitration, and—as a show of good faith—we unilaterally stood down.
>
> Unfortunately, UNITE HERE Hospitality President John Wilhelm rejected all aspects of our proposal out of hand. . . .
>
> We urge all who care about the Labor Movement to join us in saying that this fight must end, and in calling on both sides to end this dispute by agreeing to a binding arbitration process. . . .
>
> We never sought out this fight. We simply want to end it. . . .
>
> . . . We urge all who care about the Labor Movement to join us in this call for binding arbitration on all outstanding issues so this conflict can cease.[38]

There is something perverse in Stern and Raynor claiming the moral high ground and publicly rejecting internal battling and name-calling, something they began and have continued to engage in regularly. Their constant claim to be motivated by the interests of workers would be far more believable had they not embarked on a plan to financially weaken UNITE HERE, including the unconscionable stripping of the union's strike fund. The hypocrisy that underlies the campaign is revealed in the marked disparity between the public voice of the statements and the private voice evident in their planning documents. The public voice stresses unity. It is worker centered, historically oriented, and emotional. The private voice seeks discord. It is bureaucratic, strategic, and cynical. Thus, in the strategic outline prepared by The Organizing Group under the "Major Goal of Solidifying the Bases," the following tactic is suggested: "Have UNITE affiliates kick out HERE Staff in key places: Phoenix, San Antonio, Mid-Atlantic, Philly, Indy." And it takes a special appreciation for the malleability of language for them to claim "We never sought out this fight."[39]

Most union leaders recognized that the only way Workers United could become an independent force in the labor movement was through raiding areas traditionally organized by HERE. Workers United was thus seen within the movement as an instrument of SEIU jurisdictional imperialism. By the time of the UNITE HERE convention held at the end of June 2009, the labor movement seemed solidly behind UNITE HERE. Three international-union presidents addressed the convention. Gerald McEntee, the president of the huge 1.6-million-member American Federation of State County and Municipal Employees, set the tone: "For another union to come onto your turf, to come into a city like Vegas where you've worked 25 years to take advantage of what you've built . . . that is piracy. Piracy on the seas of organized labor."[40]

Terry O'Sullivan of the Laborers' International Union drew a standing ovation when he declared: "I believe that . . . what happens in this fight that . . . we have with SEIU will determine what kind of labor movement we have because when somebody comes after UNITE HERE, they're coming after the Laborers and all of us and we've got to stick together and fight together to make sure that we win together. . . . If you have a problem anywhere in North America, anywhere in your union, you call the general right here and I'm going to unleash the LIUNA [Laborers' International Union of North America] Army to be there shoulder to shoulder, step by step with members of UNITE HERE."[41] He got another standing ovation when he declared that "there is no goddamn way I would ever agree to binding arbitration when it's dependent on the future of my organization and my core jurisdiction, not a chance in the world, Brothers and Sisters."

At its convention UNITE HERE posted a statement signed by twenty-four union presidents pledging "to support UNITE HERE, both materially and morally, against a raid by any union." The statement concluded: "We stand in solidarity with UNITE HERE."[42]

The most fiery speech in support of UNITE HERE came from Vincent Giblin, the president of the International Union of Operating Engineers. He characterized the battle with the SEIU as "a story of how so-called labor leaders transformed themselves into the equivalent of corporate raiders. And these are the people who claim to be on the cutting edge of progress in the labor movement."[43]

Giblin paid special tribute to Joe Daugherty, recalling his "extraordinary, one of kind" leadership of the Frontier strike. He condemned those "former leaders" who subjected him to torture by shouting directly into his ears with a bullhorn all night. He then witheringly described Raynor as "an egotistical wannabe top dog who at his core is both self-absorbed and anti-democrat." Throughout his address Giblin referred to Raynor as the "alleged labor leader."

He was even more critical of Stern, whom he referred to as "the raider, who in some circles is known not affectionately as Darth Vader of the labor movement." He described Stern as an elitist hustler and a bully: "The raider thought he would win because his union had lots of money and is big. Most bullies and raiders think this way. It was another big mistake."

He concluded on a note of anger and defiance: "The International Union of Operating Engineers is prepared to walk shoulder to shoulder with you through this fight. . . . We are not going to rest until we rid this movement from the likes of those two individuals[, who are] a disgrace to working people of organized labor in this country."

Although Raynor and Stern have been hammered by labor leaders, they have been treated with respect, almost deference, by progressive pro-union commentators. Those who have addressed the battle almost invariably have done so from a neutral, this-is-bad-for-the-cause-of-labor, unions-need-solidarity perspective. Typical of the equal-praise, equal-note-of-disappointment writing is Harold Myerson's otherwise knowledgeable and insightful article "Disunite There" in the *American Prospect:* "Some of the savviest and most dedicated union leaders and staffers ever to work in American labor are savaging each other as the UNITE side of the union endeavors to break away from the larger HERE side and a custody battle rages over the union's financial assets. For people who believe in the American labor movement, and who've seen the positive changes that these unions have made in the lives of their members, watching this battle unfold is like watching two good friends caught up in a vicious divorce. Sometimes one is right and sometimes the other is, but after a while, the battle takes on a life of its own, and the merits of each side's case become a secondary issue."[44]

Similarly, Peter Dreier's article "Divorce—Union Style," which appeared in the *Nation,* is evenhanded in both praise and condemnation. There is no singling out, no outrage at any of the tactics used by Raynor, and only a limited suggestion that Stern exceeded the bounds of propriety. The only reference to destructive tactics employed by the SEIU is the statement that "Stern views the battle as a tug of war between different factions of UNITE HERE for the loyalty of its members, but he admits that some of the attacks on Wilhelm's division 'went too far.'" The article also criticizes Wilhelm and UNITE HERE for their tactics: "In retaliation, UNITE HERE engaged in harassment of Workers United. Wilhelm wrote letters to employers urging them not to negotiate new contracts with Workers United locals and not to forward dues to those locals."[45]

The Daily Kos has put its political influence behind the campaign urging binding arbitration of the dispute.[46] It has covered the dispute on a regular basis but with no real criticism of Raynor and with implied criticism of Wilhelm for his unwillingness to compromise.

Overall, with a few exceptions,[47] Raynor has been treated gently and has regularly been equated with Wilhelm as a progressive union leader. There is little outrage expressed at his vicious tactics, his abuse of the office of president, or his mishandling of funds. It is not clear why. To some extent, Raynor has probably benefited from the illustrious history of the garment unions that merged to form UNITE. He has probably also been treated with special respect because of his own legendary status as an organizing icon as a result of the J. P. Stevens campaign and the movie *Norma Rae,* which was based on that campaign. His positive role in the J. P. Stevens battle is widely accepted. He has won several prestigious awards at least in part because of it. For example, Raynor was the recipient of the 1999 Judge William B. Groat Alumni Award from Cornell's School of Industrial and Labor Relations. His commendation concluded: "In the late 1970s, the TWU [Textile Workers Union] merged with the Amalgamated Clothing Workers of America to become ACTWU. Raynor became a leader of ACTWU and played a major part in the union's successful drive to organize workers at J. P. Stevens, dramatized in the Oscar-winning 1979 movie 'Norma Rae.'"[48]

The J. P. Stevens campaign and his connection to the film *Norma Rae* are mentioned in all favorable biographical material about Raynor. And the image captured in the film of the Northern Jewish intellectual organizer battling to organize the South is likely part of the reason why criticism of Raynor from liberals and progressives is so rare. It is a role that Raynor played with relish. When Crystal Lee Sutton, the inspiration for Norma Rae, died in September 2009, it was Raynor to whom the press turned for encomiums. And he responded with a strong, eloquent statement: "Crystal was an amazing symbol of workers standing up in the South against overwhelming odds."[49]

But the organizer portrayed in *Norma Rae* seemed so different from the Raynor of the UNITE HERE battle that I called Crystal Lee a few months before she died. What she related was a portrait of Raynor that emphasized his ego, jealousy, and hostility: "He did not like me at all. He did not like it when the news reporters and all were coming to town, TV reporters, and they were coming to talk to me and to watch me when we were handing out leaflets and all and just talking union. He told me when those reporters came, for me not to talk to them, to send them over to him. And I tried to do it, but they wouldn't do it. They always said no, we're here to talk to you and to watch you in this thing. And he would get so angry, very angry, very hateful, and I learned to despise the man because it was all me, me, me. No matter where I was when he came, he tried to cause trouble for me, he was just so hateful. . . . Bruce was a horrible man, and I'll never understand how he got to become president of that union."

Ray Rogers, credited by many with developing the corporate campaign in the Stevens organizing drive, describes Raynor as "a complete fraud." A long-time union activist who has followed Raynor's career described him as "an egotistical lunatic and a narcissist."

Raynor's relationship to the great garment-workers tradition that he regularly cites is also far more troublesome than the biographical statements suggest. For example, in the summer of 2009, a group of former ILGWU workers issued an open letter attacking Raynor for his treatment of them and other union retirees:

Dear Brothers and Sisters of the U.S. Labor Movement:

We write on behalf of the almost 200 current members of the Retired Officers of the International Ladies' Garment Workers' Union. . . . Our average age exceeds 80, with many . . . members in their late 80's and 90's. We go back to the early thirties and fought in all of the major labor battles. . . .

Having lost our retirement income security as a result of the selfish and unprincipled conduct of Bruce Raynor, we must bring to public attention the anti-worker, anti-retiree policies of this self-described labor "leader."

We are particularly disgusted by the crocodile tears Raynor sheds publicly over the alleged attempted "takeover" by UNITE HERE of valuable assets and real estate. . . .

After spending our working lives building the ILGWU into one of the largest, wealthiest, and most powerful unions in the nation, and after being repeatedly told "not to worry about your below-market wages—we'll take care of you when you retire," we were devastated when UNITE, under Raynor's direction, summarily reduced our union life insurance benefits by an average of 95%.

[The letter goes on to detail the story of ninety-three-year-old Sally Eisenberg and her deceased husband, Sam. Their retirement fund was reduced from $118,000 to $50,000. She recalls her husband's reaction.] "Those sons of bitches. They [Raynor and cronies] came into our Union and took our money and have no regard for us as Union people. To do this to people that worked their whole life and to look forward to something, should I pass, that my wife should be able to get along, for a human being to do this is unbelievable. Unbelievable." [Then] we received this letter, it happens to be maybe five or six months before he passed away, that they're reducing—it was bad enough they did it to $50,000, now they're reducing it to $5,000, which doesn't even pay for funeral services. . . .

Ironically, at around the same time that he pushed through the virtual elimination of our retirement security, Raynor raised his own salary as UNITE's president. . . . Raynor, who supposedly worked *full-time* as UNITE HERE's general president, . . . apparently, does not want the membership to know that he receives almost $100 thousand per year from the Amalgamated Bank in addition to his union salary. . . .

. . . We abhor the "top down" leadership style of Bruce Raynor. . . .

On the other hand, we view favorably the "bottom up" style of democratic union leadership represented by John Wilhelm. . . . Unlike Raynor, who has refused over the years to meet with the ILGers, John Wilhelm has sought us out, met with us, knows about the history of our dear union. . . .

. . . Raynor is a banker first and foremost. Wilhelm is a trade unionist.[50]

By the summer of 2009, Workers United probably had about 100,000 members, roughly 50,000 fewer than Raynor and Stern had anticipated. It is very unlikely that Wilhelm will change his position on binding arbitration. That means that the future of Workers United turns on its ability to raid or organize in competition with UNITE HERE.

Widespread success in raiding UNITE HERE appears very unlikely. Those whom Raynor has constantly attacked as Wilhelm's "small band of zealots" provide UNITE HERE with a powerful shield against raids in key cities. Many in the zealot band were protégés of Vinnie Sirabella. In addition to Wilhelm himself, the Sirabella protégés singled out as targets by Raynor include Sherri Chiesa, D. Taylor, Paul Clifford, Bill Granfield, Joe Daugherty, Henry Tamarin, and Karl Lechow. Those not directly trained by Sirabella include Mike Casey, Tho Thi Do (of Local 2), Maria Elena Durazo, Tom Walsh (the current leader of Local 11), Eric Gill (of Local 5 in Hawaii), Geoconda Arguello Kline, and Peter Ward, all of whom have worked closely and effectively with Wilhelm. The unions led by the "zealots" control much of the major hotel markets in key cities. They are all formidable organizers and leaders.

Local 1 in Chicago is led by Henry Tamarin, who was recruited into the union in 1973 by Vinnie Sirabella. In 2003 the *Chicago Tribune Magazine* did an extensive, admiring profile of him which stressed his dedication to the union and his willingness to stay a tough course. It concludes: "He arrived in Chicago three years ago to clean up the mess at one of city's major labor organizations—Local 1 of the Hotel Employees and Restaurant Employees International Union. . . . Tamarin would go on to pull it off, leading his ragtag army in a mass march up Michigan Avenue last summer and ultimately to victory in contract talks with 25 of the city's hotels. In the process, he remade a weak and floundering union local into a rising star in the slowly brightening firmament of the Chicago labor movement."[51]

A major HERE stronghold is Local 2 in San Francisco, Hugo Ernst's one-time local, now led by Mike Casey. Union density in the city is near 85 percent. The union has been so effective in organizing that owners frequently contact Casey before they build new hotels in the San Francisco area (see chapter 10). Even former dissidents acknowledge Casey's effectiveness. Marc Norton, a former Alliance of Rank and File activist, recently told me, "I've been a member since 1976. I've seen a variety of leaders and kinds of leaders. At the moment, I would say that the leadership we have now is the best that I've seen." The former secretary-treasurer of Local 2 is Tho Thi Do, a Vietnamese refugee and longtime community organizer described by several of my informants as an "incredible organizer." Given the quality of the leadership and the excellence of their contracts, it is difficult to imagine that a majority or even a significant minority of the members of Local 2 would choose a new, untried union.

Down the coast in Los Angeles is Local 11, which has been the subject of a fierce attack on fixourunion.org. Maria Elena Durazo, another of the defendants in Raynor's lawsuit, recently gave up the leadership of the local to lead the 800,000-member Los Angeles County Federation of Labor—probably the strongest federation in the country. Durazo remains on the executive board of UNITE HERE. The daughter of immigrant migrant farmworkers who worked in the fields of California until she was in high school, Durazo, together with her husband, the legendary United Farm Workers organizer, Miguel Contreras, transformed Local 11 in Los Angles from a bastion of Anglo dominance to a major fighter for immigrant rights. She led the Immigrant Workers Freedom Ride and was national cochair of the Obama campaign. She played a major role in the election of Hilda Solis, now the secretary of labor, to Congress. She has long been a strong supporter of Wilhelm.[52] Her work is being carried on successfully by the current president, Tom Walsh, whose ethnic background —half Irish, half Mexican—seems to represent the local's past and current makeup.

Workers United's chances seem virtually nonexistent in New York, where Peter Ward leads Local 6. Local 6 has a long history of militancy and success. It was one of the first unions to take an active role in the civil-rights movement. As Wilhelm explained to me: "Peter Ward, only the third leader in the history of Local 6 and the Hotel Trades Council, has modernized and improved the union, but that legacy shines brightly. Under Peter's leadership, the Local

6 contract has become the best hotel contract on the planet. In 1985, under the leadership of Vito Pitta, Local 6 became the first local in our union to negotiate card-check [agreements] for all future hotels owned or managed by any union hotel. The combination of the card-check agreement together with Peter's aggressive organizing program has resulted in density of 90 percent or greater for full-service hotels in New York City."

Supporting Local 6 in the area of food services is Local 100, led by Bill Granfield, the onetime Farm Workers organizer who played a key role in turning Local 100 around.

HERE appears to be invulnerable in Las Vegas, where D. Taylor and Geoconda Arguello Kline lead the mighty Culinary, a union far easier to attack on a Web site than to defeat. The union that battled the Elardis for six years and has taken on MGM, Sheldon Adelson, and the Hilton chain and selected and trained hundreds of rank-and-file organizers—and which has organized both Las Vegas and Atlantic City—is likely to prove invulnerable to the SEIU and Workers United.

D. Taylor's achievements as secretary of the Culinary have been well recognized both by its members and by outsiders. The union's successes have been the subject of frequent newspaper[53] and scholarly[54] articles. There is fierce loyalty between the local's current president, Geoconda Kline, and D. Taylor, who first recognized her ability and persuaded her to become active in the union. As Kline later recalled, "We were together for a long time. D. really understands, you know, what the working people need and is willing to fight for everything that we need."

The political power of the Culinary was shown in the 2008 political election. Wilhelm pointed this out in a letter to the entire membership: "Our program in Nevada led the move of that state from Republican to Democrat, won the state by double digits for Obama, captured a congressional seat from a three-term Republican incumbent, outperformed every other state in the Latino vote, and recaptured the State Senate with the result that our own Steven Horsford becomes the State Senate Majority Leader. 78 percent of Latinos voted for Obama, higher than the national average of 66 percent, and higher than every other state including California, Colorado, and New Mexico. This program was led by Executive Vice President D. Taylor, Vice President Geoconda Arguello Kline, and Local 226 Political Director Pilar Weiss, with assistance from Local 165 and several other affiliates."[55]

Nor would Local 26 in Boston be easy pickings for the SEIU. Wilhelm helped transform the local in the early 1980s. As reported by Betsy Aron: "In

1982 Wilhelm came to Boston to help the new leadership of Local 26 negotiate its first contract. Wilhelm mapped out a strategy . . . which predated by 20 years the organizing innovations now associated with leading-edge union locals. TRUST was a keystone of the process. . . . Trust led to the slow but steady irrelevance of occupational divisions."[56] In 2001, led by the formidable Janice Loux, the local played a key role in the union's ability to survive the severe downturn in the hospitality industry after 9/11.[57] At one point, Loux had card-check agreements with over seventeen area hotels.

In fact, Workers United has made no real effort to raid any of these locations. It did attempt to harass Tom Walsh and the new leadership of Los Angeles Local 11, which had proposed a dues increase—always a possible source of division. Workers United and SEIU operatives ran a campaign urging members of Local 11 to vote against the increase. According to one Local 11 staff member: "SEIU sent multiple mailings to our members, leafleted some of our shops and robo-called repeatedly our membership, telling them to vote no on the increase. They use tactics that probably would most impact their own organization, but they, like the boss, underestimate the rank-and-file leadership. The 'air war' from SEIU ironically gave our leaders more motivation to win and win big. Well over 90 percent of the membership voted to approve the increase."

There was a battle in Detroit, where wages were low and new jobs scarce. But Joe Daugherty is not someone to pick a fight with. His record in Las Vegas is by now legendary. His remarkable commitment was described in a 1998 article in the *New York Times:*

> Joseph Daugherty . . . has not taken a day off since Sept. 21, 1991, when 550 workers—maids, cocktail waitresses, bartenders, cooks—walked off their jobs at the Frontier hotel. . . .
>
> . . . He did not realize that the walkout, the nation's longest in almost four decades, would end up lasting nearly six and a half years. . . .
>
> . . . Pickets credited Mr. Daugherty for helping to sustain morale. . . .
>
> "Joe was our glue," Ms. Preciado [a former striker] said. "We called him St. Joe."[58]

By midsummer 2009, Karl Lechow was convinced that "we beat them back in Detroit."

The big city that seemed most open to raiding when Workers United was organized was Philadelphia. Wilhelm had gone out of his way to strengthen the role of the Philadelphia Joint Board, which had jurisdiction over the area. When hotel contracts for HERE's Local 274 expired and new contracts were negotiated, the Philadelphia Joint Board was added to the certification. The leadership of Local 274 was weak. Although Warren Heyman, one of the Yale organizers, was assigned to Philadelphia on a part-time basis, his instruction from Wilhelm was to make the merger work. As a result, Local 274, which represented hotel workers, and Local 634, which represented school cafeteria workers, were put under the joint board run by Lynne Fox of UNITE. Local 274, which had contracts at sixteen or seventeen hotels, did not have a strong committee structure. Heyman's efforts to get the workers more involved were stymied because the joint board rejected his ideas for staff development and worker leadership.

When Workers United was formed, the *Philadelphia Inquirer* pointed out the potential struggle for membership and suggested that Workers United, led by Lynne Fox, had a significant advantage in Philadelphia: "When the unions merged, the area hospitality workers' local, HERE Local 274, was in disarray. Lynne Fox, the leader of the city's UNITE textile organization, took over and cleaned up the union."[59]

Heyman, who is a first-rate organizer, had not established a separate identity for the locals, separate from that of the joint board. When, after the formation of Workers United, Wilhelm asked him whether they could hold Philadelphia, he said, "Probably not." He was surprised when the leaders of the cafeteria workers told him, "'Look, we don't want to leave UNITE HERE. We want to leave the joint board, though, because we hate the joint board.' The entire executive committee voted to stay with UNITE HERE as long as they could be separated from the joint board. Wilhelm agreed."[60]

The cafeteria workers' stories of abuse surprised Heyman, who had just begun to spend a portion of his time in Philadelphia: "When we merged, what I knew of UNITE was what I read in *Labor Notes* and the newspaper and their general reputation that they had of being a decent, progressive union. You know, I didn't really know, because in the places where I had worked I had really never came across them and certainly never had an opportunity to get inside the union and look carefully at what was going on."

The Philadelphia Joint Board, after voting to become part of Workers United, immediately scheduled a series of votes, ostensibly to determine whether the workers wished to secede. The announced results were overwhelmingly in favor of secession. The whole process seemed of questionable veracity. UNITE HERE created a video in which a group of UNITE HERE loyalists discuss the vote. The material below is taken from the video; comments in parenthesis were added by UNITE HERE:

TIM O'TOOLE, RADISSON PLAZA WARWICK: They were going around telling everybody we're going to lose our contracts, we're going to lose our insurance, the dues were going to go through the roof, everything they were saying was a lie, everything.

NICOLE: The vote was that we disaffiliate from the Philadelphia Joint Board and stay with UNITE HERE. The vote was unanimous.

(SEIU ignored our vote and held its own.)

PAUL MINNITI, RADISSON PLAZA WARWICK: At 11 a.m. I went up to vote, they said I can't vote now, I have to wait. So, 11:15 a.m. I went up there to vote again, they said no, you have to wait. So at 11:30 again, I tried to vote, they said no, you have to wait one more time. So 11:40 I tried for my last time, I said I'm ready to vote. They said no, you have to wait.

TIM O'TOOLE: They were bringing people in that didn't even work at the hotel.

(SEIU claims we voted 42–12 to join them.)

TIM O'TOOLE: I ran over to the union hall right after that and we printed up some petitions and I came back and I got as many people as I can who voted no. I asked them if you vote no sign here. We ended up getting about 35 signatures that said they voted no.[61]

Four months after the vote, Heyman was certain that the workers at the Hyatt and the Radisson were solidly loyal to UNITE HERE because they were the two hotels in which Local 274 had successfully organized large worker committees. In other locations he acknowledged a close battle for worker support.

Early in 2009 Workers United petitioned for an election with the Pennsylvania Labor Relations Board seeking to displace UNITE HERE Local 634 as the bargaining representative. An election was scheduled for October 28, 2009. Both sides treated the forthcoming election as an important indicator of their strength. The SEIU, using its wealth and large staff, was able to commit between one hundred and two hundred organizers to the battle. In house calls and in its literature the SEIU attacked both Warren Heyman and Doris Smith, the longtime president of the local. Heyman told me early in the campaign: "I'm reading stuff they are putting out about me in Philadelphia. Their materials are right out of the management playbook." The attacks on Heyman and Smith were at best a risky tactic. My experience in conducting field studies of union organizing campaigns convinces me that using personal insults against people whom the workers know is a bad way to organize and a good way to antagonize workers.

HERE did not have the same number of organizers, but the union did have a more experienced cadre that included not only Heyman but also Wendy

Walsh, once a member of Yale's graduate-student union, who had just been elected president of UNITE HERE's Florida local. Walsh, in typical HERE fashion, recruited a large team of rank-and-file organizers from the membership of Local 634. According to Heyman, these volunteers were the heart of the UNITE HERE campaign. During their off time they went door to door announcing that their goal was to protect and rebuild the local.

Everyone expected a close vote. But—as Heyman exultantly told me—when the election was held, "we kicked their ass." The final vote was 1,121 votes for UNITE HERE Local 634, 551 votes for the SEIU Philadelphia Joint Board, and 10 votes for no union. According to a UNITE HERE press release, "This is the third noteworthy victory for Unite Here in recent months in its struggle against SEIU. In August 2000, Delaware North company food service workers ratified a contract with Unite Here, thwarting a[n] SEIU raid in the process. Three weeks ago, 2300 members of Local 74 in St. Louis voted to reaffirm their affiliation with Unite Here."[62]

The tone of the SEIU and Workers United campaign caused divisions within the SEIU. In May 2009 Fred Ross, a leading SEIU organizer who had begun his career with the Farm Workers, resigned his position with the SEIU. He issued a bitter statement explaining his actions:

> I have been an organizer since 1970, when I first started organizing with Cesar Chavez and the United Farm Workers (UFW). I know a little bit about struggle and the terrible cost of internal union conflicts. . . .
>
> . . . I am deeply disappointed that SEIU president Andy Stern is financing and helping staff a disruptive attack on the leaders and members at UNITE HERE around the country—the worst instance of a union undermining another union since the Teamsters sought to undermine Cesar Chavez and the United Farm Workers in the late 1960s and 1970s. Last month I decided to leave SEIU, in part because of these attacks.[63]

Texas at one time seemed like a likely place for Workers United to establish a beachhead in the hospitality industry. Texas has three of the nation's most populated cities—Dallas, San Antonio, and Houston—with fast-growing, hotel-rich, politically liberal Austin located between them. Each of the major cities, and San Antonio in particular, has many hotels. HERE had not really organized in Texas. It had targeted San Antonio for an organizing drive in 2006, and one of its major targets was the River Walk Hyatt, which agreed to grant recognition on the basis of a card-check majority. UNITE HERE began serious organizing efforts in 2007. Its drive was conducted in the name of the

South Western Regional Joint Board. Around the time that a card-check majority was achieved, the joint board voted to secede from UNITE HERE and affiliate with Workers United. Willie Gonzalez, a ten-year UNITE organizer and leader who had been the state director of UNITE, claimed bargaining rights on behalf of Workers United. The hotel's management immediately accepted his claim. However, before the parties could come to an agreement, Gonzalez left Workers United and rejoined UNITE HERE.

Gonzalez was an experienced, skillful, bilingual organizer. He had begun working for UNITE organizing laundries with a dynamic group of young organizers: "We all came in around the same time—myself, Scott Cooper, Mario Rodriguez, Rob Murray, Meredith Stewart, and it was an exciting program." His decision to quit Workers United highlights the self-destructive quality of some of Raynor's tactics. Gonzalez's unhappiness with Raynor began when he was instructed to fire the HERE-trained organizers on his staff. They were a first-rate group of organizers led by Danna Schneider, a 1992 Yale graduate and longtime student activist. Schneider was attracted to the idea of labor organizing because of her admiration for Lucille Dickess, the dynamic first president of Local 34. She was initially recruited and trained by Warren Heyman and at a key point in her career was inspired by Andrea van den Heever. She was assigned as field leader of the San Antonio organizing drive because of her proven success as an organizer. She and Gonzalez worked very well together, and he was stunned by the instruction to fire her and the other HERE-trained organizers working on the project:

> I had been asked twice to throw them out. I asked them, Why am I going to throw them out, they are helping organize? Well, they are evil. But they weren't doing anything political. Everybody was focused on organizing the hotel, which they did a great job of and have continued to do a good job of. I've been told a couple of times we need to kick them out. But there was no conflict going on in this city. We were working along fine. We were all focused on the campaign. But when I kept getting asked to throw everybody out, I thought, Wait a minute, this isn't about them. I told them no. I said I would not do it. That's what led me being sent up to New York to speak with Bruce [Raynor]. He turned on the charm. But some of the stuff he was telling me about HERE, [about] the people I knew, was way out, way off the mark. I realized it was really about him.

It was after this meeting that Gonzalez began to seriously consider splitting with Workers United and rejoining UNITE HERE. It was not an easy decision. He confessed his confusion to a local union leader—a woman whose judgment he respected: "So I had a conversation with her and told her I wasn't sure what to do, and she said, 'Look, whatever you do, make sure it is something you are proud of later.'"

That standard made sense to Gonzalez, who decided that he would not be proud of staying with Workers United: "The whole process was wrong. The whole way we had done it. We all knew this was a political deal, about the presidency. And sometimes you have politics in organizations, that happens. You've got to live with it, but you don't rip apart the very organization you have been building. No one person is bigger than the union itself. It had become very distasteful to me, things like the fixourunion stuff. They crossed the line there. I knew for sure I cannot be part of that."

Gonzalez has no second thoughts about his decision. He has since learned that the organizers with whom he identified in UNITE have all rejected Workers United: "All those people I was talking to you about at the laundries—they either stayed with UNITE HERE or went somewhere else, but none of them went with Workers United. They refused to be part of [the] Workers United thing."

Schneider described the impact of Gonzalez's decision as "tremendous," affecting both the staff and rank-and-file workers. With Gonzalez gone, the possibility of Workers United representing the workers at the Hyatt essentially disappeared. The forty-person organizing committee became increasingly angry with the attempts by Workers United to speak for them. They had been organized by the hotel workers union and now they were being represented by people whom they did not know on behalf of a union that had no history of representing hotel workers. At one point, members of the committee barged in on a private meeting of an SEIU staff person and members of the joint board and demanded that they leave and not continue bargaining. "We are not your committee," the committee members insisted. An effort by one former UNITE organizer who had worked on the campaign to persuade workers to sign up with Workers United failed totally.

The original bargaining between Workers United and the Hyatt was discontinued when a petition calling for an election to decertify the union was filed.[64] The UNITE HERE local petitioned to intervene in the election, whereupon Workers United, which had virtually no support, withdrew. The company commenced an intense anti-union campaign. Shortly before the election, the UNITE HERE local voluntarily withdrew. Danna Schneider believed that the vote would be close. She expected to win by a narrow margin. She was sure, however, that given the closeness of the vote, the company would file objections to the election and would be able to postpone bargaining for as long as two years. Instead of following this traditional NLRB-centered approach, the union has commenced a comprehensive campaign to obtain a neutrality agreement and card-check recognition. Schneider believes that a win obtained through struggle, though more costly and time consuming, will ultimately lead to a stronger union and a better contract than a close election victory. This is the HERE approach. It is an application of Bill Granfield's comment: "This approach of building a strong majority of workers to fight for a fair process or card check—it wasn't developed by organizers who couldn't win elections. It was developed by organizers who had won too many elections and had to sit around afterwards for years attempting to negotiate contracts. It's going to take a battle, so let's build and plan and get into the battle on our timeline." Schneider had worked with and admires Bill Granfield.

The leaders of the Hyatt local are pleased with the decision. According to Schneider, the members of the organizing committee believe that they were able to exercise power by holding off the election and that they are now ready to take part in an active campaign. She reports that in every captive-audience speech conducted by the company there are workers who speak up and challenge what is said.

Had Gonzalez, who has a strong personal following among workers and organizers, stayed, Workers United might have developed a strong presence in Texas. What seems clear now is that when the Grand Hyatt in San Antonio is unionized, it will be UNITE HERE that represents its workers.

What now appears likely is that the Hyatt organizing effort in Texas will become part of a larger battle between UNITE HERE and Hyatt Corporation. The union had long been considering taking on Hyatt nationally. It held back because of the recession and its focus on its battle with Workers United. But Hyatt's anti-worker actions in the Boston area and the response to them has provided the union with a rare opportunity to take on the company nationwide. The basic story was described in an article in *Fortune* magazine titled "A Mess: Hyatt's Housekeeping Scandal":

> What was Hyatt thinking? That no one would notice? That no one would care? Well, the privately held hotelier, which announced plans recently to go public, screwed up big-time; everybody knows that now. Even Hyatt knows, although something tells me it hasn't completely sunk in yet.
>
> "I think that we feel that there are certain aspects of the transition that we could have managed better," says Farley Kern, a Hyatt spokesperson, "and that we really do regret that."
>
> The transition? Here's what Hyatt did: At 3 o'clock on a Monday afternoon, Aug.

31, managers at two Hyatt-owned hotels in Boston and one Hyatt-managed hotel in Cambridge, in a coordinated effort, summoned their entire housekeeping staffs, fired everybody on the spot, and immediately outsourced the jobs to a staffing company based in Atlanta.

Lucine Williams, a single mom from Barbados who worked at the Boston Hyatt Regency for nearly 22 years, remembers the moment. "I could not believe my ears," she says. "I was in shock. People start crying. I start crying. And after we start crying, they say you can go get your package."

Williams's "package" was two weeks' pay plus one week for the first five years of service (never mind the other 17), for a grand total of $4,289.60. "I know you're upset," a supervisor said to her as she was leaving for the locker room to change out of her uniform, "but can I have your name tag?"

Here's what we gradually learned, beginning several days later with a front-page story in the *Boston Globe:* That most of the 98 fired housekeepers were immigrant women; that some of them had been working for Hyatt for more than 20 years; that before they were fired, they were directed to train their replacements under the guise that the newcomers would be available to spell them during vacations; that whereas the job had once paid nearly $16 an hour, it now paid minimum wage in Massachusetts, $8 an hour; and that henceforth, housekeepers would be expected to clean up to twice as many rooms in a day to meet their quotas.

. . . All hell broke loose.

Local 26 of Unite Here, the hotel workers union, which has never had a contract at any Boston-area Hyatt, nevertheless rushed to the aid of the fired workers, organizing a press conference and a big downtown demonstration.

In Chicago, about 200 union hotel workers, upset with the slow pace of contract talks in the Windy City, got themselves arrested for blocking hotel entrances and took advantage of the spotlight to publicize the plight of their sisters in Boston.

The Boston Taxi Drivers Association threatened to refuse all fares to and from Hyatt hotels in Boston. And Massachusetts Governor Deval Patrick, a Democrat facing what could be a tough reelection campaign next fall, threatened a Hyatt boycott covering anyone on state business unless the fired workers were rehired. . . .

Hyatt, now trying to defuse the situation, last week offered the fired workers a new deal. Not their old jobs back, but a choice: Either a new job with a different staffing company, at the old rate of pay, guaranteed through the end of 2010; or career counseling and job retraining, also at the old rate, through next March. Either way, they'd get to keep their health insurance coverage for six more months.

The Hyatt 100, as they're now known, thought about the offer over the weekend. Then on Monday, they voted overwhelmingly to reject it. Now the union is calling for a nationwide Hyatt boycott.

Matthew Walker, Unite Here's national director of strategic affairs, says the union has contracts at 40% of Hyatt hotels nationwide. "I wouldn't give them marks for being the worst union-busters," he says. That said, he has "never seen a wholesale elimination of the housekeeping department like they've done in these three hotels. I'm quite sure the company was interested in watching this as a case study."

Hyatt denies that. "This does not represent any kind of corporate-wide initiative," says Farley from headquarters in Chicago, taking pains to distance corporate headquarters from this mess. "It was a decision made by the managers in Boston in response to conditions in Boston."

Except that it may be too late to erase quickly the reputational damage. Already Hyatt's Wikipedia entry contains a reference to the incident. Bloggers from *The Atlantic* and *Harvard Business Review* have weighed in, unflatteringly. Now comes new pressure on Hyatt board member Penny Pritzker, whose cousin, Tom Pritzker, is chairman, and whose family controls most of the company's stock.

Pritzker was national finance chair for the Obama campaign. Once rumored to be a candidate for Commerce secretary, she settled for a seat on the President's Economic Recovery Advisory Board. Which strikes union official Walker as ironic.

"These are service sector jobs," Walker says. "These are jobs that cannot be exported, and when they pay a living wage and provide benefits, as these jobs did in Boston, they're a critical underpinning of our local economy."

Good point. Sounds like something the President's Economic Recovery Advisory Board might want to look into.[65]

The Hyatt struggle is now featured on the Hotel Workers Rising Web site. It is likely that other locations including San Antonio will be the scene of demonstrations protesting Hyatt's behavior. It is part of the movement orientation of UNITE HERE for the union to shape the battle with Hyatt in Texas as part of a larger struggle that joins them together with workers (immigrants like themselves) in other parts of the country. Moving the struggle to a higher level may delay the finish, but it might also mean a victory that secures the union's status for the foreseeable future.

By Labor Day 2009, Karl Lechow, who played a major role in coordinating the UNITE HERE campaigns, was confident of victory in almost every disputed area: "It's clear to me that we're winning this battle in one area after another. It's certainly not over, but in a place like Arizona, where it started, we [do] not just have the upper hand, we have complete control of our program and our jurisdiction. We have cleared them out of our industry in most places. We still have to engage them in some places down there in Philadelphia and some other cities."

He insisted that Workers United was playing the role historically played by company unions—offering management an opportunity to claim to be unionized at a much lower cost. He argued that many employers in the hospitality industry have become concerned with HERE's success and as a result have been eager to cut deals with Raynor and Workers United: "We represent 50 percent of food service in airports. . . . We do have 20 percent density in hotels, in gaming we have close to 50 percent. You know, in the last round of negotiations in '06 and '07 we had excellent agreements throughout the entire U.S. and Canada. So I said, Look, it is not a surprise that the companies are now looking for partners and they found them in Raynor and Stern, because those guys have said, and I'm not putting words in their mouths, We will trade standards for growth."

Not only UNITE HERE officials but labor insiders as well were convinced that UNITE HERE was winning the battle for the support of workers in the hospitality industry.

UNITE HERE has achieved its victories by continuing to use the tactics of movement. The movement emphasis was notable at UNITE HERE's 2009 convention. The battle with the SEIU was a constant theme of the proceedings, but so also were the need for immigration reform, the importance of diversity, and the need for union democracy. Wilhelm urged his membership to adopt the cause of equal rights for gay, lesbian, and transgendered workers. It was an issue bound to be controversial among many of the union's traditionally religious members. One could have taken the position that this was not the time to raise an issue that might well create a split in the union. But Wilhelm made it the first order of business on the second day of the convention. He put the blame for the union's late start on the issue on himself and others who were civil-rights activists in the 1960s and 1970s: "We didn't do the right thing in that generation, most of us, [with] some notable exceptions. In the Hotel Workers Rising campaign over the past several years, we have sought . . . to make sure that our members of the LGBT community feel like equal partners in our union. We believe so strongly in real equality for African Americans; we believe so strongly in real equality for immigrants. We believe so strongly in equality in many dimensions. I have come to believe full equality has to include our many sisters and brothers in the LGBT community."

One element of a movement approach is working closely and cooperatively with other unions. Vince Giblin, the president of the International Union of Operating Engineers, stirred the convention with his acknowledgement of past support and his pledge to "repay": "Never ever has your International Union ever tried to raid our jurisdiction. As a matter of fact, even when the employer had suggested to your leaders that they would look the other way if you wanted to sign up the Engineers and Maintenance Departments, John Wilhelm said, absolutely not. Every resource this International Union of Operating Engineers has is yours. I know you're a little short on your strike benefit and I tell you, if someone challenges you for the right, I want John Wilhelm to pick up the phone and we will fund whatever it's going to take."

Concern with union democracy might well have been ignored or even trimmed in order to make the union combat-ready. But at Wilhelm's urging the convention voted to limit the powers of the presidency (for example, no expenditures above $25,000 without approval from the executive board; regular reports to the executive board and to the members) in order to make him more accountable. The president's interpretation of the union's constitution was made subject to review: "Upon an exception taken by any member of the Executive Committee to an interpretation or construction of this Constitution by the President, the GEB [general executive board] may overrule the President." In general, the president was made subject to the overriding authority of the general executive board. The local unions were given more power.[66]

Peter Ward, the president of New York's dynamic Local 6 and the head of the Constitutional Committee, explained what Wilhelm had asked of him and other local leaders: "In February, in typical John fashion, he wrote a letter to all of the affiliate leaders in our union . . . which I thought was amazing appeal to everybody. . . . He talked about an improved system of electing our governing boards. He talked about local autonomy and process and protection from undue trusteeships and seizures of local property. He talked about fairness in the allocation of funds and resources, and I know from discussing this with John that he believes that we should try to unlock resources to organize and empower workers, protection of dissidence and a reliable process to protect their rights and absolute zero tolerance for corruption."

Ward, who is nobody's toady,[67] was high in his praise of Wilhelm's role in the amendment process: "The changes that we're making to our union, in my opinion, will give us a constitution that is by far the most progressive, the most open, the most democratic, the most transparent; it's one that empowers union officers and union members better than any other constitution that I'm aware of in the labor movement in North America. . . . None of this could have been possible if John Wilhelm was not willing to give up power. It's really that simple. I am so proud to be associated with a leader . . . the only leader that I'm aware of in the labor movement that would . . . willingly change the structure of his union to disperse power."

UNITE HERE under Wilhelm's leadership has responded to the challenge of the SEIU and Workers United by placing an even greater emphasis on internal organizing, training the rank and file, strengthening its committees, and improving contracts between local unions—all of which are movement tactics.

It seems probable that UNITE HERE will emerge from the battle larger and richer than it was before the merger. Andrea van den Heever believes that the dispute has galvanized the union so that even what she called the "nonorganizing locals" have become more militant.

Wilhelm has, not for the first time, proved himself tougher than his enemies expected or his friends feared. He has never lacked backbone. His toughness showed up early in his labor career when he refused to stay down while being beaten by a cop during the 1971 Yale maintenance-worker strike. It showed up again in Yale negotiations when he proposed a series of unorthodox bargaining tactics. It was visible in his patient leadership of Las Vegas organizing during the late 1980s and again when he urged Mike Casey to use his strike fund to organize the San Francisco Marriott.

Workers United is smaller than was first anticipated. Because of the refusal of two joint boards to go along, instead of 150,000 members it has at most 100,000 currently paying dues. And its position is precarious. Garment-industry jobs are still being lost. It is possible, indeed probable, that the courts will hold that the efforts of joint boards to sever relations with UNITE HERE are invalid. If that happens, Workers United will be poorer. What effect that would have on membership is unclear, but it might well cause additional defections. It is not surprising that Stern and Raynor are now eager to settle the battle that they, Raynor especially, started.

Each has seen his status within the ranks of organized labor diminished, although each was controversial before the battle with Wilhelm. Discussions of both Stern and Raynor have for some time included references to their overpowering egos. Their actions have given the customary accusations new force. Raynor set about destroying a union to avenge his rejection. Stern has joined in attacks on a former ally to increase his own leadership position. They have both along the way made false charges, and they joined together in attacking Wilhelm for provoking a battle that they planned, started, and carried out with deplorable zeal. Raynor's behavior has revealed an angry, destructive aspect of his personality that goes well beyond egotism. It manifests itself even when it harms his self-interest and weakens his position. What else can explain his insistence that Willie Gonzalez fire all the HERE organizers when it was apparent that Gonzalez was strongly in favor of continuing to work with them? It should have been obvious that Raynor was risking losing Gonzalez and the crucial opportunity for establishing a strong Texas presence, something that would have been of great value to Workers United. Not only did Raynor choose revenge over success but he chose the type of revenge that caused pain to those whom he perceived to be enemies over the revenge that comes with success and rewards followers.

If Raynor's behavior has been shaped by anger and the desire to appear formidable, Stern's behavior seems to be based on calculation and the desire to appear reasonable. There are in his letters and speeches no overt threats to raid. He has used instead the self-serving assumption of UNITE's right to secede, the carefully phrased claim of the right to intervene to protect the free choice of workers, and the repeated statement of disappointment at Wilhelm's refusal to compromise.

Raynor's status within the labor movement has been substantially weakened and is likely to be weakened further as his dishonorable behavior in trying to force an end to the merger becomes more widely known. His departure from the ranks of labor's influential leaders is justified and long overdue.[68]

Stern is different. He has been a significant voice for reform and progressive political causes. He understands the importance of organizing, and he cares about the status of organized labor. He has through a variety of legitimate techniques built the SEIU into a powerful union. He has led the union to stake out positions on important issues, such as the threat to workers from private-equity firms. His position that organizing should take precedence over standards deserves to be stated, debated, and given a chance to succeed. But he has lost credibility with many who once saw him as the voice of liberal unionism. The power of his ego has been recognized and his willingness to advance at the expense of onetime allies has been observed and deplored. The battle has cost him money, prestige, and staff. He is currently facing challenges to his leadership—most notably in California. Other challenges may be brewing. Organized labor could use his energy and intelligence. He remains for news media and casual observers the public voice of activist labor. But he has been irrevocably scarred with activists, union leaders, and pro-labor scholars—all of us who watched the unfolding of his ambitions with dismay. Perhaps the fallout from this battle will make him a humbler leader. That would be highly desirable.

As for UNITE HERE, it is likely to emerge from the battle as strong as ever. Its leaders have remained united and supportive of each other; its young organizers continue to find meaning and satisfaction in their tasks. Its members remain overwhelmingly loyal.

Part III **Why the NLRB Election Process Doesn't Work for Unions**

Chapter 14 The Problem
of Access

One reason that Sirabella's national organizing project failed was the inadequacy of the NLRB representation-election process. It is a complex process that has not worked well for unions. Unions generally begin the formal campaign with a large majority of card signers but often end up losing the election or even withdrawing. There is considerable debate about why. Many believe that elections are lost because of employer threats and retaliation. Some, myself included, believe that the most significant problem with Board elections is that employers have three major, related advantages: access, coverage, and delay.

THE ACCESS IMBALANCE

Soon after passage of the NLRA, the Supreme Court held that an employer has the right, under the First Amendment, to urge its employees to vote against representation.[1] This right has since been incorporated into section 8(c) of the Act. Once it was determined that the employer had the right to state its views, the question inevitably arose whether the employer, by virtue of its management and property rights, could assemble the employees, make its case against representation, and deny the union the chance to respond or to enter its premises.

In the 1956 case *NLRB v. Babcock & Wilcox Co.*,[2] the Supreme Court overturned a Board decision requiring the employer to grant limited access to its property (the parking lot) to union organizers. The Board had concluded that without access, the union would be at a serious disadvantage in getting its message to the employees. It held that the employer was guilty of "an unfair labor practice by refusing limited access to company property to union organizers." The Board ordered the employer to rescind its no-distribution order for the parking lot and walkway, subject to reasonable and nondiscriminating regulations "in the interest of plant efficiency and discipline, but not as to deny access to union representatives."

The Supreme Court reversed. It held that the Board had improperly treated organizers under the same standard that it used to determine employee rights: "It is our judgment, however, that an employer may validly post his property against nonemployee distribution of union literature if reasonable efforts by the union through other available channels of communication will enable it to reach the employees with its message and if the employer's notice or order does not discriminate against the union by allowing other distribution."

Although the Court drew a distinction between the rights of employees and the rights of nonunion organizers, it acknowledged that "the right of self-organization depends in some measure on the ability of employees to learn the advantages of self-organization from others. Consequently, if the location of a plant and the living quarters of the employees place the employees beyond the reach of reasonable union efforts to communicate with them, the employer must allow the union to approach his employees on his property."

The Court commented that the issue of access to company premises by nonemployee organizers involved a balancing of section 7 rights against the rights of ownership: "Accommodation between the two must be obtained with as little destruction of one as is consistent with the maintenance of the other. . . . When the inaccessibility of employees makes ineffective the reasonable attempts by nonemployees to communicate with them through the usual channels, the right to exclude from property has been required to yield to the extent needed to permit communication of information on the right to organize."

In *NLRB v. United Steelworkers of America*,[3] the Supreme Court held that the employer was not required to give unions the chance to respond to captive-audience speeches. Writing for the Court, Justice Felix Frankfurter concluded that the Taft-Hartley Act "does not command that labor organizations as a matter of abstract law, under all circumstances, be protected in the use of every possible means of reaching the minds of individual workers, nor that they are entitled to use a medium of communication simply because the employer is using it." Justice Frankfurter seemed to contemplate a vigorous effort by the Board to evaluate the relative ability of the parties to get their message heard: "If, by virtue of the location of the plant and of the facilities and resources available to the union, the opportunities for effectively reaching the employees with a pro-union message, in spite of a no-solicitation rule, are at least as great as the employer's ability to promote the legally authorized expression of his anti-union views, there is no basis for invalidating these otherwise valid rules."

The Court's opinion in *Nutone* (the *Steelworkers* case) did not describe how the Board was to measure whether an appropriate balance existed. The Board, lacking the ability to make quantitative judgments, sought to introduce some element of balance in 1966 when, in *Excelsior Underwear, Inc.*,[4] it ruled that "within 7 days after . . . a consent agreement or after the . . . Board has directed an election the employer must file with the Regional Director an election eligibility list," which would then be turned over to the union. In 1969, in *NLRB v. Wyman-Gordon Co.*,[5] the Supreme Court upheld the Board's authority to do so.[6]

Anyone familiar with union organizing realizes that a list of names delivered shortly before an election cannot in any way be equated with weeks or months of captive-audience speeches. Using names and addresses to make contact during nonworking time is a difficult and sensitive business. Some employees inevitably resent the intrusion. In addition, my own experience as the recipient of more than thirty *Excelsior* lists[7] suggests that they often contain wrong names and old addresses.

For many years the Board simply assumed that no imbalance exists whenever a union has some ability to reach employees through meetings, leafleting, phone calls, and home visits aided by *Excelsior* lists. In 1988, twenty years after the *Nutone* decision, the Board in *Jean Country*[8] attempted to give substantive meaning to the balancing approach suggested by the Supreme Court. Referring to the language of *Babcock,* the Board developed a general test for determining when organizers might have access to company property: "In all access cases our essential concern will be the degree of impairment of the Section 7 right if access should be denied, as it balances against the degree of impairment of the private property right if access should be granted. We view the consideration of the availability of reasonably effective alternative means as especially significant in this balancing process. In the final analysis however, there is no simple formula that will immediately determine the result in every case."

The Board applied this standard in *Lechmere, Inc.,*[9] in which it ordered the company to "cease and desist from barring the union organizers from the parking lot."[10] In *Lechmere,* the union's repeated efforts to organize employees working at a grocery store in a suburban shopping center in Connecticut were unsuccessful. The First Circuit affirmed the Board's opinion.[11] Writing for the majority, Judge Bruce M. Selya concluded that the *Jean Country* approach was well within the Board's discretion. He noted that "although the Section 7 right is the workers' right, not the union's right, unions and their agents, derivatively, enjoy the protection of Section 7."

The Supreme Court reversed.[12] Although it was willing to recognize the possibility that organizers in some limited, unusual circumstances might be entitled to some minimal access to company property, it warned that "to gain access, the union has the burden of showing that no other reasonable means of communicating its organizational message to the employees exists." This finding was not to be made on the basis of a balancing test. Justice Clarence Thomas accused the Board of "eroding *Babcock*'s general rule" that "an employer may validly post his property against nonemployee distribution of union literature." He continued, "We reaffirm that general rule today, and reject the Board's attempt to recast it as a multifactor balancing test." The Court's opinion, by virtue of its cursory analysis of the union's options, made clear how close to impossible it is for unions to show that they have no reasonable means of communicating with workers. Justice Thomas mentioned that the union could have used mailings, phone calls, and home visits. But he added that "such direct contact, of course, is not a necessary element of 'reasonably effective' communication; signs or advertising also may suffice." And he pointed out that "signs (displayed, for example, from the public grassy strip adjoining *Lechmere*'s parking lot) would have informed the employees about the union's organizational effort."

The Court did not explain why so drastic a rule was necessary or how its ruling was compatible with a statute that sought to increase the practice of collective bargaining and eliminate "inequality of bargaining power." Remarkably little weight is given to advancing the policies of the Act. If the Act is to achieve its goal of fostering free and informed choice, unions must be given access to employees. Earlier Supreme Court cases had established that the concept of employee free choice includes the ability to learn about unions. For this right to be meaningful, it must at appropriate times outweigh traditional employer property rights. That was the point of the Supreme Court's 1945 decision in *Republic Aviation Corp. v. NLRB*[13] outlawing no-solicitation rules that applied during nonworking time. The implications of the Court's reasoning in the *Republic Aviation* case were broad, but they were never turned into reality. The Court's access decisions over the years reveal a major theme in the development of the NLRA: the increasing triumph of traditional property rights over the policies of the Act. Taken together, these decisions give employers a massive advantage over unions, which employers have quickly learned to exercise.

It is the company's advantage in access that most invalidates the analogy between Board elections and political elections. The employer can use whatever work time it wishes to assemble its employees and explain why it would not be in their interest to vote for the union. Tom Woodruff, the director of the Change to Win Strategic Organizing Center and a longtime SEIU organizer, pointed this out in a slide show: "Now we're getting ready to elect a president for 2008. Let's assume this. Candidate A has a list of all the voters, names and addresses, Social Security numbers, everything about them, and has it years in advance of the election. Candidate B gets a list 30 days before the election and half the addresses are wrong. Candidate A gets to appear in all the debates, but gets to decide when the debate is, gets to make an opening statement and a closing statement, and there are no questions allowed. And Candidate B can't even appear in the debate."

According to union organizers, companies are routinely using this advantage through increasingly intense and time-consuming campaigns. This imbalance was further exacerbated when Congress passed the Driver's Privacy Protection Act (DPPA),[14] which makes it "unlawful for any person knowingly to obtain or disclose personal information, from a motor vehicle record, for any use not permitted under section 2721(b)." Union organizing is not one of the fourteen legitimate purposes set forth in section 2721. Section 2723 provides that any person who knowingly violates the Act will be fined, and section 2724 provides for hefty penalties for violations.[15]

If a union runs afoul of this section by obtaining and using names and addresses obtained through license-plate identification, heretofore a common practice, it is likely to be subject to significant damages, even if its organizers behave in an exemplary manner. Thus in *Pichler v. UNITE*,[16] the Third Circuit upheld class-based liability against UNITE for using license-plate numbers even though one of its purposes (preparation for litigation) was legitimate under the DPPA. The court also held open the possibility of punitive damages, despite the fact that there was no abusive behavior by the organizers. This statute aimed at stalkers, and probably enacted with no thought to its impact on union organizing, can be a major impediment to the primary step of getting workers and organizers together. Thus it seems that Congress, without addressing the issue, has by passing the DPPA made organizing significantly more difficult for unions.

COVERAGE

Only "employees" can vote in NLRB elections. Determining which workers are employees for purposes of the Act is crucial to the Board's role. The definition of "employee" in section 2(3) of the Act gives no guidance beyond the exclusion of certain categories. Otherwise, it simply provides that the term "employee" "shall include any employee." To make the issue even more problematic, the term has been narrowed by congressional language excluding certain categories of workers such as "supervisors" in terms that are equally difficult to define.

When the NLRA was first enacted, it was clear that the drafters meant to include the vast majority of wage earners within the protection of the Act. But the history of the Act since 1947 has included the steady narrowing of coverage on the basis of common-law notions of employment and loyalty.

During its first decade, the Board, eager to make the Act inclusive, interpreted the term "employee" in terms of giving rights to those vulnerable to economic exploitation. Accordingly, it held that newsboys who might not have been servants at common law were employees because they were dependent on the publisher for their livelihood.[17] In *NLRB v. Hearst Publications, Inc.,*[18] the Supreme Court affirmed that "the mischief at which the Act is aimed and the remedies it offers are not confined exclusively to employees 'within the traditional legal distinctions separating them from independent contractors.'" Congress responded in the 1947 Taft-Hartley amendments by specifically excluding "independent contractors" from the definition of employees. In *NLRB v. United Insurance Co. of America,*[19] the Court accepted the policy change created by the new definition. The failure to define the term "employee," a term with a rich common-law history, together with the exclusion of "independent contractors," established a statutory policy of determining employee status through common-law principles. The right of control over the way the job is performed by the claimed employee is the crucial test.

Right of control is a slippery concept. There are many jobs, such as truck driving, that are performed alone and the mechanics of which are not subject to control. If such workers are treated as independent contractors, the Act's basic policy of balancing economic power is unachievable. The extent to which the definition of "employee" under the right-of-control test can contradict the Act's policy is exemplified by port drivers. Port drivers, who have been declared independent contractors, haul cargo from ships to warehouses and rail yards. They are poor and without unionization have virtually no bargaining power. According to John Wilhelm, "Almost all immigrants [port drivers], have no benefits; they work incredible hours in order to make ends meet. They are a horrific source of pollution because, since they can barely make ends meet and they have to buy their own trucks, they have these old rattletrap trucks—they're old, they're inefficient, they are horrible." This has turned into a system of near slavery.

According to AFL-CIO general counsel John Hiatt, the widespread use of independent contractors makes it more difficult for unions to strike: "And these days in so many industries, in [the] manufacturing and service sectors, you have so many independent contractors and you have so many virtual work-places, it is much easier for employers to withstand strikes even without striker replacements than I think used to be the case."

Another category capable of removing large numbers of workers from the protection of the Act is that of supervisor. The Taft-Hartley amendments re-moved from the Act's coverage "any individual employed as a supervisor," a term defined very broadly to include "any individual having authority, in the interest of the employer, to hire, transfer, suspend, lay off, recall, promote, dis-charge, assign, reward, or discipline other employees, or responsibly to direct them, or to adjust their grievances, or effectively to recommend such action, if . . . the exercise of such authority . . . requires the use of independent judg-ment."[20]

As might be expected with a definition of this breadth, the issue whether a particular person or group constitutes supervisors arises frequently, and no clear line between supervisors and lead workers can be discerned, particularly with reference to such qualities as "responsibly to direct" or "effectively to recom-mend."[21]

Whenever skilled floor-level lead workers are found to be supervisors, they are removed from the reach of labor solidarity, which thereby diminishes the power of the strike weapon and correspondingly lessens the effectiveness of unions in collective bargaining. Supervisors, although they often favor the union's bargaining position,[22] are not permitted by law to support their fellow workers. They are regularly required to act as strike breakers by performing "struck work" and training replacement workers.[23]

The vagueness of the definition gives employers an additional benefit: the ability to delay an election by objecting to the union's proposed unit on the grounds that it includes supervisors. As every knowledgeable observer agrees, delay helps employers. Unions that have obtained a substantial majority of card signers want a quick election. Sometimes this goal is impossible to achieve because of unit issues. In order to get a speedy election, unions are frequently required to agree to remove key supporters from the unit, a concession that may well come back to haunt them if bargaining reaches an impasse.

If applied to the full extent of its language, the statutory definition of "supervisor" is broad enough to cover almost all professional employees and most lead workers. Both groups typically "direct" other workers and almost always use a degree of discretion in so doing. Thus the definition of "supervisor" is a potential linguistic Trojan horse, capable of wiping out much of the Act's intended effectiveness. This potential effect is best illustrated by a series of Supreme Court and Board decisions concerning the status of nurses under the Act. In *NLRB v. Kentucky River Community Care, Inc.,*[24] the Supreme Court ruled that nurses exercising professional judgment in dealing with other employees were supervisors: "What is at issue is the Board's contention that the policy of covering professional employees under the Act justifies the categorical exclusion of professional judgments from a term, 'independent judgment,' that naturally includes them. And further, that it justifies limiting this categorical exclusion to the supervisory function of responsibly directing other employees. These contentions contradict both the text and structure of the statute."

Under the Bush administration, the Board extended the reach of this decision in *Oakwood Healthcare,*[25] holding that "charge nurses" were supervisors. The function of charge nurses was described by the Board as follows: "Charge nurses assign other RNs, licensed practical nurses (LPNs), nursing assistants, technicians, and paramedics to patients." In all cases, this minor supervisory role was only a fraction of the charge nurses' function.

The decision to exclude the charge nurses was by a 3 to 2 vote. The Board majority focused on the language of the statute and ignored the fact that an expansive reading had the capacity to remove most of the nursing profession from the scope of the Act. The majority said that its function was to interpret language, not to consider policy in applying statutory definitions: "We begin our analysis with a first principle of statutory interpretation that 'in all cases involving statutory construction, our starting point must be the language employed by Congress . . . and we assume that the legislative purpose is expressed by the ordinary meaning of the words used.' . . . We eschew a results-driven approach and we start, as we must, with the words of the statute. . . . We do not, as the dissent contends, ignore potential 'real-world' consequences of our interpretations. Rather, we simply decline to engage in an analysis that seems to take as its objective a narrowing of the scope of supervisory status and to reason backward from there, relying primarily on selective excerpts from legislative history." The majority found that the charge nurses had responsibility for "assignment" as that term is used in the definition of "supervisors": "The assignment of an employee to a certain department (e.g., housewares) or to a certain shift (e.g., night) or to certain significant overall tasks (e.g., restocking shelves) would generally qualify as 'assign' within our construction."

The Board went on to define "responsibly to direct" in broad terms: "We agree with the circuit courts that have considered the issue and find that for direction to be "responsible," the person directing and performing the oversight of the employee must be accountable for the performance of the task by the other, such that some adverse consequence may befall the one providing the oversight if the tasks performed by the employee are not performed properly."

Finally, the Board undertook to consider the term "independent judgment": "In short, professional or technical judgments involving the use of independent judgment are supervisory if they involve one of the 12 supervisory functions of Section 2(11). Thus, for example, a registered nurse who makes the 'professional judgment' that a catheter needs to be changed may be performing a supervisory function when he/she responsibly directs a nursing assistant in the performance of that work."

The Board majority, for purposes of this case, declined to include rotating charge nurses, on the grounds that the employer had not provided enough evidence. But the Board's analysis made it relatively easy for employers in the future to exclude most nurses who serve as charge nurses.

The dissenters focused on the majority's refusal to consider the consequences of its ruling: "Today's decision threatens to create a new class of workers under Federal labor law: workers who have neither the genuine prerogatives of management, nor the statutory rights of ordinary employees. . . . That category . . . by 2012 could number almost 34 million, accounting for 23.3 percent of the work force."

The impact of this decision could be catastrophic for organized labor, as Stephen Colbert pointed out with his usual acuity. Purporting to praise the decision, he opined: "It's time for labor and management to come together as management to exploit labor."[26]

Despite the extraordinarily broad language of the supervisory exemption, the Board, with the support of the Supreme Court, added another major exclusionary category not found in the statute itself—managerial employees. It is an unnecessary category based solely on careful linguistic parsing. The Board concluded that the definition of "supervisor," broad as it is, does not theoretically include high-level employees whose role involves planning, articulating, or carrying out high-level policy but who have no supervisory role. It is doubtful that high-level officials exist who could not be dealt with under the supervisory exemption. But in *Ford Motor Company*,[27] the Board announced the creation of yet another new category of exempt employees whom it characterized as "managerial." The Board defined this group as those executive employees who "formulate, determine, and effectuate management policies." The Supreme Court, in *NLRB v. Bell Aerospace Co.*,[28] adopted the Board's definition and held further that all such employees are excluded from the definition of "employee."

Both supervisory and managerial exemptions are usually used to exclude certain individuals from voting and from the bargaining unit. Occasionally, however, the exclusion of a group of employees on the grounds of supervisory or managerial status will make an entire unit inappropriate.

In *NLRB v. Yeshiva University*,[29] the Supreme Court applied the concept of managerial employees to deny the Yeshiva faculty as a group, and by obvious implication almost all other university faculty members, the right to unionize under the NLRA. The Court held that all faculty members were managers because of their traditional role in university governance through faculty committees and other votes in academic bodies: "It is clear that Yeshiva and like universities must rely on their faculties to participate in the making and implementation of their policies. The large measure of independence enjoyed by faculty members can only increase the danger that divided loyalty will lead to those harms that the Board traditionally has sought to prevent."

The concern over "divided loyalty" and "harms that the Board traditionally has sought to prevent" is persuasive until one tries to focus more precisely on the harms that the Court is concerned with. Would unionized professors seek to harm a college or university's academic standing? Hardly, since that is crucial to their own professional careers. Would they vote against qualified faculty candidates on the basis of attitudes toward unionization? That worry too reflects a total misunderstanding of professorial self-interest. Indeed, what makes unionization of interest to faculty is two things—the possibility of personal gains and the hope for greater professorial voice. It seems that what the Court was worried about is having faculty play a greater role in the operation of universities. In its opinion, the Court indicated plainly that its conclusions about the critical policymaking role of the faculty were meant to apply not only to Yeshiva but to "mature educational institutions" generally. The Board has followed the Court's lead and has held faculty members to be managers when there is the appearance of collegial responsibility.

There are many reasons why the Board's fairly literal application of the *Yeshiva* exemption is unfortunate. First, active roles in university governance do not give faculty control over their own wages or many aspects of working conditions, such as hours of teaching and vacations. Second, many universities contain elaborate structures of faculty governance but limit final decision-making authority to full-time administrators. In such cases, the Board should consider the realities of academic power. Third, the *Yeshiva* decision, which was decided by a sharply divided Court (5–4), is fundamentally at odds with the basic national policy of free choice with respect to unionization. Most commentators have been critical of the opinion, pointing out that the Court ignored the extent to which faculty members are vulnerable to arbitrary decisions by university administrators.[30] Moreover, the Court in *Yeshiva* treated faculty as a unit, attributing to faculty members generally the institutional authority exercised by some of their colleagues—an approach never previously employed. The special approach undoubtedly reflects the Court's conclusion that traditional collective bargaining is particularly inappropriate for academic institutions. This does not mean, however, that the *Yeshiva* approach will be so limited.

Although the Board has thus far only rarely applied *Yeshiva* outside the academic context, a wide range of professional workers are at risk of being characterized as nonemployees—and thus as managers, supervisors, or "associates" —and could thus be deprived of the protections of the labor law. In *FHP Inc.*,[31] for example, the Board found a group of physicians to be managers because the governance system of the hospital in which they worked included committees of physicians that played a role in determining some aspects of health-care policy. The concept of employer-established committees replacing unionization was at one time clearly rejected under the NLRA as a technique for thwarting employee choice, but *Yeshiva* offers a dangerous precedent for its reemergence. In today's climate, the possibility of using committees so that nonprofessional but skilled workers are deemed to be managers should not be discounted, especially for those workers without a history of collective bargaining.

With all the exclusions and hard-to-define terms involved in establishing an appropriate unit of employees, an employer is almost always in a position to delay an election by challenging the unit claimed by the union. In larger units, employers can regularly obtain several additional months by claiming that the unit sought includes job categories and individual workers who do not have a community of interest with the group generally. Employers can also claim that the unit includes supervisors or managerial employees or confidential employees.

Chapter 15 The Regulation of Employer Campaign Conduct

THREATS

It is an unfair labor practice for an employer to threaten retaliation if the employees vote to unionize or to promise them benefits if they turn down the union. But employers otherwise have the right to state their views concerning unionization to their employees. Employers typically take advantage of their right to speak out; in almost every NLRB election campaign, employers make captive-audience speeches to convince employees that it is not in their interest to vote for unionization. In the course of these speeches, employers regularly suggest that employees may not benefit—indeed, may be economically harmed—as a result of unionizing. It is very difficult even for experts to differentiate between a lawful statement of opinion and an illegal threat of reprisal. Employer statements are rarely cast as direct threats. Indeed, employers generally announce that they will obey the law.

Employers (actually, their lawyers) typically craft campaign statements that intentionally create ambiguity about the ways in which unionization might prove to be harmful to employees. A good example is the following comment: "In the past, the company has given you all the wage increases and fringe benefits it could afford and still stay competitive. If we cannot remain competitive, there is no reason for us to stay in business." Similar statements are made in almost all representation campaigns. Are such statements likely to be interpreted by employees as predictions of harmful consequences that will flow from unionization regardless of the employer's wishes or as a threat to curtail or go out of business? If such statements are interpreted as threats, will employees be intimidated and vote against the union? Does the location of the business matter? Or the makeup of the workforce? Are immigrant workers easier to coerce than native-born workers?

These are not easy questions, and neither the NLRB nor the courts have the ability to give informed answers. Although it has been administering the NLRA for over seventy years, the Board has never investigated empirically whether a particular type of statement or action has a coercive impact. Indeed, the Board has not permitted the introduction of evidence as to whether particular conduct had a harmful impact on employees. It has said that "in evaluating the interference resulting from specific conduct, the Board does not attempt to assess its actual effect on employees, but rather concerns itself with whether it is reasonable to conclude that the conduct tended to prevent the free formation and expression of the employees' choice."[1]

The lack of reliable information about the impact of employer statements ensures that the evaluation of ambiguous statements will turn on political ideology. Historically, liberal Board members and judges assumed that employees pay careful attention and are sensitive to nuances of coercion; they regularly found ambiguous statements to be unlawful threats, parsing statements with grammatical precision and finding only the most explicit threats to be lawful. Conservative Board members have permitted employers greater latitude.

The problem of separating unlawful threats from legal expressions of opinion is made even more complicated because the constitutional boundaries of employer anti-union speech are not clear. In 1969 the Supreme Court, which has not weighed in on this topic for many years, gave its approval to strict regulation of employee speech in *NLRB v. Gissel Packing Co.*[2] The case involved an employer who argued that the union was a "strike-happy outfit" and warned that a strike could put the company in economic jeopardy and lead to its closing. The employer warned the employees to "look around Holyoke and see a lot of them out of business." The Board concluded that the employer's conduct made a fair election impossible because it "reasonably tended to convey to the employees the belief or impression that selection of the union could lead the [company] to close its plant or transfer the weaving operation." The employer argued that its statement amounted to no more than an exercise of its First Amendment right of free speech.

The Supreme Court rejected this contention, holding that the employer's speech contained impermissible threats of reprisal: "Any assessment of the precise scope of employer expression, of course, must be made in the context of its labor relations setting. Thus, an employer's rights cannot outweigh the equal rights of the employees to associate freely. . . . And any balancing of those rights must take into account the economic dependence of the employees on their employer and the necessary tendency of the former, because of that relationship, to pick up intended implications of the latter that might be more readily dismissed by a more disinterested ear."

Implicit in the Court's analysis is the conclusion that employees are carefully attuned to intimations of reprisal and that, faced with subtle threats, they will vote against unionization. Otherwise, the justices would not have concluded that employer statements containing no overt intention to retaliate against union supporters nevertheless infringed on employee free choice and were thus not protected by the First Amendment. The Court restricted an employer's First Amendment protection to "a prediction . . . carefully phrased on the basis of objective fact to convey an employer's belief as to demonstrably probable consequences beyond his control." It also stated that an employer was not constitutionally protected in expressing its belief that the union might lead to a plant closing even if its belief was sincere "unless, which is most improbable, the eventuality of closing is capable of proof." In responding to the employer's argument that "the line between so-called permitted predictions and proscribed threats is too vague to stand up under traditional First Amendment analysis," the Court commented that an employer "can easily make his views known without engaging in 'brinkmanship.' . . . At the least, he can avoid coercive speech simply by avoiding conscious overstatements."

Only the Court's factual assumption about the special nature of labor relations and the particular vulnerability of employees can explain why normal First Amendment protections do not apply to employer statements. In other contexts, the Court has been unwilling to assume that speech has a coercive or threatening impact. It has rejected the claims of government officials that they are able to predict the impact of speech on bystanders. It has insisted that remedies for unlawful speech be limited in such a way as to protect whatever legitimate message the speech might contain. And it has rejected the idea that the identity or position of the speaker may justify regulation.[3]

The 1969 *Gissel* decision did not, however, resolve the issue of employer free speech. In its aftermath the courts of appeals have, though citing *Gissel*, regularly rejected the standard set forth in Justice Earl Warren's opinion. The Seventh Circuit, under the leadership of Judge Richard Posner, took the boldest step in changing the *Gissel* standard. In *NLRB v. Village IX, Inc.*,[4] the employer guaranteed to the employees that if the union was voted in, the company would be out of business within a year: "The cancer will eat us up, and we will fall by the wayside. . . . I only know from my mind, from my heart and from my pocketbook how I stand on this." Judge Posner found that the *Gissel* standard was satisfied because the employer's vision of the union's economic impact, although hazy and imprecise, was consistent with respectable economic theory. The opinion ignored the fact that the employer in *Gissel* had more of a factual basis for the statements, found by the Supreme Court to violate section 8(a)(1), than did the employer in *Village IX*, whose statement the Seventh Circuit held to be permissible.

No clear standard has emerged. The circuits vary one from the other, and often opinions vary within a single circuit. What seems clear, however, is that no circuit applies the *Gissel* approach strictly and that the general movement is toward greater permissiveness. The Board itself has regularly held to be legal speech that does not meet the standard set forth in *Gissel*.[5]

THE PRESUMED COERCIVE EFFECTS OF GRANTS AND PROMISES OF BENEFITS

From very early in its history, the Board without explanation, treated the unconditional grant or promise of benefits during the course of a union organizing campaign as an unfair labor practice. The Supreme Court in *NLRB v. Exchange Parts Co.*[6] accepted this conclusion. It announced that "the danger inherent in well-timed increases in benefits is the suggestion of a fist inside the velvet glove. Employees are not likely to miss the inference that the source of benefits now conferred is also the source from which future benefits must flow and which may dry up if it is not obliged." Thus, the authoritatively announced rationale of the law is that employees, when given or promised benefits, will react as though they were threatened.

Probably the most remarkable thing about this explanation is its view of employee thinking. Why should it take a grant or promise of benefits during a representation election to make employees aware that the employer is the source of job benefits and that it will be the source of future benefits? Could not they have deduced this from examining their paycheck?

As is often the case with limitations on employer speech and conduct, the *Exchange Parts* rationale was soon applied with very little persuasive reasoning to union promises. In *NLRB v. Savair Manufacturing Co.,*[7] the Supreme Court held that a union's offer to waive initiation fees for all employees who signed cards before an election interfered with employee free choice. The Court reasoned that employees might be tempted to sign a card to avoid the initiation fee and might then feel compelled to support the union because their having signed a card would become known. The Court also viewed the practice as improper because it would permit the union to claim support it did not have. The Court assumed that such a misleading claim of support would help the union and that any votes it thereby acquired would not be an expression of free choice. Finally, the Court concluded that "the failure to sign a recognition slip may well seem ominous to nonunionists who fear that, if they do not sign, they will face a wrathful regime should the union win."

The Court's explanation reflects the same patronizing view of employees that the Court exhibited in its *Exchange Parts* decision. Why, for example, would employees who know of the conditional offer assume that other employees who signed cards were not doing so to take advantage of the offer? Why would they be persuaded to vote contrary to their own attitudes toward unionization in any case? The fear of a wrathful union regime, if it is at all a reason why employees sign cards—and existing data suggest it is not—should be the same whether or not the union offered a conditional waiver. Some of the language of *Savair* suggests that even an unconditional waiver would be improper. That conclusion might have a major impact on union campaigns because most unions currently do not require dues or initiation fees until the union wins the election and a contract is signed. The Board, however, held that such general waivers are not covered by *Savair;* its holding has been upheld on appeal.[8]

THE "LABORATORY CONDITIONS" DOCTRINE

For over sixty years, both conservative and liberal Boards have claimed the authority to set elections aside and to find unfair labor practices on the basis of a complex set of rules referred to as the "laboratory conditions" doctrine. The idea that its election process should be treated as comparable to a laboratory experiment was announced by the Board in 1948 in *General Shoe Corp.,*[9] in which the Board declared, "It is the Board's function to provide a laboratory in which an experiment may be conducted, under conditions as nearly ideal as possible, to determine the uninhibited desires of the employees. . . . When, in the rare extreme case, the standards drop too low, . . . laboratory conditions are not present and the experiment must be conducted over again." It is difficult to imagine a more inexact or confusing metaphor. It describes neither how the Board functions nor what the actual standard is or should be.

The metaphor suggests a need for pristine purity and shutting out improper influences—when the Act contains no warrant for such a standard but seems rather to have contemplated a rough-and-tumble atmosphere common to labor relations.[10] The laboratory image, reinforced by the use of the term "experiment," suggests an environment in which events can be observed easily and causality definitively determined by the Board. Neither is so, however, since the Board does not investigate the impact of campaign tactics. Thus, there was a "man behind the curtain" quality to the doctrine from its inception. The doctrine has been used, however, to set aside elections, typically but not solely employer victories, on the basis of conduct that the Board concluded violated the proper degree of campaign purity.

The main use of the doctrine has been as a makeweight in finding that employer speech interfered with free choice by improperly suggesting negative consequences from unionization.[11]

The doctrine has also been employed in the context of the interrogation of employees concerning their attitudes toward the union. Unless they are counseled, employers or their representatives will often question employees either about their support for the union or about the grievances that gave rise to the organizing effort. Although there are many reasons other than the desire to coerce that might lead to this interrogation, traditionally the Board has held that both types of questioning violate the statute—the former as an implied threat; the latter as an implied promise. The courts of appeals have always been uneasy about the Board's categorical treatment of interrogation,[12] but they have generally gone along with the Board's basic approach, which has been that interrogation is unlawful unless it contains certain safeguards such as assurances against reprisal and an agreement to grant recognition if a majority favors representation.[13]

If these requirements were not met, the Board would hold that the employer's actions constituted an unfair labor practice, regardless of the employer's motivation and regardless of whether the circumstances otherwise indicated that the employees questioned felt threatened. An employer that simply assured its employees that it would not retaliate would not meet these standards, and its questioning would therefore constitute a violation.[14]

APPEALS TO PREJUDICE

In *Sewell Manufacturing Co.*,[15] the Board said that it would set aside elections in which one or the other party used "appeals or arguments . . . to inflame the racial feelings of voters in the election." The Board justified its decision on the grounds that it "has the responsibility to ensure that the voters cast their ballots . . . in an atmosphere conducive to the sober and informed exercise of the franchise." The Board distinguished for these purposes between statements "temperate in tone" and those "not intended or calculated to encourage the reasoning faculty." The initial effect of the decision was to set aside elections in which employers used appeals to bigotry to defeat unionization. However, with the passage of the 1964 Civil Rights Act and changing attitudes about race, shortly after the *Sewell* decision these appeals ceased, in part because workforces became more integrated, in part because these statements supplied evidence of discrimination, and in large part because bigotry became less acceptable. Much of the litigation following *Sewell* has concerned union efforts to appeal to employees on the basis of racial or ethnic solidarity, a technique particularly likely to be employed when the workforce is largely black or made up of members of an ethnic minority. The Board has generally permitted unions to raise racial issues in this fashion, distinguishing between appeals to bigotry and appeals to racial pride. The courts of appeals have been less accepting than the Board of these union tactics,[16] probably reasoning that if racial appeals are improper when used by an employer, they also should be improper when used by a union.

The entire line of cases demonstrates the inevitable difficulty of the Board's and the courts' assumption of the role of censor. Why should employees be denied a union because racial feelings were expressed during the course of the campaign? Why do unions need protection against racist comments, which leave the employer open to the union response that it is the employer's goal to keep the employees separated whereas the union joins them together?[17]

RETALIATION

The law with respect to retaliation is clear. Employers may not discharge or otherwise retaliate against employees who support the union. Yet many scholars believe that discriminatory discharges are common and are increasing. There are several reasons why an employer may not feel bound to follow the law. First, an employer can often mask its motive by pretending that the discharge was for cause—the worker violated a rule or has performed poorly. It can litigate this issue in a variety of forums over a long period of time. It can argue its case first to the general counsel, then to the administrative law judge, then to the Board, and then to a court of appeals. Years are likely to go by before a final judgment is reached, and if there is any evidence of wrongdoing on the part of the employee, the employer has a good chance of winning its case. The courts of appeals in particular are reluctant to order the reinstatement of employees who, they are convinced, deserved to be terminated.[18] Second, even if the employer loses the case, the cost in back pay is likely to be small—what the employee would have earned less what he or she did earn or could have earned if he or she were diligent in seeking other employment. When the employer has been found to have discriminatorily discharged a union supporter, the remedy includes reinstatement. Several studies have shown that such employees rarely return, however, and that even when they do, they are likely to quit soon afterward.[19] Thus, to the extent that employers are tempted to discharge employees in order to coerce employees into voting against representation, the law is unlikely to be much of a deterrent.

Chapter 16 The Duty to Bargain and the Protection of Employee Choice

Winning an NLRB election is only a step toward unionizing. To secure meaningful representation, the union must be able, after the election, to negotiate a collective-bargaining agreement acceptable to its members. The law provides almost no help toward achieving this goal. The NLRA requires only that the employer "meet at reasonable times and confer in good faith" with the union. Section 8(d) specifically states that good faith "does not compel either party to agree to a proposal or require the making of a concession." It is easy for an employer to use the mandatory bargaining process as a device to rid itself of the union by making demands that it knows the union will not accept and by rejecting proposals that the union cannot abandon without losing its members' support. Bargaining to avoid an agreement without violating the NLRA is a common technique of employer counsel, particularly during first-contract negotiations.[1]

First-contract negotiations are almost invariably difficult and contentious. Unions come to the table seeking massive changes in every aspect of the employment relationship. A union will typically propose contract terms that include higher wages, improved benefits, widespread use of seniority, a grievance system ending in binding arbitration, a union-security clause that seems to require membership, a dues-checkoff provision, and a clause denying management's right to discipline employees unless it has good cause. Employers enter first-contract negotiations with a view to ceding as little power as possible and with a goal of limiting cost. Employers are likely to oppose every change that the union is seeking.[2]

Given the basic difference in starting points and goals, it is not surprising that first-contract negotiations often turn out to be tough, antagonistic, and prolonged. If no agreement is reached, the union may file charges alleging that the employer has breached its duty to bargain in good faith. The Board and the courts are then required to determine whether the employer engaged in hard bargaining or bad-faith bargaining. Not surprisingly, their decisions are confusing and contradictory.

Courts and commentators agree that an employer acts in bad faith when its behavior indicates an unwillingness to come to agreement.[3] But that is difficult to prove. The vast majority of employers, even those seeking to oust the union, make some proposals and would be willing to sign an agreement maintaining their unilaterally set wages and working conditions, especially if the proposed contract also contains a broad no-strike clause. A contract limited to these clauses would put the union in a weaker position and the employer in a stronger position than they would be in if no agreement were reached.[4]

The Board rarely examines the reasonableness of management's position in evaluating its good faith. Some courts of appeals, the Fifth Circuit in particular, have shown great reluctance to ever consider reasonableness.[5] An employer that alters its proposals and makes minor concessions such as a small wage increase is probably safe in most circuits, particularly if it is willing to meet with the union and explain its resistance to the union's proposals.

In those rare cases in which an employer is found to have violated its duty to bargain, by failing to bargain in good faith, the penalty is so weak as to be essentially meaningless.[6] Despite the broad remedial language of section 10, the Supreme Court held, in *H. K. Porter Co. v. NLRB*,[7] that the Board did not have the authority to order an employer to accept a contract clause, even when it was the failure to accept that very clause that constituted the unfair labor practice. The Court's opinion in *H. K. Porter* made clear that under no circumstance was the Board permitted to remedy a violation by ordering that the employer add (or remove) a clause that it has not agreed to at the bargaining table. The Court held that such a remedy would "violate the fundamental premise" of the Act—namely, "freedom of contract." Why the Court chose to describe freedom of contract as more fundamental than the policy favoring good-faith collective bargaining is not explained, and it is far from obvious.

The Board has since taken the position that *H. K. Porter* denies it the authority to issue a make-whole remedy under which employees would be compensated for what they lost economically by virtue of the employer's bad faith.[8] This conclusion, although harsh, is in keeping with the Court's language. And it further eliminates the possibility of obtaining a meaningful remedy for the employer's rejection of its obligations under the Act. In most cases, the only penalty is an order requiring the employer to cease and desist from bargaining in bad faith and to post a notice so stating. *H. K. Porter* thus enshrines the conclusion that an employer has the power to refuse to make any concession that it "prefers not to,"[9] as long as it is willing to face a strike.

The weakness of the duty to bargain and the absence of meaningful remedies mean that employers can frequently rid themselves of a union by simply refusing to come to an agreement. Roland Samson, formerly the Northeast organizing coordinator of the United Steelworkers, has seen some of his organizing victories vitiated in this way. As he told me, "If you are successful, and you do win the election, then they will say anything to drag negotiations out for more than a year. In that year's time, a lot of the folks that wanted the union are gonna get dissatisfied because they haven't got a contract yet and quit the union, and then you can't do anything."

The law provides no remedy for a union faced with an employer that is unwilling to sign an acceptable agreement. Why don't all employers who want to avoid unionization follow this course? Why are some first contracts negotiated successfully? In the vast majority of cases, it is the threat of a strike or its actual use that motivates an employer to make bargaining concessions. The more the law strengthens the right to strike, the more successful unions will be in collective bargaining; the weaker the right to strike, the easier it is for employers to forestall unionization. As is discussed more fully in part 4, the strike weapon is both powerful and dangerous. It gets its strength from worker solidarity and effective strategy and not from the law.

Chapter 17 NLRA Organizing:
Law and Reality

Union leaders believe that employers win elections by retaliating and instilling fear. Employers claim that they win through persuasion. The issue has provoked scholarly dispute, in which I have been an active participant. During the 1970s I took part in the first major empirical effort to study the dynamics of NLRB campaigns. Along with Professors Stephen B. Goldberg and Jeanne Brett (Herman), I conducted a study of employee voting behavior in NLRB elections. We interviewed employee voters in over thirty-one NLRB campaigns that were chosen because they promised, and turned out, to be hard fought and to include a significant amount of illegal behavior.

We conducted our study in two waves. The first wave occurred soon after an NLRB election was scheduled, and the second wave just after the election. During first-wave interviews, employees were asked how they felt about their working conditions and about unions. We asked whether they signed an authorization card and how they would vote if the election were held the next day. In second-wave interviews, we asked the same employees to recall the content of the campaign and to disclose how they voted and why. A very high percentage of employees agreed to be interviewed and answered our questions fully and honestly.[1] We also interviewed company and union representatives in each election and obtained information about the strategy and tactics that they employed. We studied only elections in which both sides agreed to speak with us, describe their tactics, and give us copies of propaganda and drafts of speeches. To determine whether there was illegal behavior, we submitted our findings to Melvin J. Welles, an administrative law judge and a well-recognized expert on NLRB law.

One of our major findings was that most voting behavior was correlated more strongly with attitudes than with campaign tactics.[2] We formed indexes from the employees' answers that measured job satisfaction and attitude toward unions. These indexes accurately predicted roughly 81 percent of the vote. For example, employees with a satisfaction score below 18 voted three to one (303–99) for union representation; those who scored 18 or above voted three to one (453–149) against union representation. Thus, knowing whether an employee's satisfaction score was greater or less than 18 allowed us to predict the vote with 75 percent accuracy.[3] We concluded that "employee attitudes, measured prior to intense pre-election campaigning, thus form strong and stable predispositions to vote for or against union representation."

The relationship between predispositions and vote was not only powerful but also broadly general. Attitudes and intent predicted the vote in Midwestern farm communities, urban ghettos, and rural Kentucky towns, among employees working in factories, warehouses, retail stores, nursing homes, and offices, in units ranging from four to nearly four hundred employees. Attitudes and intent predicted the vote for men and women; whites, blacks, and Hispanics; the old and the young; and the well and poorly educated. They predicted the vote when local unemployment was low and when it was high.

This conclusion was and remains at odds with both Board and court decisions and the writings of commentators, much of which rests on the assumption that employee choice is easily manipulated during a campaign, particularly when employers try to instill fear of reprisal.

Precampaign attitudes did not predict the vote of roughly 19 percent of employee voters. The majority of these were voters whose precampaign attitudes suggested that they would vote for the union but who voted against representation. Job-satisfaction scores for those employees were higher after the campaign than before the campaign. Similarly, they became less favorable toward unions. The implication of these data is that successful employer campaigns make employees feel better about their jobs or less positive toward unions. It is noteworthy in this regard that the only company theme reported by substantially more company voters than union voters was that the employer had treated employees well.

THE IMPACT OF ACCESS

We measured the familiarity of voters with the campaign. The result demonstrated the advantage that companies have because of their ability to make captive-audience speeches. Both union and company voters showed familiarity with the employer's campaign. Union voters, however, were significantly more familiar with the union campaign than were company voters. Familiarity with the themes of the union campaign was almost three times greater among employees who attended union meetings than among those who did not. Why didn't more employees attend union meetings? The most common reason for not attending was that meetings were "held at an inconvenient time or place." Had more undecided voters attended union meetings, it is likely that several union losses would have been victories. Undecided voters who voted for representation were significantly more familiar with the union campaign than those who voted for the company.

Our findings gave strong support to the argument that rules concerning access to employees, which permit captive-audience speeches and deny unions a right to reply, give employers a significant advantage that is capable of determining the outcome. It is an advantage that employers have learned to exploit with increasing effectiveness. As Tom Woodruff, the director of the Change to Win Strategic Organizing Center, explained to me, it is increasingly common "for employers to turn a place upside down and do nothing but campaign for a couple of weeks."

THREATS AND REPRISALS

The Board, the courts, and most commentators assume that employees will recognize implied threats and that the perception of threats will cause them to vote against representation. Judge Learned Hand explained the rationale for this theory in *NLRB v. Federbush Co.:*[4] "What to an outsider will be no more than the vigorous presentation of a conviction, to an employee may be the manifestation of a determination which it is not safe to thwart."[5]

This view is widely shared. It is believed by company consultants, union organizers, most commentators, and most scholars. John Wilhelm, with his many years of organizing experience, believes that when an employer devotes precious time to speeches and union bashing its purpose is not to convince but to intimidate. He described a Canadian representation election in which the union had cards signed from 80 percent of the membership: "Twenty-four hours later the company has an American union buster on the premises, so they stopped production for five days and harangued the people for five days. And the basic point they made was if we close down our factory for five days just to harangue you about the election, think what we might do if you actually have a union. And the union got slaughtered, even though they had 80 percent of the cards."

But Wilhelm's conclusion attributing the defeat to fear of retaliation does not follow automatically from his story. It could be that after five days of uninterrupted access, the employees were convinced either that the company was more concerned with their welfare or that the union was more likely to prove a hindrance to them and to the company than they believed when they signed a card.

The accepted truth that fear of reprisal shapes Board elections is contradicted by our data.

If fear of reprisal is the reason card signers vote no, the fear should have been manifested in a variety of ways in the elections we studied. Unions should have lost a higher percentage of elections in which threats were used than elections in which they were not. Employees should have reported more threats in those elections. They should have mentioned them more frequently in explaining both their votes and the votes of other employees. In our analysis, none of these manifestations of the impact of threats occurred. We found no basis for concluding that employers won elections by creating fear of unlawful reprisal.

Union organizers are often convinced that a precampaign majority turned into a vote against representation because the employer cleverly suggested that it would retaliate in the case of a union victory. But organizers get a skewed view of the election. What they learn about the dynamics of a campaign overwhelmingly comes from union voters—those who remained loyal. But union voters far more than employer voters perceived the employer to be making threats. For example, 47 percent of union voters reported that the employer raised the possibility that a union victory could lead to job loss. Only 24 percent of company voters mentioned this argument even though it was a standard part of all employer campaigns. Employees who were most strongly anti-union tended to report the least adversarial of the employer's comments—for example, "He told us to make up our own minds. The decision was up to us." This standard employer statement, aimed at demonstrating fairness, is usually followed by a strong attack on the union. Employees who voted no rarely reported the hostile aspect of its campaign.

Our findings suggested that the most effective employer tactic was to use the campaign to increase job satisfaction. Employers regularly do this in a variety of ways, pointing to past benefits, referring to employees by first name, suggesting without promising that it will improve things, and generally trying to convey the message "We hear you. Give us another chance."

This is not to say that fear of retaliation is irrelevant to unionization. Concerns about the economic consequences of unionization and the possibility of employer retaliation are present before organizing ever begins. Indeed, these concerns often prevent employees from seriously considering unionization until their dissatisfaction or concern about existing conditions becomes great enough to overcome their fear. It is precisely because these fears are present before and throughout the campaign that they are so little affected by most employer campaign tactics.

In the course of our study, we concluded that the effort to protect employee free choice by limiting employer speech was futile and likely would remain so.[6] Inevitably, it led the Board to make distinctions that had no basis in reality. No matter where the line between threats and prediction is drawn, carefully crafted employer propaganda will be able to convey the dangers of unionism and the promise of benefits as effectively as prohibited speech. Further, restrictions on employer speech inevitably lead to Board and court restrictions on union speech. It is true that fewer union victories are set aside than employer victories, but the consequences of setting aside union victories are more serious. Setting aside an employer victory is almost always meaningless because the employer remains in control of wages and working conditions. Setting aside a union victory because of perceived promises, threats, or appeals to racial feelings reverses the expressed will of the employees: they voted for a union but continue to work without one.

In addition, restrictions on employer speech in the organizing context invite reciprocal regulation of union speech in strikes and picketing. The Supreme Court has made clear on several occasions that reciprocity is a major factor underlying the Court's willingness to uphold restrictions on union actions, such as peaceful picketing, that might otherwise be ruled unconstitutional. Under any analysis consistent with First Amendment holdings in other areas, the provisions of sections 8(b)(4) and 8(b)(7) (the secondary-boycott and organizational-picketing prohibitions) should both be held unconstitutional. But the

Supreme Court continues to apply them and to assume their validity at least partly on the basis that labor law is an area of properly balanced speech regulations.

On the basis of our data, and our conclusion that regulation of employer speech did not provide protection for employees but did create unnecessary limitations on union speech and picketing, we suggested a significant deregulation of employer speech. This suggestion was from the first controversial.[7] Our conclusions were praised by some scholars[8] and attacked by others.[9] Most union supporters doubted our factual conclusions and rejected our recommendations on the grounds that they would leave employees with no protection against predatory employers that use threats to thwart unionization efforts.

Amid the flurry of interest, we made our raw data available to William T. Dickens, then an assistant professor at the University of California. After reevaluating our data using probit analysis, a technique that we did not employ, he concluded that "employer threats and actions taken against union supporters, along with written communications, and captive-audience speeches all have statistically significant effects on voting."[10] Insofar as Dickens found that written communications and captive-audience speeches have an effect on voting, his conclusion was consistent with our findings. Dickens also agreed with our conclusion that predisposition determines a great deal of vote: "Workers' disposition toward unions is by far the most important influence on their vote." Workers who signed a card and said they were for the union at that time were considerably more likely to vote union than those who refused to sign a card or those who signed a card but said they were not for the union at that time.[11]

Dickens also concluded that "supervisors talking individually with each worker about an election would lower the probability of the average worker voting union by nearly 13 percent." This conclusion is consistent with John Wilhelm's opinion that one-on-one meetings between supervisors and workers are the employer's most effective tactic. It is used increasingly. Dickens's major conclusion was that a tough, but legal, company campaign would likely have a significant impact: "A set of simulations were run in which every company ran the representative strong campaign, but employed only legal tactics. The results show that the legal tactics probably have a substantial effect."

With respect to illegal speech, Dickens's difference from us is rather small, and it is tentative. His analysis shows that one form of illegal speech—threats made against union supporters—may have a significant effect in discouraging workers from voting union, although its effect is confounded by the effect of actions taken against union supporters.

Dickens's article, in the great tradition of academic reviews, stressed his disagreement with our finding concerning a single aspect of case law and ignores our much greater area of agreement with respect to the great majority of rules under the laboratory-conditions doctrine and the fact that the employer's most effective advantage over the union stems from its ability to give speeches, write letters, and enlist its supervisors to help defeat the union. We responded to Dickens with respect to the area of disagreement.[12] But even if one accepts the validity of Dickens's reevaluation, the issue that it most forcibly presents is not the problem of employer intimidation but the problem of unequal access. An intelligent management representative who studied both *Union Representation Elections: Law and Reality* and Dickens's reevaluation would recognize that an employer's best strategy for defeating unions would be to increase the number of captive-audience speeches and supervisor meetings. This is, in fact, what has since happened.

Among those who rejected our findings were Professors Richard B. Freeman and James L. Medoff in their influential book *What Do Unions Do?*[13] They attribute to us the view that although "company opposition reduced the probability workers would vote union, it did not do so by what they viewed as statistically significant amounts." But our conclusion was not that company opposition did not affect the vote but rather that unfair-labor-practice campaigns were no more successful than legal campaigns. Thus, their comment that our analysis was faulty because "Dickens . . . found that some forms of company opposition do indeed have statistically significant effects" is irrelevant to our conclusion. Freeman and Medoff estimated a significant impact for unfair labor practices—first, they noted that "for every 10 percent change in unfair labor practices per election our estimates suggest that unionization of new workers falls from about three percent to six percent," and second, that "from 1950 to 1980 . . . unfair labor practices per election increased by sixfold." They included a table that records this conclusion but offered no direct cites to studies and no discussion of methodology.[14] It all sounds very scientific, but their charts and tables contain no checkable data source supporting this conclusion.

The case for the efficacy of threats has also been strongly supported in the influential work of Dr. Kate Bronfenbrenner, the director of labor education research at Cornell University, who has done pathbreaking work on organizing techniques and conducted a study of the "impact of plant closings and plant closing threats for a random sample of more than 400 NLRB elections." In her article "Uneasy Terrain: The Impact of Capital Mobility on Workers,

Wages, and Union Organizing," Bronfenbrenner found that "the election win rate associated with campaigns where the employer made plant closing threats is, at 38 percent, significantly lower than the 51 percent win rate found in units where no threats occurred." "The study found that not only are threats of plant closing an extremely pervasive part of employer campaigns, they are also very effective."[15] She found that such threats were even more pervasive and effective after the passage of the North American Free Trade Agreement (NAFTA).

There are, however, two major problems with her report. First, it does not separate illegal threats from those statements protected by the NLRA and the First Amendment. Bronfenbrenner uses the term "threat" more broadly than the Board or the courts: "Given that direct unambiguous threats to close the plant in response to union organizing activity are often found in violation of labor law, most of the employers chose to make their threats indirectly and verbally." Still, according to Bronfenbrenner, "11 percent of the election campaigns with threats included specific unambiguous written threats ranging from newspaper articles, posters, and videos of union plants that had closed, to letters and leaflets which specifically mentioned that the plant would close if the union came in. Another 51 percent involved specific and unambiguous verbal threats such as the employer stating clearly in captive audience meetings that, if the employees voted in favor of union representation, the plant might shut down, or supervisors asking individual workers whether their families were ready to move to Mexico."

Bronfenbrenner gave the following as examples of explicit threats: "One advertisement features [a] picture of a nuclear explosion with the caption, 'There's more than one way to destroy a community. Vote NO.' Another advertisement shows a group of workers standing outside of a plant gate with the sign 'closed' hanging on the gate. The caption reads, 'In the past decade, scores of textile plants have closed in North Carolina. Thousands of workers have lost their jobs. Fieldcrest Cannon lost $41 million last year. Vote NO.'"

Neither of these statements contains anything like a direct threat to retaliate against union supporters. And neither is clearly unlawful.

Most significantly, Bronfenbrenner's fact-finding technique was questionable. She described her fact-finding process as follows: "Lead organizers in these campaigns were mailed surveys asking them a series of questions about bargaining unit demographics, employer characteristics and employer tactics during the organizing campaigns, including questions about plant closings and the threat of plant closings."[16] This is not a methodology likely to lead to accurate results. As discussed above, organizers are unreliable witnesses with respect to the employer's campaign tactics; they tend to exaggerate the harshness and illegality.

This should not be surprising. Lead organizers do not hear the speeches; they get reports on them from union supporters, who are most likely to perceive threats whether they are made or not. If the employees from whom the organizer gets information are inaccurate, the organizer is likely to be misled. For example, in one of the campaigns we studied in which the employees voted against representation after the union had obtained a card majority, the organizer told us that he thought the management campaign was effective in large part because the employer pointed out that employees were subject to arbitrary treatment and unreasonable fines under the international union's constitution. But during postelection interviews, only four employees mentioned this issue—and all of them had voted for the union. The organizer obviously thought that this issue was effective because it stirred up some of his most loyal supporters.

The net result of the combined work of Professors Freeman, Medoff, and Bronfenbrenner has been to leave most pro-union commentators with the conclusion that NLRB elections are lost because of fear heightened by employer threats and the increasing resort to discriminatory discharges. And these studies are regularly cited for their conclusion on this issue. But nothing in their combined work establishes the truth of the conclusion.

If threats do not coerce, why do captive-audience speeches work? Repetition from an authoritative source is important. In addition, employers' arguments are likely to be persuasive to employees, particularly those concerned about the consequences of unionization. The employer can regularly reiterate these arguments, and many employees who are undecided or mildly favorable to the union will never get to hear the union's most effective response. Many employers' typical arguments about unions are not easy to refute, and they are likely to be prepared by a professional who has crafted the arguments in ways that have proved effective with other employees in other elections. For example, as noted earlier, employers regularly seek to exploit the fear of strikes. They announce that they will bargain hard, that they are not required to make concessions, and that the union's only weapon to force concessions is to strike. As Woodruff told me, "The best line the employer has is 'Go ahead and get the union. I don't have to give you anything in negotiations. And all you can do is go on strike and I'm gonna replace you.'" This is not an obviously erroneous argument. It has a basis in law, and the employer's statement that strikers can be permanently replaced is accurate. Thus, without threatening illegal reprisals or a refusal to obey the law, an employer can suggest that voting for the union risks jobs. The employer can also do this by talking about the impact of unionization and increased wages on other enterprises. It can also make allegations about the union that might be troublesome to undecided voters. In a HERE election, for example, the employer could quote government reports and eminent scholars referring to past allegations of corruption.

The employer can also win votes by appealing to loyalty and by suggesting, without making explicit promises, that it understands the employees' desire for improved wages and working conditions and will make an effort to improve things in the future. The message "We hear you, give us another chance" is a powerful one, particularly for employees who are concerned about the consequences of unionization.[17] Unions have arguments to defuse the effect of this employer theme, but often employees do not get to hear them.

The debate over the impact of employer anti-union speech is relevant to the issue of labor-law reform. If management is prevailing primarily because of its advantage in terms of getting its message heard, then the election process can be significantly improved by adding equal-access provisions, together with significantly tougher penalties for discriminatory discharges. If it is fear of reprisal instigated by management speeches that accounts for union election failures, then there is no available remedy. If employees are in fact sensitive to nuances of coercion, then an employer's First Amendment rights will permit it to frighten employees into voting against the union in almost every case, since employers can increase employee fear of reprisal and they can do so without directly, or often even indirectly, threatening workers.

Professor Paul Weiler, in fact, concluded that the only effective way to protect employees against intimidation is by adopting the system used in some Canadian provinces whereby a union is entitled to recognition on the basis of a card majority.[18] This plan is now in the forefront of union advocacy as the Employee Free Choice Act, discussed in chapter 21. Weiler did not, however, deal with the issue of access. But granting unions access to employees on the employer's premises would have a double effect: it would give unions a chance to answer employer arguments, and it would limit the employer's ability to use its normal control of the premises as a union-defeating device.

RETALIATION

The most complex and controversial issue with respect to union organizing is the impact of employer retaliation. According to the prevailing view of unions and union supporters, not only do discharges deprive unions of supporters but they also frighten other employees into voting against representation in order to prevent future acts of retaliation. This was one of the main assumptions that we tested in the Getman-Goldberg-Herman study. We found that discharges during the course of a representation campaign did not significantly affect the voting behavior of employees generally.[19] Professor Dickens's reevaluation seems to differ mildly from our conclusion, although he did not engage in an independent analysis of the issue. But Professor Paul Weiler took the opposite position in his enormously influential article "Promises to Keep."[20] He concluded that discriminatory discharges are ubiquitous and that they are likely the major reason why union density is declining.[21] There has been an ongoing debate about the prevalence of discharges in representative campaigns. With respect to the causal link between these facts, Weiler argued first that "it would seem plausible to suppose the decline in union organizing success . . . was indeed affected by the concurrent rise in discriminatory discharges."

Weiler acknowledged that our findings "pose a major challenge to my argument that discriminatory discharges . . . have significantly contributed to the steep decline in union success." However, he argued that our conclusion was not supported by our data. We had, he argued, overestimated the significance of the lack of a significant correlation between discharge and voting: "It may be legitimate for Getman and his coauthors to conclude that their own data do not demonstrate with certainty that employer coercion affects employee voting, but it is entirely unjustified to infer from that fact alone that the contrary was true." Weiler's point might have been well taken had we simply based our conclusion on the lack of correlation between discharge and voting, but in fact our conclusion was based on a wide variety of different analyses. For example, employees in each election were asked why they had voted for or against union representation. Of 452 employees who voted against unionization, less than 1 percent gave reasons for doing so that were related to unlawful employer campaign tactics; those few were evenly distributed among lawful and unlawful elections. Those who gave reasons other than unlawful campaigning did not attribute the anti-union votes of others to unlawful campaign tactics.

Even assuming that our conclusions were not supported by adequate analysis, Weiler had no empirical support for concluding that discriminatory discharges were a major factor in persuading employees to vote against representation. He sought to overcome this problem with a deft use of academic jujitsu, arguing that our findings actually supported his conclusion. His argument was based on Dickens's reevaluation of our data: "Ironically, then, the raw data that

Getman and his coauthors so carefully gathered point to precisely the opposite conclusion from the one they drew. A protracted representation campaign, punctuated by discriminatory discharges and other reprisals against union supporters, can have a pronounced effect on the ultimate election verdict."

This statement constitutes a significant misreading both of our findings and of Dickens's reanalysis. Since Dickens agrees with us about the importance of intent, job satisfaction, and attitudes toward unions and about the advantage to employers from access to employees, it is totally misleading to suggest that his analysis "point[s] to precisely the opposite conclusion from the one [we] drew." Further, we did not dispute the conclusion that a protracted campaign can have a pronounced effect on the ultimate election verdict. Indeed, that is why we recommended giving unions a chance to respond in kind to employer meetings.

Most significantly at odds with Weiler's argument is the fact that Dickens did not separately analyze the impact of employer retaliation. He actually lumped it together with illegal conduct generally in coming to the conclusion that it might have a small negative impact on organizing. It is noteworthy that Dickens, in his article explaining the demise of unions between 1950 and 1980 published shortly after "Promises to Keep,"[22] does not even mention employer unfair labor practices as an independent variable.[23] The second major factor was "the decline in unions' organizing activity." The least significant of the factors mentioned was success rate, which accounts for only about 17 percent of the decline in unionization. Perhaps the most surprising conclusion reached in this article is that "even if unions had continued to win representation rights for the same percentage of voters in certification elections as they did in 1950–54 (a period of great growth), their share of employment would still have fallen nearly as much as it actually did." In fact, "the percent organized would have fallen even if unions had won every election they were involved in since 1950." This conclusion supports the contention of union commentators like Vinnie Sirabella and John Wilhelm, who stressed the lack of commitment by organized labor to organizing. The issue of how much of labor's money and effort should be devoted to organizing remains a contentious debate within organized labor.[24]

There are newer studies that purport to show that unlawful behavior by employers is widespread and that it is effective. For example, Chirag Mehta and Nik Theodore, of the Center for Urban Economic Development of the University of Illinois at Chicago, issued a report prepared for American Rights at Work in December 2005.[25] Their basic conclusion was that employer interference, characterized by the comprehensive use of various legal and illegal anti-union campaigns, is both pervasive and effective. Among employers faced with organizing campaigns, 30 percent fired workers who engaged in union activities, and 49 percent threatened to close or relocate all or part of the business. Mehta and Theodore announced that "the specific tactics that appear to be most effective at undermining workers' support for unionization include promising to improve workers' wages, offering workers bribes and special favors, and threatening to shift production if workers elect for unionization." They found that 59 percent promised to improve wages, 51 percent offered bribes, and 49 percent threatened to close down.

Unfortunately, however, this study shares the methodological flaws of Bronfenbrenner's work, which the authors cite as a model. It does not have a trustworthy method for establishing what actually happened in the campaigns. Mehta and Theodore's second problem is separating the effect of illegal and legal behavior. Most of the employer themes that they referred to as being regularly used are in fact legal and even legitimate. They say, for example:

> More than 70 percent of employers in the CRC [Chicago Representation Campaign] Survey focused on the following messages in their communication strategy:
> • Give the employer another chance.
> • The union will take you out on strike.
> • Unions charge dues, fines, and assessments.
> • Unions cannot guarantee anything.
> • The union is a third party that interferes in the employment relationship.

These are arguments that the unions expect and that any decent organizer can respond to effectively. Mehta and Theodore have no reliable way of knowing which tactics in fact worked and why.

The most significant empirical study of the impact of illegal behavior following the publication of *Law and Reality* was undertaken by Professor Laura Cooper of the University of Minnesota.[26] She studied a total of 760 elections held between 1978 and 1980 in a single region. The overall success rate of unions during the period of the study was 48.2 percent, and employer unfair labor practices were found in 53 (7 percent) of the elections conducted. The employer was found to have violated section 8(a)(3) of the NLRA by discriminating against union supporters, mostly through discriminatory discharges, in 21 cases. The Board found section 8(a)(1) violations (typically threats or interrogation) in 36 cases. Professor Cooper found the following with respect to the relationship between unfair labor practices and voting:

In elections in which employer unfair labor practices occurred, the union lost less support than it did in clean elections, although this difference is not statistically significant. . . . The results provide no support for the NLRB's assumption that employer unfair labor practices substantially decrease union support. In close elections, where unfair labor practices were committed, unions gained an average of 7.9 percent; yet where no unfair labor practices were committed, unions lost an average of 8.1 percent of their support. . . . The evidence is completely contrary to the Board's assumption that employer unfair labor practices cause unions to lose support. Of course, this study provided no means to ascertain why employer unfair labor practices tended to increase support for the union in these elections. Nevertheless, one can speculate that perhaps employees, rather than being intimidated out of voting for the union by the employer's actions, considered such actions further cause for seeking the protection of a union.[27]

She concluded that "the results here substantially replicate the conclusions of the Getman, Goldberg, and Herman study of election behavior, which found that unions 'did not lose significantly more support in unlawful elections than in clean elections' and that employees 'who intended to vote union were more likely to report unlawful campaign tactics than employees who intended to vote company.'"

Professor Cooper's conclusion about the law's irrelevance was supported by Richard Bensinger, a former director of the AFL-CIO Organizing Institute, who testified before the Commission on the Future of Worker-Management Relations (often referred to as the Dunlop Commission) that "under current law any employer who expends maximum (and even not so maximum) effort to defeat a union campaign can win, any time anywhere."[28] D. Taylor, the highly successful leader of the Culinary Workers Union, told me that an employer can win an election "by scaring them to death or by loving them to death." Tom Woodruff agrees.

BOARD REMEDIES

In remedying preelection misconduct, the Board under current law has a variety of ineffective options. The first and most widely used is setting aside the election and ordering the employer to post a notice saying that it will not interfere with employee rights in the future. This response is essentially meaningless because the employer continues to have unilateral control over wages, hours, and conditions of employment. When the employer punishes employees for supporting the union, the Board can order its action set aside and the status quo restored. When discharge is involved, the remedy of reinstatement has turned out to be too slow, too uncertain, and not sufficiently costly to deter; discharge also leaves the affected employees too vulnerable. Employers can challenge the Board's finding of discrimination in the courts of appeals. The process takes years, and the courts have regularly rejected the Board's factual conclusion that a discharge was based on union activity and not, as the employer claimed, on misconduct.[29]

If a member of the inside organizing committee is discharged, the union can file charges on that employee's behalf. But unless the union files a request to proceed, the election will be halted until the charges are investigated and, if appropriate, validly remedied. This may take years; the additional time between organization and election will almost surely be used to dissipate the union's majority. If the union requests that the Board proceed with the election, it loses the support and the vote of the discharged employees who, according to studies, are unlikely ever to work for the employer again. In addition, it is likely that the possibility of discharge, which is well known to employees, has a general impact that makes workers fearful of getting involved with unions in the first place. Thus, the policy of protecting employees against discriminatory discharges remains a matter of simple justice for employees and important to the success of the statute.

If the NLRA is to be rehabilitated, it must provide quicker and stiffer penalties for acts of retaliation in general and discriminatory discharges in particular. There is no reason why discharges during an organizing campaign should be treated less seriously than secondary boycotts. If the Board after a quick investigation believes it likely that an employee was discharged for union activity (which should be the presumption), the Board should be able to obtain an injunction ordering that employee back to work. If the employer is found guilty of a discriminatory discharge, the Board should invoke a heavy penalty—treble damages. Repeat violators should be denied the right to enter into government contracts.

The most seemingly powerful, and controversial, of the Board's remedies is the bargaining order. In *NLRB v Gissel Packing Co.,*[30] the Supreme Court held that the Board could order an employer to bargain with a union in cases in which the union at one time had a majority that was dissipated by extensive unfair labor practices. As the Court asserted, "If the Board finds that the possibility of erasing the effects of past practices and of ensuring a fair election . . . is slight and that employee sentiment once expressed through cards would, on balance, be better protected by a bargaining order, then such an order should issue."

Once again, the standard is vague and the factual determinations required are far beyond the ability of the Board to make with any degree of certainty—and far beyond the ability of the courts to review. What has happened in practice has been a marked variation in the issuance of bargaining orders by the Board depending on its political orientation and a general reluctance of courts to affirm the Board's order because the bargaining order is always in opposition to expressed employee choice. Bargaining orders are inevitably challenged and regularly denied by the courts of appeals, very often on the grounds that the Board's fact-finding was perfunctory, as indeed it always is since the Board lacks the ability to make specific findings with regard to impact or lasting effect. When they are issued, bargaining orders almost never lead to a stable bargaining relationship.

The bargaining-order remedy has been a prolific source of litigation, and it has spawned a great deal of scholarly writing.[31] It is unlikely, however, that this remedy has significantly affected labor relations. Bargaining orders are issued on behalf of unions that do not represent a current majority long after the organizing campaign has ended. These unions generally do not have the ability to bargain effectively because they cannot, credibly, threaten to strike. Sometimes they do not even try to bargain; other times the bargaining is likely to fail to produce an agreement or to lead to an agreement in which the employer's power to act unilaterally is maintained. Professor Weiler, in "Promises to Keep," explained why: "What can the union do with the bargaining order? Although the order requires the employers to sit down at the negotiating table and go through the motions of trying to reach an agreement, the governing principle of freedom of contract under the NLRA means that the employer is not required to consent to any significant changes in working conditions. The Board cannot direct the employer to make a reasonable contract offer. If a decent employment package is to be extracted from a recalcitrant employer, it must come through the efforts of the workers themselves."[32]

What the studies indicate is that an employer can in most cases thwart unionization through a combination of captive-audience speeches and delay. It is in a position to help its case by manipulating the unit. Further, a union victory is nowhere near a guarantee that the union will obtain a favorable contract. A recalcitrant employer can easily refuse agreement and force a union to either strike or submit to its demands. In either case, the union is likely to be gone when the dust settles.

Part IV **The Strike Weapon**

Chapter 18 Restructuring the Strike Weapon

Strikes, protest marches, job actions, civil disobedience, and slow-downs are all parts of comprehensive campaigns. These actions require worker solidarity to be successful.

Solidarity is made up of comradeship, commitment, and belief. Comradeship is the sense of mutual trust and common destiny that joins the participants. Strikes and their hardships often breed comradeship. The terms "brother" and "sister" regularly used at union meetings take on a deep, heartfelt significance. Commitment refers to the willingness of workers to devote their time, skill, effort, and passion to the struggle. Belief refers to the idea that struggle is intended to achieve ideals broader and more profound than the economic interests of the strikers. It is reflected in the union rallying cry "an injury to one is an injury to all." Important strikes transcend the immediate and inevitably imbue the strikers with the feeling that what they do will affect the lives of working people generally.[1]

Solidarity can be an overwhelming force. Workers have sacrificed their jobs, their homes, even their lives in its name. That is why there is no term so revered in the ranks of organized labor. People proclaim it in their dress, sing about it in union songs, and often end their letters to each other "In Solidarity." One of the fundamental responsibilities of union leaders during the difficult times of sacrifice and loss is to maintain the spirit of solidarity with which strikes are normally begun.

Solidarity is the inside component of union success. There is an outside component as well. Unions today need allies in both organizing and collective bargaining. It is no longer the case (if it ever was) that strikes can be won at a single facility by withholding labor and persuading customers and truck drivers to honor a picket line. Powerful corporations can almost invariably continue to operate despite the presence of a picket line at one or even several facilities. Some unions have, as a result, essentially abandoned the strike weapon.[2] But strikes can be won by unions using a mix of solidarity and outreach.

The six-year, four-month strike at the Frontier Hotel required an unusual combination of solidarity and outside support. Solidarity remained so strong that in 76 months not a single striker crossed the line despite physical attacks and secret offers. Credit for this achievement belongs to the strikers themselves and their understanding of the importance of their strike. But the leaders of HERE and the Culinary Workers Union also deserve credit as do members and leaders of other unions who went out of their way to make sure that the strikers never felt abandoned. The members of the nonstriking units of the Culinary doubled their dues to provide livable strike benefits to the Frontier workers. Thousands of union people—teachers, ironworkers, steelworkers, municipal workers, teamsters, people of every color and ethnicity—walked the picket line with them.

During one march, 6,000 green-clad union members of the American Federation of State, County, and Municipal Employees (AFSCME), led by the union's national president Gerald McEntee, marched through the streets of Las Vegas to join with the strikers. The picketers were fed free of charge by supporters, and additional donations of food and money were made by the United Food and Commercial Workers. The AFL-CIO held one of its conventions in Las Vegas during the strike, and the strikers marched into the hall to the cheers of the delegates. AFL-CIO president Linda Chavez Thompson felt "enveloped" by the feeling that "this was my strike."

The Frontier strikers knew that they were doing something momentous. Some later said that they would miss the picket line. That is why a striker declared toward the end of the strike, "This experience has changed me spiritually, mentally, and morally."[3] She spoke, I believe, for all the activists. This is not to say that the six years of the strike did not take an awful toll. The strikers all had their moments of depression. But in the end, solidarity, combined with political pressure and public support, won out.

The 1987–1988 paperworkers strike by Local 14 of the United Paperworkers International Union in Jay, Maine, against International Paper Company demonstrates that comprehensive campaigns can be effective even when used by an isolated local union battling a Goliath company.[4] The campaign that Local 14 waged was all the more remarkable because the tactical innovations were often improvised and spontaneous.[5]

The strike might well have ended in an easy victory for International Paper, the largest paper company in the world and the largest landowner in the United States. The company had trained lawyers, a large human-resources staff, and a well-funded public-relations department. Local 14 had $15,000 in its treasury and a cadre of angry, confused members who, at the start of their strike, knew little about strike tactics beyond the need to maintain a picket line and threaten replacement workers.

The comprehensive campaign was developed largely by an outsider, Peter Kellman, who had learned organizational strategy during his years in the civil-rights movement. Kellman was a "red-diaper baby" raised to be an activist. He is an intellectual but also a worker. He left college in the 1960s and traveled to the South to register voters. He worked in factories and paper mills in the 1970s. During the 1980s he worked as a machine operator in a shoe factory, did construction work at a saw mill, and was a painter at various paper mills. He was hired to advise the local by the Maine AFL-CIO just before the strike began.

Kellman's approach was remarkably similar to that used by HERE—a combination of internal organizing and community outreach. He began by transforming anger and confusion into activity. He and Local 14 president Bill Meserve made sure that everyone they could recruit had a specific role to play. One of his first moves was to enlist Louise Parker, once a semiprofessional country singer, telling her that "with every fight, you need music to uplift people." She became a regular part of the union's Wednesday-night public meetings, developing a repertoire of union songs and recruiting other musicians into a group known as the Union Picketers.

Brent Gay, one of the strikers, later told me, "He [Kellman] was great at getting people to do things. In fact, we had something called being 'Kellmanized,' which meant you suggested something, and then all of a sudden you were in charge of the project." Within a few months, the union had amassed a new phalanx of committed activists. Many had never before taken an interest in its affairs. One of them was Ruth Lebel: "I knew I was paying dues, that there were those that walked around saying they represented us, but I wasn't involved. But the first time I was ever in the hall, Peter was there. All you gotta do is hang around Peter for a little while and it's contagious. All of a sudden I got caught up in that sense of togetherness. Then I started going down to the union hall every day, and I really got caught up in it." Lebel and several others became effective in working with the media, which by the end of the strike had come to trust them far more than they trusted the company's public-relations officials.

Many of the activities for which the strikers were recruited involved developing new skills, which, once learned, provided a strategically important ego boost. The constant activity and excitement fed the developing feeling of solidarity, which was enhanced by the union's regular raucous Wednesday-night public meetings. Through these meetings, the entire community became aware of the union's activities and learned of its victories and shared its concerns. Kellman later told me that it was "teaching the labor movement what I learned from the civil-rights movement that they learned from the labor movement."[6]

The strikers became more and more active in union and community-based activities. Ray Pineau, a Vietnam veteran who later served in the Maine legislature, found the strike to be a turning point in his life. He told me, "Someone did a study at one point, and found out that over eight hundred of our members were active doing something. Something like thirty retired, so that left hardly anybody not doing anything. We had an army like Peter speaks of, eight hundred people out there pounding the streets."

With its members mobilized, the union went on the offensive on a whole range of nonlabor issues. The one with the most bite was the claim that the mill as run by the replacement workers was an environmental menace. The offensive began when the members of the local's health-and-safety committee made a trip to the Maine Department of Environmental Protection to protest International Paper's waste-disposal practices and the department's failure to be more vigorous in policing the company's practices.

As union vice president Robby Lucarelli told me, "You know what got the most general support? It wasn't that a big company was shitting on a small union or wages or anything. The thing that got the most general public sympathy is environmental issues that affected everybody. We exposed IP's [International Paper's] pollution; the general public doesn't like that."

As the strike progressed, the workers' sense of their cause broadened. A speech by Jesse Jackson, who was invited by Kellman, was the crucial event in this transformation. The theme struck by Jackson was that the strike was part of a broader struggle for fairness and dignity that united Local 14 with all who struggle against oppression. This feeling was illustrated eloquently in a letter that Louise Parker sent to union members at a nonstriking mill: "We have a saying in Jay. 'Whatever it takes for as long as it takes.' This saying comes from our hearts to all people who are struggling for fairness, dignity and justice, union and non-union alike."

Local 14's regular Wednesday-night meetings became famous throughout New England. After the first few months, Local 14 had to limit the number of speakers at the meetings and the amount of time they could talk. So many visitors showed up that they had to be brought to the podium en masse to receive the traditional standing ovation. It became the place to be for liberal students in New England. Amy Carter, then a student at Brown University, showed up with two friends on December 18, 1987. She sat in the bleachers until near the end of the meeting when, "cheered and finally coaxed to the stage, she said, 'This applause is misplaced. You shouldn't be thanking me—I should be thanking you.'" The structure of the meetings increasingly resembled the civil-rights rallies that Kellman had attended in the 1960s. The audience arrived to the music of the Union Picketers. When the speaking ended, everyone rose and, led by Louise Parker, sang "Solidarity Forever" while holding hands and swaying back and forth. Years after the strike, Joan Fuller, a schoolteacher whose husband and son were both strikers, wrote in response to my questionnaire, "I cannot hear 'Solidarity Forever' without crying."

At Kellman's urging, the union submitted a series of proposals to the Jay selectmen to be voted on at a town meeting in August 1987.[7] The most significant of these was an ordinance that required town officials to enforce federal and state environmental laws. Paper mills in Maine historically operated with an unstated exemption from environmental law, but the mill could be shut down or substantially fined if the town were to start enforcing the law.

The ordinances were presented to a town meeting and quickly passed. International Paper challenged the ordinances in federal court, claiming that they violated federal labor law and were intended to make the town a party to the labor dispute. The court upheld the right of the town to pass an environmental ordinance that simply restated federal standards.[8] Kellman quickly spread the word about it to various mill towns where union members and their supporters had political power. The other major paper companies in Maine became increasingly concerned and pressured International Paper to settle the strike, according to town attorney Mike Gentile.

Local 14's health-and-safety committee drew the attention of state and federal agencies to environmental, health, and safety problems at the mill.[9] Because the mill was being operated by untrained personnel working under great stress, a large number of incidents occurred. The union's media committee saw to it that these incidents were brought to the attention of newspaper, radio, and television reporters.[10]

The leadership of Local 14 learned the dynamics of the comprehensive campaign, even though they would not have been familiar with the term. In November 1987, the local leadership demanded that Ray Rogers, generally considered the father of the corporate campaign, be hired to assist them. The national union leadership was not happy with this turn of events but was in no position to openly take on Local 14, which had by then become a symbol of steadfast solidarity to the union's national membership. Rogers undertook a campaign aimed at forcing one or more of International Paper's board members to resign. It failed to achieve its goal, but it brought publicity, money, and increased activism to the union.

The Metevier brothers, Armand and Maurice, became especially active during the corporate campaign. Maurice, who had once prided himself on being a "company man," found his new activities liberating:

> For me to be involved with it was a great honor. We were always asked who picked you, and I'd say nobody picked me. I picked me. I wasn't very articulate till the strike. I'm a loner, [a] very quiet individual. I discovered that I could speak to people. It was a high. The people we talked to couldn't understand. We shouldn't be so happy. Bullshit. I hadn't had this much fun in a long time. I listened to a woman of Chinese origin speaking of the troubles of her family life and how she felt about unionism. At one rally we were entertained by Yiddish musicians. We stayed at a railroad striker's sister's house; he lost everything he had but still wanted to help. We stayed with socialists, were put up by a woman and her son in Jamaica Plain in Boston. She lived on a meager income but put my brother-in-law and myself up for two days and gave us five dollars for the cause when we left. We met some terrific people on the caravan. The three months I traveled on the caravan was the most enjoyable and memorable parts of the strike for me.

In the end, the comprehensive campaign was called off by the union's national leaders, and the strike ended. That should have been the end of the battle—the union was defeated and without continuing support or any apparent way to apply pressure on International Paper. But in fact, solidarity and anger, together with the workers' new tactical sophistication, gave the battle a momentum that continued well after the strike officially ended.

When the strike ended, the replacement workers remained on the job but, under the *Laidlaw* doctrine,[11] the former strikers were placed on a list by seniority for returning to the mill.[12] A year after the strike had ended roughly one hundred had been recalled. They continued the struggle by refusing to share their know-how with the replacement workers and by denying the company the benefit of their experience and ingenuity. They even published an underground newspaper. Those former strikers who had been active in the campaigns never adjusted to the defeat.

Bruce Moran, a millwright, explained to me, "Every time you see a brother or sister that hasn't got their job back, you feel a very sick feeling, knowing the only way they will get their job is if a scab dies or quits." Laurier Poulin, who was the last person to walk the picket line, left the mill in 1993:

> I just retired last spring. And one of the scabs said, "You gonna shake my hand before you leave?"
>
> And I said, "No, I didn't shake your hand when I came here, and I sure as hell am not gonna do it on the way out."
>
> He said, "What are you gonna do, carry it to the grave?"
>
> I says, "Yep, I told my wife to put it right in the paper, in the obituaries. I want it in my obituary that I'm not a scab."

Inevitably, the continuing hostility affected productivity. In fact, the mill lost money regularly after the strike. The manager of human resources in January 1989 agreed that "things were in a state of total upheaval."

Thus, in the aftermath of the strike, a once-profitable enterprise became a financial and labor-relations disaster. John Georges, the CEO of International Paper, concluded that the labor policy that led to the replacement of the strikers was a major mistake that cost the company over a billion dollars.

For the next decade, the strike was the subject of many articles and books, almost all critical of International Paper. Not only did the union cooperate with scholars and reporters interested in telling the story of the strike but the strikers, under Peter Kellman's leadership, published *Pain on Their Faces,* a book of their experiences.[13]

Ten years after the strike, the University of Southern Maine held a conference to reappraise the strike. The conference was more like a strike rally than an academic discussion and was highlighted by an impromptu statement from the daughter of a striker, now a student at the university, explaining how proud she was of her father for remaining loyal to the union.

In the aftermath of the strike, the union underwent a series of changes. It merged first with the Oil, Chemical, and Atomic Workers Union to become

PACE (the Paper, Allied-Industrial, Chemical, and Energy Workers International Union), which then merged with and became a branch of the United Steelworkers. Anger and hostility continued to mark relations at the mill during this time.[14]

The continuing struggle finally caused International Paper to change course. The transformation was explained to me by Richard LaCosse, vice president of the Steelworkers:

> John Feracci, who was the CEO of IP, contacted Leo Gerard, who was the president of the Steelworkers, and congratulated him on the merger and said that he'd like to get together at some point in time and just have a chat—visit about where things were and where they might be able to go. That first initial meeting took place in Pittsburgh. I was at that meeting, and it was a productive meeting. Leo Gerard told them in no uncertain terms that he was not looking for a fight but they would never, ever do to our merged union what they did to the UPIU [United Paperworkers International Union]: "John, I want to tell you, you will never do that to us as a merged union. It will never ever happen again." Feracci said that he was at the helm now and that he wanted a better relationship.
>
> At that meeting we agreed to get together again, which we did—that's when the bargaining process began for a master understanding or a master agreement. And so, after a year of bargaining, we had put together a proposal for the locals, and we brought it back to them. It passed by a very significant margin. It granted successor language to every local union in the event the facility was sold; the contract had to go with the sale. That was a very strong must-have for us. We raised the health care from a 75-25 cost sharing to an 80-20 cost sharing. We got a big hit for us in pensions. There was language put in place for wage rationalizations. Some of their facilities were acquired where their wage rates were way, way out of whack. And we agreed that we would have new hires come in at a uniform rate, a better rate that made more sense.[15]

There is no doubt that the new positive agreement was the result of the long comprehensive campaign conducted by the Jay workers. Although most of the Jay strikers never got their jobs back, they ultimately won a victory for their union brothers and sisters all over the country.

Chapter 19 Strikes, Picketing, Comprehensive Campaigns, and the Law

THE STRIKE WEAPON

The drafters of the Wagner Act of 1935 (the original NLRA) intended to create a rough equality between the economic power of employers and unions. To achieve this goal, they legalized the strike. The right to strike was proclaimed in two different sections of the Act. Section 7 empowered employees to "engage in . . . concerted activities for the purpose of collective bargaining or other mutual aid"; interference with this right by employers was made an unfair labor practice. Section 13 specified that "nothing in this Act . . . shall be construed so as either to interfere with or impede or diminish in any way the right to strike."

Despite its importance to the policies of the NLRA over the seventy-plus years of the Act's existence, the strike weapon has been consistently weakened by congressional amendment and judicial decision.

Judicial weakening of the right to strike began soon after the Act's passage. In 1938, in *NLRB v. Mackay Radio & Telegraph Co.*,[1] the

Supreme Court announced that the NLRA did not prevent employers from hiring permanent replacements to take the jobs of the striking workers. The *Mackay* doctrine, as it is known, means that workers who exercise their right to strike risk losing their jobs. The *Mackay* Court neither explained its rationale nor justified its result.[2] Although the result was consistent with the NLRB's expectations,[3] had the Court undertaken a careful analysis of the issue in terms of the policies of section 7, together with those of sections 8(a)(1) and (3), it might well have come out differently or at least qualified its holding. A very strained use of language is required to conclude that hiring permanent replacements does not "interfere" with section 7 rights, which is made an unfair labor practice by section 8(a)(1), or that it is not unlawful discrimination under section 8(a)(3), which prohibits "discrimination in regard to hire or tenure of employment or any term or condition of employment to encourage or discourage membership in any labor organization."

Whatever legal justification existed for the dictum at the time was later rejected by the Court.[4] In later cases construing section 8(a)(3), the Court developed a system of analysis that if applied would clearly establish the illegality of hiring permanent strike replacements. The decision most relevant to strike replacement is *NLRB v Erie Resistor Corp.*[5] The company in that case granted superseniority to replacement workers. It claimed that its action did not violate section 8(a)(3) because it was motivated by business considerations and not by anti-union sentiments. The Board rejected this argument, explaining that "to excuse such conduct would greatly diminish, if not destroy, the right to strike guaranteed by the Act, and would run directly counter to the guarantees of Sections 8(a)(1) and (3) that employees shall not be discriminated against for engaging in protected concerted activities."

The Supreme Court specifically rejected the employer's argument that the Board had to make a finding about motive: "His conduct does speak for itself —it is discriminatory and it does discourage union membership, and, whatever the claimed overriding justification may be, it carries with it unavoidable consequences."[6] The Court pointed out the ways in which the grant of superseniority discouraged union activity. Every factor that the Court listed applies with at least equal force to the hiring of permanent strike replacements. For example, the Court mentioned that a superseniority award "necessarily operates to the detriment of those who participated in the strike as compared to nonstrikers." Surely, the hiring of permanent replacements does the same, only more strongly.

The Supreme Court addressed the proper method for analyzing employer responses to strikes, under section 8(a)(3), once again a few years later in *NLRB v Great Dane Trailers, Inc.*[7] The employer in that case denied vacation pay to former strikers. The Court upheld the Board's finding of a violation. Purporting to distill the essence of its previous opinions dealing with section 8(a)(3), the Court announced "several principles of controlling importance": "First, if it can reasonably be concluded that the employer's discriminatory conduct was 'inherently destructive' of important employee rights, no proof of an anti-union motivation is needed, and the Board can find an unfair labor practice even if the employer introduces evidence that the conduct was motivated by business considerations. Second, if the adverse effect of the discriminatory conduct on employee rights is 'comparatively slight,' an anti-union motivation must be proved to sustain the charge if the employer has come forward with evidence of legitimate and substantial business justifications for the conduct."

Since there is no action more "inherently destructive of important employee rights" than the hiring of permanent replacement workers to take the jobs of strikers, it seems clear that if the *Mackay* doctrine were evaluated by current 8(a)(3) standards, the hiring of permanent replacements would constitute a violation. Nevertheless, the Court has continued to treat the right to hire permanent replacements as settled law. Thus, an ancient dictum controls the law despite its inconsistency with both the language and policy of the NLRA.

PARTIAL STRIKES

The *Mackay* doctrine, together with the law's general concern with the protection of property rights, makes most strikes risky for the union and the workers. Powerful corporations can almost invariably continue to operate despite the presence of a picket line at one or even several facilities. They can hire permanent replacements and reassign workers and managers from other facilities. They can obtain injunctions against mass picketing, and they can fire strikers who resort to violence on the picket line. As a result of all these obstacles, many unions have largely abandoned the strike weapon. And when strikes do occur, they are often intentionally provoked by management, which seeks to use them as a way of ousting or taming unions.

Unions have sought to find ways other than striking to exert economic pressure on employers. John Wilhelm believes that partial strikes such as slowdowns (working strictly according to the employer's rules) and sick-outs, or what HERE calls "work and walk," which do not involve walking off the job, can be very effective techniques for unions. These campaigns, if they can be conducted over a long period, put pressure on the employer but do not require giving up salary or health benefits. When the Yale strikers returned to work in December 1984 they explained, "We're bringing the strike inside." The administration found this possibility more unnerving than the threat of a conventional strike and soon made proposals that led to an agreement.

Such tactics can be effective, but their legal status is tenuous. Generally, partial strikes are thought to be unprotected by section 7, so employees found to be engaged in such activity can be immediately fired—even without the hiring of replacement workers. That is why HERE's official position is to discourage such tactics.[8]

There is no persuasive reason why partial strikes should be unprotected.[9] As concerted actions for mutual aid and protection, partial strikes fit easily under the language of section 7. Jeff Fielder's explanation for the questionable status of a partial strike under the NLRA is that "all this shit's outlawed because it's effective." In fact, the law is not as clear as Fiedler suggests. Early in the Act's history, the Supreme Court in *Automobile Workers Local 232 v. Wisconsin Employment Relations Board* (commonly known as the *Briggs-Stratton* case)[10] held that partial strikes were not protected concerted activity under section 7. But the assumption on which that decision rested was that employers could not protect themselves against intermittent work stoppages since at that time it was generally thought that lockouts were illegal. But today the employer can respond to partial strikes and job actions by locking out the workers and turning the battle into a primary strike.

In recognition of the changing legal landscape with regard to employer action, the Supreme Court in *Lodge 76, International Association of Machinists & Aerospace Workers v. Wisconsin Employment Relations Commission*[11] invited the NLRB to reexamine the status of partial strike activity: "It may be that case-by-case adjudication by the federal Board will ultimately result in the conclusion that some partial strike activities . . . are 'protected activities.'" The Board has been slow to accept this invitation as a general matter. The Board should reexamine this issue and recognize that partial strikes are within the language of, and supported by the policy of, section 7.

SECONDARY BOYCOTTS

To overcome the current weakness of the traditional single-unit strike in dealing with huge multifacility enterprises, unions today—especially those like HERE and the SEIU, which use comprehensive-campaign tactics—seek to spread the conflict to other locations where the employer is doing business. This is what HERE did in its battle against the Las Vegas Hilton in 1984 and against the MGM Grand a decade later. The effort to spread the field of battle is an application of Jeff Fiedler's conclusion that even major companies are not prepared to deal with multiple simultaneous strikes. This was a tactic widely used in the first years of the NLRA from 1935 to 1947. It was understood that employees in different facilities had a legitimate mutual interest in each other's success.

However, the policy of mutual reciprocal solidarity contained in section 7 was severely limited in 1947 when Congress passed the Taft-Hartley amendments to the NLRA.[12] The Taft-Hartley Act added union unfair labor practices to the NLRA; the most significant was section 8(b)(4), which was intended to prohibit secondary boycotts—although it did not actually use the term. The concept of secondary boycotts is a vague one. In general, it refers to a union applying economic pressure on a primary employer—the one whose labor policies the union is contesting. In secondary-boycott situations, the employer being pressured has some dealing—either as a customer, distributor, or supplier —with the primary employer, which puts it in a position to harm the primary employer by withdrawing its business or services. If the primary employer manufactures widgets, the secondary might sell widgets or supply parts for their manufacture.

Essentially, there are three types of activity prohibited by section 8 (b)(4): refusals by secondary employees to do their jobs; appeals to secondary employees to refuse to do their jobs; and appeals to customers not to patronize the secondary employer. The first two situations are covered by section 8(b)(4)(i), which makes it an unfair labor practice for a union "to engage in, or to induce . . . any [employee] to engage in, a strike or a refusal . . . to . . . transport, or otherwise handle or work on any goods, . . . or to perform any services." Appeals to the public not to patronize are dealt with under (8)(b)(4)(ii), which makes it an unfair labor practice "to threaten, coerce, or restrain any person" for the purpose of disrupting relations between two employers.

During the strike by the Paperworkers against International Paper Company, if the strikers had picketed at Office Depot stores and appealed to employees of Office Depot not to stack, handle, or sell International Paper products, that would have been a violation of section 8(b)(4)(i). If they had picketed customer entrances and urged those intending to enter the store to shop elsewhere until Office Depot stopped selling International Paper products, they would have been in violation of section (8)(b)(4)(ii).

However, in two important cases the Supreme Court, motivated by constitutional concerns, limited the reach of section (8)(b)(4)(ii) and permitted unions to appeal to consumers. The first decision was *NLRB v. Fruit & Vegetable Packers & Warehousemen Local 760* (known among labor lawyers as the *Tree Fruits* decision).[13] The Court held that consumer picketing limited to persuading consumers not to buy the struck product did not "coerce or restrain." Writing for the Court, Justice William J. Brennan said that Congress was concerned only with "consumer picketing to shut off all trade with the secondary employer," which "is poles apart from such picketing which only persuades his customers not to buy the struck product."[14] The ability of unions to enlist aid from consumers was greatly strengthened in *Edward J. DeBartolo Corp. v. Florida Gulf Coast Building & Construction Trades Council*,[15] in which the Court held that distributing handbills, as opposed to picketing, is not coercive and therefore not covered by section (8)(b)(4)(ii). The result of these opinions is to make it legal for unions to seek support from customers of primary or secondary employers through refusals to patronize—something that is frequently done in comprehensive campaigns. On the other hand, unions are forbidden to seek aid from secondary employees. This is a major reason why, as noted earlier, the comprehensive campaign is more effective if the target employer is vulnerable to consumer appeals and union-instigated boycotts.

Although appeals to consumers can now generally be achieved by well-counseled unions, the law continues to forbid unions to make or seek to make common cause with each other during a strike. This creates a major obstacle to combined action. The law dealing with secondary boycotts is highly technical and riddled with confusing doctrinal twists. It is common for unions to violate it inadvertently. If they do, under section 303 of the NLRA, they are liable in damages to any party injured through their actions.

During the 1950s and 1960s, secondary-boycott law had only a limited effect on the ability of unions to strike effectively. Most employers were individual entities that could not withstand the loss of profits and productivity that came with a strike. Unions could often win strikes through an effective picket line at the premises of the struck employer. Generally, faced with a unified strike, an employer would be forced to shut down. If it attempted to continue operations with replacement workers, crossovers, or supervisors, productivity was bound to suffer and its operations were likely to be hurt significantly by the refusal of organized teamsters to make pickups and deliveries. But today, the struck employer is likely to be part of a conglomerate that can increase productivity elsewhere. It can more easily acquire replacement workers through what are known as "rat contractors." And the Teamsters are smaller and weaker. Its members no longer have the contractual option of refusing pickups and deliveries. As a result, comprehensive campaigns, in which the union broadens the locus of its activities, are often necessary if the union is to have a chance of victory.

THE COMPREHENSIVE CAMPAIGN
AND SECTION (8)(B)(7)

Under Jimmy Hoffa's leadership, the Teamsters would frequently organize small employers by picketing them, or more often by threatening to picket, until they agreed to sign up their workers. Congress referred to this technique as "blackmail picketing." In 1959 the Landrum-Griffin amendments to the NLRA attempted to outlaw this tactic. The new section 8(b)(7) made it an unfair labor practice for unions "to picket or . . . threaten to picket or cause to be picketed, any employer where an object thereof is forcing or requiring an employer to recognize or bargain with a labor organization . . . or forcing or requiring the employees . . . to accept or select such labor organization as their collective bargaining representative."

The section's prohibition against organizational picketing is eased by paragraph (C), which gives a union up to thirty days to picket in most situations before it is in violation of the Act. One of the lurking questions in connection with the legal status of comprehensive campaigns is whether peaceful picketing seeking a neutrality agreement and card-check recognition comes within the prohibitions of section (8)(b)(7). Unions have a strong case in arguing that it does not. Employees are not "forced or required" to select a union under a card-check agreement. They still must decide whether to sign a card. And the employer is not forced to bargain—only to accept the decision if a majority of its employees indicate their desire for a union. Nevertheless, during George W. Bush's presidency, the Board's general counsel, in a case against the SEIU and the Justice for Janitors program, took the position that section (8)(b)(7) does apply:

> Union picketing of an unorganized employer, which has as its goal either the organization of the employer's employees, or voluntary recognition by the employer, violates Section 8(b)(7)(C) when it is conducted without an election petition being filed within a reasonable period of time from its commencement, not to exceed 30 days. In determining whether union picketing is for an object proscribed by Section 8(b)(7)(C), the Board considers the totality of the circumstances. Recognition

or organization need not be the sole object of picketing for a violation of Section 8(b)(7)(C) to arise; rather it need only be one of the reasons for the picketing.

As a threshold matter, we agree with the Region that the Union had an organizational and recognitional object. Thus, "an" object of the Union conduct was obtaining a neutrality agreement from the Employer to assist the Union in its effort to organize the Employer's employees and to ultimately obtain recognition. While the agreement urged by the Union would not require immediate recognition, as evidenced by the sample agreements provided to the Employer, such an agreement would require the Employer to give up its right to an election and to recognize the Union if presented with a verified card majority. Such an ultimate recognitional object is proscribed by Section 8(b)(7)(C).[16]

It seems likely that this determination will be overturned, either by the general counsel or by the Board itself, once President Obama's appointees rule on the issue. However, there is no telling what the courts will do if the issue comes before them. Even if picketing for card-check and neutrality agreements is ultimately held by the courts to fall within the recognitional and representational purposes regulated by section (8)(b)(7), it is possible for unions applying pressure for card check to avoid violating the section. The simplest way would be to leaflet and not picket. Another technique for unions is to limit their picketing to thirty days, which of course limits the potential reach and time of the comprehensive campaign. A union can also generally avoid the application of section (8)(b)(7) by structuring its picketing so that it has another apparent objective, such as to protest against employer actions. Of course, the Board and the courts may conclude that despite the language of their picket signs, the real objective remains recognitional or organizational. Activist unions like HERE would therefore welcome a conclusion from the Board, upheld by the courts, that picketing for a card-check agreement is not covered by section (8)(b)(7). This is probably an area in which conservative and liberal Boards will fundamentally differ as long as the statute remains unamended.

THE CONSTITUTIONAL STATUS OF LABOR PICKETING

Both section 8(b)(4) and section 8(b)(7) exist on the thin edge of constitutionality. They each make it unlawful for unions to use picketing in circumstances in which other types of appeals would be constitutionally protected. They rest in significant part on the conclusion that labor picketing is uniquely coercive.

The constitutional status of labor picketing has a long, confusing history. In 1940 the Supreme Court, in *Thornhill v Alabama*,[17] struck down an Alabama statute that prohibited picketing for the purpose of furthering a boycott. The Court's opinion, which was direct and unqualified, said that labor speech was an important part of public discussion and that labor picketing was constitutionally protected. But the Court quickly retreated from its reasoning in *Thornhill*, upholding state laws outlawing organizational picketing, on the grounds that picketing as used by labor unions is both speech and a technique of coercion. This concept was expressed most famously by Justice William O. Douglas in *Bakery & Pastry Drivers & Helpers Local 802 v. Wohl*:[18] "Picketing by an organized group is more than free speech, since it involves patrol of a particular locality and since the very presence of a picket line may induce action of one kind or another, quite irrespective of the nature of the ideas which are being disseminated."

There is reason to believe that Justice Douglas eventually came to rue this statement, but it continues to be quoted and echoed in cases perfunctorily upholding NRLA restrictions. The judges who cite it do not explore its meaning, which is far from clear. The "patrol of a locality" clause, to the extent that it equates picketing with physical intimidation, does not provide a basis for upholding section 8(b)(7) or section 8(b)(4), for neither section requires that a hint of physical intimidation be present. Neither of these sections requires a significant number of people nor anything resembling patrol.

Courts have regularly held that picketing can take place without numbers or movement or any indication of physical intimidation.[19] In fact, stationary people holding signs have been characterized as picketers, and the Court in quoting Justice Douglas's language has never investigated the circumstances to determine whether an element of physical intimidation is present.

The second clause of the Douglas quotation is even more confusing. Does it refer to the fact that those being appealed to are likely to honor a picket line out of fear of physical attack, a highly questionable assumption as shown under circumstances present in many labor cases? Imagine three union members, none of imposing height or build, standing in front of a store and urging consumers not to patronize it because it sells a product produced by strikers. Are Justice Douglas and those who quote him really suggesting that those who honor the picket line are likely to do so because of fear or coercion? Would they hold the same if the picketers were right-to-lifers complaining because the facility sells morning-after pills?

The Douglas statement fails to distinguish picketing from other union-authorized inducements to boycott such as leaflets, newspaper ads, or speeches. The fact that people might respond to picketing because of their general attitude toward labor is not different from the fact that people respond to many forms of expression because of their own views or the causes with which the expression is associated. Other forms of communication that are constitutionally protected, such as wearing an armband, refusing to salute the flag, or holding a Ku Klux Klan rally, may elicit a similar response.

Although statutory limits on labor picketing have existed for over half a century, the Supreme Court has never satisfactorily addressed the constitutional issue. In refusing constitutional protection for picketing, the Court's opinions rely on both the special nature of picketing just discussed and on Congress's right to prohibit the spread of strikes and boycotts to secondary employers. Thus, in *NLRB v. Retail Store Employees Union, Local 1001*,[20] the Court upheld a ban on peaceful picketing aimed at persuading consumers not to purchase a struck product. It dismissed the First Amendment claim in a short, conclusory paragraph focusing on the purpose of the picketing: "Congress may prohibit secondary picketing. . . . Such picketing spreads labor discord by coercing a neutral party to join the fray. . . . A prohibition on 'picketing in furtherance of such unlawful objectives' [does] not offend the First Amendment." But subsequently, the Court held that distributing handbills, which has similar consequences, is constitutionally protected.

In other contests not involving unions, picketing is given greater constitutional protection, as shown by the Supreme Court's unanimous opinion in *NAACP v. Claiborne Hardware Co.*[21] The case involved a boycott of white-owned businesses by black residents of Claiborne County, Mississippi. The boycott was conducted in order to secure compliance with specific demands, including "the desegregation of all public schools and public facilities, the hiring of black policemen, public improvements in black residential areas, selection of blacks for jury duty, integration of bus stations so that blacks could use all facilities, and an end to verbal abuse by law enforcement officers." The leaders of the boycott sometimes enlisted participants through threats and acts of violence; Charles Evers, the field secretary of the NAACP, delivered a speech in which he said that boycott violators would be disciplined by their own people and warned that the sheriff could not "sleep with boycott violators at night." Because the boycott leaders used force, violence, and threats, the Mississippi Supreme Court found that the boycott was a tortious interference with the merchant's business. The court did not find a violation of the state secondary-boycott law but only because that statute was enacted two years after the boycott began.

The U.S. Supreme Court reversed. It noted that the boycott was furthered by speech and picketing, which, citing *Thornhill*, it described as being "ordinarily safeguarded by the First Amendment."

In delineating the state's limited role, the Court found that Evers's speeches were beyond the state's power to regulate even though his comments included an implicit threat: "If that language had been followed by acts of violence, a substantial question would be presented whether Evers could be held liable." Because no violence immediately followed Evers's speech, however, the Court found it to be protected by a "profound national commitment" that "debate on public issues should be uninhibited, robust, and wide-open." The Court asserted: "Strong and effective extemporaneous rhetoric cannot be nicely channeled in purely dulcet phrases. An advocate must be free to stimulate his audience with spontaneous and emotional appeals for unity and action in a common cause. When such appeals do not incite lawless action, they must be regarded as protected speech."

Unions have cause to be confused. Why is their picketing judged by different standards? Why is the policy of robust debate so rarely mentioned and replaced instead by the "delicate balance," the "laboratory," the policy of "peacefully resolving disputes," and the unthinking assumption of coercion? The majority opinion in *Claiborne Hardware* attempted to distinguish the case before it from cases of union picketing. In labor cases, the Court said, regulation of speech is permissible because of the "strong governmental interest in certain forms of economic regulation even though such regulation may have an incidental effect on rights of speech and association." Thus, "secondary boycotts and picketing by labor unions may be prohibited." The picketing involved in *Claiborne Hardware*, on the other hand, rested on a higher constitutional plane: "While States have broad power to regulate economic activity, we do not find a comparable right to prohibit peaceful political activity such as that found in the boycott in this case. This Court has recognized that expression on public issues 'has always rested on the highest rung of the hierarchy of First Amendment values.'"

The distinction drawn between the economic activity involved in the labor cases and the political activity relating to public issues is analytically unsound, historically inaccurate, and culturally myopic. What, for example, distinguishes the retail-store employees' appeal to the public for support, which the Court held was not constitutionally protected in the *Retail Store Employees Union* case, from the public boycott that the Court protected in the *Clairborne Hardware*? Both cases involve appeals aimed at achieving immediate economic benefits for a limited group, and both appeals were ultimately premised on a broader goal of redistributing economic benefits: to blacks in one case, to labor in the other. To suggest that one goal is of greater public concern than the other is to view labor through the Court's artificially created prism by which collective bargaining becomes dissociated from any broader, nobler, more enduring purpose.

Claiborne Hardware and cases of union secondary picketing can be distinguished only by focusing on the immediate objective in one and the long-term objective in the other.

CARD-CHECK AGREEMENTS UNDER THE NLRA

In *Shaw's Supermarkets,*[22] the Labor Board, controlled by George W. Bush appointees, cast doubt on the legality of card-check agreements, stating: "We have some policy concerns as to whether an employer can waive the employees' fundamental right to vote in a Board election. It is clear that the Board's election machinery is the preferred way to resolve the question of whether employees desire union representation. That method, as compared to a card-check, offers a secret ballot choice under the watchful supervision of a Board agent."

The Bush Board further expressed its disapproval of recognition through card-check majorities in *Dana Corporation,*[23] which changed the law to encourage challenges to a collective-bargaining relationship based on a card-check majority:

> We find that the immediate post-recognition imposition of an election bar does not give sufficient weight to the protection of the statutory rights of affected employees to exercise their choice on collective-bargaining representation through the preferred method of a Board-conducted election.
>
> In order to achieve a "finer balance" of interests that better protects employees' free choice, we herein modify the Board's recognition-bar doctrine and hold that no election bar will be imposed after a card-based recognition unless (1) employees in the bargaining unit receive notice of the recognition and of their right, within 45 days of the notice, to file a decertification petition or to support the filing of a petition by a rival union, and (2) 45 days pass from the date of notice without the filing of a valid petition. If a valid petition supported by 30 percent or more of the unit employees is filed within 45 days of the notice, the petition will be processed. The requisite showing of interest in support of a petition may include employee signatures obtained before as well as after the recognition. These principles will govern regardless of whether a card-check and/or neutrality agreement preceded the union's recognition.

The Board claimed to be protecting employee free choice by channeling issues of representation into its own election process, which it announced is the preferred method of protecting employee choice. Since it is well established that card-check agreements are more likely to lead to collective bargaining than the Board's election process, it seems clear that the right that the Board was intent on protecting is the right not to have a union and not to engage in collective bargaining. This is the very opposite of the right that the NLRA was initially passed to protect and the process of collective bargaining that it was meant to advance.

It is true that the Act recognizes a right to refrain from exercising section 7 rights, and the Board seems concerned that this interest will not be adequately protected through card-check or "labor peace" agreements. But there is nothing in a card-check agreement that requires an employee to sign up; nor does a card-check agreement prevent employees from urging their colleagues not to sign up. All of this suggests rather strongly that the interest the Bush Board was protecting is the interest of the employer in stating the case against unions through captive-audience speeches. When employers sign card-check agreements, they do generally (though not always) agree not to try to influence employee votes. They give up their right to speak against unions in the interests of labor peace. It seems like a trade they should be able to make and unions should be able to influence.

Chapter 20 Comprehensive Campaigns and RICO

In 1994 and 1997 the United Food and Commercial Workers International Union (UFCW) attempted to organize workers of Smithfield Packing Company's Tar Heel plant. Smithfield responded in each case with anti-union campaigns that the NLRB found involved widespread use of threats, harassment, and retaliation through suspensions and discharges. The Board's findings were upheld by the D.C. Circuit Court of Appeals, which summarized Smithfield's unfair labor practices as follows: "The company threatened to fire employees who voted for the Union, to freeze wages and shut the plant if the employees unionized, and to discipline employees who engaged in union activity. It also interrogated employees about their union support, confiscated union materials, and videotaped and otherwise spied on its employees' union activities."[1]

Smithfield's behavior, according to former U.S. secretary of labor F. Ray Marshall, "was so extreme as to be shocking by the standards of the 1990s."[2]

Sometime in the summer of 2006, the UFCW began a corporate campaign to force the same Smithfield plant to agree to procedures, including card check, to be used in future organizing efforts. In February 2008 Smithfield responded by bringing a suit under the Racketeer Influenced and Corrupt Organizations Act (RICO) against the union, Change to Win, Research Associates of America (headed by Jeff Fiedler),[3] and various union officials, including Andy Stern, the president of the SEIU, and Tom Woodruff, the director of the Change to Win Strategic Organizing Center.[4] In order to maintain a RICO suit, a plaintiff must show "a pattern of racketeering activity" based on at least two predicate criminal acts "involving listed crimes which include murder, kidnapping, gambling, arson, and extortion." Smithfield alleged that the defendants had been guilty of extortion under North Carolina and Virginia law. Generally, the crime of extortion involves efforts to obtain property by threats of unlawful acts. Smithfield's suit followed several previous successful efforts to derail comprehensive campaigns through RICO suits.[5]

Among Smithfield's attorneys and advisers was Notre Dame law professor G. Robert Blakey, one of the key drafters of the RICO statute. The essence of the complaint, as described by Judge Robert E. Payne, was that "defendants, conspiring together, devised an unlawful scheme to extort an agreement from Smithfield to recognize UFCW and Local 400 as the exclusive bargaining agents of the hourly employees of the Tar Heel plant."

According to Judge Payne, the most serious allegations of misconduct to achieve this goal were the following:

(1) UFCW retained Research Associates of America to prepare and release a false report to the public entitled "Packaged with Abuse: Safety and Health Conditions at Smithfield Packing's Tar Heel Plant."[6] It is further alleged that the defendants intentionally and maliciously caused the false report to be published regarding the working conditions in the Tar Heel plant.

(2) The Defendants allegedly interfered with Smithfield's business relationship with Harris Teeter, one of Smithfield's largest customers. Defendants are alleged to have continually and repeatedly attempted to cause Harris Teeter to cease doing business with Smithfield, inter alia, by organizing "Days of Action" which called for demonstrations to take place at Harris Teeter grocery stores across the southeast. The protests allegedly focused on Smithfield's treatment of its workers and accused Smithfield of racial bias with respect to Smithfield's African-American and Latino workers. All of these charges are alleged to be false.

(3) Smithfield alleges that the Defendants attempted to interfere with Smithfield's business relationships with numerous other grocery stores nationwide by sponsoring protests in Ann Arbor, Atlanta, Boston, and Nashville. The protests are alleged to have been based on falsified grounds.

(4) UFCW allegedly issued a nationwide directive in August 2007 to all of its affil-

iated local unions regarding the commencement of a "National Boycott" of Smithfield products. Each affiliated local union was directed to contact retailers in its local jurisdiction that carry Smithfield's products and instruct them to discontinue sales of Smithfield's products or face demonstration activity. The retailers allegedly were given false information to justify the boycott.

(5) The Defendants allegedly interfered with Smithfield's business relationship with celebrity chef Paula Deen, who had entered a contractual agreement to promote Smithfield's products on her cooking shows. In an effort to interfere with the business relationship, the Defendants are said to have sponsored, and caused to take place, a series of demonstrations at "Paula Deen Live Tour" events and book signings in several cities. These demonstrations too are alleged to have propounded false information.

(6) The Defendants allegedly encouraged cities to effect and publish resolutions condemning Smithfield and banning the sale of its products within their municipal jurisdictions. The Defendants also encouraged members of the Potomac Association of the Central Atlantic Conference of the United Church of Christ to effect and publish a similar resolution condemning Smithfield. The information provided in pursuit of these resolutions allegedly was untrue.

(7) The Defendants allegedly attempted to devalue Smithfield's stock by mailing letters containing falsely disparaging information about the company to financial analysts who follow publicly traded companies in the food industry.

(8) The Defendants also are alleged to have orchestrated, sponsored, and conducted protests against Smithfield which took place at the company's 2006 and 2007 shareholders' meetings.

(9) In or around June 2006, the Defendants issued untrue and misleading press releases in numerous markets as part of the so-called "Justice at Smithfield" campaign. Such conduct, Smithfield alleged, violated the Racketeer Influenced and Corrupt Organizations Act.

The defendants argued that since what is at stake is essentially the ground rules for granting union recognition, the case did not involve extorting "money, property, or pecuniary benefit" under Virginia law; nor did they "threaten" as that term is used under North Carolina law with the "intention thereby wrongfully to obtain anything of value or any acquittance, advantage, or immunity" under North Carolina law. Indeed, without the constant injection of the term "falsely" it would be obvious that Smithfield was basing its claim on traditional concerted labor-union activities protected by section 7 of the NLRA. There was no allegation of violence or threats of violence. The defendants accordingly moved to dismiss the complaint.

In support of their motion, the defendants relied heavily on the case of *Schei-*

dler v. National Organization for Women.[7] The defendants in *Scheidler* had attempted to shut down abortion clinics through a series of actions including criminal violations. The Supreme Court held that their actions did not violate RICO because, as Chief Justice William Rehnquist explained, "we have construed the extortion provision of the Hobbs Act at issue in these cases to require not only the deprivation but also the acquisition of property." He continued: "It is undisputed that petitioners interfered with, disrupted, and in some instances completely deprived respondents of their ability to exercise their property rights. Likewise, petitioners' counsel has acknowledged that aspects of his clients' conduct were criminal. But even when their acts of interference and disruption achieved their ultimate goal of shutting down an abortion clinic, such acts did not constitute extortion because petitioners did not 'obtain' respondents' property. Petitioners may have deprived or sought to deprive respondents of their alleged property right of exclusive control of their business assets, but they did not acquire any such property. They neither pursued nor received 'something of value from' respondents that they could exercise, transfer, or sell."

The defendants in the *Smithfield* case argued that Justice Rehnquist's reasoning applied with equal force to Smithfield's claim and thus eliminated the alleged extortion predicate for Smithfield's complaint since there was no allegation that they had obtained any property belonging to Smithfield. The defendants also relied on the Supreme Court's earlier decision in *United States v. Enmons,*[8] which held that even violent union action seeking to force an employer to agree to a legitimate union collective-bargaining objective did not constitute extortion under the Hobbs Act, which defines extortion as "the obtaining of property from another with his consent, induced by wrongful use of actual or threatened force, violence, or fear." The Court in *Enmons* concluded that the word "wrongful" applies both to the means used and the goal sought, so violence committed during an otherwise lawful strike would not constitute extortion.

The conduct in which both the *Scheidler* and *Enmons* defendants engaged seems significantly more serious than that in which the UFCW engaged, even in the unlikely event that the plaintiff's characterization of the union's purpose —instant recognition—was correct. In fact, the union claimed in support of its motion for summary judgment that the undisputed evidence demonstrated that it was not seeking immediate top-down recognition but rather a neutrality agreement followed by an election to be supervised by a mutually agreed-upon neutral. Jeff Fiedler insisted that there was not a scintilla of evidence to support Smithfield's allegation in this regard. The likelihood that Fiedler was in error is minuscule. The standard approach of Change to Win unions using a comprehensive campaign is to call for an expression of majority support. Otherwise, the union's recognition can easily be set aside by the Labor Board. Judge Payne did not take issue with the union's denial in this regard. Nevertheless, he denied the defendant's motion for summary judgment on the grounds that

> the union was seeking to take away from the employer its right to recognize or not a union based on the union's majority status. The right to recognize a union (or not), especially when employees have rejected the union's organizing efforts, is a matter of considerable import and the exercise of that right carries with it significant consequences, fiscal and operational, for the employer and its employees. The right is intangible. But, of course, businesses have a host of intangible rights, the exercise of which are critical to the viability of the business, and, without doubt, those rights are the property of the proprietor—the business owner. For example, business owners have, among others, the right to invest (or not) in new equipment, to open or close manufacturing facilities, to hire and fire employees, to vote the shares that the company owns, and to provide (or not) pay raises, bonuses or other financial incentives to employees.
>
> In reality, the right to recognize (or not) a union as bargaining representative is among the most valuable and important of rights possessed by business owners. The very existence of the Corporate Campaign concept is founded on the recognition that the exercise of that right is of great import and of great consequence. Like the host of other rights mentioned above, the right of voluntary recognition cannot, standing alone, be bought or sold or exercised by a third party. That certainly does not mean either that the right is not valuable or that it is any less of a property right than the other rights that compromise the essence of business ownership.

Judge Payne seems to have it backward. The NLRA did not create a property right for employers with regard to union recognition. Indeed, if anything, it did the opposite, taking away from employers their common-law right to grant or withhold recognition as they chose. Section 9(a) specifies that a labor organization selected by a majority of workers in an appropriate unit is entitled to recognition whether the employer wants to recognize it or not. The NLRA, which governs issues of union recognition, contains no provision for employer rights. All rights concerning representation belong to employees. The property right that Judge Payne found in the interstices of statutory obligations is a property right with no statutory mention, no right of transfer, and no direct legal protection.

Employee choice, not management prerogative, is the basis for rights concerning representation under the Act. If a majority of employees in an appropriate unit so choose, they are entitled to representation. If only a minority favor union representation, the employer violates the Act by granting recognition. The question of when a union violates the NLRA in seeking recognition is a complex issue covered by section 8(b)(7), which has established procedures and its own remedial scheme, including injunctions and unfair-labor-practices findings.

If followed, Judge Payne's opinion in the *Smithfield* case would turn RICO into a labor-relations statute. Employers might not find this to their liking. Judge Payne's reasoning would give unions a strong basis for arguing that serious employer unfair labor practices aimed at overturning a union's majority status also violate RICO. After all, unlike the employer right enunciated by Judge Payne, the right of a majority of employees to choose union representation is clearly spelled out in sections 7 and 9 of the NLRA. Unlawful employer acts trading on fear to deprive employees of that right could easily be interpreted as extortion and therefore as predicate offenses for application of RICO. Unions would be well advised to use Judge Payne's reasoning as a precedent for RICO suits of their own.

Another disturbing feature of Judge Payne's opinion is the importance that it gives to allegations of false and misleading statements. In the absence of such allegations, it would have been apparent that much of what the union did was typical First Amendment protected speech and protest. For example, Smithfield alleged that "the Defendants issued untrue and misleading press releases in numerous markets as part of the so-called 'Justice at Smithfield' campaign." Smithfield also alleged that "the Defendants . . . encouraged members of the Potomac Association of the Central Atlantic Conference of the United Church of Christ to effect and publish a similar resolution condemning Smithfield. The information provided in pursuit of these resolutions allegedly was untrue."

The law already provides remedies for maliciously false statements that harm a business. If RICO were to be available as a remedy for false statements, it could easily become a regulator of political campaigns, product advertising, and official statements by government officials.

The potential First Amendment implications of the opinion were recognized in a satirical article in the *New York Times* by Adam Liptak, which began with a note of bewilderment at "the theory that speaking out about labor, environmental and safety issues in order to pressure the company to unionize amounts to extortion like that used by organized crime."[9] Liptak quoted Professor

Blakey's justification for the use of RICO: "'It's economic warfare,' explained G. Robert Blakey, one of Smithfield's lawyers. 'It's actually the same thing as what John Gotti used to do. What the union is saying in effect to Smithfield is, "You've got to partner up with us to run your company."'" It is difficult to understand how two such different behaviors can be equated by a legal scholar. The union is seeking not monetary gain but increased rights for workers. It is not using violence or threats of violence. It is seeking the same kind of moral and economic mobilization that the civil-rights movement employed throughout the 1960s, most notably during the Birmingham boycott.[10]

Liptak's article illustrates the anti-democratic nature of the holding:

> But the most striking assertion in the suit, one Smithfield devotes five pages to, is that the union was engaged in racketeering when it urged local governments in New York, Boston and other cities to pass resolutions condemning the company. After meeting with the union in 2006, a dozen members of the New York City Council sponsored a resolution calling for the city to stop buying meat from Smithfield's Tar Heel factory "until the company ends all forms of abuse, intimidation and violence against its workers," citing a ruling by a federal appeals court in Washington that Smithfield had engaged in "intense and widespread coercion" in battling unionization at its Tar Heel plant.
>
> Councilwoman Melissa Mark-Viverito was a sponsor of the resolution, and she said she had been happy to meet with representatives of labor and business groups to hear their concerns. The practice Smithfield calls racketeering is, Ms. Mark-Viverito said, what others call lobbying.

There is reason to believe that Judge Payne was uncomfortable with the publicity that the case received. He strongly encouraged the parties to settle the dispute, which they did before the case went to trial. The terms of the settlement were not spelled out. As reported by the Bureau of National Affairs: "In a joint statement, the parties announced that they have agreed on 'a fair election process' by which workers at Smithfield's pork processing plant in Tar Heel, N.C., can choose whether or not to be represented by UFCW. In return, UFCW agreed 'to end its public campaign against Smithfield,' in which the union has employed a variety of tactics, including product boycotts, to pressure the company to agree to a card-check recognition process. Smithfield and UFCW also agreed to establish and jointly fund and administer a feed the hungry program."[11]

Although the parties kept the terms of the agreement secret, it was clear from their tone that the union defendants were pleased with the result. On December 10, 2008, the employees voted to unionize.

The widespread use of RICO suits to counter union organizing campaigns was dealt a blow in January 2009 when Judge Dennis Hurley, in a well-reasoned opinion, dismissed a RICO suit by Wackenhut against the SEIU for failure to state a claim.[12] The SEIU had engaged in a typical concerted campaign against Wackenhut in an effort to organize its employees. Wackenhut argued that the union's violations of the Hobbs Act established the predicate offenses for a RICO complaint. Among the many allegations made by Wackenhut was that the SEIU, through a "shell organization," had undertaken "to harass and unfairly disparage Wackenhut with 'dozens of demonstrations at facilities of Wackenhut customers, at board of director meetings, shareholder meetings and other gatherings.'" The complaint further alleged that the SEIU had used its shell entity to "make a series of false statement about Wackenhut designed to shake public confidence in its ability to provide security to America's large corporations after the September 11, 2001, tragedy." Wackenhut also accused the SEIU of "flooding stakeholders with false and disparaging communications via mail, fax, websites, newsletters, newspaper advertisements, fake annual reports, and anti-Wackenhut letters sent to investors and stock analysts."

Under Judge Payne's analysis in the *Smithfield* case, a RICO suit would likely have been sustained. However, accepting as true "all of the factual allegations," Judge Hurley dismissed the complaint on the basis of the Supreme Court's decision in *Scheidler.* He held that the allegations "did not allege that SEIU obtained any of Wackenhut's right or property. At most, [Wackenhut] claims that SEIU improperly coerced or attempted to coerce it to do something which it was not otherwise inclined or required to do." Judge Hurley's reasoning marks a major step forward, although his *Wackenhut* opinion did not end the use of RICO claims against unions in strikes and organizing campaigns. Statutes other than the Hobbs Act may be used to establish predicate offenses, as was done in *Smithfield,* and employers will probably be able to convince courts in some cases that the element of "obtaining property" was an aspect of particular union campaigns.

A further blow to the once-promising employer technique of countering corporate and comprehensive campaigns with RICO lawsuits was delivered in an opinion by Judge William H. Pauley in *Cintas v. UNITE HERE.*[13] Cintas is the largest maker of uniforms in the country. UNITE HERE and the Teamsters undertook a campaign to pressure Cintas into agreeing to a neutrality and card-check agreement. Cintas claimed that

> Defendants have engaged in a so-called "Corporate Campaign" against Cintas, which includes "[f]alsely portraying Cintas as a company with 'a long history of anti-union-

ism' that 'bullies, harasses, intimidates and terminates workers who want to join unions,' [and painting] Cintas as a company bent on racist, sexist and illegal acts." (Amended Complaint ¶ 94.) Defendants reached out to Cintas's customers, especially small minority owned businesses to pressure Cintas. (Amended Complaint ¶ 98.) Defendants also communicated "disparaging information about Cintas to Cintas's stakeholders by mailing and faxing letters and flyers containing misleading and/or negative statements about Cintas, distributing newsletters, posting press releases, creating web pages, and sending anti-Cintas letters to investors and stock analysts." (Amended Complaint ¶ 102.)

Judge Pauley rejected the effort to tie card-check campaigns with extortion:

> Because Cintas would receive some benefit from a card-check/neutrality agreement, it must show that it has a right to pursue its business free from Defendants' activities. However, Cintas does not have a right to operate free from any criticism, organized or otherwise. . . . ("[W]ithin the labor context, in seeking to exert social pressure on [plaintiff], the Union's methods may be harassing, upsetting or coercive, but unless we are to depart from settled First Amendment principles, they are constitutionally protected.") . . . ("[T]he prime directive in the Union [organizing] campaign, a boycott of [the target employer] is . . . constitutionally safeguarded," as is the accompanying "activity of peaceful pamphleteering."). To the extent that any of Defendants' statements are defamatory, then Cintas can pursue those claims under state tort laws. Accordingly, Cintas's allegations do not rise to the level of criminal extortion.

Despite these positive developments, RICO remains a potential threat to the right to strike in a variety of different situations. Much turns on whether the Supreme Court will affirm and extend the policy implications of its decision in *United States v. Enmons.*

In *United States v. Thordarson,*[14] the Ninth Circuit specifically held that *Enmons* did not reflect a broad policy of limiting the application of federal criminal laws in strike situations. In *Thordarson,* Teamster officials and staff members were indicted under various federal criminal statutes, including RICO, on the grounds that they had been part of a conspiracy to destroy trucks of Redman Moving and Storage Company "in an effort to coerce Redman into recognizing the Teamsters." The charges included the use of explosives to damage vehicles used in interstate commerce, arson in violation of the Travel Act, and conspiracy to conduct the affairs of an enterprise through a pattern of racketeering activity in violation of RICO. The district court below dismissed all the violence-related charges on the basis of *Enmons,* which the judge read as "preclud[ing] federal criminal prosecution for violent activity which occurs during the course of a legitimate labor dispute" in the absence of specific authorization from Congress.

The Ninth Circuit reversed, stating that "there is no basis in the Court's decision or its underlying rationale for the creation of an '*Enmons* doctrine' of immunity. . . . We read *Enmons* as holding only that the use of violence to secure legitimate collective bargaining objectives is beyond the reach of the Hobbs Act." The court held that defendants involved in an organizing effort could be charged under the Travel Act, the Hobbs Act, and RICO.

RICO remains a menace to unions, particularly in strikes. A pattern of racketeering may be found on the basis of two criminal acts over a ten-year period, and there are a vast number of crimes that qualify. When illegal acts, attributable to the union, are committed by its members during a strike, the predicates for a RICO claim will frequently exist. The scope of remedies available under RICO is extremely broad; remedies range from treble damages to injunctions of the sort once thought to have been outlawed by both the Norris-LaGuardia Act and the NLRA.

RICO casts a broad linguistic net in an avowed effort to combat organized crime. The language is so broad that courts have regularly expressed concern even as they have applied it. If RICO makes sense in dealing with organized crime (a debatable conclusion), it is a terrible tool for regulating strike misconduct. The statute creates a new, serious crime—with heavy penalties—that can be based on a small number of minor infractions. Long strikes often involve enough instances of violence to subject the union and its leaders to a broad range of criminal and civil penalties. In addition, the general language of RICO, together with the vague notion of "conspiracy," makes a union and its leaders potentially liable whenever acts of violence take place. The likelihood of attribution is great because of the erroneous assumption, often indulged by courts, that strike violence occurs only because union leaders want it to.

Relatively minor strike misconduct such as placing "jack rocks" on roads—a regular feature of bitter strikes and a violation of the Highway Act—can provide the predicate offense. And the requirement of a "pattern" of activity, which in some nonlabor situations places a check on the application of RICO, will easily be found in strikes where multiple similar acts are engaged in for a similar purpose. The impact of a RICO claim will likely fall not on the perpetrators of the misconduct but on the unions, whose treasury and structure will be vulnerable to the Act's broad remedies, and on union leaders, who may be found guilty of crimes on the basis of the conduct of others.

One of the first cases to apply RICO in a strike situation was *MHC, Inc. v.*

International Union, United Mine Workers of America,[15] a case that stemmed from a strike for recognition by a local of the Mine Workers that had won a representation election at the mine when it was owned by another company. The recognition strike was marred by violence by both sides. The district court found that union members—among other acts of violence—"threw nails and spiked boards in front of coal trucks." A RICO action was brought against the international union. The court held that application of RICO in this circumstance was not preempted by the NLRA because it was not necessary for the court to construe the NLRA in determining whether RICO was violated. It rejected the claim of preemption on the grounds that the policy of the NLRA is intended to encourage peaceful settlement of labor disputes and not to protect violence.[16]

A case that vividly indicates the potential connection between the Hobbs Act and RICO in organizing situations is *C&W Construction Co. v. Brotherhood of Carpenters and Joiners, Local 745.*[17] The case involved an effort by the defendant unions and leaders to organize a construction company. According to the complaint, union officials threatened the company's president with picketing and violence if C&W did not sign a union contract. He refused, whereupon, at the direction of the union president, union members began picketing three of the company's job sites. After the first week, the employees agreed to work and crossed the picket lines.

Thereafter, pursuant to the provisions of section 8(b)(7) of the NLRA, the NLRB held a representation election at the company's request. C&W's employees voted to reject the union as their representative. The NLRB regional director issued complaints alleging that the union's pickets at C&W's job sites were illegal, and the Board brought suit in federal court. The union continued to picket C&W's job sites for more than three months. There was no allegation of violence during the picketing.

During the period of the picketing, union business agents attempted to persuade various suppliers not to deliver materials to C&W's job sites. In some cases they were successful. In the NLRB proceedings, two union officials were found to have lied and were later convicted of perjury. The company alleged that the union's conduct caused it both financial harm and emotional distress.

The company filed suit against the union. The complaint contained eleven claims for relief, including both federal and state antitrust violations, interference with the company's business, civil RICO claims, intentional and negligent infliction of emotional distress, and violations of the NLRA.

Although the court held that certain of the plaintiff's claims were barred by the statute of limitations, it found that the defendants were potentially liable under all the theories set out by the plaintiff. The defendants argued on the basis of *Enmons* that Hobbs Act violations could not, in the context of a labor dispute, form the predicate for applying RICO. The court rejected this argument, citing *Thordarson*. It concluded that the defendant unions and their officers could be guilty of a RICO violation on the basis of either the perjury committed by the union officers before the NLRB or violations of the Hobbs Act. The court limited the *Enmons* decision to cases of traditional collective bargaining: "Unlike the union in *Enmons,* the union in this case did not have a contract with C&W. Moreover, the union here was not on strike against C&W. The boycott was secondary, not primary. Thus, the union's activities did not entail 'legitimate collective bargaining objectives.'"

Although the defendants violated the NLRA by attempting to interfere with the employees' free choice with respect to unionization, the Act itself already provides for adequate relief. To the extent that the union used unlawful secondary pressures to achieve its objective, the NLRA provides for mandatory injunctions and for monetary relief to "whoever shall be injured in his business or property by reason" of an illegal secondary boycott.

By applying a variety of other theories of liability, the court ignored the carefully constructed scheme of the Labor Act. The NLRA does not outlaw all efforts by unions to use economic pressure in support of organizing but rather has worked out a complex system of rules to deal with this issue. If courts address the legality of union organizing as a prelude to determining whether to apply the Hobbs Act and RICO, the likelihood of their making significant errors is great. And the liability imposed on unions will be far greater than that imposed on employers who violate the basic rights of their employees. By making unions subject to both of these federal statutes as well as to a wide variety of other causes of action, the courts inevitably increase the advantages that the law gives to employers in organizing situations. Beyond that, the courts are setting the stage for expansion of both the Hobbs Act and RICO to strike situations in which the union as an institution is guilty only of some technical violation of labor law.

Judge Bernice B. Donald's opinion in *Overnite Transportation Co. v. International Brotherhood of Teamsters*[18] best recognizes the potential of RICO to significantly impair union rights. The case grew out of a major organizing effort by the Teamsters against Overnite, which, according to the RICO complaint, included threats and acts of violence. In denying part of the RICO claim, Judge Donald said:

The Court is troubled by the consequences of incorporating such an overly broad interpretation of extortion in RICO. If any coercive conduct on the part of picketers and strikers constitutes extortion, seemingly every "garden variety" unfair labor practice will be swept into the fold of RICO. As a result, an overly broad interpretation of state extortion laws will cripple union activity with the specter of treble damages, destroy the delicate balance of labor/management relations forged by the NLRA, and force the federal district courts to police every strike, every picket line, and every labor dispute.

Whereas, Congress's specific purpose for enacting RICO was the eradication of organized crime, not the revamping of the federal labor law landscape.

In *United States v. Enmons,* the Supreme Court refused to uphold the indictment of striking employees for extortion under the Hobbs Act, even when these employees engaged in significant property destruction. The Supreme Court recognized that violence, property damage, and extortion often went hand-in-hand with "lawful" strikes and was willing to exempt such conduct from the debilitating penalties of tough federal laws. In essence, the Supreme Court impliedly recognized the unique circumstances of labor disputes, and the reality that extortion is an integral part of the labor landscape. Any overly broad interpretation of extortion incorporated into the federal laws reaching labor disputes would illegalize all overtly coercive conduct occurring during a strike and destroy the healthy balance forged by the NLRA between labor and management. In the light of the Supreme Court's emphasis on the special characteristics of extortion in the labor context, this Court concludes that the restricted scope of extortion under the Hobbs Act is extended to limit similarly the scope of all of RICO's extortion provisions including those under the Travel Act and state law.

It is a sensible analysis and should be followed regularly. The courts should recognize that RICO has no legitimate role in policing labor-management relations where a legitimate union is engaged in collective bargaining or organizing activities.

Part V **The Need to**

Change the Law

Chapter 21 Organized Labor and the Employee Free Choice Act

From 2006 to 2009, the main legislative goal of organized labor has been passage of the Employee Free Choice Act (EFCA).[1] The EFCA mandates certification of a union that demonstrates a card majority. It also provides for first-contract arbitration and increases penalties for employer unfair labor practices intended to prevent unionization. The key provisions of the EFCA are sections 2 and 3.

Section 2 provides that the NLRB can certify an organization without an election: "Whenever a petition shall have been filed by an employee or group of employees or any individual or labor organization acting in their behalf alleging that a majority of employees in a unit appropriate for the purposes of collective bargaining wish to be represented by an individual or labor organization for such purposes, the Board shall investigate the petition. If the Board finds that a majority of the employees in a unit appropriate for bargaining has signed valid authorizations designating the individual or labor organization specified in the petition as their bargaining representative . . . the Board shall not direct an election but shall certify the individual or labor organization as the representative."

Section 3 of the EFCA provides for mediation and arbitration for first-contract impasse:

(2) If after the expiration of the 90-day period beginning on the date on which bargaining is commenced, . . . the parties have failed to reach an agreement, either party may notify the Federal Mediation and Conciliation Service of the existence of a dispute and request mediation.

(3) If after the expiration of the 30-day period beginning on the date on which the request for mediation is made under paragraph (2), . . . the Service is not able to bring the parties to agreement by conciliation, the Service shall refer the dispute to an arbitration board established in accordance with such regulations as may be prescribed by the Service. The arbitration panel shall render a decision settling the dispute and such decision shall be binding upon the parties for a period of 2 years, unless amended during such period by written consent of the parties.

In addition, the EFCA calls for doubling back-pay awards and for possibly severe penalties for employers who willfully or repeatedly violate the NLRA to prevent unionization: "Any employer who willfully or repeatedly commits any unfair labor practice within the meaning of subsections (a)(1) or (a)(3) of section 8 while employees of the employer are seeking representation by a labor organization or during the period after a labor organization has been recognized as a representative defined in subsection (a) of section 9 until the first collective bargaining contract is entered into between the employer and the representative shall, in addition to any make-whole remedy ordered, be subject to a civil penalty of not to exceed $20,000 for each violation."

The bill has been bitterly attacked by employer groups and by commentators who argue that moving from elections to card check is an insult to the democratic process. It has been the target of numerous op-ed attacks and negative commercials. Most of the attacks focus on the perceived likelihood of unions coercing workers to sign cards. Typical of the negative attacks is an op-ed article by George Will urging Republicans to make the EFCA a major campaign issue in the 2008 election. Will described the consequences of passing the bill as follows: "The exquisitely misnamed Employee Free Choice Act would strip from workers their right to secret ballots in unionization elections. Instead, unions could use the 'card check' system: Once a majority of a company's employees—each person confronted one-on-one by a union organizer in an inherently coercive setting—sign cards expressing consent, the union would be certified as the bargaining agent for all workers."[2]

Will rejected out of hand the claim that the EFCA is needed as a response to employer coercion, arguing that "there are, however, ample protections against employer pressures that really are abusive." He does not spell out what the protections are. One can only imagine what he would say if he were somehow required to spell them out. Similar editorial comment abounds. Among others, the moderate *Chicago Sun Times* sees the EFCA as a cure that is worse than the malady it is supposed to correct. George McGovern, writing in the *Wall Street Journal,* put his liberal prestige behind the anti-EFCA arguments:

> There are many documented cases where workers have been pressured, harassed, tricked, and intimidated into signing cards that have led to mandatory payment of dues.
>
> Under EFCA, workers could lose the freedom to express their will in private, the right to make a decision without anyone peering over their shoulder, free from fear of reprisal. . . .
>
> To my friends supporting EFCA I say this: We cannot be a party that strips working Americans of the right to a secret-ballot election. We are the party that has always defended the rights of the working class. To fail to ensure the right to vote free of intimidation and coercion from all sides would be a betrayal of what we have always championed.[3]

McGovern too is short on documentation. He does not describe any of the "many documented cases" of union abuse. We do not know how many he refers to, when they occurred, or what resulted from their being exposed. Indeed, it is not easy to locate in recent case reports these "many documented cases." Nor does he consider what the effect of documented coercion on recognition would be if the EFCA were passed.

EFCA opponents see the likelihood of coercion in any interaction between organizers and workers. It is not difficult to visualize their image of the EFCA-enabled organizer. He (always a he) is not a visionary arguing for worker solidarity but is a menacing, shadowy figure, strong of arm and with limited verbal skills. The point is illustrated in a frequently shown anti-EFCA commercial featuring the actor who played the mob boss Johnny Sac on *The Sopranos* as the organizer insisting, in his familiarly menacing voice to the worker he is soliciting, "Just sign the card." The implication is clear: failure to sign will result in a brutal attack on the worker or his family—perhaps his aging mother.

The anti-EFCA writers seem to be blissfully ignorant of how organizing works and how it would work under the bill. They know little or nothing about today's organizers, who are increasingly a mix of idealistic college students and dedicated union workers—their main task is not to frighten but to reassure. Opponents of the EFCA also seem ignorant of the limited ability of professional organizers to make contact with workers. Nor do they seem to recognize the employer's continuing ability to use captive-audience speeches inculcating fear of retaliation. Nevertheless, because they have managed to frame the EFCA debate in terms of the importance of the secret ballot, a concept dear to Americans, the opponents of the bill have substantially influenced public opinion. As this is being written, the chances for passage of the EFCA in anything like its original form seem remote.

The labor movement has fought back. It has, with success, solicited friends to sign statements and to write op-ed articles favoring the EFCA. Pro-EFCA articles and statements have been abundant, but they generally ignore or finesse the secret-ballot issue and stress the value of unions and the weaknesses of the Labor Board's election processes.[4]

Some pro-EFCA statements suggest that the bill would not eliminate the secret ballot. This approach was taken in an op-ed article by John Sweeney and Mark Love: "The Employee Free Choice Act would level the playing field for workers and restore workers' freedom to form unions and bargain in three ways. It would strengthen penalties for companies that coerce or intimidate employees, establish mediation and binding arbitration when the employer and workers cannot agree on a first contract, and enable employees to form unions when a majority signs cards authorizing a union to represent them. If workers choose to have a government-sponsored election, they can still do so. The legislation does not change that process. It simply gives workers, not employers, the power to decide how they will choose to form a union."[5]

The attempt to reconcile the EFCA with the secret ballot is, however, misleading. The point of the EFCA is to replace the NLRB election process. Unions do not petition for elections without signing up a majority, and if the EFCA were law, once they had a majority, there would be no reason for an election. They would be entitled to recognition immediately. It is difficult to imagine a situation in which an election would be held if the EFCA were passed. Of course, unions could make the decision to go to election after achieving a card majority, but why would they? The whole point of the EFCA is to make it unnecessary. There is not much in either piece that would explain to an interested observer how the EFCA would work.

Another pro-EFCA article appeared in the *Wall Street Journal,* written by Thomas Frank, the author of *What's the Matter with Kansas?* Frank too based the case for the bill on the prevalence of employer unfair labor practices, which he says have been "scrutinized by academics and quantified with scientific precision, most notably in a 2000 study written by Kate Bronfenbrenner of Cornell University and submitted to the U.S. Trade Deficit Review Commission."[6]

Frank also cited Professor Bronfenbrenner for the conclusion that "there has been no such thing as a secret ballot for the 20 years I've been studying elections. . . . Employers know exactly which way an employee is going to vote." I have interviewed many employees. This statement is an exaggeration. It is true that employers and unions alike evaluate employee sentiment during the campaign and usually have a pretty good idea of voter sentiment. This is particularly easy with respect to employees who wear buttons or engage in public argument. But in any good-sized unit there will be some employees who give no clear indication of their preference and some who make up their minds in the voting booth without either side being aware. It is not an argument against the secret ballot that the parties often (although not always) have a good idea of how the vote will come out. What is important is that the workers believe the ballot to be secret, and overwhelmingly they do.[7] Of course it is important that voters, worried about possible repercussions, believe the ballot to be secret so that they can safely vote their true choice. I have earlier in this book expressed my doubts about the reliability of much research on the impact of employer tactics. There is no body of scholarly work that measures the prevalence of unfair labor practices with scholarly precision.

The debate over the EFCA is misleading on both sides. The opponents paint a picture of routine union bullying that is most unlikely to happen and which, if it did, would be grounds for setting aside a certification. Pro-union writers assume that the EFCA will make union organizing success common, in part by eliminating the threats and reprisals that are believed to be the prime reasons for employer success under the current system.

What is surprising about both news stories and opinion pieces about the EFCA is that they so rarely explore how it would work in practice. Whereas both union supporters and opponents assume that it would be a major boon to organization, I have my doubts because of two aspects of the EFCA. First, the bill is unlikely to eliminate representation campaigns in units of any size. Second, if there were campaigns, the EFCA would not significantly eliminate the employer's advantages. For example, there is nothing in the bill that would permit union organizers greater access to employees and nothing that would eliminate or reduce the employer's ability to make captive-audience speeches or to have its supervisors campaign against the union. As Tom Woodruff, the director of the Change to Win Organizing Center, said, it is the campaign, not the election, that poses the problem for unions: "The issue is not to me elections versus majority sign-up; the issue is not having the interference of the employer."

It is true that under the current system a good part, probably a majority, of the employer campaign typically takes place after a union has obtained a card majority. This is why Stewart Acuff, the director of organizing for the AFL-CIO, believes that it will be a great boon to organizing. As he explained to me: "We will still have campaigns and it will still be difficult, but it will be a much shortened process because when we get 50 percent on cards, we'll file for certification."

Acuff assumes that unions would be able to sign up a card majority as quickly after passage of the EFCA as they can now. But that is far from clear because employers would be motivated to campaign against card signing as soon as, or even before, they learn of the union's presence. Acuff anticipates organizing drives that essentially finish before the employer learns of them: "I think that you do careful committee selection and you spend time training the committee. There's not going to be a lot of evidence of union activity until you're ready. There will be some."

Surely, some units would be organized, as Acuff suggests, "before the boss knows." But it stands to reason that these would be small, discrete unions where general access can be achieved away from the employer's premises and not the large units that unions need to organize in order to grow in size and strength. If Acuff and others in the labor movement are wrong about the prevalence of quick, one-sided campaigns that take place before the employer is aware, then the EFCA's impact on organizing might well be minor, perhaps even negative.

In a larger unit of one hundred employees or more, the selection of an employee committee is crucial to organizing, and the process of identifying leaders and forming the committee takes a considerable amount of time. So does the card campaign that follows. In large units, employers almost always know about the campaign even before the committee is fully staffed. "Loyal" employees or supervisors typically bring organizing drives to the attention of labor-relations staff. If the EFCA were passed in its current form, employers would warn their supervisors to be aware of and report any discussion of unions or card signing or the formation of committees. As Roland Samson, formerly the Northeast organizing coordinator of the United Steelworkers, told me, "Today, if you go to a shop with a hundred or more people, and you've got two organizers working on it, it's going to take you a long time just to get the signatures. The company is likely to be running its campaign in the meantime." And without the signposts of the election process, they would surely begin their campaign earlier, perhaps before the union is on the scene. If widespread employer campaigns became prevalent before unionizing begins, the EFCA could actually have a negative impact.

Acuff believes that loyal employees would be less likely to report to the employer if the activity consisted only of choosing and training a committee. But even if that were so under current conditions, it seems almost certain that employers would solicit and train employees to inform them of any hint of union activity—whispered discussions, sudden silences when supervisors come into view. It is also likely that the courts would expand the employer's ability to interrogate employees about union activity so that they would be able to state the case against unionization before a majority has signed up.

The EFCA would not prevent employers from making captive-audience speeches urging employees not to sign cards or to revoke those they have already signed.[8] Once the organizing campaign became public, why would workers feel freer to sign a card than they would to vote yes in a secret ballot?

Perhaps the EFCA would make employers less likely to commit unfair labor practices given the long-overdue harsher penalties for violation. But that is questionable. It is unlikely that many employers who would otherwise commit unfair labor practices would be inhibited by the passage of the EFCA. Employers would still be able to litigate the issue of their guilt for years. In cases of discriminatory discharges, or other acts of retaliation, they would still routinely get a chance to argue that their actions were motivated by business considerations. Employers would win a fair percentage of such cases, at least as many as they do now. The courts of appeals have long been hostile to NLRB findings of discrimination where the employer is able to produce some evidence of employee misbehavior or wrongdoing. As the penalties rise, courts are likely to be even tougher in reviewing Board findings of discrimination. Even if employers were held liable, the amounts of money involved would generally be small. Back-pay awards are calculated on the basis of loss of pay, less money earned or that could have been earned. And even if, counter to my prediction, employers were to give up the weapon of discriminatory discharge, they would still have the more valuable advantage of immediate and constant access to the employees.

In sum, it seems unlikely that EFCA would eliminate the battle for employee sympathies without a pledge of neutrality, which the EFCA does not require; and there is little reason to be optimistic about the likely results of such battles. Two of the hotels that Vinnie Sirabella and his team of future all-star organizers attempted in vain to organize had card-check agreements. As Sirabella recounted to me: "We went one-on-one with Marriott in New York and lost. There isn't a better labor town than New York, and we had a card check and couldn't get the 51 percent. The other example was the combat we're having with Marriott in San Francisco. Here we have again, card check. The mayor has come out foursquare in support of the union, not just lip service. We have a good team of organizers; the woman who runs it out there, Sherri Chiesa, is one of our best. We still haven't been able to get a majority. The San Francisco thing isn't over; we're at it now for over a year, [but] we haven't accomplished very much."

Ironically, a sign-up battle under the EFCA with an employer might well create new difficulties for the union. Currently, organizers and the organizing committee can promise that the names of card signers will not be turned over to the employer. But if signed cards were determinative of unionization, the courts might well allow an employer to view the list in order to challenge the inclusion of individual employees.

The issue of revocation promises further complication. The EFCA is silent on the subject, but it is difficult to believe that the Board and courts would ignore evidence that card signers have changed their minds. Employers would undoubtedly urge card signers to revoke their authorization. The issue of what constitutes an adequate revocation would likely arise. A letter to the union with a copy to the employer should be effective. But what if the employee notified only the employer or some third party? Would the employer be able to rely on manifest revocation not communicated to the union? If an employer solicited employees to notify it of revocation, would its action be viewed as a form of coercion with a hint of reprisal? It seems likely that the courts would require the Board to investigate claims that a card majority does not reflect current employee sentiment. If the employer had any factual basis for its claim, would the Board certify and the courts enforce solely on the basis of cards signed over a period of time, particularly if the length of time were significant?

Perhaps unions base their commitment to the EFCA on the theory that EFCA-based campaigns would have no cutoff point similar to the election. Perhaps they hope to store authorization cards until they have a majority in an appropriate unit. It seems highly unlikely that the courts would adopt, or permit the Board to adopt, an assumption of continuing validity of authorization cards across long time periods. The question of how long cards should be treated as valid would be bound to arise.[9]

The EFCA would require a petition for an "appropriate unit." Employers would regularly challenge the appropriateness of the unit claimed. This challenge could be mounted before the Board to urge denial of certification and before the courts by simply refusing to bargain after certification. Unit questions always arise, and many are difficult—for example, it is almost always possible for employers to argue that the unit sought is inappropriate because it includes supervisors or managerial employees. If the union were found to be wrong on unit questions, would the Board readjust the unit and certify the union or would the Board simply deny certification? It is impossible to tell in advance. The EFCA would almost certainly add to the intensity of and time committed to litigating questions of unit. It seems likely that the courts, rarely a friend of labor, would be particularly hostile to nonelection certification. One way that they could manifest their unhappiness would be to reject certifications for what they concluded were inappropriate units. Thus the EFCA would likely lead to further legal complications and more stringent court review of the Labor Board's unit determination.

Perhaps unions believe that they would have an advantage under the EFCA because card signers would be more reluctant to publicly revoke than they would be to vote no in a secret ballot. This is a thin reed on which to base so much hope and political effort. In any case, employers might develop non-public ways for employees to indicate a change of mind, likely by notifying the Board.

More significantly, the EFCA would likely lead to earlier and perhaps more militant employer anti-union campaigns. The one certainty is that the EFCA would be a boon to anti-union consultants who would use the publicity and the debate about the Act's potential impact to persuade employers to hire them in advance of an organizing campaign. "Don't wait till it's too late," they would argue, and employers would likely be swayed. In Ontario, where card check is mandated, anti-union employers have responded by hiring consultants and beginning their anti-union campaigns before unions even begin asking employees to sign cards. If employers start early, they can mobilize fear and make arguments against unions before card signing begins. That was one of the problems with Vinnie Sirabella's national organizing campaign, as Paul Clifford, the head of the HERE local in Toronto, later explained to me: "He actually announced that we were coming to town. So the employers were prepared. They had anti-union consultants already prepping the employers."

Even those who don't hire consultants would beef up staff, make anti-union speeches earlier, and pay more attention to complaints. This is what Clifford predicts would happen if the EFCA were passed: "More and more of them will do it in-house, by strengthening their internal HR function." Clifford pointed out that, even in a liberal city like Toronto, "employers still run anti-union campaigns which are probably more preemptive." And according to the Canadian labor expert Roy Adams, "Union density and bargaining coverage are falling even in provinces such as Saskatchewan and Quebec that have card check and first contract arbitration clauses in effect."[10]

Some unions might be able to organize quickly through an organizing blitz. But this would not be easy in large units. Kirk Adams, the organizing director of the SEIU, told me that he believes that the EFCA would be most valuable in small health-care units and that its impact would be temporary: "I think it can be effective for the SEIU probably more than anybody else because I could imagine the health-care industry coming to terms with it more easily than, let's say, the fast-food industry, or hotel restaurant. I think two things are gonna happen. One is we are gonna organize really fast and pick up a good chunk of health care, and two, companies are gonna give raises to their employees to buy them off. There will be a period of time that we can rock and roll, but that could be as little as a year, maybe less. It has always been neutrality rather than a card check. We much prefer neutrality rather than a card check."

Assuming that some units would be organized quickly if the EFCA were passed, they would likely be small, nonmilitant units and would likely not be in a position to bargain effectively. Those units would need the binding-arbitration provision of the EFCA to be effective. First-contract arbitration might well be the most significant part of the EFCA. It is also highly controversial. Given the shaky status of the EFCA politically, it is hard to imagine that, even with large Democratic majorities, both card check and first-contract arbitration will be passed as is. First-contract arbitration would undoubtedly solidify some organizing victories that might otherwise have ended in failure. On the other hand, first-contract arbitration has its own drawbacks.[11] An employer displeased by the decision of an arbitrator could simply refuse to implement the award, claiming that it is unfair, biased, or contrary to public policy. The union would have to seek court enforcement. Courts have historically been reluctant to enforce agency or arbitration awards without reviewing them on the merits. Courts would likely develop limits on arbitral discretion, and in so doing, they would likely postpone many contracts, amend some, and reject a few.

It would be more difficult to develop and maintain rank-and-file militancy if the first contract were not earned through solidarity but achieved through third-party fiat. The best way for unions to overcome employer unwillingness to negotiate fairly is through their own power. That is why amending the law to increase union bargaining power should be labor's primary goal.

There is little basis for assuming that the EFCA would make a major change in union organizing success. Why then is organized labor so strongly behind it? Why do some expect that its passage would lead to millions of new members? Partly, the answer is that card-check agreements have been the major source of organizing in recent years. Where card check has been achieved, organizing success has followed. Some may assume that giving all unions the benefit of card check would give them the same advantages that unions get from persuading employers to sign them. The problem with this reasoning is that it is not the card-check agreement but the card-check agreement plus neutrality after a comprehensive campaign that has proved so effective. The organizing approach adopted by HERE and other unions achieves card check through a combination of negotiation pressure and worker solidarity. By the time card check is achieved, the employer has concluded that it is in its interest not to battle further against the union. But the EFCA cannot legislate this employer conclusion. The passage of the EFCA could lead employers to conclude that they need to battle harder, and they would retain all the advantages that they currently have under the NLRB's election process.

It is difficult to tell what the effect of the increased remedies would be if the EFCA were enacted. In particular cases, employers might be penalized severely depending on the way the term "each violation" were interpreted. Increased penalties would likely lead the courts to be more rigorous and, in some cases, more hostile to Board findings. Most likely, the increase in penalties would reduce the number of discriminatory discharges and increase the amount of traditional anti-union campaigning. If that happened, it is quite possible that the effect would be to increase the efficacy of employer campaigns. In this regard, the conclusions of the Getman-Goldberg-Herman study and the Dickens reevaluation are in accord:[12] it is the amount of activity that most determines the effectiveness of the employer's campaign.

Chapter 22 Changing the Law of Representation Campaigns and Striker Replacement

The law should be amended to reduce the amount of time that employers can devote to captive-audience speeches and to provide unions with an equal opportunity to address employees. Equal time would permit unions to respond to employer arguments. Unions have responses to every argument that employers make. They can reduce concerns about dues in the vast majority of cases by pointing out that dues will not be charged until the union has obtained an agreement that increases the workers' income by more than the amount of dues. They can point out that union officials cannot drag workers out on strike. In most unions, strikes require a vote of the membership, usually a two-thirds vote. Moreover, equal-time responses would demonstrate the ability of the law to reduce the employer's previous unlimited power over the workplace.

The law should increase penalties for serious employer unfair labor practices during an organizing campaign. One of the problems with the current reinstatement remedy is that it can be delayed for years. Injunctions against discriminatory discharges would permit employee activists to play a major role in the campaign. Speeding up elections would make them less subject to manipulation and more of a reflection of employee choice. Another desirable major change would be adding significant penalties, including requiring standard contract terms, to remedy employer refusals to bargain. Congress should also amend the Driver's Privacy Protection Act so that it is lawful for organizers to obtain and use address information from license plates.

But the most beneficial change would be to overturn the *Mackay* doctrine and declare it illegal for employers to permanently replace striking workers. According to Kirk Adams, when the EFCA was first formulated in the halls of the AFL-CIO, prohibiting striker replacement was one of the four elements. Somewhere along the line, it dropped out. Adams is not sure why: "I don't know whether there was too much of a heavy list or what." I believe that organized labor made a major mistake in dropping the prohibition against striker replacement in favor of card check. Prohibiting the hiring of permanent strike replacements would have been far more likely to win popular support than doing away with the secret ballot. It is straightforward and easily understood, and its core principles persuasive. Workers should not lose their jobs for exercising their basic statutory rights. Polls show that it would have public support. According to organizers with whom I have spoken, it would be far more popular with union rank and filers than the EFCA or direct amendment of the election process. It would help unions in organizing, in bargaining, and in winning strikes. And it would encourage local unions to come to each other's aid.

Historically, union growth has been strongly correlated with successful strikes. The early New Deal period, which laid the foundation for the powerful labor movement of the 1950s and 1960s, was a period of tumultuous, unorthodox, successful strikes. HERE grew at its most rapid rate during the 1930s, and the strike was one of its major organizing weapons. Its recent organizing accomplishments in Las Vegas were given enormous impetus by its successful strike at the Frontier Hotel. Its successes in San Francisco, Los Angeles, and New York were also based on successful strikes. The Frontier strike demonstrated that victorious strikes breed solidarity and a sense of empowerment in a way that neither organization through cards nor contracts obtained through arbitration can possibly do. Eliminating the *Mackay* doctrine would strengthen collective bargaining and the desire of workers to take part in it.

The possibility of permanent replacement is a key element of the typical employer anti-union campaign. As Tom Woodruff stated to me, "The best line the employer has is 'go ahead and get the union. I don't have to give you anything in negotiations. And all you can do is go on strike, and I'm going to replace you.' That's a good line." A reasonable pro-union employee might well vote against union representation to avoid having to choose between his or her coworkers' desire to strike and his or her job. Changing the law to outlaw replacement would eliminate this employer argument and would protect striking workers, who are the frontline troops of the union movement.

The *Mackay* doctrine, together with the weakness of the law governing bargaining, frequently gives the employer a motive not to reach an agreement but rather to force a strike so that it can permanently rid itself of union supporters and very possibly the union itself. When employers permanently replace strikers, the results are often devastating. In the strike against International Paper Company by Local 14 of the United Paperworkers International Union (UPIU) in Jay, Maine,[1] the pain inflicted on the community—workers, children, families—by the hiring of permanent replacement workers was comparable to what might have happened had Jay been invaded by a hostile army. It is only when unions are in a position to strike effectively that employers are deterred from using this tactic.

The permanent replacement of a community of strikers is a yet-unrecognized human-rights violation—one that continues to work its evil long after the strike ends. I witnessed this in my study of the strike by Local 14. The strike, almost surely intentionally provoked by the company's drastic bargaining demands,[2] lasted from the summer of 1987 to the fall of 1988. Its repercussions have never stopped blighting the lives of the strikers, their families, and the community.

Before the strike, Jay and nearby Livermore Falls were models of the working-class version of the American dream. Most of the employees at the Androscoggin mill had lived in the Jay area all their lives and had started to work at the mill right after high school. They had relatives and friends in the workforce and were following in the footsteps of fathers and grandfathers who worked for International Paper before them. They referred to the company as "Mother IP" and proudly wore company jackets. The long-standing ties between the company and some of the Jay families were exemplified by Maurice Poulin, who traced his relationship to the company after the strike and realized that starting with his maternal grandfather, "the total years that my family has given to . . . IP comes to a grand total of 379 years." The employees believed that years of loyal service had created an unalterable bond between them and the company. Joe Gatz, a former mill worker, described it to me as "an organizational bond, indeed an emotional and psychological attachment that connected employer and employee in this area for the past ninety years."

The UPIU had represented the bulk of the paperworkers at International Paper's predecessor mill since 1937. By 1987 the average seniority was seventeen years. Most of the floor-level management came from the ranks of the hourly workers, and many had relatives among the union's rank and file. Supervisors and rank-and-file employees were often friends. The nature of the relationship was described to me by John Wall, a floor-level supervisor: "You went fishing with your crew; you went bowling or hunting or something like that. It was a community sort of thing. They'd see you in town, and you knew everybody."

All of this was changed by the loss of over a thousand jobs to permanent replacement workers who have never become assimilated into the community. The devastation that the hiring of permanent replacement workers caused is best expressed by the strikers themselves in answers they gave to a questionnaire that I sent out seven years after the strike ended. One answer came from Earl B. Fuller, formerly a machine tender with forty-three years and nine months' seniority. At age sixty-eight, he was working as a "maintenance man at McDonalds." When asked to describe the impact of the loss of jobs on the area, he responded, "Total disaster. Property doesn't move. Businesses are not profitable. Schools are not what they were. Sense of community is gone. Area has become undesirable. Many deaths, broken marriages, lost homes, etc." David Hutchinson, a millwright with thirty-one years' seniority before the strike, reported that before he left town he was filled with "uncertainty, depression, anger." Robert Hiscock, a maintenance worker with thirty-five years' seniority, reported the impact on the community with one word: "HATRED." It is the word most frequently mentioned by the former strikers in describing their feelings toward the mill, the company, and the replacement workers.

When asked what he remembers about the strike, Pete Bernard, a waste-treatment operator with nineteen and a half years' seniority, wrote, "The immorality of permanent replacement." He wrote that the community was "still feeling the effect of it both monetarily and emotionally and will for many years to come. There are so many bitter feelings, even among our children."

It is true that not all the jobs were lost permanently. Replaced strikers, under what is known as the *Laidlaw* doctrine, have a right to fill openings. After four years, roughly a quarter of the workforce consisted of former strikers. But the former strikers returned to the mill in misery to work alongside replacement workers whom they hated. Among the returnees was Maurice Metevier, a friendly Sunday-school teacher who had once proudly proclaimed himself a company man. When he first returned to the mill, Metevier considered any socializing with the replacement workers an act of disloyalty toward those on the outside: "I go in every day with the same thought—just because I've got my job doesn't mean it's over. I've still got 600–800 friends on the outside and until they're back I refuse to be friendly with these people." When asked how the strike changed his life, he replied, "Made me miserable. Not a day goes by we don't deal with the issues of the strike."

Gerald Ouellette, a quality-control paper tester with ten years' seniority, was back in the mill but with a continuing sense of grievance. When he thinks about the strike, what he remembers is "the good people who lost their homes, breakup of families, loss of savings, all of the tragic things." What he recalls in personal terms is "depression, loss of self-esteem, loss of income, loss of savings —selling of my home." Another anonymous striker back at work, which he hated, reported that "anytime you see a brother or sister that hasn't got their job back you feel very sick, knowing the only way they will get their job is if a scab dies or quits." The widow of Franklin Nichols filled out my questionnaire and reported that "it killed my husband. He had a massive heart attack after the strike was over and he had returned to work. It changed his personality and he became a very frustrated and emotional man."

Twenty years afterward, the strike remained salient for those who had experienced it. According to Roland Samson, whom I interviewed in 2008, "The bitterness has not gone." Every answer that I received contained bitterness, contempt for the replacement workers, hatred for the company, distrust and disappointment with the national union, and anger at the legal system. But surprisingly, the answers also revealed a continuing feeling of support for and pride in the local union and fellow strikers and something approaching nostalgia for the solidarity and sense of importance that the strike brought them. When asked what he recalled about the strike, Earl Fuller answered, "The great feeling of togetherness." Dick Cook mentioned the local's public meetings and "the solidarity you felt when you walked into the room." Asked what the most interesting thing was that happened to him during the strike, he answered, "I met a lot of great union brothers and sisters." Gary McGrane recalled, "Solidarity, sticking together, supporting one another, a feeling of strength and power." Bay Gosselin recalled, "The feeling of being among friends. Being supported by union members from across the country. Knowing we were right. We had a good bunch of people who knew how to stick together." Even the wife of Franklin Nichols, who blames the strike for his death, recalled the "determination, solidarity, and commitment of the strikers." Despite the loss, bitterness, and hatred, the vast majority retained their allegiance to the cause of labor. Barry McDonald, one of the younger workers (both his father and his grandfather worked for International Paper), was typical: "I still believe that a union is the best tool or vehicle to get fair wages and benefits for workers."

These answers demonstrate the ability of strikes to create a lasting sense of solidarity on the part of workers who had never before seen their union as part of a cause worthy of their allegiance. Overwhelmingly, the Jay strikers maintained their belief in unionism and their allegiance to the local union even though they felt betrayed by the international union. Pete Bernard expressed the common view: "The local union has my full support. The UPIU can jump in the river."

The tragic result of the strike had a legal root in the *Mackay* doctrine. The strikers were aware of this and as a result, during the strike, against the advice of AFL-CIO leaders, they instigated legislation, which was narrowly defeated by filibuster in the Senate, to overturn the doctrine. In so doing, they reflected the powerful feeling of the community, which, by the time the strike had ended, had come to see the law as their enemy.

If the *Mackay* doctrine had been overturned, the strike might still have been lost, but the loss would not have had as devastating an impact on individuals, families, and the Jay and Livermore Falls communities. The *Mackay* doctrine darkened the lives of those who crossed the line as well as those who stood fast. It was because of *Mackay* and International Paper's use of it that Darrel House, a longtime worker facing a family crisis (his wife's illness), had to choose between protecting the economic interests of his family and being loyal to his fellow strikers. He chose to return to work and became a pariah hated by his former friends. Ten years after the strike, he left Jay and went to live in Alaska. Five years later, he wrote to me expressing his continuing bitterness toward the law and the *Mackay* doctrine: "I think it's a shame that this country is allowing the backbone of the country, the working man, the blue-collar man, to be run over, torn down by big business because of a law that won't allow them to stand up to big business. The company should have had to keep that mill down or run it with salaried people."

The impact of the *Mackay* doctrine was also felt by the supervisors who could keep their jobs only by training and working with those who had replaced their friends and relatives. This dilemma was made vivid in my interview with Richard Parker, who recalled, "I could see them losing their jobs. I'd come home and I'd tell my wife, 'They're losing their jobs,' and I'd cry." He paused for a moment, and then added, "The only place I can go now is heaven, 'cause I've been through hell."

Charles Noonan, the town manager of Jay, testified before Congress in favor of the anti-striker-replacement bill: "I suggest that before you pronounce the permanent replacement issue 'not broke' and working well, you journey to Jay. I don't have a lot of experience with strikes, and I certainly hope I never have to go through another one—but I have been talking to a number of town managers who have seen strikes, and the difference appears to be, when you add that element of the permanent replacement worker, that the level of violence, the bitterness, the desperation on those picket lines goes up considerably, because every one of those replacement workers who goes in is taking someone's job."[3]

The bargaining positions taken by Local 14 before the strike reflected the attitudes of the employees the union represented. The process by which the union reached its decision to strike was a democratic one; it involved meetings, discussions, and widespread participation by the union's members. All the former strikers with whom I have spoken have said unequivocally that under these circumstances, even if they had had serious disagreements with the union, they would have felt morally bound to honor a strike called by the union as long as the necessary two-thirds of the employees agreed.

No other course was morally acceptable to the great majority of paperworkers at the Androscoggin mill. Each would have benefited if the union had won the strike. Each felt bound by family ties, loyalty, history, and mutual commitment to the others in the group. In short, they behaved as loyal members of the group that was entrusted by law with their claims and aspirations as well as those of their fellow employees.

Encouraging employees to participate in the process of collective bargaining through the union cannot be adequately justified absent a strong policy of free choice that insulates the employees' jobs from their union activity.[4] The NLRA, in recognition of this obvious truth, clearly sets forth such a policy, and the Supreme Court has clearly articulated it. However, the *Mackay* doctrine is inconsistent with that policy. To establish a system under which employees are encouraged to work through their unions, and to simultaneously provide that they risk their jobs by so doing, is both manifestly unfair and inconsistent with the policy of free choice that lies at the heart of the NLRA and that the Supreme Court has forcefully articulated.

Chapter 23 Is the NLRA
Worth Saving?

Many union leaders have turned against the NLRA, advocating its repeal. Jeff Fiedler, for example, told me, "I would personally return to the law of the jungle before anything else." The same contempt was expressed by Richard Trumka, now president of the AFL-CIO: "I say abolish the Act. Abolish the affirmative protections of labor that it promises but does not deliver as well as the secondary boycott provisions that hamstring labor at every turn."[1]

These are provocative, powerful statements. Taken literally, however, they make little sense. For as both Fiedler and Trumka know, if the NLRA were in fact repealed, union activity would continue to be regulated by a combination of state and federal law—state labor statutes, state tort and criminal law, the Norris-LaGuardia anti-injunction statute, and nonlabor federal statutes, plus RICO and the Hobbs Act, among others. Not only would this mark the demise of a single coherent labor policy that the NLRA initially promised but it would leave much union activity of the type favored—indeed developed—by Fiedler subject to the vagaries of state law. It would mean that for HERE to effectuate its plans to organize in Texas, for instance, it would have to confront the public-policy attitudes of the Texas Supreme Court. No one with Fiedler's values would wish that on unions seeking to organize.

I take Fiedler's comments as saying something different and deeper. He prefers the comprehensive campaign to any legalistic process. The comprehensive campaign requires mobilization of and action by workers. When it succeeds, it means that they have demonstrated their power and that the employer will be anxious to avoid future conflict. It leads to cooperation based on mutual respect. The law cannot provide a peaceful, nonpressured process that can do the same. If that is what Fiedler is getting at, I think it is accurate and insightful. But the law can be amended to protect and support the comprehensive campaign. If the secondary-boycott provisions of the Act were either amended or repealed, comprehensive campaigns would be more clearly legal under the NLRA and better protected against state law. As one prominent HERE organizer told me, "If you said to me what would be the one thing you'd like to change in labor law, I'd say secondary boycotts. Fuck EFCA. You take away secondary boycotts, I'll organize 30,000 hotel workers in a year."

A few scholars, Professor Ellen Dannin prominent among them, believe that the NLRA can be restored to its original purpose through creative lawyering and without major legislative changes. That is the central theme of her 2006 book *Taking Back the Workers' Law.* She argues that the current state of labor law is similar to the state of constitutional interpretation during the separate-but-equal reign of *Plessy v. Ferguson.* Both situations were created by courts ignoring basic individual rights:

> The courts rewrote the NLRA to permit employers to exit collective bargaining and dictate the terms of work. An employer can retaliate against workers by taking away their jobs through a lockout or through permanent replacement if they strike. Moreover, the courts say that Section 10(c) may give only the most limited of remedies.
>
> In doing so, judges have taken away the rights the law gave to workers and have given employers virtually irresistible incentives and opportunities to avoid unions and collective bargaining. What employer would bargain when the law says it can insist on what it wants even if it is unreasonable and that it can reach impasse, implement its final offer, lock out workers, replace strikers—and use all this as a tool to de-unionize and to send a cautionary message to other workers about what happens to employees who vote for a union?[2]

She points out that the law permitting segregation was overcome by the forceful legal strategy of the NAACP Legal Defense Fund under the strategic leadership of Charles Houston, Thurgood Marshall, and their advisers, who step-by-step and case-by-case demonstrated that segregation was inherently unequal. Labor unions, she argues, should develop a comparable litigation strategy with the goal of remaking the NLRA into the worker- and union-friendly statute it was meant to be. "A litigation strategy can achieve these goals without the need to campaign for new legislation." Professor Dannin argues that it is not the words of the statute that are the problem: Board and court interpretation—particularly decisions by the Supreme Court—is the problem.

If the civil-rights movement could change the law in its favor, so can the labor movement, she argues:

> [It] provide[s] models that can be used to target judicial decisions that created striker replacement, restricted the right to strike, undermined the right to bargain, denied the NLRA rights of worker freedom of association and speech, and weakened remedies. These and other decisions have perverted the plain language and express intent of the NLRA. The NAACP experience provides inspiration and helpful guidance. In the 1940s, institutional and legal apartheid were the law of the land. An apartheid state was protected by state statutes and Supreme Court decisions. Brave and visionary individuals put together a multi-decade strategy of both activism and targeted litigation to remake the racial landscape of this country. While they have not yet achieved full success, the story is more one of success than of failure. And given the forces of law and power arrayed against them, it is a story of the power of the weak. The problems unions face today are serious, but unions are not as powerless or as friendless as were those civil rights activists.

According to Dannin: "Not only is the NLRB not the enemy, but unions can make it part of the solution. True, the NLRB cannot do everything for unions, but the union movement would benefit enormously by thinking creatively about how to make the best use of the NLRB and the NLRA, rather than throwing them away because they are not perfect."

She believes that the courts can be persuaded to change their approach to issues of workers' rights by cogent arguments backed by sophisticated research, much the way courts were educated about the realities of segregation: "There is evidence from recent court cases that courts will respond to thoughtfully developed records. To give two recent examples, the D.C. Circuit Court of Appeals said that academic research and arguments made to it by the Board had led it to conclude that it might be appropriate to give the implementation-upon-impasse doctrine a second look. In other words, the D.C. Circuit said it was willing to reconsider a judicial amendment whose origins go back to the 1940s. The Ninth Circuit recently relied on expert testimony and research in issuing a decision about union dues that was favorable to unions."

The evidence she cites is very slim when measured against the body of judicial opinions interpreting the NLRA. Her thesis assumes that court opinions are to some extent the result of inadequate argument that can be overcome by a new strategy of litigation that will teach the courts about the reality of labor relations. She suggests that part of the problem lies in the overly technical way that labor cases have been tried by Board and union lawyers:

> The insularity with which NLRA cases are tried must be overcome. . . . Every aspect of NLRA cases must be presented with a consciousness that the very purpose of the Act was to supplant key parts of the law that controlled the workplace and that are still the default mode for controlling workplace relations. . . . Anyone trying an NLRB case must do so in a way that will help non-labor lawyers learn to think like labor lawyers. . . . NLRB cases could be tried, briefed, and argued in a way that highlights the NLRA's express policies: creating equality of bargaining power, promoting collective bargaining. . . . There must be evidence from social scientists and others who have done and who will do research on these issues. Expert evidence can come from union representatives, mediators, lawyers, and employees whose experiences qualify them as experts.

I find Dannin's approach to litigation admirable, but I do not share her hope that good lawyering can make so profound a difference in the enforcement of the law. The worst features of current labor law—favoring employer property rights over collective bargaining or the right to strike, strictly limiting union access to employees while permitting employers to make captive-audience speeches, and imposing pitiful remedies for employer violations—are all cemented into the law; they are supported by generations of Supreme Court precedents and legislative acceptance. The system of unequal access, based on traditional property rights, has by now been reaffirmed in four Supreme Court opinions.[3]

The union and Board lawyers who have suffered fundamental defeats at the hand of the courts have been first-rate advocates. They have lost key cases because the courts and the Board itself periodically have rejected the anti-market doctrines that both Dannin and I recognize were implicit in the NLRA as it was originally passed. I have no hope that good lawyers, even great lawyers, can persuade courts not otherwise sympathetic to organized labor to reverse years of precedent interpreting the NLRA to do the least damage possible to the unregulated market. Remember: the judiciary that presided over the constant erosion of employee rights has been regularly enforced with adherents to the view that whatever interferes with the workings of the free market is necessarily undesirable.

The case against the *Mackay* doctrine, its unfairness to employees and its inconsistency with the statute, has been presented in cases, in eloquent testimony by victims, in countless law-review articles, and in books—all to no avail. The *Mackay* doctrine has been regularly reaffirmed, and it has remained the law for more than seventy years. It is doubtful that the Supreme Court can be made to reconsider it at this time. If it did, it might well refuse to address the merits; instead, it might conclude that after so many years, if change is to come it must come from Congress.

The Court did not take this position with regard to *Plessy* because *Plessy* and its progeny affected the political process and because its victims were a distinct and downtrodden minority. It had its roots in slavery, the most pernicious institution in American history. The civil-rights legal movement had only one opinion to target—*Plessy v. Ferguson*—an opinion grounded in the notion that separation based on race was consistent with equality. The inequality that *Plessy* permitted and gave rise to was evident on a daily, life-destroying basis in states throughout the South, as Charles Black so ably showed.[4] Over eighty years and two world wars later, its inhumanity was evident as were its roots in the doctrine of white supremacy and its incompatibility with the notion of equality contained in the Fourteenth Amendment. Yet it still took thirty years for the litigation strategy to be vindicated. The cause of unions is not equivalent in the minds of liberals and progressives to the cause of racial equality. Separate but equal was a visible, constant denial of our basic national ideal—the equality of all human beings. It was an idea fundamental to the country's formation and the underlying cause of our greatest national conflict, the Civil War. Segregation was rooted in the concept of inequality and justified by the absurd argument that its inherent inequality was a product of the faulty thinking of black people and their supporters.

Anti-union opinions are rooted in much more stable concepts—the importance of private property, the interests of shareholders, and the widely shared view that society works best when government lets the free market alone. As long as those attitudes are powerful in society generally, and predominate in the judiciary, it would be foolish to expect the Court to overturn the *Mackay* doctrine, which Dannin properly uses as her example of the havoc wrought by the judiciary on the basic ideas of the NLRA.

For a variety of reasons, only the courts were in a position to dismantle the system of white supremacy built on the doctrine of separate but equal. But Congress could easily, and in 1992 almost did, overturn *Mackay*. It is far more difficult to control the flow of labor litigation than it was for the NAACP to control the flow of segregation litigation. In the 1940s and 1950s judges cared deeply about the issues of racial equality that were involved in the segregation opinions. There is no suggestion of similar judicial concern with the rights of labor. There is something to George Schatzki's argument that courts and unions are inherently antagonistic entities—one elitist by nature and the other anti-elitist.[5] Another significant difference is that the number of labor cases in the courts is far greater than the number of separate-but-equal cases in the 1940s and early 1950s, which means that it would be extremely difficult to develop a strategy that step-by-step eats away at the basic concepts that Dannin rightly attacks.[6]

Nevertheless, Professor Dannin may be correct in urging labor supporters not to abandon the NLRA. She is correct that the statute's language, in section 7 in particular, is a stirring statement of employee rights that could become the basis for a pro-worker policy. It is also true that the idea of a coherent national policy developed from that language by labor-relations experts is a worthy goal.

A harsher critique of the NLRA in its current form is contained in a widely cited article by Professor Cynthia Estlund, *The Ossification of American Labor Law,* in which Estlund argues that "the core of American labor law has been essentially sealed off—to a remarkably complete extent and for a remarkably long time—both from democratic revision and renewal and from local experimentation and innovation. The basic statutory language, and many of the intermediate level principles and procedures through which the essentials of self-organization and collective bargaining are put into practice, have been nearly frozen, or ossified, for over fifty years."[7]

Estlund argues that ossification has been caused primarily by a combination of increasing judicial hostility to "the collectivist premises of the New Deal labor law regime" and the failure of Congress to amend the aging statute to give it more contemporary relevance. The original scheme of the statute is itself outdated in a variety of ways. One is limiting remedies to those ordered by the NLRB. She argues that "the absence of a private right of action to enforce basic employee rights excludes the energies of private plaintiffs and their attorneys, and the creative role of courts."[8] Ossification has also resulted from the concept of preemption because "even incremental state and local reform efforts run headlong into the wall of federal labor law preemption." If not preempted, state law might have made valuable contributions by providing alternatives to the strike weapon and limiting the use of strike replacements. Professor Estlund sees a positive aspect of ossification in forcing organized labor to begin using tactics similar to those urged by Richard McCracken in his 1984 presentation to the Food and Allied Service Trades Department of the AFL-CIO urging adoption of the comprehensive-campaign strategy:

> By finally rendering the law nearly useless to workers seeking a collective voice at work, the ossification of the labor laws is impelling those workers to construct a new labor law from the ground up—outside the walls of the established order, as it were. Their building blocks include the First Amendment. The building blocks include other less ossified bodies of state and federal law—both laws regulating employment and laws that are completely unrelated to employment, such as environmental law and corporate law—by which pressure may be brought to bear on employers.
>
> As with any successor regime, the building blocks of this new labor law include some elements of the existing regime—especially section 7 rights. That brings us to a paradoxical conclusion: Ossification can be labor's friend. Ossification has helped to assure the survival of the New Deal's inscription of labor's basic rights of association and collective action in the federal statute books. Some of the surviving statutory language that emerged out of that era—labor's pinnacle of power and public support—is more supportive of collective action than anything one can imagine emerging in the current political climate, or perhaps at any time since the New Deal. Organized labor has little choice but to use that language for all it is worth, even if it is worth only a fraction of what it once was.

Estlund tentatively predicts a thawing of the current labor laws through the use of these tactics: "On the other hand, if this cobbled-together regime of quasi-self-help actually does succeed in arousing the public passions on which it relies, and in disrupting business as usual, it is a fair bet that labor law reform will be back on the table. Labor would then have some bargaining chips, and management might be in a mood to make a deal."

Estlund does not spell out the terms of a deal that would make the NLRA valuable once again, but her article suggests some basic elements: first, a lesser role for the Board; second, greater leeway for state law; third, more flexibility for employers in establishing alternate forms of employee workplace participation. All of these are interesting, and, taken together, they raise a crucial question about labor-law reform: Should the Labor Board be abolished or transformed in some fundamental way? Should its basic function be transferred to the courts or perhaps to the states?

Getting rid of the Board has appeal, at least viscerally, in the immediate aftermath of the toxically anti-labor Bush Labor Board. Far from being an expert tribunal concerned with the rights of workers, the Bush Board demonstrated both ignorance of labor relations and hostility to unions and workers. But the problem is not limited to the Bush Board.

Through most of its history, the NLRB has been politically motivated and legalistically oriented. Its opinions have far more often been based on conjecture and surmise than on an understanding of the realities of labor-management relations.

There are a variety of reasons why the Board so little resembles the vision of its earliest advocates. One is the political nature of the appointment process, which sometimes has been used to reward labor for its support and sometimes has been used as a way of punishing labor for opposing the president's policies. The judicial nature of the Board's task has mandated the appointment of lawyers, which historically has meant politicians with little or no labor-relations background, former Board employees, or those with only partisan experience. The vague, contradictory, and complex language of the statute has permitted the Board to express its policy decisions through a myriad of technical doctrines and subdoctrines that have increased the complexity of the law even as they have limited and reduced the rights of workers.

All of this might be less significant if the personnel and procedures of the Board were such as to permit it to develop true institutional expertise so that it could ultimately draw on its own experience and whatever is known about labor relations by scholars and experienced people in the field. Unfortunately, this is not the case. Those who are responsible for announcing the Board's policies and applying its decisions have very little to do with those who have field experience, who interview employees, or who hear the cases. Those who investigate an unfair labor practice are part of the regional office staff responsible to the general counsel, not to the Board.

Cases are tried not by the Board members but by administrative law judges. For reasons of administrative neutrality, Board members have little contact with the regional offices or the administrative law judges. Although it has been administering the NLRA for over seventy years, the Board has never engaged in an effort to determine empirically the impact of the law on employer or union conduct. As it has acknowledged: "In evaluating the interference resulting from specific conduct, the Board does not attempt to assess its actual effect on employees, but rather concerns itself with whether it is reasonable to conclude that the conduct tended to prevent the free formation and expression of the employees' choice." Thus, the elaborate structure of Board rules is not grounded in any respect on data. Rather, it rests largely on guesses, assumptions, and politics. There is nothing in the collective activities or experiences of the Board that ensures the accuracy of the assumptions upon which these rules are based.

To read through a volume of Board opinions is to be struck by the perfunctory nature of its opinions and the lack of sophisticated analysis when the Board does undertake to analyze a labor-law issue. Its effort is almost always confined to elaborating its own doctrine and treating as established reality its previous assumptions.

The Board has had to apply its myriad doctrines and subdoctrines to the complex facts of labor-management relations. The result would be confusion and uncertainty even if there were significant continuity on the Board. Given the political nature of the Board and its tendency to change complexion with the political environment, however, the problem becomes magnified many times. New Boards are always in a position to distinguish most of the precedent that is inconsistent with their political values and to refuse to accept much of the rest. The matter is further complicated by the fact that the Board often attempts to adjust its doctrine or to articulate it in such a way as to avoid judicial rejection. This has meant a significant difference between doctrines as announced and as applied. For those reasons, the Board has supplied neither expertise nor clear doctrine nor consistency.

A second major problem is the cumbersome process that the statutory scheme provides for. This is most apparent in the problem of protecting employees from retaliation. A discharged employee must first convince the Board's regional office that the discharge was discriminatory. After that comes a hearing before an administrative law judge, then review by the Board. These steps alone are likely to take more than a year. But even if all these determinations are favorable to the employee, he or she does not have a legally binding ruling. The Board may order reinstatement and back pay, but the order does not become mandatory until it is enforced by a decision by a court of appeals—which will typically take at least another year. Of course, as a matter of economic survival, most workers will find alternate employment in the meantime. This diminishes the likelihood that they will actually be returned to the job from which they were fired, and it reduces, usually significantly, the amount of back pay that is recoverable.

Thus, the idea of a quicker, less legally cumbersome process has considerable appeal. But how would such an idea be implemented? If the Labor Board were eliminated, who would make decisions in the first instance about the meaning and application of the NLRA? Perhaps the federal courts. It is hard to see how this would be an improvement. Given the number of judges, doctrinal confusion and contradiction would be inevitable. Federal courts have less chance than the Board of developing a consistent body of doctrine that is consistently applied, and if the courts were to try the cases initially, it would place a major burden on their time. Perhaps we could eliminate the Board and give administrative law judges the same authority that the Board now has. This would eliminate one part of the time-consuming process, but it would reduce the consistency of decisions. And the administrative law judges are an uneven group in terms of knowledge of the law, competence, and bias. There are too many of them to hope for consistency, which the Board has on rare occasion supplied. There is much to be said for having the law developed through an independent body of neutral labor-relations experts. The problem with the Board is that it has rarely, if ever, been such a body. And as long as the Board is chosen as it now is, it will continue to be a politically biased group lacking in understanding of labor law.

Remaking the Labor Board is possible. There exists a group of essentially nonbiased experts whose independence and neutrality have been market tested —experienced labor arbitrators. To understand why this is so, one must have a basic understanding of how labor arbitration works.

The vast majority of collective-bargaining agreements provide that unions may formally grieve management decisions that they claim to be prohibited by the agreement. The vast majority of agreements set forth a process for resolving grievances. The process typically involves a series of steps culminating in binding arbitration. The agreements also provide a system for choosing the arbitrator, which typically involves getting a list of potential arbitrators from an arbitration service such as the American Arbitration Association or the Federal Mediation and Conciliation Service. The names submitted are of private parties who desire to serve as arbitrators and who have, in the great majority of cases, been selected in the past. Thus, labor arbitration is a private system of adjudication in which the judges are private individuals selected by the parties. Each party has the ability to eliminate any person that it believes to be biased. Almost every student of labor-management relations believes that the arbitration process has been successful. In part, the success of labor arbitration is due to the selection process, which, because of the desire of arbitrators to be acceptable to both sides, ensures the development of decision makers who are not only unbiased but attuned to the priorities of the parties as well.[9]

Experienced arbitrators learn useful lessons about labor relations. They come to understand the basic concern of both labor and management and inevitably develop an understanding of how individual workers have an interest separate from both. If members of the NLRB were chosen from the ranks of experienced, successful arbitrators from panels of names submitted from the National

Academy of Arbitrators, for example, we could be reasonably assured that they would be neutral and knowledgeable about the basic aspects of collective bargaining. They would understand how unions work and what the needs of employers are.

It would be in the best interests of both sides to amend the law so that members of the NLRB are chosen from the ranks of experienced arbitrators. A proposal to that effect might well be supported by liberals and conservatives, unions, and employers. After all, they choose arbitrators when they have the chance to mutually select judges to rule on the meaning of their agreements.

Even if the Board were composed of labor experts, the law would still be subject to the rulings of the courts of appeals. Their performance overall has been only slightly better than the Board's. To make the NLRA work better, labor and management need a special court for labor appeals that would function similarly to the way the Court of Appeals for the Federal Circuit functions with respect to issues of patent and copyright.

Another approach, one that would reduce the role of the Board, was made by Professor Benjamin Sachs, a onetime union lawyer. Sachs, pointing to the recognized weaknesses of the NLRA, particularly its remedial failures, suggests a new non-NLRA system as part of what he calls the "great trade." Workers would have greater, more powerfully protected rights to protest, which would lead to a great array of union-like organizations. In return, there would be no bargaining requirement on the part of management. He uses as examples organizing efforts like the Restaurant Opportunities Center that developed through non-NLRA laws such as the Fair Labor Standards Act and anti-discrimination laws:

> This new regime would operate by galvanizing and insulating the early stages of collective action in order to set in motion dynamics of efficacy and reciprocity that can generate subsequent organizational development. Such a new labor law might, like the NLRA, offer workers a broad statutory right to act collectively to improve their work lives. Or the new regime might expand the range of substantive, enumerated rights around which workers have a protected right to organize. In either case, the new regime would protect the right to collective action with employment law remedies: private rights of action coupled with the availability of preliminary injunctive relief and robust damages. The regime would also deploy other mechanisms to engender reciprocity and efficacy, including expanded opportunities for communication among workers.

If this new approach improves labor law's ability to generate collective and organizational activity, the question is whether the regime might then scale back the type of regulation that has defined labor law's second project for the last 70 years. By more successfully fostering workers' collective action, that is, might the new labor law leave to the strengths and interests of the respective parties a large swath of issues currently regulated by statute? Broadly, might we place outside of labor law's reach, for example, many of the ways in which labor and management interact once workers have organized? Or the permissible content and timing of labor-management negotiations? Or the structures through which non-union employers and employees can deal with one another? Or the form that such worker organizations must take?[10]

What Sachs apparently urges labor to sacrifice is the requirement that employers bargain in good faith with a certified labor organization. This would be a minor (although not totally meaningless) sacrifice with respect to bargaining-table behavior since the law barely regulates what happens there now. However, the requirement of meeting is itself of some significance, and the conclusion of bad faith, which is made from time to time, ensures the reinstatement right of strikers. In addition, the concept of exclusivity that Sachs offers to sacrifice is often meaningful in preventing employers from taking unilateral action without dealing with the union.

Ultimately, it is not clear what unions or workers get from Sachs's deal. He argues that various forms of collective action, not easily characterized as union organizing, should be protected. But in general, concerted activity for mutual protection not aimed at traditional organizing is already protected by section 7 of the NLRA. It is not clear what activity not currently protected Sachs seeks to insulate from reprisal under his great trade. Perhaps he is simply seeking a more inclusive and more consistent definition of concerted activity. That is a worthwhile purpose, but it does not require a trade as much as it requires a less politically biased Board. He may also be arguing that the protection for legally permissible concerted activity should be greater and that penalties for employer retaliation should be stiffer. That is certainly true, but those goals too should be achievable without a great trade by amending the NLRA to make its remedial scheme more similar to that of other, more effective, regulatory statutes.

Another position that joins together many critics of the NLRA, at least in its current form, is the desire to weaken or eliminate the concept of federal preemption.[11] This position marks a significant change for commentators favorable to unions. When the NLRA was first passed, it was generally understood that it would largely preempt state regulation of labor relations. The Supreme Court quickly announced a national policy of limiting the scope of state legislation whenever there was danger of its interfering with national policy. It was not merely a policy announcing the supremacy of federal law but a policy of discouraging the application of state law. Justice Felix Frankfurter announced this policy in *San Diego Building Trades Council v. Garmon*.[12] His decision was viewed as a major benefit for unions since preemption quickly limited the ability of state courts, which were not covered by the Norris-LaGuardia Act, to issue injunctions against strikes on the basis of state policy. The doctrine of preemption was also aimed at preventing states from applying tort or criminal law to punish workers or unions that engaged in activity protected by the NLRA.

If the NLRA is working right, a broad preemption scheme would ensure the protection of workers' rights in those states (and there are many) where unions are still considered dangerous to the generally benevolent status quo. Union organizing would be strengthened more by laws changing the ground rules of the NLRA election system.

I believe it is possible to amend the NLRA to make it work the way it was originally intended to work. Amending the method of selecting Board members and the process of appeals would be only a first step. Other changes similar to those contained in the proposed Labor Reform Act of 1977 would also be critical. The Board's remedial power needs to be increased. Injunctions against employer unfair labor practices need to be regularly employed, much the way they currently are against union secondary boycotts. Unions need to be given equal time to respond to employer speeches and meetings, and the election process should be speeded up. Employees unlawfully fired during an organizing campaign should be quickly reinstated. Most significantly, strikers who engage in no serious misconduct should not be risking their jobs when they lawfully walk out.

If the NLRA were amended in such ways, the doctrine of federal preemption could be continued and workers would not be subject to the uncertainties of state law, which often denies them protection in those areas where it is most needed.

Chapter 24 Beyond Traditional Collective Bargaining

There are inevitably more people who would like to have representation than are members of collective-bargaining units. Some workers are not represented because no effort has been made to organize them; some, because they supported the union in a losing cause; some, because they have retired; some, because they are viewed as independent contractors; some, because their employers are individuals who do not command a workforce; and some, because they work in isolation. How to recruit and represent these workers and the amount of dues, if any, to charge them have been issues of increasing concern to unions. It is a sign of health in the labor movement that it is now focusing on these issues.

OPEN-SOURCE UNIONISM

From time to time pro-union commentators, discouraged by the declining rate of collective bargaining, propose techniques by which unions can grow membership without traditional organizing and representation. One recent suggestion along these lines comes from Professors Richard Freeman and Joel Rogers. They argue that surges in unionism have been "associated with changes in union form that attract previously nonorganizable groups of workers or with institutional or legal changes that greatly weaken employer opposition." The new form that they offer is a major effort at organizing members without regard to employer and bargaining units. They call the plan "open-source unionism." Here is how it would work:

> An open-source union would give its members services outside collective bargaining, including helping them at their workplaces with much the same legal status as a majority-status union. The union would use the internet to provide members with accurate and up-to-date information about economic conditions affecting them. At firm-based locals, the union would gather information from members as well as from the regular business and economic news services about the firm. At locals in a given occupation or industry, the union would gather information about wage and employment developments in the specified job markets. Since the union's first product would be information, the union website would have to provide utterly trustworthy information and develop other features that would make it a valuable site for members. It could also give information about unionism in the world writ large, for instance through access to the LabourStart website (http://www.laborstart.org). Going beyond provision of information, the open-source union would provide personalized advice to members about economic problems, such as what workers might do if an employer mistreated them, how to get an employer to offer more options for defined contribution pension moneys, or the range of pay in their area or occupation.
>
> Since an open source union would not have the clout inside the firm of a majority-status collective bargaining union at particular workplaces, it would have to use different tactics to impact obstreperous employers. It could use its reputation for providing accurate information to set the agenda in disputes with management, to shape public discourse, and to marshal resources from outside a unit to support workers in disputes. When young law associates thought that they were getting an unfair deal from major law firms in 1998, they set up a website (http://www.greedyassociations.com) that provided information to the firms' potential recruits about salaries and working conditions.[1]

It is questionable whether organizing for open-source unionism would be a good expenditure of union resources. It would initially involve large expenditures of money. It would inevitably reduce the number of organizers available for traditional collective bargaining. It is not at all obvious that the types of services being offered would attract and maintain large numbers of workers. For unions like HERE, at this point, it would be a diversion from a program that is working. For less organizing-centered unions, it would reduce the likelihood of their adopting more costly techniques such as the comprehensive campaign.

It would likely attract a different, less committed breed of organizers, not the D. Taylors, Paul Cliffords, Mike Caseys, and Joe Daughertys who see what they are doing as a mission. I think it should not be tried until unions have made more aggressive efforts at organizing for collective bargaining. The HERE model provides a new form that, if widely adopted, might significantly increase the ranks of organized labor. That seems a useful prelude to a campaign for open-source unionism.

WORKING AMERICA

A program narrower but related to open-source unionism has been undertaken by the AFL-CIO. Called Working America, it involves organizing workers for political power rather than collective bargaining. The formation and goals of the program were described to me by its director, Karen Nussbaum:

> There had been a group of us here at the AFL-CIO who had been talking for cer-
> tainly a decade, some of us longer, about ways of organizing outside of collective
> bargaining. I was one of the people who started nine to five. Similarly, it was a way
> to organize people where they were without any regard to what the normal structures
> are. And our hope here was to figure out, How do you tap into the concern of work-
> ing people . . . who have no access to information or connection to an organizing ef-
> fort? The problem had always been that there wasn't a model that got you localized
> enough so that you could exercise power and that was cost efficient enough that you
> could communicate with people.
>   We looked at this whole issue again in 2003, a group of us here at the AFL-CIO.
> What we wanted to do was marry the technique of door-to-door canvassing that
> community organizations have been using for twenty years with the very sophisti-
> cated technology that was now available both to do targeting, messaging, commu-
> nication, and to create a new level of accountability on who you were talking to and
> the system that we were dealing with our members with. So in 2003 we did a pilot
> project, and in August of 2003 the executive council approved the creation of Work-
> ing America as a community affiliate of the AFL-CIO. And here's the basic idea:
> We hire local canvassers; we hire people locally to be canvassers.
>   Now we mostly put ads in the paper. We just hire people and we train them, and
> you know, there's a job, a good job, full-time job with benefits and opportunities for
> advancement. We send teams out into essentially working-class neighborhoods with
> lists that identify the union's members. They skip those households, and they only
> talk to people who don't have a union on the job.

In approaching people, the organizers make a fairly traditional union argument about the need for workers to organize. Those who sign up are asked to

pay minimal dues (five dollars a month), but this is not required. They are mainly asked to sign up so that the union can keep in contact with them. The program has been phenomenally successful—two out of three workers approached have signed up. In less than four years, Working America signed up over two million members. The level of activity encouraged is not great, Nussbaum acknowledges, but it is not insignificant either: "One out of five people who become a member writes a letter that night or sends out a card for the Employee Free Choice Act, or they take significant action. But we do not offer and people don't expect help with their workplace problems. We are really an organization to build a new source of worker power."

Nussbaum notes that members of Working America are likely to become involved in an organizing effort when one takes place at their workplace: "We do find that our members are far more anxious to become involved in an organizing campaign and become the heart of an organizing committee. And we are just beginning now to convene meetings locally where our members can get more involved face-to-face with other members." Working America also takes advantage of the Internet: "We communicate with our members a lot, about 22 or 25 percent of our members give us their e-mail addresses, and we communicate with them by e-mail weekly on issues." The communications were general at first, but as the 2008 presidential election drew near, they became increasingly political.

One of the benefits of Working America has been the development of a cadre of committed organizers from the canvassers hired through Craigslist. The organization maintains a blog on which their organizers share experiences. Almost all represent positive experiences and convey the sense that the organization had an effect on the 2008 election. Typical is the following from a canvasser in Pennsylvania: "We were in Shaler, PA, and he was my first contact of the evening. I started out telling him my name and when I told him that I was from Working America a really big smile came across his face. He said that he received phone calls from Working America that informed him about Melissa Hart's voting record. He also talked about voting for her in the past, and not knowing that she was not for issues that concern working people. He said, 'We kicked her butt, I loved it and I love Working America!' He was just as excited about renewing his membership, which he displayed by quickly pulling out the money from his pocket and informing me that he did not need a receipt. I think he said 'I love Working America' three times before our conversation ended."[2]

A post from Ohio is similarly enthusiastic: "The other night I met a woman on turf whose husband had been laid off from his auto manufacturing job. He has not been able to find steady work and has been working for a temp agency in a desperate attempt to support his family. The woman related to me that she often doesn't have enough money to feed her children. I asked if she was registered to vote; she said no. She then asked for a voter registration form because she finally realized she could help to make change by voting."[3]

According to Karen Nussbaum, Working America was controversial within the AFL-CIO when it was first proposed because it did not seem to fit into ongoing programs, but it is highly popular today. It has also been politically effective. Its members voted overwhelmingly for Barack Obama in the 2008 election in several key states, arguably providing the margin of victory.[4] Working America may offer a better model than open-source unionism because it is less ambitious and takes fewer resources.

HOME HEALTH-CARE WORKERS

The SEIU has been particularly imaginative in mobilizing and representing groups not quite suitable for traditional collective bargaining. Probably their greatest achievement in this regard is organizing home health-care workers, a group that does not work together or have a single obvious employer. Its approach reflects the philosophy of the union's president, Andy Stern, who believes that organized labor has for far too long been fearful of nontraditional approaches to organizing.

The union's achievement in organizing home health-care workers was described to me by SEIU attorney Carol Golubock:

> The group that we started with first in the nineties were personal-care assistants who were paid by state health and welfare programs to provide services in the homes of the elderly and disabled. They provided nonmedical services—just services to help people with their daily activities.
>
> We had tried for years to get a ruling that these workers were employees of the state or of the county. We were never able to get them to be covered under the public-sector bargaining laws. So the idea became, we are going to create a public employer for these workers. And in California, we created the option for them to create a public employer that would be covered by one of public-sector bargaining laws in California.
>
> We've done this in many states. The way we started out, this was done in coalition with consumer-advocacy organizations who were very interested in what they call consumer-directed employment of these in-home care providers, and of course they work. The actual consumer is considered for many purposes, for tax purposes,

the employer of these workers, and they wanted very much to maintain that kind of control and were very concerned at the time that the state was going to turn to the use of agencies, which they saw as sort of a diminution of their authority and power. So they were called public authorities and they were governmental entities, but they were distinct from both the county and the state, and they were to have a board that was consumer controlled. So that's been our model.

What is especially noteworthy in this plan is that it combines the interests of unions in having the workers organized with the interest of consumer groups in having a voice in the setting of wages and working conditions. Also, both the union and the consumer groups on the board were favorable to improving conditions for the home-care workers. They would agree on a common proposal and then work together to get the state legislature to approve it. The SEIU's success in California was followed by success in other states, even though the bargaining format varied. According to Golubok, "In other states, we went ahead and organized statewide, and that led to some fairly enormous numbers of workers coming into our union."

An interesting example of the SEIU's creativity in regard to new forms of organization is its effort in Washington State to put health-care workers and directors into a single unit to bargain with the state. The union developed this plan because staff and directors saw themselves as closely allied, and they realized that organizing based on differences between staff and directors wasn't working.

RESTAURANT OPPORTUNITIES CENTER

The Restaurant Opportunities Center (ROC) is another organizing effort that aims to empower workers who are outside the collective-bargaining framework. It began as a union-initiated program for protecting New York restaurant workers, who were particularly vulnerable in the aftermath of 9/11.

The idea came from Bill Granfield, the president of HERE Local 100 in New York. Granfield developed a new and far-reaching plan for helping members cope with the sudden drastic downturn in the industry. HERE at that time had a decent amount of money in 501(c)(3) welfare and education funds: "We said, [We have] long-term-needs displaced workers, [and we have] some money available. Let's set [up] a long-term group." The initial concept, as explained to me by Granfield, was threefold: "Number one, helping people apply for different types of aid. Number two was figure a way to develop actual gainful employment for people, and number three was the concept of a worker-justice campaign. They were going out into the workplace and finding all these abuses, so they do worker-justice-type things so we could use a long-term thing, a long-term entity for this. We've got some talented people among the displaced workers, we've got some money, but we need someone who could be a director to run that. Someone who had the educational background to run an entity and some policy experience, an orientation towards working people and immigrants. So that was kind of where the idea of ROC came along."

The person hired as the director was Saru Jayaraman, a Yale Law School graduate and worker activist with considerable experience at worker centers. She told me how she became involved: "I got phone calls from Bill Granfield saying that they had all these workers displaced from Windows on the World and could I help to start up a new center that would initially provide support to all the workers who had lost their jobs and in the long run really begin to create a labor-friendly climate in the restaurant industry. What I didn't know at that time is that the industry is now the largest private-sector employer in the nation."

The program was successful beyond all initial expectations, and ROC became an independent factor in the restaurant industry, first in New York, where it opened its own restaurant, Colors, and then in other states throughout the country.

ROC is difficult to classify. It is not quite a union, but it undertakes job actions. It is not quite a legal-aid organization, but it brings suits on behalf of workers and seeks agreements that go beyond money and affect wages and working conditions directly.[5]

Many of its major successes have arisen from Fair Labor Standards Act cases. It brought a major suit on behalf of hundreds of workers against the Redeye Grill, a midtown-Manhattan restaurant, and the Fireman Hospitality Group, of which it is a part. The settlement was intended to change labor practices in a significant way. As reported by Stephen Greenhouse in the *New York Times:* "On Dec. 4, lawyers for the two sides signed a tentative agreement calling for a $3.9 million settlement. Under that accord, Fireman agreed not to have managers share in the tips, not to retaliate against any workers who joined the lawsuit, and to comply with New York's wage laws. The $3.9 million would be one of the largest settlements that a New York restaurant reached in a wage-and-hour dispute. The two lawsuits were part of a wave of litigation in which workers in dozens of Manhattan restaurants sought to highlight what they said was widespread lawbreaking—especially managers sharing in the tips."[6]

The group's experiences had by 2005 changed the nature of ROC and the goals of its leadership. According to Saru Jayaraman: "What was initially intended as a temporary measure of support for displaced workers from the World Trade Center has become an immigrant worker–led center with its sights set on organizing the 99 percent of New York City's restaurant workforce that does not enjoy the benefits of a union. Our long-term vision is to change the balance of power in the industry by organizing restaurant workers around strategic industry campaigns. Using protests, media pressure, research policy, and cooperative development, ROC NY has organized restaurant workers citywide."[7]

ROC New York has not yet been able to coordinate its activities with those of Local 100 in that regard. However, both groups agree that ROC's activities might eventually pave the way for unionization. Says Jayaraman: "We've always had an obvious solidarity with UNITE HERE. We've tried on a number of occasions to go to them and say, look, we've just organized all these workers in this restaurant company. They've won a settlement agreement. They will talk to them for a few times and then kind of drop the ball. They are focused on hotels and Local 100 is focused on cafeterias, and they are not that interested in restaurants right now. They don't have the capacity; they are not ready to go in that direction just yet. I think they will be at some point."

EMPLOYEE-INVOLVEMENT SCHEMES

These new forms of organization, initiated and developed by unions, are a sign of vitality. They have helped workers, made the labor movement stronger, and paved the way for further organizing. Each of them may once have been controversial within the ranks of organized labor but that is no longer the case. What continues to be controversial are employer-sponsored programs such as productivity and safety committees or quality circles. Most of these programs are currently illegal under section 8(a)(2) of the NLRA, which makes it an unfair labor practice for an employer "to dominate or interfere with the formation or administration of any labor organization or contribute . . . support to it." This broad language is made even more sweeping by the NLRA's broad definition of "labor organization" as "any organization of any kind, or any agency or employee represented committee or plan, in which employees participate and which exists for the purpose, in whole or in part, of dealing with employers concerning grievances, labor disputes, wages, rates of pay, hours of employment, or conditions of work."

In 1959 the Supreme Court announced in *NLRB v. Cabot Carbon Co.*[8] that this definition was to be interpreted as broadly as its wording suggests. The employer in that case set up a system of employee committees that met regularly with management "to consider and discuss problems of mutual interest." The NLRB held the committees to be dominated labor organizations because they were formed for the purpose, in whole or in part, of dealing with employers. The Supreme Court affirmed, stressing that the term "dealing with" should not be read as "synonymous with the more limited term 'bargaining with.'" Thus, schemes or plans that are not comparable to unions, and do not involve collective bargaining, strikes, or the settlement of grievances, may still constitute labor organizations. If an employer scheme constitutes a labor organization, the Board will order it dissolved. The *Cabot Carbon* opinion, together with the broad language of the statute, served to put in doubt the legitimacy of any employer-initiated scheme of worker involvement. It convinced many employers that the expense of setting up a new program was not worth the risk.

By the late 1970s and early 1980s, commentators began to think of section 8(a)(2) less as protecting employees and more as inhibiting innovation. Several commentators argued that section 8(a)(2) was outdated. Judge John Minor Wisdom decried what he saw as its adversarial assumptions: "An inflexible attitude of hostility toward employee committees defeats the Act. It erects an iron curtain . . . penetrable only by . . . a certified union, . . . preventing the development of a decent, honest, constructive relationship between management and labor."[9] The U.S. Court of Appeals for the Sixth Circuit in *NLRB v. Streamway Division of Scott & Fetzer Co.* declared in 1982 that "the adversarial model of labor relations is an anachronism."[10]

In 1994 the Dunlop Commission recommended that "nonunion employee participation programs should not be unlawful simply because they involve discussion of terms and conditions of work or compensation where such discussion is incidental to the broad purposes of these programs." The commission also recommended that "the law should continue to prohibit companies from setting up company dominated labor organizations." The recommendation was mild and involved at most a minimal departure from current law, but it drew a dissent from Douglas Fraser, the labor member of the commission who insisted that "section 8(a)(2) stands as a bulwark against forms of representation which are inherently illegitimate because they deny workers the right to a voice through the independent representatives of their own choosing and put the employer on 'both sides of the table.'"[11]

In 1995 Republicans in Congress proposed the Teamwork for Employees and

Management (TEAM) Act,[12] which would have added a proviso to section 8(a)(2) permitting employers to "establish, assist, maintain, or participate in any organization or entity of any kind, in which employees participate, to address matters of mutual interest—including, among others, issues of quality, productivity, and efficiency." The Act also specified that such organizations may not "claim, or seek authority to enter into or negotiate collective bargaining agreements or to amend existing collective bargaining agreements, nor may they claim or seek authority to act as the exclusive bargaining agent of employees."[13]

The Act was bitterly opposed by organized labor and was defeated. The view that section 8(a)(2) should be preserved remains the majority view of organized labor, bolstered by scholarship that purports to show a negative correlation between employee-involvement committees and union organizing victories.[14] In *Law and Reality,*[15] we found no correlation between the existence of employee programs and vote outcomes. Nor did voters themselves refer to existing committees as a reason for voting against unionization. No study has demonstrated whether unions could learn to use the existence of committees as a spur to unionization, although it stands to reason that committees should be so usable.

Intermediate forms of organization should be thought of as opportunities for organization rather than as inhibitors of unionization. The steel unions and the National Education Association both evolved in part from company unions.

When amendments to section 8(a)(2) are proposed, I believe that the wiser approach for organized labor would be not to oppose them outright but to try to structure them so that they can be used to foster union organizing. For example, section 8(a)(2) might be amended to specify programs in which employees selecting their own representatives through a secret ballot would be presumed legal. Americans trust elections, and elections would provide unions an opportunity to have their leaders or members installed as the worker representatives in such programs.

The section 8(a)(2) traditionalists have legitimate concerns about potential abuse from well-orchestrated but ultimately meaningless worker-involvement programs. Nevertheless, experiments with employee organizations, even if employer-established, seem worth the risk.

Even if new employee organizations do not lead to unionization, they could make life better for employees. Academic committees would in other situations constitute section 8(a)(2) violations. But their existence gives greater power to faculty than they would otherwise have.

It would be unwise for organized labor to assume that major changes in the construction of section 8(a)(2) were forestalled by the Board's 1992 decision in *Electromation, Inc.*[16] In that case, the employer, in the wake of an organizing drive, established a series of employer committees designed to discuss and address issues ranging from absenteeism and attendance bonuses to compensation and no-smoking policies. The Board unanimously held that the committees were dominated labor organizations. However, several of the Board members issued separate opinions explaining why they would be reluctant to apply section 8(a)(2) to bona fide employer efforts to share power. Board member Clifford R. Oviatt Jr. insisted that this decision did not apply to "management's attempt to draw on the creativity of its employees by including them in decisions that affect their work lives." Board member John N. Raudabaugh insisted that he would apply section 8(a)(2) more leniently in the future to permit employee-participation programs that were not used to stifle unionization.

The Board's subsequent opinion in *Crown Cork & Seal Co.*[17] shows a retreat from *Electromation* and a further move away from *Cabot Carbon*. The employer in that 2001 case established a series of work teams with considerable voice in working conditions. The Board held that because the managerial functions had been "flatly delegated" to the teams, they were not labor organizations. Whether unions like it or not, section 8(a)(2) is changing. The question is how much and how quickly. In my view, it behooves the labor movement to try to shape the changes and not to limit itself to resisting them. As long as unions resist changes to section 8(a)(2), they will not learn how to make worker committees part of their campaign. Once again, unions are fearful of potentially helpful change.

Andy Stern believes that organized labor was wrong to oppose the TEAM Act. As he told me: "I think we made a mistake on the TEAM Act. Sometimes when you're feeling weak, as the labor movement was, we were more fearful than we should have been that the employer would seize on the opportunity to get rid of us. I think our fear was totally legitimate, but it was out of balance with the opportunity, you know. Yes, we would have probably had certain employers using it that way, but it's almost hysterical now that we were worried management was going to form committees to frustrate us. We should be so lucky."

MINORITY UNIONS

Another suggestion for empowering unions is that they use minority bargaining status. Proponents of this idea make a variety of legal and tactical points.

First, they argue that minority-union bargaining is provided for under the law as it currently exists. They point out that the language of section 7 includes the right to bargain collectively for employees, not for unions. This argument has been advanced by a number of prominent scholars. The argument is spelled out by Charles Morris, one of the most prolific of its supporters. Morris goes over both the legal and practical arguments in favor of minority bargaining. He argues that, both before and immediately after the Wagner Act (the NLRA) was passed, minority bargaining was a common step on the path to full union representation:

> What typically happened in those days was that a group of workers—either on their own initiative or more often with the encouragement and assistance of outside union-organizers—would decide they wanted union representation and would then join a newly-forming union or one already established. They thus became union members—not just card-signers or voters—and their new union would begin to act like a union. Its representatives became the workers' spokespersons in their efforts to dialogue with management, and they would also attempt to serve as advocates of individual employee members in need of advice or support. When this new union's membership grew large enough and strong enough—even though it still represented only a minority of the employees—it would seek recognition and bargaining with the employer. The contracts that resulted from such bargaining would apply to union members only, not to nonunion employees. This combination of organizing and bargaining was frequently accompanied by a strike or a threat of a strike.
>
> The drafters took pains to ensure that all employees would have the right to bargain collectively, even at the preliminary stage of pre-majority union bargaining, for that stage was viewed as a natural stepping-stone on the path to mature, majority-based exclusivity bargaining, which was considered to be the ideal form of bargaining and the ultimate goal of the legislation.
>
> Minority-union members-only bargaining was deemed a natural and frequently necessary part of the growth process of a union becoming a majority-exclusive representative of all the workers in a bargaining unit. As originally intended, elections were only expected to be a means to resolve the question—and only when there is a question—of whether a union seeking exclusive recognition does in fact represent a majority of the bargaining-unit employees. Both members-only minority-union bargaining and exclusive majority-union bargaining were deemed complimentary parts of the statutory bargaining process.
>
> After the Act's passage, minority-union collective agreements proliferated. Members-only agreements at that time were as common as exclusivity agreements—perhaps even more common—and the record suggests that their coverage may have been more extensive. These agreements were especially prevalent in the steel, automobile, rubber, textile, and electrical industries.[18]

Thus, on the basis of statutory language and historical precedent, Morris concludes that "in workplaces where a majority/exclusive union has not yet been selected, the NLRA requires bargaining with any union of the employees' choice, including a minority union." Morris is optimistic that a new pro-labor Board in place after appointments by President Obama "will recognize that this unambiguous statutory language means exactly what it says."

Morris has been diligent in his efforts to promote this idea and, as of the time of this writing, has secured the support of many unions who have sought to get the Board to address the question of minority bargaining in a rule-making procedure. He sees the benefits of the process as twofold. First, minority unions can help improve the wages and working conditions of their members. Second, the process is likely to lead to unionization:

> What will the process of bargaining without prior majority status mean in a presently nonunion workplace? It will mean that whatever the minority union and the employer negotiate and agree upon will become binding as to union members only, and employees who prefer not to join the union will be legally free to negotiate their own individual terms of employment—which in actuality may prove meaningless. What is more likely to happen regarding the nonunion employees is that most employers will extend union-negotiated economic benefits to all similarly-situated employees—this will be the employer's voluntary decision, however, not a legal requirement. On the other hand, contractual grievance and arbitration procedures will apply only to union workers. As was true in the past, most of these minority-union contracts will likely serve only as temporary stepping-stones on the way to majority-exclusivity contracts, which will then provide the same full benefits to all employees.

In short, what Morris envisions as a result of the recognition that employers are required to bargain with minority unions is "an upsurge in the number of unionized workplaces."

I have been among the dissenters that Professor Morris refers to in passing. I doubt the legality of formal minority-bargaining agreements. My position is that a members-only contract that grants benefits to union members that are not available to nonmembers violates section 8(a)(3) of the NLRA. It constitutes discrimination that will have the inevitable effect of encouraging membership in the union. Discrimination is clear because union members and nonmembers will be treated differently. Indeed, Morris himself so states: "On the other hand, contractual grievance and arbitration procedures will apply only to union workers." The encouragement of union membership is also spelled out in his article: "Grievance and arbitration procedures will apply only to union workers. As was true in the past, most of these minority-union contracts will likely serve only as temporary stepping-stones on the way to majority-exclusivity contracts. . . ."

In addition, there is the problem of bargaining strength. If majority unions cannot achieve meaningful agreements in 40 percent of new contract negotiations, why should unions not capable of achieving majority support succeed?

The complexities, confusion, and potential burden of an employer's having to deal with every group that declares itself the representative of some of its employees will undoubtedly cause the courts to look hostilely on the entire business and to try to limit its scope—if they do not declare the whole business illegal. It is an idea that, if accepted by the courts, may do some good for workers and unions, but it seems unlikely that any major benefit can come from it.

CONCLUSION

There are a variety of techniques short of collective bargaining that can give workers more control over their economic fortunes. All of these are valuable, and all can be useful adjuncts to a vital union movement. None of these however, involve workers taking charge of their own economic destiny. None except minority bargaining are or would be worker led. They will not, except marginally, help create a worker-centered union movement.

Part VI **Summing Up**

Chapter 25 The Difference between Labor Organization and Labor Movement

If you had asked a large group of union organizers in 1985 why organized labor was losing membership, almost all would have responded with a version of Dorothee Benz's explanation: "hostile employers and inadequate labor laws."[1]

Vinnie Sirabella, by contrast, devoted most of his criticism to the labor movement itself, focusing on the lack of planning and the lack of organizing passion. John Wilhelm later recalled Sirabella's "insistence that we can organize successfully in spite of all the obstacles, his impatience with those who blamed the lack of organizing on external forces, like the NLRB." Sirabella, doubtless unfairly, considered the failure to commit to organizing as evidence of a character deficiency prevalent among labor leaders: "When people say you can't galvanize the workers, I say that's nonsense. That's the position of some people unwilling to rock the boat, unwilling to effect change, who worry about the political consequences of change."

In the 1970s and 1980s, he was in a state of constant outrage at the failure of union leaders to recognize the need for change and the opportunities for new organizing: "I just think they were resistant to change; they were doing their thing their way and everything was fine, but they didn't see the storm clouds ahead. The building trades in those years wouldn't, for example, organize a contractor who had nonunion workers, and they wouldn't take the contractor's workers into the union. Anyone who had any vision about the future would have known that it was utter folly. I had a reputation as a radical who would raise issues like this. I'd get up on the floor and talk about this at regional meetings all over the country and so they used to say, he's a radical, he's an agitator, he's a troublemaker, he's not stable."

Sirabella did not change his views when he became one of the union's general officers. He related to me with relish how he upset his fellow organizing directors at a meeting at AFL-CIO headquarters: "I told them, forget those political hacks you got in your organization, you got as organizers, get rid of them or red circle them. The whole structure of organizers has revolved around nepotism or hacks you want to get rid of. This is just terrible. They have no vision or energy. If we're going to revolutionize the American labor movement to make it more responsive to the times, it means radicalizing the structure."

In the early 1980s, a high-level committee led by Harvard professor James Medoff proposed a new form of union membership for workers not represented for purposes of collective bargaining. These new "associate members" would be recruited through union services such as insurance, travel planning, and discount credit cards.[2] Sirabella was contemptuous: "I think that Medoff's proposal illustrates the dilemma the AFL-CIO is in. They are so desperate, groping so badly for something. They latched on to anything that came by to demonstrate that they are going to do some things differently. It's not fueled with any passionate desire for change; it's fueled with a sense of business concern. Some guys don't give a shit if they never organize anything. But where is that human spirit that used to propel us? Where is it? Why don't they express it in those terms? Nobody but me is talking about the proper selection, the proper training, the proper this, and the proper environment in which they work. Nobody is talking about that. Kirkland didn't talk about it, Medoff didn't talk about it, the international presidents won't talk about it."

Sherri Chiesa, one of Vinnie's protégés and now the secretary-treasurer of UNITE HERE, finds the same attitudes that troubled Sirabella still present and still harmful to the labor movement: "There are international-union presidents who actually have publicly said, 'We can't organize unless there is labor-law reform. We just can't.' So, what they believe their mission is, is politics."

Even when his organizing drive failed to produce the results that he had anticipated, Sirabella blamed himself for following "the Yale model" and not using the street power of the union: "I take culpability for that—can't lay that on the young people. Things can be done if we have a vision and if we are willing to play unsafe and do the unorthodox by today's standards. People say the sitdowns are dead, don't work anymore. That's nonsense. Many of them still work if we rework them." As his statement shows, as the drive ended, Sirabella was moving toward the new comprehensive-campaign model that the union later adopted.

Unions are right to be outraged at the NLRB election process, which has made successful organizing so difficult. But it is a great mistake for them to ignore their own failures. Focusing on external difficulties inhibits needed change, and sweeping change is needed. As part 2 shows, new methods of the type developed by HERE have led to successful organizing. This is not surprising. Unions throughout history have been able to organize and strike successfully, even in the face of repressive laws, as long as they have had the determination and willingness to take chances. Examples in modern times include movements in South Africa during apartheid and in Poland during the early days of Communist rule. Solidarity, a movement that changed the world, was organized by people violating the law and risking imprisonment (almost all for the second time) for going into the factories distributing a "workers' bill of rights."[3] At a time when strikes were illegal, its members faced imprisonment when they struck.[4]

Although their stories are not as dramatic as the stories of Poland and South Africa, organizers and members in the United States have often exhibited a similar spirit of resistance to anti-labor, anti-democratic power. While some unions put organizing efforts on hold, others including HERE, the SEIU, the United Food and Commercial Workers (UFCW), the Communication Workers of America (CWA), and the Teamsters increased their efforts and organized successfully. Rich McCracken, HERE's main outside lawyer, told me in 2005 that he did not spend much time worrying about whether the Employee Free Choice Act would pass: "We're getting what we need done without it. And it might be better if we had it, but I'm not going to wait for it to be passed." Jeff Fiedler, whom John Wilhelm describes as the guru of the comprehensive campaign, is much like Sirabella in his refusal to focus on the law as the problem: "The Board is inconsequential to me. If the workers want to organize and you understand the company, you can win."

HERE's organizing successes came shortly after its failed national organiz-

ing campaign, which was Sirabella's great final disappointment. During the
1980s I closely followed the organizing project, and in 1996 I published an article in which I referred to the organizing campaign as a "heartbreaking union
failure."[5]

I sent a copy of my article to John Wilhelm, who responded with a long,
thoughtful letter disagreeing with my characterization. He argued that the
union's growing success was, in significant ways, the result of Vinnie's efforts:

> I am not comfortable with the depiction in your opening line of Vinnie's organiz-
> ing projects as "heartbreaking union failures."
>
> In personal terms, for Vinnie, the projects were indeed heartbreaking. He was
> not well during the last 2–3 years of his life, and as he saw his career and life end-
> ing, he was enormously frustrated that he had not been able, in spite of strong back-
> ing from the International President, to achieve more successful organizing.
>
> The point for the movement—as distinguished from the point for Vinnie per-
> sonally—is, in my view, that his vision and tenacity and his hiring of so many as-
> piring organizers, directly laid the foundation for substantial organizing successes
> which have been occurring in HERE for a decade.
>
> Two things happened as the direct result of the early period of these projects, and
> I am certain that Vinnie would share this perspective if he had lived. First, we learned
> a great deal about what it takes to organize successfully in our industry given the
> fierce opposition of employers, as well as the familiar inadequacies of the law. We
> learned two fundamental points:
>
> 1. Workers will ordinarily lose, no matter how heroic their struggle, if they are left by
>   the union's strategy to go one-on-one with their employer. The union needs to have
>   a comprehensive strategy which has the organization and struggle of the workers as
>   its foundation, but which includes other elements of pressure sufficiently strong to
>   modify the employer's behavior. These pressures can be corporate, community, cus-
>   tomer, political, or other kinds of pressure; they must be developed based on an ac-
>   curate understanding of the strengths and weaknesses of both the employer and
>   the union in a given situation. Without an ability to modify the employer's behav-
>   ior, we are unlikely to organize successfully, and certainly unlikely to gain a first
>   contract.
> 2. Existing union members must be involved in organizing; and for that reason, we
>   are more likely to be successful where the union already has a base than in areas
>   where we have no base. There are several levels of importance in the involvement
>   of present union members in organizing: they are by far the most credible per-
>   suaders of non-union workers, far more credible than paid organizers; the repu-
>   tation of the union among those already in it is an important determinant of the
>   feelings of non-union workers in the same community about unionization; and

the mobilization of the membership can provide crucial person power for pressure on the targeted employers.

The projects enabled Vinnie to hire another generation of young organizers. They are now providing the leadership of increasingly successful organizing. In Nevada, HERE has the most successful private-sector organizing program in the labor movement. We have organized 11,000 new members, under contract, since this program was launched in 1987. We will, without any exaggeration at all, add 10,000 more new members in Nevada this year. Organizers Vinnie recruited and trained provide the backbone of this remarkable program: D. Taylor, Joe Daugherty, Julie Pearlman, Jo Marie Agriesti, and Steve Janowicz were all 1985 project hires. I have directed the project, and of course Vinnie hired and trained me, and Karl Lechow has played a key role as well.[6]

The chief lesson that the union learned during the mid-1980s, starting with Vinnie's program and continuing in Las Vegas, San Francisco, and Los Angeles, was that organizing is a complex process and that at its heart is the effective mobilization of the membership and the application of relentless pressure on recalcitrant employers. It was the message that Sirabella passed on to Wilhelm and the other young organizers that he hired. It was put into action when Wilhelm, Joe Daugherty, and D. Taylor prepared for the forthcoming battle for survival in Las Vegas through the intense mobilization of their membership. This was not an easy task. Many people at the time thought that it could not be done since the union had so many disparate elements: senior, well-paid white workers; Hispanic workers, many of them illegal, from different locations; and many African Americans. The Culinary was able to unite this racially, ethnically, linguistically, and functionally mixed group. In doing so, union leaders were repeating what Sirabella had done in creating solidarity in Local 35 when he became the business agent for Yale's maintenance workers. This focus on member involvement continues. It is what newcomer Sarah Julian was taught when she joined the staff of Local 19 in 2003—and it illustrates Mike Casey's comment to me: "There are people who don't even know Vinnie who are his disciples today."

Mobilizing existing membership for purposes of organizing may seem obvious. Virtually all unions today regularly talk the talk of grassroots, bottom-up organizing and member mobilization. But that is not how the vast majority operate. HERE has been almost unique in its commitment to rank-and-file power, involvement, and voice. It is a movement union, growing, and well led, a far cry from the unfocused organization of self-aggrandizing leaders described by the federal monitor in 1998.

For a union to grow, its current members must feel a personal stake in the organizing process. Such a feeling is what enabled the members of Yale's Local 35 to stand firm in support of the organizing effort and strike by the clerical workers in Local 34. The strike could easily have been defeated had the members of Local 35 felt aggrieved by the attention lavished on their white-collar sister local. As Sirabella pointed out, "John and the whole team quite naturally immersed themselves in Local 34, and they let 35 do it by themselves." It was Sirabella's constant preaching about labor unity that made Local 35 members see the organization of the white-collar workers as crucial to their own success.

Given the weakness of the NLRA process and the success of comprehensive campaigns, it is a mystery why so few unions actually use comprehensive campaigns and even fewer use them in an organized, comprehensive fashion. Why, for example, do the Steelworkers continue to rely on hot-shop organizing? The United Steelworkers is a union with a rich tradition, and, through the merger with PACE, it has acquired targets like box factories that might well yield significant results if approached through a comprehensive campaign. Is it fear of failure, fear of legal consequences, fear of squandering money that might well be needed to support other activities? Why didn't the United Auto Workers (UAW) use a comprehensive campaign and more aggressive tactics in its unsuccessful efforts to organize Japanese and Korean auto companies? This was a failure of major and lasting importance.

The unions that are not trying different approaches to organizing are not obviously failing, but they are not learning either. Perhaps they are awaiting changes in the law, but even a significantly revised NLRA would, at best, present an opportunity. It would not ensure success without risk and experimentation. Organizing campaigns are the graduate-study programs of unions. They are critical to organization development. There will be no success until unions generally are willing to risk failure, as HERE did and as the CWA did in its battle to survive in the late 1980s.

In 1986 I asked Sirabella how he explained the fact that few labor leaders looked to the success of Locals 217, 35, and 34 as a model for organizing. He shook his head dejectedly and said, "You have to remember that, first of all, most labor leaders are conservatives. They get into these positions of authority, power, and influence and comfort, large incomes, and all the other things, and they insulate themselves from any possibility of being deposed or even challenged. What they do is play it safe. . . . I think that the greatest deficit of the labor movement is this lack of vision and basic planning that any organization must do."

COMPETING MODELS OF WORKER POWER

During my second year as a professor at Yale Law School, a group of secretaries asked me whether they should join one of the unions trying to organize Yale's clerical workers and, if so, which one.

"Yes," I said, "but which unions are you talking about?"

"Well, both the UAW and the Hotel and Restaurant Employees union are trying to get us to sign up."

The answer now seemed obvious. "You should by all means sign up with the UAW," I told them. "They are more powerful, more socially conscious, and have no history of corruption. The Hotel Workers have no experience representing secretaries, and they have a reputation of being mob connected." It was the answer almost any "expert" would have given. The UAW was the shining face of industrial unionism, led by Walter Reuther, who had fought the bosses, the Communists, and the mob. It had played a key role in the passage of the 1964 Civil Rights Act. HERE was discussed mainly in stories of union corruption.

They thanked me, and I left feeling that I had used my knowledge of labor to good purpose. About a month later, I was in the same secretarial office. "What have you guys decided?" I asked.

"We've decided to go with the Hotel and Restaurant Workers."

"Really?" I hoped my voice did not show my disappointment. "Why HERE over the UAW?"

"We like their organizers better. They really care about us. They want to hear what we think. The UAW guys just kind of lecture us."

I was surprised and disappointed. Why had they ignored my advice and made such a blunder?

But now, three decades later, it seems obvious to me that the secretaries not only were right but were on to something important that labor experts (myself included) would eventually learn. The face of the HERE organizers was the face of labor's future. The UAW represented the militant but inadequately understood past. After the strike, one of the organizers described why Lucille Dickess, the president of Local 34, did not sign on with the UAW: "I think it was because they always talked about 'their union' and we talked about 'her union,' so she said, 'Okay if it's going to my union, I'm going to get involved and do it.'" Lucille, an eloquent speaker, became an inspiration to others, such as Yale graduate Danna Schneider, who now leads UNITE HERE's organizing drive in San Antonio.

This difference was understood by the Yale human-relations manager I interviewed (who wished to remain unnamed), who recognized both the strength of Local 34 and the weakness of the UAW organizers:

> Local 34 built a strong core of people who really have a sense of religion about the union movement—or if not the international union, at least the union at Yale. There's a hierarchy and the clerical and technical people are at the bottom of it, so what do they do, they get together and say hey, we're important, and they put their arms around it, and they wine-and-cheesed it at the start. [They] used to go up to the science area, and they talked to each other and they reinforced each other, and if you see the original group together, there's a real bond of affection and there's a little bit of the values of the women's movement in it.
>
> UAW sent in people who knew nothing about Yale University, didn't try to learn anything about the university. . . . [They] took the standard industrial-labor program to Yale, and it went over like a lead balloon. John Wilhelm and Paul Clifford, two recent Yale grads, didn't make the mistakes that UAW did. Also, they learned from Sirabella that the way to get to Yale is through the media, make events, call in the television cameras. That has more significance for the labor movement than for just the campus. If they want to get white-collar people, they can't use blue-collar tactics.

Even when I came to appreciate the skill and commitment of Local 34's organizers, I thought of the UAW-HERE comparison at Yale as isolated and unique, since each union was operating away from its core constituencies. I now see the Yale story as prophetic. My conversation with the secretaries took place around 1980. Shortly thereafter, each union would be confronted with major organizing challenges. The UAW faced opposition from the increasing number of foreign car companies building cars in the United States. HERE was confronted with the combined efforts of major hotels to reduce or eliminate its power in key cities, including Las Vegas, San Francisco, and Los Angeles. It also faced the task of restructuring its organizing tactics after the failure of Sirabella's national organizing campaign.

HERE has met its challenges. Before the recent economic collapse, it was stronger than ever in each of the cities mentioned. It has grown despite a series of major problems, including the devastating impact of 9/11.

The UAW has failed repeatedly to organize the foreign car companies, and it has continued to use old-fashioned NLRB-oriented organizing tactics. Doubtless, the answer is complex and multifaceted, but I believe that HERE's success is attributable at least in significant part to the excellence of its leadership, and that in turn is a reflection of the union's diversity and its openness to people from outside its ranks. This openness is one of Sirabella's major contributions to the union. It has brought into the union people as varied as John Wilhelm, Karl Lechow, Maria Elena Durazo, and Joe Daugherty. This was no accident. Sirabella believed that the union needed an infusion of the idealism that he saw and recognized in the anti-war and civil-rights movements.

This infusion was almost universally unpopular with the union's then-current staff and could never have happened without the support of Ed Hanley, as Sirabella recognized: "Hanley bit the bullet; that's why he deserves enormous credit for doing what he did because it was not a popular thing to bring these hot-shot young kids in the numbers that I brought them in."

The UAW has required that organizers come from within its own ranks. This is the current policy of most AFL-CIO unions. It has served to inhibit innovation. In an interview with me, Mike Casey insisted that diversity among organizers is the key to success: "I remember about eight or ten years ago, there was about an eight-month period where our hotel division was all men and they were young and older, good organizers and stuff, but they were all guys. I used to just dread going into those meetings and talking to them about shit because there just was not a mix, and it's not just gender, it's ethnicity, it's age, it's where you come from, your experience, and all that. People talk about hiring for diversity because it's the politically correct thing. Or the right thing to do. I say that's fine, but that's not the reason you do it. Because it's the most practical, the best, most effective way."

Tom Woodruff believes that the failure to hire outsiders as organizers reflects a basic misunderstanding of the process: "I used to argue with the UAW and the Steelworkers. I would say, you hire accountants, you hire lawyers, you hire office managers. And the response was, yeah, but those are all skilled jobs. That's why you're never going to be able to organize anybody because your view of an organizer is that it's an unskilled job. It's probably the most skilled job in the union."[7]

The importance of Sirabella's action in recruiting organizers like Wilhelm and Lechow was recognized by Betsy Aron, who has spent years studying HERE:

> In this story a (former rank-and-file) working-class leader, Sirabella, makes an unpopular and risky decision to recruit student activists, whom he then protects from political retribution by disapproving local leaders for the first decade of their union tenure while they mastered the techniques of representation and organizing strategies. Sirabella's most important contribution was not only the energy and ideas and incentives for organizing that he created; in addition, he buffered his acolytes from

the negative sanctions that other union leaders would have otherwise deployed against them, as they did . . . against innovative organizing initiatives. As an official reformist he legitimized their autonomy and provided some measure of protection for scaled-up collective action. Both the positive incentives and the buffering matter, but the first helps little without the second. Sirabella looked for three things in his 1973 recruits: intelligence, guts, and an understanding of the class struggle.[8]

The organizers whom Sirabella recruited into the union now provide the core of its leadership. They have kept the union in a constant organizing mode while other unions have focused on alternative programs and political activity. As Mike Casey pointed out to me, "Almost all of us are organizers, right? We weren't business agents, we weren't researchers, we were organizers, and so we naturally focused on organizing." There is no doubt some pride in his description of himself and other leaders of HERE as organizers and in his recognition that not all labor leaders are organizers. As Joe Daugherty told me, "I think he [Sirabella] would be quite pleased about how well his leadership development went."

Top organizers are, as Casey suggests, a special breed. Recognizing and recruiting them is crucial to the success of the labor movement. Everyone I've talked to has a somewhat different explanation of what makes someone a first-rate organizer. One of the most thoughtful answers came from Kris Rondeau of the Harvard Union of Technical and Clerical Workers (HUCTW) in an interview I conducted in 1986:

> I believe that to be a good organizer there are two things that you have to not only do well but be comfortable with. One is you have to have a strong, comfortable sense of yourself, and if you don't have that, your organizing will always be tainted. The other piece of it is connected to that. It is emotionally draining work. You have to be like an athlete in terms of your ability to not only know yourself but to empathize with somebody else. It's like the ability that writers talk about to become the object that you write about, to put themselves in somebody else's shoes that Shakespeare, for example, valued so highly—"where the bee sucks there suck I." Organizers have to be able to feel what somebody else feels in order to be really good at it, and it's not simple, it's not simple at all, to have to be on their toes all the time. I think you have to have a belief in happiness. You wouldn't ever, I think, become a union organizer if you didn't believe that there was a potential for happiness.

During the period that the HUCTW was affiliated with the UAW, Rondeau believed that the organizers she dealt with lacked this basic ability "to the point where I went home at night [and] I would cry on a regular basis." The

UAW organizers seemed to have little understanding of the importance to the union of organizing Harvard. They went out of their way to emphasize this point to Rondeau, now a major figure in organized labor. She made this clear in a letter to Owen Bieber, then the president of the UAW:

> I filed organizing report after organizing report with dozens of supplemental reports beyond what is required by organizers in the UAW. Later I was told by [a UAW official] that he had never read any of these reports. Incredibly I never had even one meeting about Harvard with . . . the director of organizing for Region 9A. Each time we did meet with Ted he told me and others involved in the Harvard UAW campaign directly, "Harvard may be important to you, but to me it's the least important project in the Region."
>
> [Union officials] were repeatedly invited to meetings of all kinds at Harvard—committee meetings, organizer training, strategy meetings, and big meetings of over 500 workers. Not once did one of them ever attend and they never met even one Harvard worker.[9]

It is difficult to imagine anything other than a feeling of separateness or perhaps incompetence in the presence of Harvard and its highly educated staff that could have led to such self-defeating behavior.

By contrast, the diversity of backgrounds and attitudes has provided an opportunity for HERE's leaders to learn from and teach each other. A perfect example of this dividend from diversity is Karl Lechow's relationships with Ed Hanley, from whom he learned, and Maria Elena Durazo, whom he instructed.

Lechow was a "red-diaper baby" who taught hatred for the boss when he was first hired by Sirabella. As he explained to me, he learned a different approach to organizing from Ed Hanley, whom he came to see as a mentor: "Ed Hanley came out of a different culture than Vinnie or John and I for sure. I found his approach to stuff not irritating but very perplexing to me. I would say, I think we should be tougher or more oppositional or engage in more in-your-face tactics. He was actually over a course of ten or fifteen years very, very helpful in showing us how to gain by being cooperative as well as by being oppositional. He introduced some tools to us—look, guys, there are a number of ways of skinning a cat and you know these people we're dealing with are very powerful. It may be worthwhile not only to have some struggle but also to have some cooperation."

And Lechow was able to pass on a more class-oriented approach to Maria Elena Durazo, now one of the most powerful people in the labor movement, who recalls his mentoring with affection. Lechow recounted some of the advice he gave Durazo:

In the late eighties, early nineties, I had talks with Maria Elena about everything—the movement, the world. One time we were in a Chinese restaurant. I said, Maria Elena, why did you get into this stuff? She said, well, I'm Chicano, I really felt that my people should be really backed up. And I said, that's laudable, but I didn't get into the movement because of the Jews. Now, there are a lot of Jews in New York, and they are in the working class. That's not what brought me. I really think of it as working people. When I help in San Francisco, it's Chinese, and in Chicago, its African Americans, in here it's Latinos. I don't even speak the language, but I don't give a damn. When I did Yale, it was women, so you have got to really broaden your reasons for doing this. Because I said it's not always going to be Latino here. I said, Maria Elena, I'm going to fight for Latinos because 80 percent of the workers here are Latino. But I want to have the Asians that are leaders and the African Americans that are leaders and the whites that are leaders, and we are going to have the staff people who are the best, and if they come from El Salvador instead of Mexico, we are going to promote them. So you've got to understand that that is where I'm coming from. I think that's where you should be coming from. She was learning. She's brilliant now. She leads the immigrant workers—she's wonderful.

The organizers whom Sirabella hired for Local 217 and for the organizing project were almost all outsiders, with the partial exception of D. Taylor, who was both a college student and a waiter. Sirabella told me in 1990 that he wished he had recruited more from the union's rank and file. Since then, most organizer hiring has focused on insiders, immigrants, and people with working-class backgrounds. Taylor, for example, who is constantly on the alert for organizers, limits his search to members. But there are enough idealistic young people fresh from college, like Sarah Julian, to keep a healthy mix.

Geoconda Arguello Kline, the president (the number-two position) of the Culinary, came from the ranks, as did almost all its new organizers. Taylor and Lechow are constantly on the watch for potential organizers. Julian is now seeking out new organizers from the rank and file. Some organizers have come from the union summer program. The essential fact is that HERE is constantly seeking new organizers and making a conscious effort to strike an appropriate balance of insiders (from the workforce) and outsiders. John Wilhelm believes that it is important to have leaders and organizers from a variety of different backgrounds. This creates the danger of discord, cliques, and power struggles. That it hasn't done so in HERE is undoubtedly due in part to the special skills of harmonizing people and making them feel good about themselves that Wilhelm possesses to a remarkable extent.

Why haven't other unions followed a similar path? Why do the majority of

AFL-CIO unions still recruit organizers solely from the rank and file? According to Stewart Acuff, the AFL-CIO's director of organizing, it is a combination of "tradition and ideology." I suspect that there is also an element of fear, the worry that Sirabella rejected when he hired Wilhelm: "When Vinnie hired me, one of the things he drummed into me from the beginning is that the biggest problem in the labor movement was insecurity. People are afraid to develop leaders because they would feel threatened by it. And to the extent that we've been able to avoid that trap, hopefully I've contributed. I think it's Vinnie's legacy."

Of course, it would be a mistake to overuse students or outside intellectuals and to develop the attitude that those with degrees are by virtue of their education bound to be better organizers than workers. Steve Early, a graduate of the New Left, has expressed concern with what he seems to believe is a disturbing trend in both the SEIU and UNITE HERE: "Over-reliance on former students often goes hand-in-hand with underutilization of workers themselves —both organized and unorganized in union campaigns. It avoids the hard, politically challenging work of creating a new organizing culture rooted in local unions and their communities. It also perpetuates the technocratic myth that deploying more professional staff is the key to success in organizing, bargaining, and politics. Any strategy for rebuilding union strength that relies so heavily on an infusion of paid help is deeply flawed."[10]

Early seems to have HERE in his sights as one of the guilty parties creating the danger of a top-down technocratic culture staffed by "paid help." As proof he cites a HERE recruitment brochure that reads "No experience is necessary. You provide the commitment to justice for working people and good communication skills. . . . We provide salary and excellent benefits plus constant training and endless opportunity for growth and leadership."

The problem with Early's critique is that it does not respond to the reality of HERE's approach to organizing, which is rooted in precisely what he advocates and which deplores the absence of "the hard . . . work of creating a new organizing culture rooted in local unions and their communities." How does he think the union succeeded in Las Vegas? How does he account for the remarkable solidarity of the Frontier strike, the emergence of Geoconda Kline, the leadership of Maria Elena Durazo, the remarkable success of Local 2? Surely he is aware of the union's diverse structure in Boston and Los Angeles. In fact, the former college students who have risen to positions of authority in HERE —among others, D. Taylor in Las Vegas, Paul Clifford in Toronto, and Henry Tamarin in Chicago—have been meticulous in searching out and recruiting rank-and-file organizers. This same approach is carried on today by Sarah Julian in Santa Clara. As she recounted to me, her first assignment was to help locate and train rank-and-file activists: "I was one of the only internal organizer reps for the first year or so after I started, and I ended up recruiting one of my leaders out of the committees to be an organizer in our local. We are always looking at who can be an organizer in the future. These leaders that are taking on these huge fights as part of our committees will be future organizers to be developing that leadership, people not only leading their workplace but to be leading the union . . . to be able to inspire someone. That is something else that is really satisfying."

The idea that HERE has somehow sinned against the concept of working-class unity by bringing in people like Julian or, for that matter, Wilhelm elevates class-based social theory over reality. Early's article drew a response from Lance Compa, an academic, labor reformer, and onetime United Electrical Workers organizer who was a Yale law student during the early 1970s: "I was lucky to watch Vinnie Sirabella and John Wilhelm work in the Yale strikes and organizing campaigns of the 1970s. . . . The insider-outsider combination epitomized by Sirabella and Wilhelm . . . is a model for the labor movement, not something to be scorned because former students are involved in key roles."[11] I agreed with Compa during my time at Yale, and I believe it even more strongly today.

The insider-outsider combination is what Yale-educated Paul Clifford, now the head of the Toronto local, sees as the great continuing source of strength for HERE: "I think the combination of John and Vinnie, one being Yale educated and one a grade ten or grade nine being together, I think together it's a pretty big tent. The wonderful thing about HERE is its ability to have people really respect each other; no matter where they came from within the labor movement, they learn from each other. The combination is really important, so we got leaders and staff from all the different backgrounds. A lot of our emphasis in Toronto now is immigrant workers, so recent hires have come from Eritrea and Guyana and Jamaica, and we've got people from all over the world all on our staff here in Toronto."

HERE, with its strong cadre of former student activists, makes certain to project the face of its members as the face of the union.

The UAW, with its tradition of hiring from inside, does not. With the fate of the U.S. auto industry seemingly in the balance, I watched and heard Ron Gettelfinger making his way from television news show to news show speaking in his serious, somewhat bureaucratic style, trying to explain why the UAW should not immediately accept the same wages and benefits as those granted by foreign automakers in America. He was earnest and knowledgeable but not very effective. I thought to myself that he should be accompanied by autoworkers who would talk about their mortgages, their kids' educational needs, their struggle to maintain a decent lifestyle with fewer hours and almost no overtime. They could have been far more effective than Gettelfinger. I asked a knowledgeable labor person whether my reaction was unfair. He responded, "You're not being overly harsh at all. This is enormously frustrating. He should have hundreds of autoworkers with him at all times."

TAKING THE MOVEMENT OUT
OF THE LABOR MOVEMENT

Union Politics

Unions are inevitably political institutions. At their best, they reflect the views and interests of their members. This can be achieved only by a democratic political process that gives members the power to decide on priorities and actions. There is, however, a less noble but constantly present aspect to union politics. It involves those with power who cut ethical corners to remain in power, thwart opposition, and stifle different points of view. Harmful union politics is largely about the competition for advancement and recognition. Sometimes it involves existing staff resisting the infusion of new people with new ideas. Sometimes it reflects those with more education and status treating rank-and-file workers with contempt. Having spent more than half my life in academia, I am well acquainted with the harmful potential impact of intellectual rivalries, constant competitive ambition, destructive concern with status, and overcoddled egos in high positions. And yet nowhere that I know of are the negative aspects of politics more prevalent or more destructive than in the labor movement. I have witnessed union politics' constantly occurring malevolent impact in labor education programs, organizing drives, staff appointments, leadership decisions, and strikes. I have spoken to union members, staff, and leaders about its impact. No one has denied its presence or tried to minimize its impact. It has been a constant factor in the campaigns and struggles described in this book. It threatened to tear apart the valuable merger between UNITE and HERE. It has led to bitter attacks on John Wilhelm by those who should be his allies. It played a major—and harmful—role in the International Paper strike, causing union leaders and staff to fear rather than applaud the creativity of the comprehensive campaign developed by Local 14.

During the strike against International Paper, this concern was manifested most clearly by the negative reaction of the staff and officers to former civil-rights activist Peter Kellman and his ally Local 14 president Bill Meserve. It was Kellman who turned the Jay strike into a crusade. Bill Meserve told me: "The organization we had here, it was great. In all due respect, it was not because of me. It was Peter Kellman. Peter is probably the world's best organizer." Robby Lucarelli, the union's vice president, concluded that "because of Peter, we had, from what I know of different strikes in the country, in my opinion, the best-organized strike from all points of view."[12]

Kellman's approach would have won the approval of Sirabella. Each saw the key to victory in the mobilization of the membership. Each step in the comprehensive campaign developed during the strike involved participation of the membership.

Not a single one of the international union's leaders gave Kellman credit for the immense and original organizing that he did. The union's vice president with jurisdiction over New England thought that he had too much influence, and another vice president told me that Kellman "was not the sort of person I wanted to be associated with." An officer of one of the Mobile, Alabama, locals told me that "the one the international [union] was really not fond of was Pete Kellman."

Bill Meserve, Local 14's president, was viewed with suspicion by those in the international union who feared his popularity with the union's rank and file. Richard Thomas, then a young union staff member, told me that Meserve's popularity with the rank and file frightened union officials: "What I see as one of the greatest shames within our union is the fact that some of our executive officers in the UPIU [United Paperworkers International Union] misconceived these people's determination and enthusiasm for a coup attempt, and in all actuality it never was a coup attempt. It was determination and dedication to fight off the evils of [International Paper]. The international [union] hadn't seen nothing in all our years with that much emotion, and that scared them. They did the best they could to get away from them."

In this, as in so many areas, Vinnie Sirabella was unusually perceptive. He believed that internal union politics made union leaders fearful. As he explained to me, he made sure to pass this message to John Wilhelm very early in their relationship:

John, you have brains, you can read, you can write, you can think, you have a nice personality and a nice presence. All that is advantageous, but it doesn't mean a piss-hole in the snow if you don't learn the politics. First, last, and always, the labor movement is a political institution. Don't ever forget that. And you have to know what the political parameters are under which you can function. Particularly an outsider. I came from the rank and file, and even I have difficulty with those kinds of problems. And you've got to understand there are a lot of people that don't think like we do. And we can't be looking down on them making snide remarks etcetera, etcetera —that will get you only a ticket to oblivion.

But you know in the best sense John is a good politician. He really is. He is what I like to call—what I used to call myself—a practical idealist. That may sound like some form of hypocrisy, but it really isn't, because if you are part and parcel of a political institution . . . [and if] you don't understand that, you're not going to accomplish anything.

Sirabella believed that internal politics played a large role in thwarting the national organizing drive that he developed: "When these kids went out into the city, they learned some of the political facts of life, that not every one of these local union leaders welcomed us. Moreover, some of their staffs were uneasy about these kids being around for fear they might take their job in some unknown way." He was sure that the impact of union politics was not adequately understood by his trainees. He told me at the time, "John is very seasoned. These kids aren't. He can't transfer his political skills, for example, to them. Nor can I, as a matter of fact." When Sirabella decided that "trying to do what we did at Yale wasn't working," he set up two conferences in Las Vegas during the summer of 1987 to "analyz[e] what we had done up to that point." He concluded the meeting by telling the young organizers, "If I were to drop dead in the next five minutes, I want to leave you with one message you should never forget: learn the politics of the labor movement, because you will never make it otherwise. I don't care how smart you are, how dedicated you are. If you don't understand the politics, it won't work. They will kill you. The politicians running the labor movement will kill you."

Sirabella's "kids" are now the key leaders of the union, and they, together with Wilhelm, have made a major effort to keep political infighting to a minimum in their jurisdictions. When HERE was an independent union, they were largely successful. Wilhelm set an example of openness, which Paul Clifford described to me: "I think of John in terms of his ability to look at things comprehensively and sort of enjoying figuring out strategy and enjoying engaging people in discussions of strategy. He is really good at that. I think of his selflessness and lack of ego, patience, keeping things in perspective, believing that things will work out in the long run if you do the right thing—sort of a sense of integrity, not motivated to do anything for his own selfish interest."

Jeff Fiedler considered the relationship between Wilhelm and his lieutenants unique and a powerful factor: "It's very different from what I've experienced with other unions. People are loyal to John. John is loyal to them. It is not this typical Washington kiss up, kick down. It is not just loyalty to John, it's others, too. People don't seem to me, in all my experience with all those folks over all those years, burning white-phosphorus hot with ambition for position. They are burning to accomplish something and are content to know more than many other unions that they will achieve position by accomplishment."

All of which makes the battles between John Wilhelm and Bruce Raynor and between Wilhelm and Andy Stern, as well as the attacks by Steve Rosenthal, surprising. How did Wilhelm, a preacher of unity, a distributor of praise, a seeker of compromise, become the target of personal attack from people who were thought by many to be the intellectual leaders of organized labor?

Perhaps increased political infighting is a natural result of increasing the number of credentialed intellectuals in the leadership. According to Fiedler, intellectuals in the labor movement are the ones most likely to be seduced by the indicia of power: memberships on public boards, trips to the White House, being quoted in newspapers and interviewed on television. They act, not surprisingly, much like academics. As he told me, "Intellectuals have got the fucking problem. Almost uniformly. They're seduced." It is clear from many statements that he considers Wilhelm an exception. He did not give me his views of either Raynor or Stern. But I have conducted enough interviews to know that both are famous for their egos and for their ambition. John too is ambitious, although his ambition is tied very much to the success of his union.

It seems strange, almost bizarre, to sympathetic observers that a movement based on solidarity, committed to values of beneficence, and so in need of revitalization should be expending its energy in mutual anger, recrimination, and destructiveness. But angry political battling is so prevalent, especially in the higher ranks of organized labor, as to make one wonder whether there is something more than the normal competitive aspects of human nature at work. Labor leaders claim to hold themselves to a higher, more value-based standard of behavior. And therein may lie the problem. The altruistic foundation of the movement may provide both a motive and an excuse for internecine warfare. If Steve Rosenthal believes that he is in fact "repairing the world" in his battle with John Wilhelm, it is imperative that he succeed so that the world may be made better. And any harm inflicted on those who stand in the way of this noble purpose is more than justified by the importance of the goal. If the harmful effects of such internal political battling are to be overcome, they will have to be acknowledged and dealt with directly by union officials.

Professionalism and Autocratic Leadership

During the strike against International Paper, leaders of Local 14 proposed sending out teams of strikers to win support from workers at other International Paper mills, but UPIU president Wayne Glenn rejected the idea: "I don't think it necessary to have groups traveling around the country. I think it would be much less expensive if we let our trained staff handle work on this problem in each location."[13] Later, when strikers from Local 14 developed a plan to write letters to mobilize paperworkers at other locations, the international union refused to make names and addresses available to them.

Glenn's behavior is illustrative of the antipathy that many union leaders have toward member involvement. They believe that unions work better when professionals handle delicate matters than when the membership gets involved. I understand that point of view. Members are frequently ill informed, untrained, and confused about the issues that unions confront.

When I was the chief negotiator for the Connecticut State Police Union, it was the union's policy to encourage the members of the bargaining unit to sit in on negotiations. Afterward, many would have suggestions about negotiating positions and strategies that they were eager to tell me about. Most of the time their ideas reflected a lack of understanding of collective bargaining. For example, they repeatedly urged me to reopen settled issues on which the union had compromised. Their involvement took up time and rarely added ideas that the bargaining committee had not considered. They were, as one of the committee members put it, "a regular pain in the ass." We all spent a good deal of time informing the members about the negotiating process. The police union's democratic approach was costly in terms of time and emotion. But it paid off when the union conducted an original job action that involved stopping and warning speeding motorists but not ticketing them. The entire membership participated, which made disciplining those who took part impossible. And it was this display of solidarity that forced the state to make far more concessions than it originally contemplated.

Another reason that union leaders often discourage member involvement in union activities is their desire to control the union's positions. For example, Wayne Glenn did not want sympathy strikes to take place at other International Paper facilities. As long as the staff controlled events, he could be sure that his policy would be followed. But if the Jay strikers met with paperworkers at other mills, they might encourage all kinds of sympathy strikes and different types of job actions that would endanger his efforts to negotiate a compromise. Movements are more exciting and ultimately more effective than tightly run organizations, but they are far harder to control.

Success and the Spirit of Movement

As surprising as it may seem at first, success is often the inhibitor of movement building. When leadership is competent, employers are fair, employment is full, wages are high, and jobs are secure, it is difficult to maintain the spirit of movement. Members under these circumstances will be content to let the leaders make needed decisions while they attend to family or personal concerns. According to rank-and-file activist Marc Norton, the current successful leadership of Mike Casey in San Francisco makes the once highly volatile membership passive. Back in the early 1980s, when there was great dissatisfaction with the leadership of the trustee Joseph Belardi, "there were a lot of different groups, there was a lot of different points of view, there was a lot of dissension." But under the successful leadership of Mike Casey, he finds the membership far more passive:

> Democracy is a good thing. But if they are delivering the bacon, you don't care that much. And that's sort of the attitude that I see these days in our union. Both in the international union, as far as I can see, but particularly on the local level. Democracy is just a game everybody talks about, but in some ways it's sort of a *Godfather-ish* sort of thing. They do well by us, okay.
>
> The key is they deliver the bacon. There's not like any material reason that people would have to fight over anything unless they have a very different point of view and they have a way of expressing it, and it just doesn't happen very often. When I walked into this union in '76, there was several different caucuses, there was an active rank-and-file movement, people were questioning lots of things, it was a different period in history. That's not there now. There's no independent rank-and-file movement anymore.
>
> Mike is the best thing we've had as long as I've been around. But that doesn't mean that everything's perfect and everything's the way I wish it would be. . . . There is no real vehicle for presenting an alternative point of view. I mean, you are free to disagree, but it's not like you'll get anywhere with that, because the union is good at what they do. There hasn't been a seriously contested election since 1985. And you can take that as a sign of satisfaction, which is true, and you can take it as a sign of a lack of democracy, which is also true.

Conclusion

For organized labor to play its proper role in turning the American dream into reality, the labor movement must be not only for the people, as most unions are, but also of the people, in ways that most unions are not. Workers should be involved in organizing and bargaining and in the selection of their leaders. They should feel that the union is theirs and is worthy of their devotion, support, and participation. This does not mean that union leadership must come solely from the workforce, but it does mean that workers should take part at every level of leadership. Members must believe, on the basis of established fact, that they have the opportunity to shape the union's actions and priorities. This is what Vinnie Sirabella practiced and preached. It is what he passed on to John Wilhelm. It is at the heart of UNITE HERE's approach to organizing and bargaining.

Member-centered unionism is not always the easiest way for unions to grow. Sometimes organizing is more easily accomplished through negotiation between union leaders and management officials eager for industrial peace. Still, it is not unreasonable to believe that workers can sometimes be brought into the process of governance once they are organized and have the opportunity to learn the advantages of unionization. Although top-down organizing is in rhetorical disfavor, it may on occasion be the only process available. But member-based organizing leads to stronger unions, and member-based collective bargaining leads to better contracts. Member involvement may make the process of bargaining and organizing longer, but in the long run it will pay for itself by increasing the overall strength of the union. John Wilhelm's view of how the process works at its best is described by Betsy Aron: "Its potential is greater than that of the staff. The committee attracts and creates leadership. They alone create an environment of courage and solidarity. Then the committee builds the cadre, who build the local, who build the labor movement."[1]

For a variety of reasons, it is easy for union leaders to forget that member involvement cannot be limited to periods of contract negotiation and strikes. Professionalism is valuable for union staff, but leaders must be vigilant to ensure that it is not purchased at the cost of member sovereignty. Member sovereignty is what makes organized labor a movement.

The technicality of the law is one reason why professionalism sometimes takes precedence over movement. It is one of the reasons why most unions understandably see the law as their enemy. Change along the lines suggested in earlier chapters can reduce the cost of organizing and bargaining. But there is no magic pill—certainly not the Employee Free Choice Act, which by replacing comprehensive campaigns would have the perverse effect of removing workers from the organizing process. The change in the law that would most encourage worker involvement would be to eliminate the danger of permanent replacement. But a new law on strike replacement would not provide instant solidarity nor ensure that the strike weapon is properly used.

Solidarity and involvement will remain the key to victorious strikes. As Sherri Chiesa told me when comparing the union's strike in 1984 with its strike in 1986, "But, bottom line is, all the tactics aside, the only reason we could carry it out is because we organized the members. And that is what was different from the 1984 strike."

Notes

I began doing research for this book many years ago while I was on the faculty of Yale Law School. During the late 1970s and early 1980s, I witnessed the organizing drive of the university's clerical and technical workers by Local 34 of the Hotel Employees & Restaurant Employees International Union (HERE). The drive was followed by a long, bitter, and ultimately successful strike. I became intrigued with the union's member-centered approach, which was far different from the approach used by organizers of other unions. Because I found Local 34's organizing methods unique and effective, I undertook to interview both organizers and members. I learned that the local's methodology came from the ideas of Vincent Sirabella and his then-disciple John Wilhelm. Between 1984 and 1990, I interviewed both Wilhelm and Sirabella on numerous occasions. I had in mind a book on union organizing. The following people were interviewed as part of my study of HERE and new approaches to organizing:

Vincent Sirabella
John Wilhelm
Paul Clifford, organizer
Karl Lechow, vice president
Warren Heyman, organizer
Ellen Thomson, organizer
Richard Bensinger, director of the AFL-CIO Organizing Institute
Lucille Dickess, president of Local 34

Deborah Chernoff, Local 34 member
Michael Boyle, Local 34 member
Lee Berman, Local 34 member
Molly Ladd-Taylor, Yale student
Kris Rondeau, president of the Harvard Union of Technical and Clerical Workers
Morty Miller, HERE organizer, Local 34
Vicki Saporta, director of organizing (IBT), 1980s

When in 2005 I undertook to write this book, I continued my study of HERE, by then essentially the hospitality division of UNITE HERE, and broadened my inquiry into the tactics of other unions and labor leaders. The following people were interviewed between 2005 and 2009:

AFL-CIO:
John Sweeney, president (Jan. 22, 2008)
John Hiatt, general counsel (Apr. 16, 2008)
Stewart Acuff, director of organizing (Nov. 12, 2008 and Apr. 15, 2008)
Karen Nussbaum, director of Working America (Dec. 20, 2007)

SEIU:
Andy Stern, president (Nov. 7, 2007)
Carol Golubock, SEIU attorney (Aug. 1, 2008)
Kirk Adams, director of organizing (Oct. 26, 2007 and Aug. 15, 2009)
Anna Burger, chair of Change to Win (Nov. 7, 2007)
Tom Woodruff, director of the Change to Win Strategic Organizing Center (Nov. 21, 2007)
Judy Scott, general counsel (three interviews from May 7, 2008 to Sept. 23, 2008)

UNITE HERE:
John Wilhelm, president of HERE and copresident of UNITE HERE (three interviews from Oct. 10, 2007 to Nov. 25, 2008)
Tom Snyder, political director (Apr. 8, 2008)
Sherri Chiesa, secretary-treasurer (Dec. 6, 2007)
Sarah Julian, HERE organizer (Aug. 5, 2008)
Paul Clifford, head of Toronto local (Dec. 22, 2008)
D. Taylor, secretary-treasurer of the Culinary Workers Union (Nov. 27, 2007, Apr. 30, 2008, and Feb. 25, 2009)
Bill Granfield, president of New York Local 100 (Apr. 17, 2008 and Sept. 4, 2008)
Geoconda Arguello Kline, president of the Culinary Workers Union (May 1, 2008)
Joe Daugherty, mission director of UNITE HERE, Detroit, Michigan (Sept. 2, 2008)
David Prouty, general counsel (Feb. 12, 2008)
Peter Ward, president of New York Local 6 (Nov. 12, 2008)
Mike Casey, president of San Francisco Local 2 (Nov. 7, 2008)

Maria Elena Durazo, executive secretary-treasurer of the Los Angeles County Federation of Labor (Feb. 21, 2008)

Karl Lechow, international vice president (Jan. 31, 2008 to Sept. 20, 2009)

Marc Norton, member of San Francisco Local 2 (summer 2009)

Danna Schneider, organizer (Sept. 15, 2009)

Willie Gonzalez, Texas state director (Sept. 20, 2009)

Andrea van den Heever, director of the Connecticut Center for a New Economy (Apr. 18, 2008)

Jim DuPont, leader (Sept. 4, 2009)

Fran Stone, legal director (Sept. 15, 2009)

Trent LeonLierman, organizer (Feb. 19, 2009)

Attorneys:

Richard McCracken, labor lawyer at the law firm of Davis, Cowell & Bowe (Dec. 6, 2007)

From 2007 to 2009, I interviewed the following people:

HERE:

John Wilhelm, president

D. Taylor, secretary-treasurer of the Culinary Workers Union

Karl Lechow, director of organizing

Geoconda Arguello Kline, president of the Culinary Workers Union

Joe Daugherty, coordinator of the Detroit Region

David Prouty, general counsel

Peter Ward, president, New York Local 6

Mike Casey, president, San Francisco Local 2

Tom Snyder, political director

Paul Clifford, head of Toronto local

Bill Granfield, president of New York Local 100

Sarah Julian, HERE organizer

Andrea van den Heever, director of the Connecticut Center for a New Economy

Jeff Fiedler, president of Research Associates of America

Cecil Roberts, president of the United Mine Workers of America

AFL-CIO:

John Sweeney, president

John Hiatt, general counsel

Stewart Acuff, director of organizing

Karen Nussbaum, director of Working America

SEIU:

Andy Stern, president

Judy Scott, general counsel
Katherine Lev, management attorney

Others:
Peter Kellman, president of the Southern Maine Labor Council (July 9, 2008)
Roland Samson, organizing coordinator of the United Steelworkers (July 4, 2008)
Jeff Fiedler, former president of Research Associates of America (eight interviews between
    May 28, 2008 and Apr. 1, 2009)
Richard LaCosse, vice president of the United Steelworkers (May 8, 2008)
Saru Jayaraman, Restaurant Opportunities Center (July 16, 2008)
Ray Rogers, Corporate Campaigns Inc. (Jan. 11, 2008 and Mar. 31, 2009)
Cecil Roberts, president of the United Mine Workers of America (May 27, 2008)
Crystal Lee Sutton, union activist and inspiration for the movie character Norma Rae
    (Apr. 28, 2009)

I also received e-mails from the following people:

John Wilhelm
Judy Scott
Tom Snyder
D. Taylor

All the quotations in this book from any of the named persons are from the interviews
and e-mails unless otherwise noted.

PREFACE

1. *Getman v. NLRB,* 450 F.2d 670 (D.C. Cir. 1971). Judge Wright said that "the Board's position suffers from the obvious self-justifying tendency of an institution which in over 30
   years has itself never engaged in the kind of much needed systematic empirical effort to
   determine the dynamics of an election campaign or the type of conduct which actually
   has a coercive impact. The public interest need for such an empirical investigation into
   the assumptions underlying the Board's regulation of campaign tactics has for some time
   been recognized by labor law scholars. This particular study has been reviewed and supported by virtually every major scholar in the labor law field."

CHAPTER 1. THE NEED FOR UNIONS

1. Robert J. Lalonde and Bernard D. Meltzer, "Hard Times for Unions: Another Look at
   the Significance of Employer Illegalities," 58 *U. Chi. L. Rev.* 953 (1991). Unions represent
   only 13.5 percent of the workforce and less than 10 percent in the private sector. *See* Dan
   Clawson, *The Next Upsurge: Labor and the New Social Movements* 1 (2003).
2. *See* Russ Roberts, Op-Ed, "Workers Are Fine with Fewer Unions," *L.A. Times,* Feb. 17,
   2007.

3. *See* Lawrence Mishel, Jared Bernstein, and John Schmitt, *The State of Working America: 1996–1997,* at 3 (1998).

4. CEOs and schoolteachers both typically have master's degrees, but schoolteachers have seen only modest gains since 1973, whereas CEOs have seen their income rise from about thirty times that of the average worker in 1970 to more than three hundred times as much today. Paul Krugman, *The Conscience of a Liberal* 136 (2007).

5. *See* Harvard Researchers Link Medical Costs to Bankruptcy, Posting of John Amato to Crooks and Liars, http://crooksandliars.com/john-amato/harvard-researchers-links-medical-costs (June 5, 2009, 4:00 p.m.).

6. Krugman, *supra* note 4, at 149.

7. Michael Yates, *Why Unions Matter* 17 (1998).

8. *The Employee Free Choice Act: Restoring Economic Opportunity for Working Families; Hearing before the Senate Committee on Health, Education, Labor, and Pensions,* 110th Cong. 22 (2007) [hereinafter *EFCA Hearings*] (prepared statement of Lawrence Mishel), *available at* http://www.gpo.gov/fdsys/pkg/CHRG-110shrg508/pdf/CHRG-110shrg508.pdf.

9. *Strengthening America's Middle Class through the Employee Free Choice Act: Hearing before the Subcommittee on Health, Employment, Labor, and Pensions of the House Committee on Education and Labor,* 110th Cong. 72 (2007) (statement of Harley Shaiken), *available at* http://www.gpo.gov/fdsys/pkg/CHRG-110hhrg11032906/html/CHRG-110hhrg 11032906.pdf.

10. Donald W. Beachler, "Race, God, and Guns: Union Voting in the 2004 Presidential Election," 10 *Working USA* 311 (2007). Beachler notes that in the 2006 senatorial elections, the six Democrats that defeated incumbent Republicans ran campaigns with strong populist elements.

11. *Id.* In each of the past three presidential elections, the Democratic candidate won 59 percent of the vote. Had union membership been slightly higher in either 2000 or 2004, Bush would not have been able to claim victory.

12. Krugman, *supra* note 4, at 69.

13. Jody Carlson, *George C. Wallace and the Politics of Powerlessness: The Wallace Campaigns for the Presidency, 1964–1976,* at 33 (1981). A classic example was the role of the Indiana AFL-CIO in combating the presidential campaign of George Wallace in 1964. The labor movement changed the focus of attack and pointed out that wages were low and unions were weak in right-to-work Alabama. The attack worked well enough that Wallace felt compelled to respond by trumpeting his support from Alabama unions. It was the best that he could do. But labor's attack had forced him to do battle on an issue on which he was comparatively weak. As a result, he received less than 30 percent of the Democratic vote and less than 20 percent of the total vote. He was weaker among union voters than among voters generally.

14. Clayton Sinyai, *Schools of Democracy: A Political History of the American Labor Movement* 205–207 (2006).

15. HERE Local 6, *The History of New York City Hotel Workers in the 20th Century* (2001) (on file with author).

16. *Id.*

17. Michael D. Yates, *Why Unions Matter* 20 (1998).

18. And workers contribute little to the improvement of methods and processes. Studies show that workers fear that suggesting improvement will lead to adverse results.

19. He was a guest speaker at a class taught at the Stanford Business School by Professor Robert Flannagan and me in 1976. He made this remark in response to a student who wondered how he could favor a law like the NLRA that rejected market principles.

20. *EFCA Hearings, supra* note 8, at 21 (prepared statement of Lawrence Mishel).

21. According to the Worker Representation and Participation Survey reported by the U.S. Department of Labor Appendix A, 90 percent of current union members would vote to keep the union in a new representation election. The Worker Representation and Participation Survey was directed by Richard Freeman and Joel Rogers and conducted by Princeton Survey Research Associates in the fall of 1994.

CHAPTER 2. THE FALL OF ORGANIZED LABOR

1. I taught at Indiana University during this period and was a member of the Labor Advisory Committee.

2. Lee Cross, who was an attorney and the labor-relations adviser to Cummings Engine, which was headquartered in Columbus, Indiana, and was one of the state's largest nonunion manufacturing companies, told me that he regularly matched whatever increases the autoworkers obtained.

3. Vincent J. Sirabella, Remarks at the Hotel Restaurant and Catering Trade Group Conference of the International Union of Food and Allied Workers Association in Limassol, Cyprus (Nov. 11, 1987). Sirabella, however, did not share that view. As he explained, "I never shared that view then nor do I now; and those who did began to preside over the liquidation of their unions in one way or another."

4. Dale Belman and Paula B. Voos, "Changes in Union Wage Effects by Industry: A Fresh Look at the Evidence," 43 *Industrial Relations* 491 (2004). From the mid-1980s to the mid-1990s, the percentage of unionized private-sector employees dropped from 21.6 percent to 10.2 percent. This drop was accompanied by a drop in benefits, real hourly wages, and employment security, as well as an increase in work hours for union employees.

5. *See* David Moberg, "The U.S. Labor Movement Faces the Twenty-first Century," *in Which Direction for Organized Labor? Essays on Organizing, Outreach, and Internal Transformations* 21 (Bruce Nissen ed., 1999).

6. Ronald I. McKinnon, "Government Deficits and the Deindustrialization of America," *Economists' Voice,* vol. 1, issue 3, article 1 (2004), http://www.bepress.com/ev/vol1/iss3/art1/. McKinnon notes that since the 1960s, the percentage of the workforce employed in the manufacturing sector has fallen from 24 percent to just 10.5 percent. This problem has been exacerbated as the United States consumes products made by cheaper, nonunion overseas labor. He estimates that the trade deficit caused by this consumption equals the loss of 4.7 million manufacturing jobs.

7. Leo Troy, "Reflections on Getman's 'Another Look at Labor and the Law,'" *in The Future of Labor Unions: Organized Labor in the 21st Century* 157 (Julius G. Getman and F. Ray Marshall eds., 2004).

8. Paul Krugman, *The Conscience of a Liberal* 150 (2007).

9. Dorothee Benz, "Labor's Ace in the Hole: Casino Organizing in Las Vegas," 26 *New Pol. Sci.* 525 (2004).

10. Daisy Rooks, "Cowboy Mentality: Organizers and Occupational Commitment in the New Labor Movement," *Lab. Stud. J.,* Sept. 2003, at 33.

11. Benz, *supra* note 9.

12. *See* David Witwer, *Corruption and Reform of the Teamsters Union* 3–4 (2003).

13. During his 2000 election campaign, Al Gore was accused of favoring special interest groups with his support of organized labor. He responded by arguing that he was frequently attacked by organized labor for his positions. This reflects a long-standing enmity between unions and environmentalists, an enmity that has done credit to neither group.

14. Richard E. Walton, Joel E. Cutcher-Gershenfeld, and Robert B. McKersie, *Strategic Negotiations: A Theory of Change in Labor-Management Relations* 7 (2000).

15. Many commentators attribute the origin of this plan to Ronald Reagan's dismissal of the air-traffic controllers and the subsequent demise of their union.

16. International Paper Company, once the model for progressive labor-management relations, set the groundwork for a union-destroying strike by forcing the United Paperworkers International Union to disband its multi-mill bargaining units. This led to a major sixteen-month strike.

17. *See* Abraham K. Turkson, *Save American Jobs: New Business Ideas to Retain Jobs in America* 131 (2005). In the past twenty years, employment in the steel industry in the United States has dropped 80 percent.

18. William F. Averyt and K. Ramagopal, "Strategic Disruption and Transaction Cost Economics: The Case of the American Auto Industry and Japanese Competition," 8 *Int'l Bus. Rev.* 39, 44–45 (1999). These automakers operate primarily with nonunion labor in states like Tennessee that limit labor contracts. This move essentially defeats the goal of American automakers of luring Japanese manufacturers to the United States to subject them to the higher labor costs experienced by American automakers.

CHAPTER 3. THE NLRA ORGANIZING PROCESS

1. In *NLRB v Gissel Packing Co.,* 395 U.S. 575 (1969), the Supreme Court affirmed the right of management to refuse to recognize a card majority. Before the early 1960s, management could legally refuse recognition and insist on an election by claiming to have a good-faith doubt about the validity of the cards.

2. NLRB, *About Us, Representation Elections.*

3. The employer speech or handout would often state something like "The union will pull you out on strike."

4. This quotation and other quotations from management campaigns come from material collected between 1971 and 1976 as part of the study of union representation campaigns that I conducted together with professors Stephen Goldberg and Jeanne Brett (Herman). *See* Julius G. Getman, Stephen B. Goldberg, and Jeanne B. Herman, *Union Representation Elections: Law and Reality* (1976). (This study is discussed in chapter 17.) I checked on the continuing relevance of these discussions with Stewart Acuff, the director of organizing at the AFL-CIO.

5. Statements of this type, of course, carry a hint of reprisal, but they are permissible under current law. The employer can argue that once a collective-bargaining agreement is signed, it can no longer do small favors for the employees.

6. Some unions issue guarantee letters of their own, promising that no strike will be called except by a two-thirds vote of the employees and pledging not to collect dues until a collective-bargaining agreement is signed with benefits far greater than the dues.

7. *Quoted in* Peter Drier, "Why He Was In Memphis," *American Prospect* (Web only), Jan. 15, 2007, http://www.prospect.org/cs/articles?articleId=12380.

8. From material collected during my six-year study of union and representation elections.

9. Tom Woodruff, the director of organizing for the labor confederation Change to Win, believes that the one significant change in management campaigns during the past fifteen years is that they have become more time consuming and are more prone to hammer away at the basic themes discussed in this chapter.

10. I later attended a seminar by the firm of Jackson Lewis on how to defeat unions. The messages were sensible but neither illegal nor creative.

CHAPTER 4. HERE AND ITS HISTORY

1. The early history is largely taken from Matthew Josephson, *Union House, Union Bar: The History of the Hotel and Restaurant Employees and Bartenders International Union* (1956).

2. Indeed, over half the members were bartenders.

3. Josephson, *supra* note 1, at 102.

4. According to the union's rules, one could hold a single position for only six months. As a result, Ernst shuttled back and forth between his paid job as secretary and his unpaid position as president of the local. When he was president, he worked as a waiter.

5. Josephson, *supra* note 1, at 140.

6. *Id.* at 136–140.

7. *Id.* at 145.

8. According to Josephson, a particularly heated battle erupted in Cleveland, a HERE stronghold with a well-run local and a history of good relations with management. In July 1930, the Cleveland Hotel Association sent a curt letter to the union announcing that it would "not continue, renew, or enter into any contract or relations." A long, nationally significant strike and lockout followed. Both the national union and the local spent almost all their funds in the battle. But when it ended, the local was intact and the loyalty of the membership secured for the next half century.

9. As reported by Josephson, it had been "one of the richest in the union with reserve funds of about $15,000 in 1930. By 1932 this was all gone, since the members had voted to pay cash relief to the unemployed." Josephson, *supra* note 1, at 188.

10. Jean Maddern Pitrone, *Myra* 23–28 (1980).

11. Many old locals were organized by craft, but new unions were amalgamations of crafts, as urged by the Congress of Industrial Organizations (CIO). But even as it grew and changed, HERE was locked in battle with the more left-wing Food Workers Industrial Union. And battles between old-fashioned unionists and racketeers who had become in-

terested in the union during the days of Prohibition continued. It had become a mixed union in terms of the eternal battle of craft versus industrial organization.

12. Josephson, *supra* note 1, at 25–27. The convention renominated Flore and raised the stature of Ernst, who was elected secretary-treasurer, Jere Sullivan's old position. McLane, then a vice president and member of the union's executive board, lost his position to Ed S. Miller of Kansas City, who was himself destined to become president of the union. McLane also lost his position as head of Chicago-based Local 278, which was taken over by a mob-appointed successor named Louis Romano.

13. He opposed the war in Vietnam and the purge of Communists and their supporters.

14. He thought that organized labor had responded defensively to the challenge of the civil-rights movement. Sirabella himself was a founder of the New Haven chapter of the Urban League and a member of the NAACP.

15. He was the single nationwide labor liaison for Community Progress, Inc., the Ford Foundation's (and the nation's largest) pioneering anti-poverty and manpower organization. He was for many years the vice chairman of the Connecticut State Board of Mediation and Arbitration and a city alderman. He was on the board of the United Way and a half-dozen other civic organizations. He built housing for the working-class community. Under his leadership, the New Haven Labor Council became the first labor organization in the country to sponsor a not-for-profit community HMO, the Community Health Care Center Plan. He ran at least twenty political campaigns, including one for himself for mayor of New Haven. (The voter registration chairman of the Sirabella for Mayor campaign was then Yale law student Bill Clinton!)

16. Betsy Aron, "The Ecology of Trade Unionism in New England" (1998) (unpublished dissertation, Brandeis University) (on file with author).

17. Wilhelm's family encouraged social activism. He was also nourished by some of his professors at Yale. Among them was "Bob Cook, who taught in the Sociology Department and who ran for Congress on a third-party anti-war ticket in 1966 and 1968 and who quit Yale and teaching. [Later, he] became an ironworker. I worked on both of those campaigns. He's a wonderful guy; his whole family are wonderful people. I learned an enormous amount from him about life I guess. He was very interested in the lives of ordinary people."

18. Letter from John Wilhelm to author (Mar. 17, 1996).

19. John Wilhelm, "A Short History of Unionization at Yale," *Social Text*, Winter 1996, at 13.

20. Churchill famously said that he did not become prime minister to preside over the dissolution of the British Empire.

21. He had, among other things, given an important and well-received speech on the New Haven Green on Moratorium Day in 1969.

22. Report by Vincent J. Sirabella to the General Executive Board, Miami Beach, Florida, June 12, 1972.

23. According to the union's constitution, any local was entitled to appear before the executive board. Few took advantage. Sirabella appeared regularly.

CHAPTER 5. THE REJUVENATION OF HERE LOCAL 2

1. Marc Norton, "High Stakes in Hotel Worker Battle," *Beyond Chron,* Sept. 4, 2006, http://www.beyondchron.org/news/index.php?itemid=3644.
2. Sherri Chiesa is now the secretary-treasurer and international vice president of the union.

CHAPTER 6. ORGANIZING YALE'S CLERICAL AND TECHNICAL WORKERS

1. The members of Local 35, who understood that a sister local of clerical workers would increase their bargaining power, voted to increase their own dues to support the effort.
2. Among its members were Karl Lechow, Warren Heyman, Ellen Thomson, Morty Miller, Kim McLaughlin, and Paul Clifford. I conducted interviews with Thomson, Clifford, Lechow, and Heyman in 1984. I also conducted interviews with Lee Berman, Lucille Dickess, and Andrea Ross (now Andrea van den Heever) during 1984 and 1985. Unless otherwise indicated, all statements attributed to these individuals come from these interviews.
3. Conversation with A. Bartlett Giamatti, President of Yale University, in New Haven, Conn. (1980). He asked whether I thought it was a good idea, and I said no, arguing that their actions would violate the concept of academic community.
4. For example, longtime union supporter Isabel Poludnawicz, the British-born secretary to the dean of the law school, was not challenged as a managerial employee. She played a key role in organizing the law-school staff.
5. *A Report to the Community from the Members of Local 34, Federation of University Employees, AFL-CIO* (Sept. 1984), *quoted in* Molly Ladd-Taylor, "Women Workers and the Yale Strike," 11 *Feminist Stud.* 465 (1985).
6. Linda L. Anderson, "On Strike Against Yale," *Frontiers,* vol. 8, no. 3, at 26 (1986).
7. Both are now distinguished law professors at New York University. Cindy Estlund is a nationally prominent labor-relations scholar and was a leading member of President Obama's labor transition team. Sam Issacharoff is a procedure, voting-rights, and constitutional-law maven who is recognized as one of the leading scholars of his generation.
8. Toni Gilpin et al., *On Strike for Respect: The Clerical and Technical Workers' Strike at Yale University, 1984–85,* at 33 (1995). To prepare for the negotiation, the University dismissed Siegel and O'Connor, its local counsel, and instead hired the Chicago-based firm of Seyfarth, Shaw, Fairweather and Geraldson. The person who negotiated for the university administration was a young lawyer named Jay Swardensky. The use of Seyfarth Shaw quickly became an issue. The union declared the firm to be "one of the most notorious anti-union law firms in the country." Fears were expressed that the firm would use the negotiations to provoke a strike. Swardensky, a former student of mine from the University of Chicago, quit.
9. Rhode was a strong proponent of the idea of comparable worth, which was very much a union issue on campus.
10. *N.Y. Times,* Oct. 27, 1984.
11. Paul Bass, "Yale Strike Also Takes a Break," *N.Y. Times,* Dec. 9, 1984.

CHAPTER 7. THE NEED FOR A NEW ORGANIZING MODEL

1. John W. Wilhelm, Eulogy for Vincent J. Sirabella on behalf of the Hotel Employees & Restaurant Employees International Union in Washington, D.C. (Apr. 13, 1993). As Wilhelm recounted, "When I heard the news of President Hanley's appointment of Vinnie to that position, my heart overflowed. I thought back to a conversation I had with Vinnie several times over the years. He used to tell me—philosophically, not in any envious or bitter way—that his life's ambition was to become the director of organization but that of course he knew he would never be able to realize that ambition."

2. In 1987 he held a final training and evaluation session with the trainees in Las Vegas. He issued a solemn warning to those who would devote their future lives to the union: "If I were to drop dead in the next five minutes, I want to leave you with one message you should never forget: learn the politics of the labor movement, because you will never make it otherwise. I don't care how smart you are, how dedicated you are. If you don't understand the politics, it won't work. They will kill you. The politicians running the labor movement will kill you."

3. I witnessed Sirabella's counterproductive behavior when he met with a group of San Antonio, Texas, activists who were interested in helping organize San Antonio's riverfront hotels. Sirabella treated the idea disdainfully, and when one of the Hispanic attendees protested his attitude and mentioned his "fancy suit," Sirabella erupted and began to shout about his poverty-stricken childhood. This was not the Vinnie Sirabella I had watched calmly winning point after point in a debate with Yale's director of human resources.

4. Vincent J. Sirabella, Remarks at the Hotel, Restaurant, and Catering Trade Group Conference of the International Union of Food and Allied Workers Association in Limassol, Cyprus (Nov. 11, 1987).

5. All the organizers stressed the importance of a strong internal organizing committee and then suggested ways to achieve it.

CHAPTER 8. THE CULINARY UNION AND THE DEVELOPMENT OF THE COMPREHENSIVE CAMPAIGN

1. *See* Timothy J. Minchin, "Organizing a Labor Law Violator: The J. P. Stevens Campaign and the Struggle to Unionize the U.S. South, 1963–1983," 50 *Int'l Rev. Soc. Hist.* 27 (2005).

2. See Julius Getman, *The Betrayal of Local 14* (1998), for a fuller explanation of his tactics and battles.

3. Fiedler's guerilla style of organizing was not very different from the tactics that Vinnie Sirabella had used many years before to organize restaurant workers in New Haven, the tactics that Local 35 had employed during its 1970s strikes.

4. Richard McCracken, "Comprehensive Strategic Offensives" (paper presented at the 1984 UFCW Attorneys Conference).

5. The only traditional labor technique that McCracken endorsed was the secondary boycott, which has the advantage of creating possible friction between the target employer

and another that it does business with. He noted that all the tactics he mentioned "shared the characteristic of looking beyond the immediate employment relationship for power."

6. There is really nothing new to the idea of corporate campaigns, except system. For many years, labor lawyers have been exploiting power sources outside labor law in order to gain advantage in labor disputes. The process has, however, been very erratic, by and large.

7. He concluded: "I believe that two fundamental concepts underlie the idea of the corporate campaign. The first is the use of new sources of power. The second is systematic corporate research. The potential power that is available to the labor movement is virtually unlimited except by our ability to exploit it. Present-day business is an incredibly dense mass of business relationships involving individuals and organizations. These relationships are highly interdependent. Pressure at one point is transmitted widely throughout the mass."

8. McCracken lost faith in the Board after representing unions in a series of cases in which employers withdrew recognition from unions, claiming that they no longer represented a majority. The unions fought the cases through the NLRB and the courts; they were victorious legally but were defeated practically. "It's because we couldn't function during the entire time, the very long time that these cases were pending. And the result was, the workers saw no union, there was no effective representation, and so even though the union won in the end, by the time the bargaining orders were final, it had no members, it had no organization, it could go to the bargaining table but it didn't have anything to work with. So eventually basically what happened was the union just walked away from most of the places. They were finally decerted in the one where it had any kind of activity. So what I saw was in the space of the seven years it took to get from unfair-labor-practice charge to final NLRB order we won every stage. We were doing a wonderful job legally, but the law was so totally ineffective that it was worthless organizationally. I declared, that's it for me and the NLRB."

9. Dorothee Benz, "Labor's Ace in the Hole: Casino Organizing in Las Vegas," 26 *New Pol. Sci.* 525 (2004).

10. "The injunction was converted to a statute applicable to all labor picketing in 1985. It was declared unconstitutional in a suit we brought in 1989. The judge who issued the injunction ran for election to the [Nevada] Supreme Court. We campaigned against him and he was trounced."

11. Local officers and an international-union team led by Vinnie Sirabella encouraged them to ignore the injunction. The union undertook a massive campaign of civil disobedience, disobeying the injunction at a central location, the intersection of the Strip and the Flamingo.

12. Eight of the hotels that had hired replacement workers did not sign on. The union was decertified at six of the unsigned hotels and rendered ineffective at the other two. It lost thousands of members, large amounts of money, and once-valuable bargaining relationships.

13. Sara Mosle, "Letter from Las Vegas: How the Maids Fought Back," *New Yorker,* Feb. 26, 1996, at 148.

14. *One Day Longer: The Story of the Frontier Strike* (1999).

15. The *New Yorker* story continues:

> The Elardis stopped deducting members' union dues from their paychecks, refused to contribute to the union's health-and-welfare fund, and, in July of 1991, suspended all contributions to the workers' pension plans. . . .
>
> On the morning of September 21st, some five hundred and fifty workers, members of the Culinary Union and three other unions, walked out. Four and a half years later, they are still on strike. During that time, not a single striker has crossed the picket line to go back inside, and, in a show of solidarity rarely seen in labor these days, Culinary Union members voted to double their dues to support the strike fund. Arnodo told me how workers' lives had changed over the course of the strike: "Ninety children have been born, seven people have died, many more have gotten married, and a few moved from town." Strikers have strategically set up "shacks," which look like newspaper kiosks, at points of heavy traffic on the hotel's periphery. They congregate at the shacks and pass out leaflets explaining the issues of the strike; a tape player blares voices of workers chanting inspirational slogans; and, at any given moment, a few workers walk between the stations, carrying their signs.

16. Benz, *supra* note 9.

17. *Id.*

18. The SEIU too learned that its comprehensive campaigns were most effective when attached to offers of cooperation. It also learned that employers were enticed with the idea of getting workers from the union. As explained to me by Kirk Adams: "We can be partners certainly in industries that depend on state funding or federal funding. We can be partners with that industry or employer in that regard not only because we have political power, but in some cases it can be a more positive pitch to the legislature or Congress if it's a labor-management pitch than if it's just a management pitch. That's one thing. There are others in terms of recruitment or training or workforce—that's an incredibly important thing to [employees]."

19. Steven Greenhouse, "Local 226, 'The Culinary,' Makes Las Vegas the Land of the Living Wage," *N.Y. Times,* June 3, 2004.

CHAPTER 9. FROM HANLEY TO WILHELM

1. President's Commission on Organized Crime, *The Edge: Organized Crime, Business, and Labor Unions; Report to the President and the Attorney General,* Section Four: Hotel Employees and Restaurant Employees International Union (1986), *available at* http://www.thelaborers.net/documents/REPORTS/Commission_HERE.html.

2. This litigation and its predicates are described in James B Jacobs, *Mobsters, Unions, and Feds: The Mafia and the American Labor Movement* 214–220 (2006).

3. The review board consisted of Muellenberg, along with Archbishop James P. Keleher of Kansas City and James R. Thompson, a former governor of Illinois, who was designated as chairman.

4. Kurt Muellenberg, *Final Report as Monitor of HEREIU* (Aug. 26 1998). He explained his review process thus: "I have reviewed the operations and actions of the International

Union in a systematic way. In doing this, I have relied on the Consent Decree's mandate that the International Union give me unfettered access to all records or documents and officials, agents, employees, and members of the International Union and its constituent entities. Investigators from my office have conducted reviews of select local unions and the International Union headquarters. Investigations have also been conducted in response to unsolicited complaints and allegations. Finally, investigators from my office have conducted investigations regarding specific programs, issues, topics, and individuals associated with the International Union. . . . I am pleased to report that the International Union has been very cooperative in submitting matters to me for review and has given members of my staff unfettered access to records."

5. He concluded:

1. Many of the local unions do not obey their bylaws.
2. Notice to membership meetings is not adequate, resulting in lack of quorums for General Membership meetings.
3. Expenses are not presented to the membership for approval as required, or, if presented, are vague or not presented in the full context of the expenditures.
4. Raises and bonuses are not presented to the membership for approval as required, in many instances, they were not even presented to the local union's Executive Board.
5. Per capita taxes are delinquent with no effort to make arrangements for payment to the International Union.
6. Personal expenses are placed on union credit cards, including personal meal and beverage expenses.
7. Expenses are charged to the union without adequate documentation to verify that the expense was necessary for conducting union business.
8. Automobiles are provided for employees who only use them to commute to and from work.
9. Training of officers, business agents, and organizers is minimal or nonexistent.
10. Organizing projects are not coordinated or supervised.
11. Severance and insurance programs are set up for the officers, which are not in the best interest of the membership.
12. Members are not permitted to inspect LM-2 reports as required by the Labor Management Reporting and Disclosure Act, and, in many cases, members are unaware they exist.
13. Personnel policies, salary pay scales, job descriptions, performance standards do not exist.
14. The International Union's audit program is not properly designed to detect fraud or abuse by officers and employees of local unions.
15. Many local unions do not require Business Agents to file any documentation or weekly report describing what they did during the preceding week.
16. Executive Board members have little or no understanding of their fiduciary obligation to ensure that the local's funds are spent solely in the best interests of the membership.
17. Many locals do not have an annual audit despite the requirement for such an audit in the HEREIU Constitution.

6. Jacobs, *supra* note 2, at 221.

7. To labor scholars familiar with Wilhelm's past, his support alone is reason for reevaluating Hanley. Wilhelm's entire history has been a long and effective battle for reform, from the civil-rights movement to the anti-war movement to the labor movement.

8. The monitor was very critical of the special treatment of Local 1 in Chicago (Hanley's local), which was permitted to remain delinquent for many years with respect to its per capita dues payments. I hope that the new national leadership will give HERE the national and international attention it deserves. Local 1 should have been placed in trusteeship many years ago. I am informed by Wilhelm that Local 1 is currently timely on both per capita dues payments and loan repayment.

9. Ricky Baldwin, "Striking Chicago Hotel Workers Celebrate Labor Day in the Rain, Sitting on Michigan Avenue," *Lab. Notes,* Oct. 2003, *available at* http://www.labornotes.org/node/1025.

10. "South Florida Local Bosses Ousted by Internal Ethics Board," National Legal and Policy Center, May 21, 2007, http://www.nlpc.org/stories/2007/05/21/south-florida-local-bosses-ousted-internal-ethics-board.

CHAPTER 10. REFINING THE COMPREHENSIVE CAMPAIGN

1. Sheila Muto, "For Hoteliers, the Word for Today Is: Cooperation," *Wall St. J.,* Apr. 8, 1998.

2. The Hotel Trades Council is a group that bargains on behalf of different unions that have contracts with hotels.

3. Harry Katz, Rosemary Batt, and Jeffrey Keefe, "The Revitalization of the CWA: Integrating Collective Bargaining, Political Action, and Organizing," 56 *Indus. & Lab. Rel. Rev.* 573 (2003).

4. *Id.*

5. *See* Wikipedia, Communication Workers of America, http://en.wikipedia.org/wiki/Communications_Workers_of_America (last visited Oct. 13, 2009); Communication Workers of America, http://www.cwa-union.org (last visited Oct. 13, 2009).

6. *See Dana Corp.,* 351 N.L.R.B. 434 (2007).

7. Vanessa Tait, *Poor Workers' Unions* 206 (2005). This incident is also described in Richard Bensinger, *Not Your Father's Labor Movement* 27 (1998).

8. With respect to the dynamism of its current leadership, see Jim Green, "Camp Solidarity: The United Mine Workers, the Pittston Strike, and the New 'People's Movement,'" *in Building Bridges: The Emerging Grassroots Coalition of Labor and Community* 15 (Jeremy Brecher and Tim Costello eds., 1990).

CHAPTER 11. THE IMMIGRATION ISSUE

1. *See generally* Leah Haus, "Openings in the Wall: Transnational Migrants, Labor Unions, and U.S. Immigration Policy," 49 *Int'l Org.* 285 (1995).

2. David Bacon, "The AFL-CIO Reverses Course on Immigration," *LaborNet Newsline,* Oct. 17, 1999, http://www.labornet.org/news/111499/01.html.

3. Kent Wong and Carolyn Bank Munoz, "Don't Miss the Bus," *New Lab. Forum,* Summer 2004, at 61.

CHAPTER 12. HERE IN THE TWENTY-FIRST CENTURY

1. Granfield had worked as a farmworker organizer before being hired for HERE by Vinnie Sirabella during his period on the West Coast. Granfield came east to work with Sirabella when Vinnie was appointed trustee of Local 100 in 1993 and once again called on Granfield, whose dedication and honesty were beyond approach. Granfield became president of Local 100 in October 2001. Before that, he was the secretary-treasurer of the local.

2. Immigration policy has remained an important and controversial issue since. Some old-line unions and union supporters continue to oppose anything resembling amnesty. Wilhelm has maintained his strong pro-immigrant stand. He served on the Independent Task Force on Immigration and America's Future, chaired by former senator Spencer Abraham and former representative Lee Hamilton, which made a careful study of the impact of immigration on the U.S. economy and concluded that

> the benefits of immigration far outweigh its disadvantages and that immigration is essential to U.S. national interests and will become even more so in the years ahead. But to harness the benefits, the United States must fundamentally rethink its policies and overhaul its system for managing immigration. . . .
>
> . . . Without immigration, we cannot sustain the growth and prosperity to which we have become accustomed.

Immigration and America's Future: A New Chapter; Report of the Independent Task Force on Immigration and America's Future (2006), *available at* http://www.migrationpolicy.org/task_force/new_chapter_summary.pdf.

3. Melody Hanatani, "UCLA Students Take Wild Ride for Worker Freedom," *Daily Bruin,* Oct. 10, 2003.

4. Kent Wong and Carolyn Bank Munoz, "Don't Miss the Bus," *New Lab. Forum,* Summer 2004, at 61. HERE made two DVDs of the ride—one showing riders from Los Angeles and the other, riders from Las Vegas.

5. John McCann, "Not Just a Latino Thing," *Herald Sun* (Durham, N.C.), Oct. 10, 2003.

6. Ricardo Pimentel, "It's Time for Fear to Get off the Bus," *Ariz. Republic,* Oct. 7, 2003.

7. "I know of at least two rank-and-file riders on the Las Vegas bus, one of whom (Leonora Rhem) became a staff organizer and one (Josefa Osorio) who regularly takes leave from the job to do union work. I am sure there are others." E-mail from Tom Snyder (one of the ride's organizers) to author (Apr. 9, 2008).

8. Wikipedia, International Ladies' Garment Workers' Union, http://en.wikipedia.org/wiki/International_Ladies%27_Garment_Workers%27_Union (last visited Oct. 3, 2009). It was the union my father, a cutter, joined in 1912.

9. Obituary, "Crystal Lee Sutton, 68: Labor Organizer Was Inspiration for 'Norma Rae,'" *Wash. Post,* Sept. 16, 2009.

10. "We represent basically the same type of people. The makeup of their membership, the

demographics of their membership is virtually identical to ours; the philosophy is quite similar. We're two of the leading unions on immigration and civil rights issues, and so it's almost a no-brainer." Interview by Kent Wong with John Wilhelm, *in New Lab. Forum,* Spring 2005, at 79. UNITE, which owned the Amalgamated Bank of New York, also had substantial resources.

11. Sweeney had immediately upon election created a new organizing department and increased the budget of the Organizing Institute. The director of the institute was Richard Bensinger of the SEIU, an open critic of the AFL-CIO's previous lack of focus on the issue. Many of Bensinger's criticisms of organized labor were similar to those made earlier by Vinnie Sirabella. Like Sirabella, Bensinger was eager to go outside the ranks of organized labor to recruit new organizers. He recruited at colleges and sought activists from progressive social movements.

In 1998, Bensinger was abruptly fired by Sweeney. This action was not well received by organizing activists. A series of disagreements about organizing followed.

12. The tension between local unions and the international leadership emerged most powerfully in the battle between the SEIU's national leadership and one of its largest locals, United Healthcare Workers West (UHW), a local of over 150,000 members led by the longtime activist Sal Rosselli. The dispute received a great deal of attention from labor leaders, commentators, and activists. Rosselli, thought to be the underdog, emerged as a hero of left-wing labor blogs. *See, e.g.,* Matt Smith, "Stern Reprimand: SEIU Members in Northern California Challenge the National Boss over His Collaboration with Employers," *SFWeely.com,* June 12, 2007, http://www.sfweekly.com/2007-06-13/news/stern-reprimand/print. Pro-Rosselli postings were answered by labor activists supportive of Stern. In February 2008 Rosselli resigned from the executive board of the SEIU. His letter of resignation accused Stern of behaving undemocratically. Letter from Sal Rosselli to Andrew L. Stern (Feb. 9, 2008), *available at* http://www.thenation.com/special/pdf/SEIU/RosselliResignationLetter.pdf.

13. The lockout was settled with considerable help from San Francisco mayor Gavin Newsom.

14. DVD: Sharing the Banquet (Hotel Workers Rising, Aug. 2006).

15. Barbara Sternal, "Hotel Workers Rising," *Dollars and Cents,* Sept. 1, 2006.

CHAPTER 13. SOLIDARITY REBUFFED

1. John Wilhelm explained the conflict to me in 2007: "There is a real tension, not just in our union, but in the labor movement . . . around the question of whether or not, in order for the labor movement to grow faster than it is growing, we need to substantially dilute the notion of good collective-bargaining agreements. Bruce [Raynor] is a strong advocate of this point of view, that in order to ameliorate employer anti-union behavior we need to move away from the notion of contract standards. That is neither my view nor the view of most of us in the former HERE."

2. Harold Myerson, "Disunite There: Civil War at UNITE-HERE, One of America's Stellar Unions," *American Prospect* (Web only), Feb. 27, 2009, http://www.prospect.org/cs/articles?article=disunite_there.

344   Notes to Pages 139–144

3. I witnessed Wilhelm's consensus-building approach in action as an observer at the union caucus, during negotiations between Local 34 and the Yale administration in 1983. At one point, a member of the committee told Wilhelm that she would defer to him on a point of strategy because he knew so much more than she did. "That's not the way we do things in this union," he told her. "You make your point, I'll make mine, and then we'll argue till we all agree."

4. Dupont's comment about Raynor's treatment of the staff was supported by a former UNITE department director who told me that in ten years Raynor "never said hello to me, never made eye contact." She contrasted Raynor with Wilhelm, who instantly knew her name, regularly chatted with her, and "always treated me with the utmost respect."

5. Proceedings, UNITE HERE 2nd General Convention 2009, at 72–73 [hereinafter Convention Proceedings] (on file with author).

6. Paul Abowd, "Pre-Convention Battle: Detroit UNITE HERE Local Seized," *Lab. Notes,* Feb. 2009, *available at* http://labornotes.org/node/2067.

7. Michael Mishak, "Big Union Reels as Card-Check Fight Looms: Culinary Leader in Vegas Calls Parent Union Chief's Actions 'Undemocratic,'" *Las Vegas Sun,* Jan. 29, 2009.

8. Complaint at 2, 4, *Raynor v. Wilhelm,* No. 09-268 (E.D.N.Y. Jan. 22, 2009), *available at* http://labornotes.org/files/pdfs/raynor.v.wilhelm.pdf.

9. He is married to Eileen Kirlin, an SEIU vice president.

10. E-mail from Thomas Snyder to author (Apr. 2, 2009).

11. Stories of Greed, fixourunion.org, http://www.fixourunion.org/soc.html (last visited Aug. 23, 2009).

12. Ann Gerhart, "Ground War: Steve Rosenthal Wages a $100 Million Battle to Line Up Democratic Votes," *Wash. Post,* July 6, 2004.

13. Interview with Danna Schneider, UNITE HERE organizer (July 31, 2009).

14. Steven Greenhouse, "Two Unions in Marriage Now Face Divorce Talks," *N.Y. Times,* Feb. 7, 2009.

15. Its signers, in addition to the named defendants in Raynor's lawsuit, included Jo Marie Agriesti, Geoconda Arguello Kline (the president of the Culinary), Paul Clifford (one of the Yale organizers and now the president of Local 75 in Toronto), Joe Daugherty, Tho Thi Do (a Vietnamese refugee, community organizer, and the secretary-treasurer of Local 2), Warren Heyman (a former Yale organizer), and Janice Loux (the president of Boston Local 26 and the national union vice president). The statement is available online at http://unitehere8.org/docs/Statement%20020409%20From%20IU%20Ex%20Board .pdf.

16. The statement went on to criticize Raynor's unilateral actions in the preceding couple of months:

1. With no advance notice, the elected leadership of Phoenix Local 631 was cast out of its offices and subjected to an undemocratic takeover by the WRJB [Western Regional Joint Board].

2. With no advance notice, the elected leadership of Detroit Local 24 was cast out of its offices and subjected to an undemocratic takeover by the CMRJB [Chicago Midwest Regional Joint Board]. . . .

5. Raynor, acting in his capacity as Chair of the Amalgamated Bank Board of Directors, is attempting to rob the International Union of control over the union's largest asset by first, without any notice, passing undemocratic supermajority provisions and then, after hiring a witch hunting law firm to interrogate them, throwing John Wilhelm and Matthew Walker off the Board.

6. Raynor has filed a lawsuit against his own elected Executive Committee.

17. Raynor included the same content in a posting to the Huffington Post: The UNITE HERE Merger—A Missed Opportunity, Posting of Bruce Raynor to the Huffington Post, http://www.huffingtonpost.com/bruce-raynor/the-unite-here-merger—-a_b_165290.html (Feb. 9, 2009, 2:06 p.m.).

18. It was Wilhelm who led the AFL-CIO to adopt a more pro-immigrant policy and Wilhelm who devoted key resources of HERE to the Immigrant Workers Freedom Ride.

19. Letter from the Retired Officers of the ILGWU Executive Committee to Brothers and Sisters of the U.S. Labor Movement (Aug. 6, 2009), *available at* http://www.unitehere.org/roipenletter080609.pdf.

20. *Gillis v Wilhelm,* No. 09-01116 (S.D.N.Y. filed Feb. 6, 2009).

21. Letter from Andy Stern to Bruce Raynor and John Wilhelm (Jan. 30, 2009), *available at* http://labornotes.org/files/pdfs/stern.to.unite.here.pdf.

22. Letter from Andy Stern to the SEIU Executive Board (Mar. 10, 2009) (on file with author).

23. Juan Gonzalez, "Union Fighting over Bank," *N.Y. Daily News,* Feb. 20, 2009.

24. The counterclaim accuses Raynor of "1) converting and secreting money, property, and assets of UNITE HERE to which they are not entitled; 2) failing to hold the money and property of UNITE HERE solely for the benefit of UNITE HERE and its members; 3) failing to manage, invest, and expend the money and property of UNITE HERE in accordance with the UNITE HERE's Constitution and bylaws and with resolutions of its General Executive Board; 4) dealing with UNITE HERE as an adverse party and on behalf of an adverse parties in matters connected to counterclaim-defendants' duties; and 5) holding and acquiring a pecuniary and personal interest which conflicts with the interests of UNITE HERE."

25. Press Release, SEIU, SEIU and Workers United Announce Affiliation (Mar. 23, 2009), *available at* http://www.seiu.org/2009/03/seiu-and-workers-united-announce-affiliation.php.

26. Letter from Andy Stern to John Wilhelm and Bruce Raynor (Mar. 23, 2009) (on file with author).

27. Press Release, UNITE HERE, UNITE HERE International Union Suspends Its President (Apr. 21, 2009), *available at* http://www.reuters.com/article/pressRelease/idUS213174+21-Apr-2009+BW20090421.

28. Officers negotiate and administer their own contracts with employers, maintain their own offices and financial accounts and records, own their own real estate and real-estate corporations, conduct their own organizing campaigns, file their own yearly tax and governmental reports, hire and fire their own staff, and generally operate as fully autonomous labor organizations. The joint boards provide a full spectrum of representational services for their members. The joint boards employ business agents and representatives and

maintain a treasury, collect dues from their members, and pay the costs of representing their current members.

29. Workers United has had success in a series of cases before the Labor Board concerning the right of union officers who switched allegiance to continue collecting dues. The Board has held that in the interest of continuity, employers can continue to collect dues and forward them to the joint board. Typical of the Board's approach to this issue was the decision by the Board's regional director in *Royal Laundry,* Case 20-RM-2868 (2009), *available at* http://www.nlrb.gov/shared_files/Regional%20Decisions/2009/20-RM-02868-06-12-09.pdf. The case involved a petition by an employer concerning conflicting claims by the Western States Regional Joint Board and UNITE HERE Local 2 to dues collected by a local (Local 75) that had voted to disaffiliate. The regional director dismissed the employer's petition and, citing the notion of substantial continuity, instructed the employer to continue paying dues to the joint board.

The SEIU and Workers United have claimed the Board's ruling as a major victory. It is noteworthy that the Board did not rule on the ability of joint boards or locals to disaffiliate. Thus, the issue whether Local 75's officials owe all or part of the money they collected to UNITE HERE remains open.

30. On the other hand, it is arguable that since the constitution deals directly with the issue for local unions, the constitution's failure to restrict joint boards acknowledges their ability to decide freely with whom to associate.

31. Convention Proceedings, *supra* note 5, at 161–162. It is telling that in the flurry of public statements and appeals made by Raynor and Stern after the UNITE HERE convention they did not attempt to directly refute this charge.

32. Juan Gonzalez, "Battle over $12M Splits Labor Movement UNITE HERE," *N.Y. Daily News,* June 16, 2009.

33. Memorandum from Mark H. Ayers to National and International Unions of the AFL-CIO and All Building Trades Affiliates (Mar. 2, 2009), *available at* http://www.politico.com/static/PPM110_ayers_statement.html.

34. San Diego and Imperial Counties Labor Council resolution (on file with author).

35. Press Release, SEIU, SEIU and Workers United Lay Out Clear Path to Resolving Issues and Serving Workers (Apr. 30, 2009), *available at* http://www.seiu.org/2009/04/seiu-and-workers-united-lay-out-clear-path-to-resolving-issues-and-serving-workers.php. A letter to John Wilhelm, included in the press release, contained the following proposals:

> 1. Negotiation. We have continued to take advantage of the advice of Joe Hansen in his role as mediator. We put forward to you today a comprehensive settlement offer that recognizes UNITE HERE's core jurisdiction and the leading union of hotel and gaming employees, provides UNITE HERE with a substantial financial package that allows it to remain a viable international union, and seeks to definitively resolve which union (Workers United/SEIU or UNITE HERE) that members in disputed areas will be a part of going forward. To date these discussions have not been successful, and we believe we must consider continued negotiations as you have proposed as well as other alternatives.
>
> 2. Arbitration. We are prepared now or if the negotiation process is not successful, to submit *all outstanding* issues to an independent third party for a final-offer arbitra-

tion process. We appreciate that in any dispute there are two points of view and believe that the use of an independent third party is necessary to make a final determination if we cannot do it amongst ourselves.

We are also prepared to unilaterally take four very important steps to demonstrate the sincerity of our position. Obviously, we would expect UNITE HERE to do the same.

1. No raiding commitment. In the interim, and in all of the alternatives, we are willing to continue to comply with the provisions of the CTW Constitution regarding no-raiding and will ask the Change to Win Presidents to immediately appoint a permanent, mutually-acceptable arbitrator who would be empowered to expeditiously settle all questions of raiding. We will abide by all decisions.
2. Cease membership contact. In addition, we are unilaterally ceasing any contact with the approximately 200,000 uncontested members of UNITE HERE.
3. Respect organizing campaigns. We are unilaterally willing to not interfere with any new UNITE HERE organizing efforts.
4. Employer relations. We are agreeing not to disrupt any existing employer relationships as it relates to existing contracts, contract negotiations and dues deduction in all undisputed jurisdictions.

To reiterate, we believe there are two viable alternatives for resolution of our strongly held differences all of which can lead to a thoughtful conclusion of our dispute. We are willing to attempt to finalize negotiations, and if that is not successful, we are willing to submit to arbitration as soon as feasible.

36. Letter from John W. Wilhelm to Andy Stern (May 1, 2009), *available at* http://www.one unitehere.org/files/JWWtoStern050109.pdf. Wilhelm wrote:

> You state that SEIU will continue to campaign in "disputed" areas, meaning that you will continue to try to hijack UNITE HERE members, even where members have clearly voted to stay in UNITE HERE, and even where SEIU has engaged in demonstrable fraud and voter suppression in so-called "votes."
> You also state that SEIU will not interfere in "new" UNITE HERE organizing campaigns; does that mean SEIU will continue to seek revocation of UNITE HERE authorization cards in situations like the Phoenix Sheraton Hotel?

37. Letter from John W. Wilhelm to Andy Stern (June 15, 2009), *available at* http://www.wrongwayseiu.org/files/JWWBindArbResponsetoStern.pdf.
38. Letter from Andy Stern, Bruce Raynor, and Edgar Romney to the American Labor Movement (June 3, 2009), *available at* http://www.politico.com/static/PPM110_090603_open_letter.html.
39. The effort to develop labor support for the arbitration proposal had some initial success. Calls for a peaceful resolution using mediation or arbitration were made by a variety of union leaders. On June 11, 2009, Ron Gettelfinger, the president of the United Auto Workers, wrote an open letter to Wilhelm and Raynor in which he pointed to the potential harm of the continuing battle: "The longer this fight goes on, the more it will be used against all of us by the Chamber of Commerce, NAM [National Association of Manufacturers], the National Right to Work Committee, Richard Berman, and others who are

determined to destroy everything we have fought for, together, in all our years as trade unionists." Letter from Ron Gettelfinger to Bruce Raynor and John Wilhelm (June 11, 2009), *reprinted at* http://www.workersunitedunion.org/content/letter-president-gettel finger. On June 10, 2009, actor Danny Glover, who had participated in the Hotel Workers Rising campaign, wrote, "I call on President Wilhelm to accept President Raynor and President Stern's offer to enter into binding arbitration. The sooner the better." Binding Arbitration, Sooner the Better, Posting of Danny Glover to the Huffington Post, http://www.huffingtonpost.com/danny-glover/binding-arbitration-soone_b_213883 .html (June 10, 2009, 2:38 p.m.).

40. Convention Proceedings, *supra* note 5, at 59.

41. *Id.* at 196.

42. Union Presidents' Solidarity Pledge, http://www.unitehere.org/convention_2009/presi dents_solidarity.php.

43. Convention Proceedings, *supra* note 5, at 238–242.

44. Myerson, *supra* note 2.

45. Peter Dreier, "Divorce—Union Style," *Nation,* Aug. 31, 2009, *available at* http://www .thenation.com/doc/20090831/dreier/single. There is no recognition in Dreier's article of the fact that Wilhelm's letter was based on enforcing the terms of UNITE HERE's constitution, which forbids locals from leaving the union.

46. *See* Workers and Progressives Can't Afford Labor Civil War, Posting of TomP to Daily Kos, http://www.dailykos.com/story/2009/6/19/744408/-Workers-and-Progressives-Cant -Afford-Labor-Civil-War- (Jun. 19, 2009, 7:26 a.m.).

47. The most notable exception is the attorney Randy Cross, who has written on the topic for Beyond Chron, a San Francisco Web site that deals with labor issues.

48. Linda Myers, "Textile Labor Leader Bruce Raynor Wins ILR's Groat Award," *Cornell Chronicle,* Apr. 29, 1999, http://www.news.cornell.edu/Chronicle/99/4.29.99/Raynor .html.

49. Associated Press, "Inspiration for Movie 'Norma Rae' Dies at 68: Labor Organizer Succumbed to Long Battle with Brain Cancer," MSNBC, Sept. 14, 2009, http://www.msnbc .msn.com/id/32842182/ns/business-us_business.

50. Letter from the Retired Officers of the ILGWU Executive Committee, *supra* note 19. Except for a statement by Edgar Romney that referred to the ILGWU retirees as "disgruntled former employees," I was not able to find any responses to their charges even though I asked various people associated with Workers United, including their information contact, Eric Sharfstein.

51. "Street Fighting Man: How Veteran Organizer Henry Tamarin Got a 'Dead' Union Ready to Rumble—and Win," *Chi. Tribune Magazine,* Feb. 10, 2003.

52. Part of the reason is contained in her testimony before the House Labor Committee in 1999:

> President John Wilhelm twice negotiated our citywide hotel contract covering more than 4,000 hotel workers. We won historic collective bargaining agreements, and this was unheard of in our local, and in Los Angeles the best wage increases in decades. We won for the first time a prepaid legal plan with a panel of attorneys to provide free legal

services to members. And we protected free family health insurance, which employers were threatening to take away. . . .

. . . President Wilhelm taught us to work hard to establish partnerships with employers, and we have succeeded in many cases. We also learned, though, that we must fight back if that partnership is rejected and if our members' livelihood is threatened.

Union Democracy Part VII: Government Supervision of the Hotel Employees and Restaurant Employees International Union; Hearing before the House Subcommittee on Employer-Employee Relations of the Committee on Education and the Workforce, 106th Cong. (July, 21, 1999) (statement of Maria Elena Durazo), *available at* http://commdocs.house.gov /committees/edu/hedcew6-63.000/hedcew6-63.htm.

In August 2008, Durazo was chosen by acclamation as the new chair of the UCLA Center for Research on Labor and Employment advisory committee. It seems highly unlikely that she can be either lured away from UNITE HERE or overcome by a hostile organizing drive. Nor is she likely to stay out of the struggle.

53. *See, e.g.,* Mishak, *supra* note 7. The article comments that Taylor was one of the two people who "rebuilt the Culinary after years of decline and a devastating citywide strike, making it into the country's largest and most successful union local."
54. *See, e.g.,* Dorothee Benz, "Labor's Ace in the Hole: Casino Organizing in Las Vegas," 26 *New Pol. Sci.* 525 (2004).
55. E-mail from John Wilhelm to UNITE HERE Family (Nov. 6, 2008).
56. Betsy Aron, "Who Organized the Organizers? HERE Leadership Succession at the end of the Twentieth Century." Unpublished, np; written 2000.
57. According to Wilhelm, "Local 26 in Boston, which was literally at the bargaining table with the Boston hotels on 9/11, was forced by timing to shoulder the issue of whether, in the face of this collapse of our industry, we had to negotiate concessionary contracts, and Local 26 answered with a resounding NO."
58. Sara Mosle, "Las Vegas Journal; At Hotel-Casino, Triumphant Shouts of 'Union!'" *N.Y. Times,* Feb. 5, 1998.
59. Jane M. Von Bergen, "New Union Convenes," *Phila. Inquirer,* Mar. 22, 2009.
60. Heyman was especially worried about the loyalty of the school cafeteria workers, who seemed to eye him with suspicion. But it turned out that they were suspicious of his loyalty to HERE: "Doris [the president of the local] said to me, 'You know, I didn't really know who to talk to, because I didn't know whether or not frankly I could trust you because you worked so closely with the joint board.'" Heyman then met with the executive committee of the local: "They then explained to me how disrespectful they had been treated by the joint board, in fact by Lynne Fox specifically, but also by a number of people there. And [they] told me some pretty horrendous stories, such as [that] one of the clerical workers was being sexually harassed by the building maintenance guy and the joint board was aware of this and didn't do anything about it."
61. Videotape (UNITE HERE) (on file with author).
62. Press Release, UNITE HERE, UNITE HERE Local 634 Wins Philadelphia Election (Oct. 27, 2009), *available at* http://unitehere.org/presscenter/release.php?ID=3849.
63. Fred Ross Jr., "SEIU President Andy Stern Has Crossed the Line," Beyond Chron, May 7, 2009, http://www.beyondchron.org/news/index.php?itemid=6900.

64. These are called *Dana* petitions. The name derives from the Labor Board's decision in *Dana Corp.*, 351 N.L.R.B. 434 (2007), which dealt with the rights of unions and employees in cases of "an employer's voluntary recognition of a union, in good faith and based on a demonstrated majority status." The Board, claiming to be concerned with "employee free choice," decided that "employees in the bargaining unit [must] receive notice of the recognition and of their right, within 45 days of the notice, to file a decertification petition."

65. David Whitford, "A Mess: Hyatt's Housekeeping Scandal," *Fortune,* Oct. 2, 2009.

66. The constitution provides:

> (i) The Executive Committee has the authority to include in a budget any limitation or conditions on the use of funds it deems appropriate, consistent with this Constitution;
>
> (ii) no discretionary expenditure in excess of $50,000 to any recipient or for any project may be made without prior approval by the Executive Committee; and
>
> (iii) no contract with a vendor or service provider that may require payments of over $50,000 per year or which extends beyond the fiscal year may be entered into without approval of the Executive Committee.
>
> (j) No expenditures shall be made that are not in accordance with a valid budget adopted in accordance with this Article.

67. When I suggested that Vinnie Sirabella might be responsible for the union's member-centered approach, Ward assured me that his local was involving members "when Vinnie Sirabella was still in knee pants."

68. Raynor's reputation was undoubtedly a reason why Wilhelm and others in HERE were willing to affiliate with him and accept him as general president of the merged unions. They should have investigated more carefully.

CHAPTER 14. THE PROBLEM OF ACCESS

1. *NLRB v. Virginia Electric & Power Co.*, 314 U.S. 469 (1941).
2. 351 U.S. 105 (1956).
3. 357 U.S. 357 (1958).
4. 156 N.L.R.B. 1236 (1966).
5. 394 U.S. 759 (1969).
6. On the same date that it promulgated the *Excelsior* rule, the NLRB also announced its decision in *General Electric Co.,* a case that involved the denial by an employer of a union's request to respond to a captive-audience speech. The Board that had considered modifying its rules regarding union access decided not to make any change in these rules, pending a determination of the impact of *Excelsior.* The Board never made the assessment and never found an imbalance under *Nutone* in any situation in which names and addresses gave unions the opportunity to make home visits to a substantial part of the workforce.
7. I received these through a court order as part of the representation-election study described in chapter 17.

8. 291 N.L.R.B. 11 (1988).

9. 295 N.L.R.B. 94 (1988).

10. The company was required to post a notice stating "WE WILL NOT prohibit representatives of Local 919, United Food and Commercial Workers, AFL-CIO (the Union) or any other labor organization, from distributing union literature to our employees in the parking lot adjacent to our store in Newington, Connecticut, nor will we attempt to cause them to be removed from our parking lot for attempting to do so."

11. 914 F.2d 313 (1st Cir. 1990).

12. 502 U.S. 527 (1992).

13. 324 U.S. 793 (1945).

14. 18 U.S.C. §§ 2721–2725.

15. 18 U.S.C. § 2724 provides:

> (a) Cause of Action.—A person who knowingly obtains, discloses or uses personal information, from a motor vehicle record, for a purpose not permitted under this chapter shall be liable to the individual to whom the information pertains, who may bring a civil action in a United States district court.
>
> (b) Remedies.—The court may award—
>
> (1) actual damages, but not less than liquidated damages in the amount of $2,500;
>
> (2) punitive damages upon proof of willful or reckless disregard of the law;
>
> (3) reasonable attorneys' fees and other litigation costs reasonably incurred; and
>
> (4) such other preliminary and equitable relief as the court determines to be appropriate.

16. 2008 WL 4138410 (3d Cir. Sept. 9, 2008).

17. *Stockholders Publishing Co., Inc.,* 28 N.L.R.B. 1006 (1941).

18. 322 U.S. 111 (1944).

19. 390 U.S. 254 (1968).

20. Section 2(11).

21. The issue is made even more difficult by the fact that the constant or routine use of such power is not necessary for an employee to be deemed a supervisor.

22. Their wages and working conditions are inevitably improved by whatever benefits the union obtains.

23. During the strike by paperworkers at International Paper Company's Androscoggin mill in Jay, Maine, this occurred regularly for over a year. Many of the strikers and supervisors were relatives; many were friends. The strikers felt betrayed. Father McKenna, the local priest, heard the anger on a regular basis: "They are hurting us. They are training the scabs." On the other hand, he also reported that "low-level management felt bad that they had to go there and train replacements. They were depressed about that." Some supervisors quit, and some, like Dom DeMarsh, a longtime foreman, found themselves miserable: "I couldn't sleep. I found myself crying a lot. As God is my witness, I wanted to commit suicide." He was not the only one. *See* Julius Getman, *The Betrayal of Local 14* (1998).

24. 532 U.S. 706 (2001).

25. 348 N.L.R.B. 37 (2006).

26. *Colbert Report* (July 18, 2006) (word for the day: "solidarity").

27. 66 N.L.R.B. 1317 (1946).

28. 416 U.S. 267 (1974).

29. 444 U.S. 672 (1980).

30. Nor did the Court explain why the problem of union-created divided loyalty is more acute for faculty members, whose institutional commitment is normally increased by the professional standards to which the various faculty unions are committed, than for other groups of employees.

31. 274 N.L.R.B. 1141 (1985).

CHAPTER 15. THE REGULATION OF EMPLOYER CAMPAIGN CONDUCT

1. 33 N.L.R.B. Ann. Rep. 60 (1968); *see also Shovel Supply Co.*, 118 N.L.R.B. 315, 316 (1957).

2. 395 U.S. 575 (1969).

3. The Court in *Gissel* referred with evident approval to the Board's "laboratory conditions" doctrine, even though the metaphor has, over the years, generated a variety of rules that are inconsistent with general First Amendment policies. For example, elections have been set aside for minor injections of racism into a campaign by employers; for racial appeals by unions; for showing films deemed by the Board to be misleading and inconsistent with sober and reflective thought; and for discussions of unionism containing no hint of reprisal, held either in the employee's home or in the office of someone senior enough in the company for the office to be considered the "locus of final authority." Either side can suggest the futility of voting for the union.

4. 723 F.2d 1360 (7th Cir. 1983).

5. In *Birdsall Construction Co.*, 198 N.L.R.B. 163 (1972), for example, the employer told his employees that financial problems would confront the firm if the union succeeded in gaining representation. The employer had deliberately located his plant inland to obtain lower labor costs, even though this location necessitated trucking goods from Rivera Beach, Florida, to Miami and Fort Lauderdale. If required to operate under a union contract, he might as well eliminate his trucking costs and relocate on the coast, he told them. This prediction of a plant closing was deemed not to be a threat of retaliation, although it clearly would have been under either the language or approach used in *Gissel*. The employer, for example, did not know that the union demands would match those made on the coast. He had no proof that the shipping costs plus union demands would leave him in a less favorable competitive position. More recent Board decisions show a similar willingness to permit employers considerable latitude to suggest by reference to hypothetical situations that unionization will harm employees, without either specifying the harm or setting out a factual predicate.

6. 375 U.S. 405 (1964).

7. 414 U.S. 270 (1973).

8. *NLRB v. Wabash Transformer Corp.*, 509 F.2d 647 (8th Cir. 1975).

9. 77 N.L.R.B. 124 (1948).

10. This idea of a rough-and-tumble atmosphere is supported by section 8(c), which says that "the expressing of any views, argument, or opinion, or the dissemination thereof, whether

in written, printed, graphic, or visual form, shall not constitute or be evidence of an unfair labor practice under any of the provisions of this Act, if such expression contains no threat of reprisal or force or promise of benefit."

11. *See Dal-Tex Optical Co.*, 137 N.L.R.B. 1782 (1962).

12. *See NLRB v. Lorben Corp.*, 345 F.2d 346 (2d Cir. 1965).

13. *Struksnes Construction Co.*, 165 N.L.R.B. 1062 (1967). The circumstances under which a poll would be valid under *Struksnes* were as follows:

> 1. The purpose of the poll was to determine the truth of a union's claim of majority status.
> 2. This purpose was communicated to the employees.
> 3. Assurances against reprisals were given.
> 4. The employees were polled by secret ballot.
> 5. The employer had not engaged in unfair labor practices or otherwise created a coercive atmosphere.

14. In *Rossmore House*, 269 N.L.R.B. 1176 (1984), the Board explicitly adopted a more permissive approach to the interrogation of union supporters about their support for the union. In its opinion, the Board cited courts-of-appeals cases criticizing the Board for being too rigid in its application of its rules. The Board held in *Peerless Plywood Co.*, 107 N.L.R.B. 427 (1953), that any speech to a large group of employees on company premises within twenty-four hours of a scheduled election would be grounds for setting aside the election. These speeches were described as "unwholesome and unsettling" and inconsistent with "that sober and thoughtful choice which a free election is designed to reflect." The *Peerless Plywood* doctrine has not been applied to voluntary-attendance meetings, although whether a meeting was in fact voluntary is often difficult to determine after the meeting. The Board generally assumes that a meeting was not voluntary unless the employer stated specifically that employees were not required to attend.

15. 138 N.L.R.B. 66 (1962).

16. *Carrington South Health Care Center, Inc. v. NLRB*, 76 F.3d 802 (6th Cir. 1996).

17. The Board has never used its reasoning in *Sewell* as a general warrant for setting elections aside when irrational or emotional appeals have been made. It has on occasion, however, set aside an election when the employer has linked the trade-union movement to communism. The authority for this is old and unreliable.

18. *See, e.g., Mueller Brass Co. v. NLRB*, 544 F.2d 815 (9th Cir. 1977).

19. *See* Paul C. Weiler, "Promises to Keep: Securing Workers' Rights to Self-Organization under the NLRA," 96 *Harv. L. Rev.* 1769, 1787–1803 (1983).

CHAPTER 16. THE DUTY TO BARGAIN AND THE PROTECTION OF EMPLOYEE CHOICE

1. *See* Joshua L. Schwartz, "Union Organizing and Public Policy: Failure to Secure First Contracts," 40 *Indus. & Lab. Rel. Rev.* 136 (1986).

2. There are only two contract proposals that management seeks: a broad no-strike promise and a strong management-rights clause that gives it the ability to make in the future all or most of the decisions that it made in the past.

3. Judge Calvert Magruder first articulated this standard in *NLRB v. Reed Prince*, 130 F.2d 765 (1st Cir. 1942), defining bad faith as the "desire not to reach an agreement."

4. That is because, in the absence of a contract granting it the power to do so, the employer may not make unilateral changes to wages, hours, or working conditions without first bargaining to impasse with the union.

5. In *Chevron Oil Co. v. NLRB*, 442 F.2d 1067 (5th Cir. 1971), the company insisted on a broad management-rights clause, a no-strike provision, and a grievance procedure that did not provide for arbitration. The Fifth Circuit found only a case of "hard bargaining between two parties who were possessed of disparate economic power" and no "substantial evidence on the record as a whole to support the Board's finding that the company went through the motions of negotiation as an elaborate pretense with no sincere desire to reach an agreement."

6. Employers seeking to rid themselves of unions do not want to be found guilty of bargaining in bad faith, because they lose the ability to permanently replace strikers.

7. 397 U.S. 99 (1970).

8. *Ex-Cell-O Corp.*, 185 N.L.R.B. 187 (1970).

9. This may be characterized as the "Bartleby" principle, after Herman Melville's character Bartleby, the Scrivener, who regularly responded to assignments, "I prefer not to." In certain cases, the Board has awarded litigation and organizing expenses to a union, but this has been rare and restricted to cases of repeated and flagrant violations. *See Tiidee Products, Inc.*, 194 N.L.R.B. 1234 (1972).

CHAPTER 17. NLRA ORGANIZING

1. For example, we asked the voters whether they signed union authorization cards. Our reported percentage of card signers matched that of the unions that we studied.

2. Our methodology and findings were published in Julius G. Getman, Stephen B. Goldberg, and Jeanne B. Herman, *Union Representation Elections: Law and Reality* (1976).

3. The union-attitude index was similarly valuable in predicting vote. Values ranged from a low score of 8 to a high score of 32. The average union voter's score was 26; the average company voter scored 15.

4. 121 F.2d 954 (2d Cir. 1941).

5. Justice Earl Warren gave this assumption constitutional force in *NLRB v Gissel Packing Co.*, 395 U.S. 575 (1969), in which he rejected the First Amendment claims by an employer whose speech contained no overt threat of retaliation: "Any assessment of the precise scope of employer expression . . . must take into account the economic dependence of the employees on their employers, and the necessary tendency of the former, because of that relationship, to pick up intended implications of the latter that might be more readily dismissed by a more disinterested ear."

6. We used two methods to determine whether unlawful campaigning occurred. If unfairlabor-practice charges or objections to the election were filed, we relied on the Board's disposition of those charges. When charges or objections were not filed, all arguably unlawful speech and conduct were submitted on an informal basis to an NLRB administrative law judge. The judge reviewed this speech and conduct as he would have done

if they had been submitted to him in his official capacity. He decided whether the campaigning had been unlawful and, if so, the appropriate remedy. Our main concern was to measure the impact of threats, promises, and retaliation—conduct deemed illegal by the Board. The administrative law judge found the employer to have engaged in unlawful campaigning in twenty-two of the thirty-one elections we studied. The judge found campaign violations serious enough to warrant a bargaining order in nine elections. The unlawful campaign tactics that resulted in bargaining orders included reprisals, grants of benefits, interrogation, the formation and domination of an employee-representation committee, and attempted surveillance of union activities.

7. We did not urge any relaxation in Board regulation of acts of retaliation, particularly discriminatory discharges and other acts of retaliation. Whether or not it intimidates voters, such retaliatory conduct generally punishes individual employees for exercising basic statutory rights. We urged that remedies for such conduct be strengthened. Prompt and effective remedies for an employer's retaliatory conduct may serve ultimately to establish a climate in which fear of reprisal is less of a factor in some employees' initial responses to a union organizing drive.

8. Derek Bok, the president of Harvard and a major scholar in the area, wrote the introduction, in which he concluded, "I can only applaud the efforts of Professors Getman, Goldberg, and Herman."

9. *See* Edward B. Miller, "The Getman, Goldberg, and Herman Questions," 28 *Stan. L. Rev.* 1163 (1976).

10. William T. Dickens, "The Effect of Company Campaigns on Certification Elections: Law and Reality Once Again, 36 *Indus. & Lab. Rel. Rev.* 560 (1983).

11. Dickens concluded that with respect to company letters, "each written communication sent out after the first wave of interviews, on average, made workers 3 to 4 percent less likely to vote for unionization; the written communications sent out before the first wave made workers 1 to 2 percent more likely to vote for unionization. Three of the four effects are statistically significant at the .01 level. The other is significant at the .10 level. The relative importance of early and late communications is reversed for company meetings. The point estimates of the effects of meetings indicate that early meetings decrease the probability of an average worker voting union by about 5 to 7 percent. Late meetings decrease that probability by zero to 3 percent."

12. Stephen B. Goldberg, Julius Getman, and Jeanne M. Brett, "Differing Empirical Approaches," 79 *Nw. U. L. Rev.* 721 (1984).

13. Richard B. Freeman and James L. Medoff, *What Do Unions Do?* (1984).

14. Perhaps their conclusion is based on a senior thesis by Harvard student Susan Catler, which is included in their list of studies but not described and almost impossible to locate.

15. Kate Bronfenbrenner, *Uneasy Terrain: The Impact of Capital Mobility on Workers, Wages, and Union Organizing, Part II: First Contract Supplement* (submitted to the U.S. Trade Deficit Review Commission, 2001), *available at* http://digitalcommons.ilr.cornell.edu /cgi/viewcontent.cgi?article=1001&context=reports.

16. She wrote, "The study is based on surveys of lead organizers from a random sample of 600 NLRB certification elections." In doing our research for *Law and Reality*, we real-

ized that organizers tend to exaggerate the hostility of the employer campaign. In part, this is because they learn about company tactics from their supporters, who are the group most likely to perceive threats regardless of the actual statements. This is particularly true in lost elections because they provide an excuse for failure.

17. Employees who have never been in a union may be concerned because of employer propaganda, because of television or movie depictions that are rarely positive these days, or simply because unionization is bound to change the nature of an important part of their lives. Employees who have been in a union may have had bad or mixed experiences.

18. This could be accomplished by certifying a union when it presents signed authorization cards from a majority of the employees in the unit or, preferably, by holding an election immediately after a union presents enough cards to indicate substantial employee interest. Relying on cards or instant elections is by no means a novel or untried notion. Indeed, precisely that approach is embodied in Canadian labor law, which otherwise emulates the American system of establishing the union as the exclusive bargaining agent once it has been selected by a majority of the employees. Reflection on the differences between the representation procedures used in the two countries reveals certain crucial and questionable assumptions of the American system—not just about how best to determine the actual wishes of the employees with regard to collective bargaining but also about the appropriate role of the employer in that process and even about the significance of certification itself.

19. We did not study the impact of discharges before the formal campaign. If such discharges harm the union's organizing committee, they might well have a harmful impact on a campaign. Such discharges would, however, be particularly difficult to remedy.

20. Paul C. Weiler, "Promises to Keep: Securing Workers' Rights to Self-Organization under the NLRA," 96 *Harv. L. Rev.* 1769 (1983).

21. Perhaps the most remarkable phenomenon in the representation process in the past quarter century has been an astronomical increase in unfair labor practices by employers. Employees entitled to reinstatement in 1980 numbered 10,033, a 1,000-percent increase from the low point in 1957.

22. William T. Dickens and Jonathan Leonard, "Accounting for the Decline in Union Membership, 1950–1980," 38 *Indus. & Lab. Rel. Rev.* 323 (1985).

23. Dickens and his coauthor Jonathan Leonard conclude that in terms of maintaining the union movement's share of the workforce through NLRB elections, net growth (actually net loss) due to economic factors explains the greatest part of the decline in unionization.

24. Although Dickens does not analyze the impact of discriminatory discharges, his analysis suggests that the most effective employer tactic for defeating unionism is very likely the employer's refusal to bargain after a union victory. He cites a study of the results of union victories between April 1979 and March 1981: "By February 1983, first contracts had been obtained in only 63 percent of the units."

25. Chirag Mehta and Nik Theodore, *Undermining the Right to Organize: Employer Behavior During Union Representation Campaigns* (report for American Rights at Work, Dec. 2005), *available at* http://www.americanrightsatwork.org/dmdocuments/ARAWReports/UROCUEDcompressedfullreport.pdf.

26. Laura Cooper, "Authorization Cards and Union Representation Election Outcome: An

Empirical Assessment of the Assumptions Underlying the Supreme Court's *Gissel* Decision," 79 *Nw. U. L. Rev.* 87 (1984).

27. Professor Cooper also noted that her study provides support for the assumption that delay between the petition and election decreases the union's chance of victory.

28. Richard Bensinger, Statement before the Commission on the Future of Worker-Management Relations (Aug. 10, 1994), *available at* http://digitalcommons.ilr.cornell.edu /cgi/viewcontent.cgi?article=1333&context=key_workplace.

29. Back pay is calculated by subtracting what the employee has earned or what the Board believes the employee would have earned had he or she been diligent enough. In practice, reinstatement is a weak, generally meaningless remedy. Studies show that most unlawfully discharged employees don't want to return and that those who do are typically forced out after a short period.

30. 395 U.S. 575 (1969).

31. *See, e.g.,* Laura J. Cooper and Dennis R. Nolan, "The Story of *NLRB v. Gissel Packing:* The Practical Limits of Paternalism," *in Labor Law Stories* 191 (Laura J. Cooper and Catherine L. Fisk eds., 2005); James J. Brudney, "A Famous Victory: Collective Bargaining Protections and the Statutory Aging Process," 74 *N.C. L. Rev.* 939 (1996).

32. *Quoted in Labor Law Cases and Materials* 268 (Archibald Cox et al. eds., 14th ed. 2006).

CHAPTER 18. RESTRUCTURING THE STRIKE WEAPON

1. An initial feeling of commitment is easy to achieve during the first days of a strike, which often have an almost party-like atmosphere. Workers' sense of common purpose is fueled by rallies, marches, songs, chants, and expressions of support from bystanders and union drivers. Rich Trumka, the president of the AFL-CIO, has said that during the first days of a strike, workers feel as though "the weight of the world has been lifted from their shoulders." But it is difficult to sustain that feeling over a long period of time with diminished income and decreased public attention. When there is no solution after weeks or months, strikers often become disillusioned and worried about their future. And then, as Trumka notes, "the weight of the world falls back on their shoulders." In a long strike, solidarity is inevitably tested. During a long, difficult struggle, it is almost always the case that some strikers will on occasion feel defeated or abandoned. During such moments, they will be tempted to cross the picket line to reclaim their jobs. If a substantial number of strikers return to work, a strike is doomed.

2. Julius G. Getman and F. Ray Marshall, "The Continuing Assault on the Right to Strike," 79 *Tex. L. Rev.* 703 (2001). And when strikes do occur, they are often intentionally provoked by management, which seeks to use them as a way of ousting or taming unions.

3. *One Day Longer: The Story of the Frontier Strike* (1999).

4. Facts and quotations, unless otherwise indicated, come from my research on the strike. Most of the material is contained in Julius Getman, *The Betrayal of Local 14* (1998).

5. The national union's contribution was limited. It recommended that the three locals form a voting pool, which was later held to be illegal. The idea as suggested by Glenn and understood by the locals was that other International Paper unions would join the pool and the strike as their contracts expired. This never happened, largely because of the

failure of the national leaders and staff to take the steps necessary to implement this plan. The national union made regular payments of $55 a week in strike benefits, and it hired the Kamber Group to conduct a polite, behind-the-scenes public-relations campaign against the company—a campaign that almost everyone familiar with the strike agrees contributed little and which was terminated midway through the strike. In choosing the Kamber group and its limited-pressure approach, the national union specifically turned down the local's plea to hire Ray Rogers.

6. At the July 15 meeting, Dominic Bozzotto, the president of HERE Local 26, told the strikers, "Whatever you do, you have to do it together like a union. You can't applaud like individuals, you're a union." He asked the crowd to try it, and they broke into loud, disjointed applause mingled with cheers. Bozzotto shook his head disapprovingly as the audience laughed. "No! Everybody together!" He began to applaud rhythmically and the crowd began to applaud with him, louder and louder and with greater and greater power. When they finished, almost everyone was smiling and applauding together. The "solidarity clap" became a regular part of the Wednesday-night meetings. And the anger that marked the first days of the strike was transformed into a mood of earnest, somewhat self-congratulatory commitment.

7. Another provision prohibited businesses from hiring employees who had twice before been hired as striker replacements. It was held to be preempted by federal law. Another prohibited the construction of movable or temporary living quarters for ten or more people except under stringent regulation; it would have outlawed International Paper's practice of housing the replacement workers in trailers on company property.

8. *International Paper Co. v. Town of Jay,* 928 F.2d 480 (1st Cir. 1991).

9. The Occupational Safety and Health Administration (OSHA) found thirty-seven health and safety violations at the mill. Thirty-four of the violations were deemed "willful and serious," meaning that International Paper knew that hazardous conditions existed and failed to correct them.

10. On October 1, 1987, the *Lewiston Daily Sun* reported that "state environmental officials inspected International Paper Co.'s Androscoggin Mill Wednesday after an equipment failure resulted in about 80,000 gallons of mill waste being dumped into the Androscoggin River. The incident marked the third time that the Department of Environmental Protection was called in to inspect the mill's waste water treatment plant since June 16—the day a strike by 1,250 unionized paper workers began." On October 15, the paper reported that "a smoldering canister containing a dangerous chemical resulted in the evacuation of sections of International Paper Co.'s Androscoggin Mill on Saturday." On October 27, the paper reported a finding by OSHA "that IP Co. exposed workers at its Jay mill to toxic gases and hazardous chemicals without adequate protection." According to the Portland, Maine, *Portland Press Herald,* OSHA, in recommending the stiffest possible penalty on October 26, cited the company's "disregard for employee protection." OSHA cited the frequency of gas leaks at the mill and said that thirty-one employees were exposed to toxic gases "on a regular basis."

11. The name of the doctrine comes from the case that first announced this preference, *Laidlaw Corp.,* 171 N.L.R.B. 1366 (1968).

12. Many found the thought of working alongside scabs whom they hated, for a company

by which they felt betrayed, so painful that they renounced their claim in exchange for a small buyout. Most of the former strikers, however, felt that they had no real choice and awaited their recall to the mill.

13. Jay-Livermore Falls Working Class History Project, *Pain on Their Faces: Testimonies on the Paper Mill Strike, Jay, Maine, 1987–1988* (1998).

14. Interview with Bill Meserve and Sandra Lucarelli in Portland, Maine (July 20, 2007).

15. Richard LaCosse, who negotiated the agreement, is certain that the continuing battle led by the Jay strikers was the motivation for International Paper to change its approach to labor relations.

CHAPTER 19. STRIKES, PICKETING, COMPREHENSIVE CAMPAIGNS, AND THE LAW

1. 304 U.S. 333 (1938).

2. The *Mackay* decision was issued at a time when there were no union unfair labor practices and before the Court had developed the jurisprudence of section 8(a)(3). The *Mackay* doctrine became particularly disadvantageous to unions during the 1970s and 1980s, when American corporations in many industries launched concerted campaigns to weaken or destroy unions and collective bargaining.

3. *See* Julius G. Getman and Thomas C. Kohler, "The Story of *NLRB v. Mackay Radio & Telegraph Co:* The High Cost of Solidarity," *in Labor Law Stories* 13 (Laura J. Cooper and Catherine L. Fisk eds., 2005).

4. *Id.*

5. 373 U.S. 221 (1963).

6. The Court went on to affirm the ways in which the grant of superseniority had, according to the Board, diminished the right to strike:

(1) Super-seniority affects the tenure of all strikers. . . .

(2) A super-seniority award necessarily operates to the detriment of those who participated in the strike as compared to nonstrikers.

(3) Super-seniority made available to striking bargaining unit employees as well as to new employees is, in effect, offering individual benefits to the strikers to induce them to abandon the strike.

(4) Extending the benefits of super-seniority to striking bargaining unit employees as well as to new replacements deals a crippling blow to the strike effort. . . .

(5) Super-seniority renders future bargaining difficult, if not impossible . . .

It has been noted that every one of these characteristics applies with even greater force to the hiring of permanent replacement workers.

7. 388 U.S. 26 (1966).

8. The union's official position has probably been adopted to avoid responsibility for actions that may or may not be approved by union officers.

9. For a full discussion of the issue, see Julius G. Getman, "The Protection of Economic Pressure by Section 7 of the NLRA," 115 *U. Pa. L. Rev.* 1195 (1967).

10. 336 U.S. 245 (1949).

11. 427 U.S. 132 (1976).

12. The Taft-Hartley Act was the result of a rare combination: Republicans were in control of Congress, and for a period after World War II strikes were rampant. The rash of postwar strikes was an inevitable result of pressure for improvement by unionized workers, who during the war years, from 1941 to 1945, voluntarily gave up the strike weapon. Wages had not kept up with prices during the war. Many of the strikers during the early postwar period were returning G.I.'s who believed that they had earned the right to strike because of their service. Yet, spurred on by employer associations, many in society came to the conclusion that unions had become too strong and needed to be controlled. Taft-Hartley was the result.

13. 377 U.S. 58 (1964).

14. In *NLRB v. Retail Stores Employees Union, Local 1001*, 447 U.S. 607 (1980), the Court held that the *Tree Fruits* holding does not apply where the picketing is "directed against a product representing a major portion of a neutral's business."

15. 485 U.S. 568 (1988).

16. SEIU Local 3, NLRB General Counsel Advice Memorandum 09-CP-00371 (Mar. 19, 2008) (internal footnotes omitted), *available at* http://www.nlrb.gov/shared_files/Advice%20Memos/2008/09-CP-00371.pdf.

17. 310 U.S. 88 (1940).

18. 315 U.S. 769 (1942).

19. "Courts have established union conduct as picketing despite the lack of signs of conventional patrolling." Lee Modjeska, "Recognition Picketing under the NLRA," 35 *U. Fla. L. Rev.* 633 (1983). A more careful approach was taken by Judge Marsha Berzon (a former labor lawyer) in *Overstreet v. United Brotherhood of Carpenters,* 409 F.3d 1199 (9th Cir. 2005).

20. 447 U.S. 607 (1980) (Safeco Title Insurance Co.).

21. 458 U.S. 886 (1982).

22. 350 N.L.R.B. 585 (2007).

23. 351 N.L.R.B. 434 (2007).

CHAPTER 20. COMPREHENSIVE CAMPAIGNS AND RICO

1. *United Food & Commercial Workers Union Local 204 v. NLRB,* 447 F.3d 821 (D.C. Cir. 2006).

2. Report of Ray Marshall regarding *Smithfield v. UFCW* (Sept. 2008) (on file with author).

3. Research Associates of America, since disbanded, provided research and other assistance to unions engaged in or considering comprehensive campaigns.

4. *Smithfield Foods, Inc. v. United Food & Commercial Workers International Union,* 585 F. Supp. 2d 789 (E.D. Va. 2008).

5. *See* Adam Liptak, "A Corporate View of Mafia Tactics: Protesting, Lobbying and Citing Upton Sinclair," *N.Y. Times,* Feb 5, 2008.

6. The report was released in August 2006 and was rereleased in January 2007.

7. 537 U.S. 393 (2003).

8. 410 U.S. 396 (1973).

9. Liptak, *supra* note 5.

10. Of course, at the time there were those who argued that the Birmingham bus boycott was a form of extortion. It is difficult to believe that Judge Payne meant to be associated with that position.

11. "Smithfield, UFCW Settle RICO Suit, Agree to Election Using 'Fair Process,'" *BNA Daily Lab. Rep.*, Oct. 28, 2008, http://emlawcenter.bna.com/pic2/em.nsf/id/BNAP-7KULHA?OpenDocument.

12. *Wackenhut Corp. v. Service Employees International Union,* 593 F. Supp. 2d 1289 (2009).

13. No. 08-Civ-2185, 2009 WL 604099 (S.D.N.Y. Mar. 9, 2009), *also available at* http://hr.cch.com/cases/Cintas.pdf.

14. 646 F.2d 1323 (9th Cir. 1981).

15. 685 F. Supp. 1370 (E.D. Ky. 1988).

16. In *Yellow Bus Lines, Inc. v. Drivers, Chauffeurs & Helpers Local Union 639,* 883 F.2d 132 (D.C. Cir. 1989), the D.C. Circuit Court of Appeals made it clear that relatively minor strike violence could provide the predicate for a civil RICO action. The case arose out of a 1981 strike for recognition. The company alleged various acts of intimidation, and the court, in an opinion by Judge Abner Mikva, held that a RICO action would lie: "Four [of plaintiff's counts] allege direct threats to *Yellow Bus* property or employees which qualify as offenses listed in the § 1961(1) definition of racketeering activity. Additionally, these predicate acts appear to fulfill the requirement for a 'pattern' . . . [which] . . . embraces 'criminal acts that have the same or similar purposes, results, participants, victims, or methods of commission . . . and are not isolated events.' Here, appellees are accused of engaging in acts of vandalism and intimidation during a specific time period in pursuit of a unitary goal. We believe this scenario meets the statutory requirements for a 'pattern of racketeering activity.'"

17. 687 F. Supp. 1453 (D. Haw. 1988).

18. 168 F. Supp. 2d 826 (W.D. Tenn. 2001).

CHAPTER 21. ORGANIZED LABOR AND THE EMPLOYEE FREE CHOICE ACT

1. H.R. 1409, S. 560, 111th Cong. (2009).

2. George Will, "Temper Irrational Exuberance," *Austin Am. Statesman,* Sept. 25, 2008.

3. George McGovern, "My Party Should Respect Secret Union Ballots," *Wall St. J.,* Aug. 8, 2008.

4. Labor and its friends have spent lots of time thinking about ways to respond to the pro-secret-ballot editorials. Friends of labor have been urged to write their own op-ed articles explaining why passage of the EFCA would be in the public interest. The advice to EFCA supporters from AFL-CIO strategists has generally been to ignore the secret-ballot issue or to deny that the EFCA would eliminate the secret ballot.

5. John Sweeney and Mark Love, "Employees Need Choice Act to Level Playing Field," *Wichita Eagle,* May 10, 2007.

6. Thomas Frank, "Happy Labor Day. Drop Dead," *Wall St. J.,* Sept. 3, 2008. Frank continues: "Among its [the study's] findings: In 51% of union organizing drives, management made some sort of threat to close its operation down if the union won the election. Ninety-two percent of companies facing union elections made employees attend 'captive audience meetings'; 67% had employees attend weekly 'supervisor one-on-one'

meetings; 70% sent out 'anti-union letters'; 55% showed 'anti-union videos'; 34% gave 'bribes or special favors' to anti-union employees; and 25% simply fired pro-union employees. If American business was its own country, it would probably come in for sanctions from the State Department."

7. *See* Julius G. Getman, Stephen B. Goldberg, and Jeanne B. Herman, *Union Representation Elections: Law and Reality* 128 (1976).

8. The Act makes no provision for revoking cards that have already been signed.

9. The Board would have to establish an initial ruling, which would likely be tested by litigation after an employer refused to bargain with a union certified on the basis of a card majority that includes cards signed years or months earlier.

10. Kim Moody, "Card Check: Can It Organize the Unorganized?" *Lab. Notes,* Nov. 2008, at 11, *available at* http://www.labornotes.org/node/1943.

11. Some of the building-trades unions are fearful that compromise decisions by arbitrators would be used to replace negotiated master agreements with arbitral compromises over an entire area. This replacement could happen because the agreements contain clauses in which the union promises to give employers most-favored treatment—a promise that the union can easily make as long as it has the ability to insist that the terms of the earlier joint agreement be met. This binding arbitration would prohibit it from doing so.

12. These studies are discussed in chapter 17.

CHAPTER 22. CHANGING THE LAW OF REPRESENTATION CAMPAIGNS AND STRIKER REPLACEMENT

1. The strike is discussed in chapter 18. See also Julius Getman, *The Betrayal of Local 14* (1998), for the basic facts.

2. It seems likely that the company's bargaining behavior was calculated to encourage a strike but was carefully constructed to stay within the very loose standards of section 8(a)(5).

3. *Preventing Replacement of Economic Strikers: Hearings on S. 2112 before the Subcommittee on Labor of the Senate Committee on Labor and Human Resources,* 101st Cong. 274 (1990).

4. *See* Julius G. Getman, "Section 8(a)(3) of the NLRA and the Effort to Insulate Free Employee Choice," 32 *U. Chi. L. Rev.* 735 (1965).

CHAPTER 23. IS THE NLRA WORTH SAVING?

1. *Quoted in* Ellen J. Dannin, "Using the NLRB as a Resource," *Lab. Stud. J.,* Sept. 1999, at 38.

2. Ellen J. Dannin, *Taking Back the Workers' Law: How to Fight the Assault on Labor Rights* (2006).

3. For discussion of these cases and this area of law, see Cynthia L. Estlund, "Labor, Property and Sovereignty after Lechmere," 46 *Stan. L. Rev.* 305 (1994).

4. Charles Black Jr., "The Lawfulness of the Segregation Decisions," 69 *Yale L.J.* 421 (1959).

5. George Schatzki, "It's Simple: Judges Don't Like Labor Unions," 30 *Conn. L. Rev.* 1365 (1998).

6. Dannin recognizes this difference in approach and argues effectively that it would be a mistake for unions to put much hope in replacing the NLRA with a new statute such

as the EFCA, since "any new law will be subjected to the same judicial processes that have affected the NLRA." This is an important point. Any effort at pro-labor legislation should be simple and as difficult to undo as possible. A prohibition on striker replacement would be far more likely to survive judicial scrutiny with its purpose intact than the EFCA, which presents all sorts of interpretation problems (e.g., the status of revocations and employer efforts to achieve them).

7. 102 *Colum. L. Rev.* 1527 (2002).

8. Estlund argues that ossification is also created by the all-or-nothing role of section 8(a)(2), which has inhibited the development of competing, employer-sponsored forms of employee representation.

9. It seems likely that the desire to maintain acceptability plays a useful role in helping achieve the resolution that the parties would have achieved had they had the opportunity to negotiate with respect to the issues in dispute.

The parties' priorities are difficult to ascertain. The arbitrator must pay careful attention to the clues that the parties give concerning how strongly they feel about a particular case. My judgment is that the need to maintain acceptability makes arbitrators more attentive to such clues than judges are, and more likely than judges would be to use them in their decision. Arbitrators whose decisions over time accurately reflect the priorities of the parties are more likely to maintain and enhance their acceptability than arbitrators who take either a more narrowly judicial role or a more personally activist role. Thus, the process of selection will tend to produce arbitrators and a body of arbitral precedent that facilitate and extend the process of negotiation. The desire to maintain acceptability makes it important for arbitrators not to project either a pro- or anti-union bias. As a result, this desire serves to insulate the process from personal political attitudes and to prevent it from reflecting changes in governmental policies toward labor, as is characteristic of the NLRB.

The careful selection process also motivates arbitrators to try to please both sides, if possible, with their decision. Thus, the split award and the decision in which it is difficult to tell which side has won are frequent in labor relations. Although the parties constantly insist that it is contrary to their wishes, this system of giving a little bit to each side permits the process to achieve the results of successful negotiation.

10. Benjamin I. Sachs, "Employment Law as Labor Law," 29 *Cardozo L. Rev.* 2685 (2008).

11. *See, e.g.,* Michael H. Gottesman, "Rethinking Labor Law Preemption: State Laws Facilitating Unionization," 7 *Yale J. on Reg.* 355 (1990); Eileen Silverstein, "Against Preemption in Labor Law," 24 *Conn. L. Rev.* 1 (1991).

12. 359 U.S. 236 (1959).

CHAPTER 24. BEYOND TRADITIONAL COLLECTIVE BARGAINING

1. Richard B. Freeman, "Searching Outside the Box: The Road to Union Renascence and Worker Well-Being in the U.S.," *in The Future of Labor Unions: Organized Labor in the 21st Century* 75, 83–84 (Julius G. Getman and Ray Marshall eds., 2004).

2. He Totally Gets It! Posting of Ebony Taylor to Main Street, http://www.workingamerica .org/blog/2008/09/ (Sept. 8, 2008, 5:45 p.m.).

3. Old Mother Hubbard, Posting of Rebecca Hawkins to Main Street, http://www.working america.org/blog/2008/09/ (Sept. 15, 2008, 4:12 p.m.).

4. *See* Working America, *Election Report* (2008).

5. As Jayaraman told me: "Every time we win a campaign, it's a combination of money that's owed to the workers and these great policies that affect all the workers in a company. So the one we just won a few weeks ago started with 2 workers at one restaurant and ended up being 250 workers at seven restaurants all surrounding midtown, surrounding Carnegie Hall and Lincoln Center in midtown. It was a $4 million settlement, and it included a grievance procedure and a form of job security. You know, we've won in other settlements, raises, and all these kinds of things. So we found a non-NLRB path to winning agreements. In most of the agreements we are a party to the agreement as an organization, so we have the power to enforce. We use what we call an eleven-step method, which we basically created. It's a combination of organizing workers internally and also doing actions external to the restaurant—and corporate pressure and all this pressure to ultimately win settlement agreements in federal court that resemble union contracts. So we've been able to win raises and grievance procedures and job security and even paid vacation, paid sick days, paid holidays, in a contract-like settlement agreement."

6. Stephen Greenhouse, "Judge Approves Deal to Settle Suit over Wage Violations," *N.Y. Times,* June 19, 2008.

7. Saru Jayaraman, "'ROCing' the Industry: Organizing Restaurant Workers in New York," *in The New Urban Immigrant Workforce: Innovative Models for Labor Organizing* 143 (Sarumathi Jayaraman and Immanuel Ness eds., 2005).

8. 360 U.S. 203 (1959).

9. *NLRB v. Walton Manufacturing Co.,* 289 F.2d 177 (5th Cir. 1961) (Wisdom, J., dissenting).

10. 691 F.2d 288 (6th Cir. 1982).

11. Commission on the Future of Worker-Management Relations, *Final Report* (1994), *available at* http://digitalcommons.ilr.cornell.edu/cgi/viewcontent.cgi?article=1004&context =key_workplace.

12. S. 295, 104th Cong. (1995).

13. S. Rep. No. 104-259, at 3 (1996).

14. James Rundle, "Winning Hearts and Minds in the Era of Employee-Involvement Programs," *in Organizing to Win* 213 (Kate Bronfenbrenner et al. eds., 1998).

15. Julius G. Getman, Stephen B. Goldberg, and Jeanne B. Herman, *Union Representation Elections: Law and Reality* (1976). This study is discussed in chapter 17.

16. 309 N.L.R.B. 990 (1992).

17. 334 N.L.R.B. 699 (2001).

18. Charles Morris, "Where Have All the Unions Gone? Long Time Passing. When Will They Ever Return?" (2008) (draft manuscript, on file with author).

CHAPTER 25. THE DIFFERENCE BETWEEN LABOR ORGANIZATION AND LABOR MOVEMENT

1. Dorothee Benz, "Labor's Ace in the Hole: Casino Organizing in Las Vegas," 26 *New Pol. Sci.* 525 (2004).

2. The plan was tried and failed.

3. Interview with Yan Litinski and Zbigniew Bujak in Warsaw, Poland (1980). Bujak told me that when he was working at the Ursis tractor factory as an electrician, it was the workers' bill of rights and conversations with Litinski that motivated him to become an activist. Bujak had an amazing and admirable career. He co-organized a strike at the factory in 1980 and became one of the leading figures in the Solidarity movement. From 1981 to 1989, he was head of Solidarity for the Mazowsze region, and until his arrest in 1986, he was the most prominent opposition figure to avoid detention during Poland's long period of martial law. He took part in the negotiations that helped end the Soviet domination of Eastern Europe. Bujak was awarded the Robert F. Kennedy Human Rights Award in 1989.

4. Most of Solidarity's leaders were actually imprisoned by the Communist leadership in 1981. That did not stop the movement, which, led by Bujak, continued to organize underground.

5. Julius G. Getman, "The Fine Line between Success and Failure in Strikes and Organizing," 2 *U. Pa. J. Lab. & Emp. L.* 719 (2000).

6. Letter from John Wilhelm to author (Mar. 17, 1996). At the time, Wilhelm was the western regional director of the AFL-CIO.

7. Sirabella believed that Lane Kirkland, then the president of the AFL-CIO, favored bringing in newcomers of the kind that Sirabella had hired but that he was incapable of breaking through the existing bureaucracy: "Me, Lane Kirkland, and Kenny Young, who's his top assistant—the three of us were sitting down, and he said, Boy, was I impressed with those young kids today, where do you get them? I explained it, and he turns to Kenny and said wouldn't it be wonderful if we had two teams like the kids we saw today and do experimental projects in two cities where we organized around recognition without the Board, just going to the street if we have to. He couldn't say that, in my opinion, in front of his executive council."

8. Betsy Aron, "Who Organized the Organizers? HERE Leadership Succession at the end of the Twentieth Century." Unpublished, np; written 2000.

9. Letter from Kristine Rondeau, President of the Harvard Union of Clerical and Technical Workers to Owen Bieber, President of the United Auto Workers.

10. Steve Early, "Thoughts on the 'Worker-Student Alliance'—Then and Now," 44 *Lab. Hist.* 5 (2003).

11. Lance Compa, "More Thoughts on the Worker-Student Alliance: A Reply to Steve Early," *Labor: Stud. Working-Class Hist. Am.*, vol. 1, no. 2, at 15 (2004).

12. Julius Getman, *The Betrayal of Local 14*, at 82–83 (1998).

13. *Id.* at 64.

CONCLUSION

1. Betsy Aron, "Who Organized the Organizers? HERE Leadership Succession at the end of the Twentieth Century." Unpublished, np; written 2000.

Index